The Myths of the Popol Vuh
in Cosmology, Art, and Ritual

The Myths of the Popol Vuh in Cosmology, Art, and Ritual

edited by

Holley Moyes,

Allen J. Christenson,

and Frauke Sachse

UNIVERSITY PRESS OF COLORADO
Louisville

Published by University Press of Colorado
245 Century Circle, Suite 202
Louisville, Colorado 80027

ASSOCIATION
of UNIVERSITY
PRESSES
The University Press of Colorado is a proud member of
the Association of University Presses.

The University Press of Colorado is a cooperative publishing enterprise supported, in part, by Adams
State University, Colorado State University, Fort Lewis College, Metropolitan State University
of Denver, Regis University, University of Alaska Fairbanks, University of Colorado, University
of Denver, University of Northern Colorado, University of Wyoming, Utah State University, and
Western Colorado University.

ISBN: 978-1-60732-338-9 (hardcover)
ISBN: 978-1-64642-198-5 (paperback)
ISBN: 978-1-64642-199-2 (ebook)
https://doi.org/10.5876/9781646421992

Library of Congress Cataloging-in-Publication Data

Names: Moyes, Holley, editor. | Christenson, Allen J., 1957– editor. | Sachse, Frauke, editor.
Title: The myths of the Popol vuh in cosmology, art, and ritual / edited by Holley Moyes, Allen J.
  Christenson, and Frauke Sachse.
Description: Louisville, Colorado : University Press of Colorado, [2021] | Includes bibliographical
  references and index.
Identifiers: LCCN 2021021117 (print) | LCCN 2021021118 (ebook) | ISBN 9781607323389 (hard-
  cover) | ISBN 9781646421985 (paperback) | ISBN 9781646421992 (ebook)
Subjects: LCSH: Popol vuh—Criticism, Textual. | Quiché mythology. | Quiché Indians—Religion. |
  Quiché philosophy. | Central America—Antiquities.
Classification: LCC F1465.P83 M97 2021 (print) | LCC F1465.P83 (ebook) | DDC
  299.7/8423—dc23
LC record available at https://lccn.loc.gov/2021021117
LC ebook record available at https://lccn.loc.gov/2021021118

The University Press of Colorado gratefully acknowledges the support of the University of California,
Merced toward the publication of this book.

Cover illustration: folio page 1r of the Popol Vuh. Courtesy of The Newberry Library, Chicago.

Contents

PART 1: UNDERSTANDING HIGHLAND MAYA WORLDVIEWS
THROUGH THE MYTHOLOGIES OF THE POPOL VUH

PART 2: THE POPOL VUH IN UNDERSTANDING THE
ARCHAEOLOGICAL RECORD

PART 3: COMPREHENDING CLASSIC MAYA ART AND WRITING
THROUGH THE MYTHS OF THE POPOL VUH

PART 4: MYTHOLOGICAL CONTINUITIES AND CHANGE

Figures

Preface

Maya Archaeology and the Popol Vuh

An Intellectual History

MICHAEL D. COE

My involvement with the Popol Vuh and the mental world that produced it did
not come as a sudden, personal enlightenment but evolved slowly and in fits and
starts over the years. In 1950, when I was an undergraduate senior and an anthropology major at Harvard, the University of Oklahoma Press issued the great translation and commentary on the manuscript by the Guatemalan scholar Adrián
Recinos (Recinos et al. 1950). I was intrigued by it, especially the mythological part
involving the story of the Hero Twins and their conquest of Xibalba. Since J. Eric
Thompson's landmark *Maya Hieroglyphic Writing: An Introduction* had appeared
that same year, I had the nerve to write him a letter asking how this myth might
apply to Maya archaeology. He immediately replied, but alas, I never kept his letter.

In my cherished copy of Sylvanus G. Morley's *The Ancient Maya* (1946), there
were only two brief references to the Popol Vuh and none at all in Thompson's
1950 magnum opus. It appeared to me, then, that apart from the section describing
the origin and migration of the K'iche' people, it had little or no relevance to what
Maya archaeologists had been excavating or to museum collections of Maya art.

But there was one notable exception. In 1950, in the Carnegie *Notes on Middle
American Archaeology and Ethnology* series Thompson had created and edited, there
appeared an article by Frans Blom titled "A Polychrome Maya Plate from Quintana
Roo." It showed a pair of seated young blowgunners on either side of a fantastic
bird perching on what Blom describes as an "Earth Monster." In his third paragraph
Blom (1950: 405) says:

DOI: 10.5876/9781646421992.c000

So far as is known, this is the only representation of users of blowguns in Maya art, in spite of the fact that the Popol Vuh constantly refers to this weapon. The black spots on the blowgunners' bodies indicate that the men are dead. Note the sights on the guns. I have made a quick but unsuccessful search of the Popol Vuh to find a passage that would describe this scene.

Blom went on to describe and analyze the figure of the Great Bird, a passage that constitutes the first notice of what would decades later become known as the "Principal Bird Deity." It is curious that he failed to identify the bird victim as a cognate of Seven Macaw and the young men as the Hero Twins of the myth. Yet here is how he finishes his article: "The lower half of the plate has a border of hieroglyphs along the edge. I like to imagine that they are a quotation from the Popol Vuh" (Blom 1950: 406).

Frans Blom was a brilliant, tragic figure who was often ahead of his time as an innovative scholar but who often failed to follow his intuition. He was the first to describe the "E-Groups" of lowland Maya sites and their function, and he never altered his opinion that the Maya writing system had a phonetic basis. It is uncertain whether the last quote was made as a lighthearted jest or was instead a hint that he believed pottery texts might be proved to be meaningful (a view not held by any other Mayanist of his era).

Let us now pass over the next two decades, when I was successively an intelligence officer during the period of the Korean War, a Harvard graduate student, and an excavator of Early Formative sites in Mesoamerica, including the Olmec site of San Lorenzo. On the Yale faculty since 1960, I had fallen under the spell of my linguist colleague Floyd Lounsbury, to the extent that I sat in on two semesters of his graduate course on the Dresden Codex. The study of Maya hieroglyphic writing, especially the crucial role Yuri Knorosov (despised by Thompson) was playing in its decipherment, became one of my principal research interests.

Thus when I was asked, in August 1970, if I would be willing to mount a show on Maya writing at the Grolier Club in New York City, I jumped at the opportunity. I knew we would never be able to borrow the Dresden, Madrid, and Paris Codices; but many Classic Maya pictorial ceramics had glyphic texts, and we could borrow them from private collectors and public museums. This was a period in which unprecedented numbers of such vases, bowls, and dishes had begun appearing in the antiquities markets of Mesoamerica, Europe, the United States, and even Japan; most had probably been looted from graves and tombs in Guatemala and, to a lesser extent, Mexico. The ferocious and disruptive civil war in Guatemala, which began in 1960 and was to last until 1996, probably played a part, making large areas of the Peten essentially lawless.

The Grolier Club exhibit opened in April 1971. I installed it in two days, and as I proceeded, I began to see some patterns in these ceramics. Why, I wondered, were almost identical standing young men shown paired, as though they were twins? Of course, I immediately thought of the Hero Twins in the Popol Vuh. And why did the same sequence of glyphs (none of which neither I nor anyone else could then read) appear below the rims or on the body of different vessels?

Over the next two years, as I was preparing the catalog for the Grolier exhibition (Coe 1973), I gave serious attention to Maya pictorial vases in general, published or otherwise. The assumption under which I then operated was that since they all were surely found by either archaeologists or looters in graves or tombs, they must have had a funerary function. As for the repetitive painted or carved texts, the general opinion among the experts (including Thompson) was that since the artists who produced them were most likely illiterate commoners, they had no meaning. However, my analysis was able to show that since the glyphs of the texts placed along rims or in other prominent positions always kept the same order, they *did* mean something, perhaps a funerary mantra. This hypothetical explanation for my "Primary Standard Sequence" (PSS) later proved to be completely wrong.

Some of those twinned figures wore white headbands—I called these the "Headband Gods." But on one extraordinary polychrome vase shown in the exhibit (the Vase of the 31 Gods), these two were seated, and large black spots covered their cheeks and bodies; here I compared them to the twin blowgunners of the Blom Plate and concluded that they must be the Hero Twins of the Popol Vuh story.

Most of the illustrations in the Grolier catalog were either beautiful and accurate rollout drawings by Diane Griffiths Peck or standard-format photos taken by Justin Kerr. Both Justin and I lamented that a rollout camera had not yet been invented. By 1978, Justin had put together such an apparatus, and it worked. Full-color rollout images for Maya ceramics made their printed debut in the catalog of the Princeton Art Museum exhibit *Lords of the Underworld* (Coe and Kerr 1978). I was still thinking of Maya pictorial vases as funerary in function and stated in the catalog that the PSS was probably an "underworld litany." On Vase 8 (K555 in the Kerr Archive) is a complex scene involving several gods, including an enthroned Itzamnaaj; and on the far right of the unrolled image is a headbanded, black-spotted Hero Twin with a blowgun, who has shot the slumped figure of the Vulture God. In my description of this tableau, I mentioned that Peter Mathews had once suggested to me that when the putative Hero Twins appear together, the one with the black spots might be Junajpu and the counterpart with jaguar-skin markings on face and body his brother, Xb'alanke. If this held up, the defeated vulture of this vase might be cognate to Seven Macaw of the Popol Vuh.

The 1980s were (for me and my students at Yale) an exciting epoch for Maya iconography and decipherment. Major publications of that decade were *The Maya Book of the Dead: The Ceramic Codex* by Francis Robicsek and Donald Hales (1982) and Nicholas Hellmuth's *Monster und Menschen* (1987), both heavily based on Classic pictorial pottery. In 1984, David Stuart had deciphered one of the glyphs in the PSS (the one I had nicknamed "Fish") as *ka-kaw(a)*, "chocolate." It was not long before epigraphers on both sides of the Atlantic were able to read these ceramic texts as a kind of name tag, giving the vessel's dedication, sometimes the name of the artist, the shape of the vessel, its contents (often chocolate), its owners (or patron), and their titles. In other words, these vases, dishes, and plates were not funerary at all but part of daily and ritual life among Classic Maya royalty and other members of the elite class.

In my research on the Grolier catalog, I had noted the presence on many Maya vases of one or more weird chimaera-like creatures and jumped to the conclusion that they could be explained as the death gods of Xibalba as described in the Popol Vuh. However, independent of one another, Nikolai Grube, Stephen Houston, and David Stuart had "cracked" the glyph passage next to each figure as the named *way*, or spirit counterpart, possessed by the ruler of a particular city or polity. Another nail in the coffin of the "funerary ceramics" hypothesis.

In 1989 Justin and his wife, Barbara, began publishing *The Maya Vase Book* series, each volume containing many pottery rollouts followed by scholarly essays. In the first of the six volumes was my essay "The Hero Twins: Myth and Image," in which I not only used scenes on pictorial ceramics but brought in the remarkable scenes on Stela 2 and 25 at the Late Formative site of Izapa (Coe 1989). In fact, V. Garth Norman in 1976 and Gareth W. Lowe in 1982 had already suggested that these scenes most probably illustrate the first encounter of the Hero Twins with the monster bird Seven Macaw of the Popol Vuh and Junajpu's loss of his arm to the bird. Beginning with a 1976 article by Lawrence W. Bardawil (then a Yale undergraduate), this avian in its appearances during Formative and Classic times is better known as the "Principal Bird Deity" (PBD) and has been well established by more recent scholarship as the avian form of the great deity Itzamnaaj.

Looking back over the past seven decades, I am still puzzled that Thompson, discussing Maya day names and glyphs in his great 1950 volume, failed to see the significance of the fact that both the K'iche' and the Ixil name for *Ajaw*, the last day in the list of twenty days, is *Junajpu*. Or that the Poqomchi' name for that same day is *Ajpu*, meaning "he of the blowgun." Or that the head form glyph for the day in the Classic stone inscriptions shows the profile face of a young man with a black spot or spots on the cheek, just like the two young blowgunners of the polychrome plate illustrated by Frans Blom in an article Thompson had edited. Amazingly, "Popol Vuh" appears nowhere in the voluminous index to the book.

One question needs to be answered: Why do recognizable depictions of the Hero Twins and their defeat of the PBD and the lords of Xibalba never seem to show up on Classic Maya stone reliefs—stelae, panels, lintels, and so forth? The answer is that these monuments had an entirely different function from pictorial ceramics: largely for public display, they were produced under the authority of dynastic rulers to assert their origin, genealogy, accession to office, notable events such as military victories, and the performance of royal rituals and were usually geared to the Long Count calendar—in other words, to what was virtually linear time.

In contrast, Popol Vuh–related scenes and individuals seem pretty much restricted to ceramics and to cave paintings (as in the Naj Tunich cave; see Stone 1995). These vases, bowls, and dishes belonged to the world of palaces and elite residences and covered a huge range of subject matter—everything from actual palace interiors to complex mythologies including and extending far beyond the Hero Twins saga and even scenes of drunkenness and enema-taking.

The most explicit representations of the Hero Twins, their defeated brothers the Monkey-man scribal gods, and the blowgun episode are on what I dubbed "Codex-Style" pottery, since it looked to me as though the scribal artists who painted it had also painted codices. Many hundreds of such vessels are known, and they originated in the area of the Peten and Campeche controlled by the Late Classic rulers of the Kaan ("Snake") kingdom. But no Classic codices survived the Classic Maya collapse and the Spanish invasion in the sixteenth century. These codices must have held the bulk of their history, mythology, and astronomical knowledge. As the latest translator of the Popol Vuh has said regarding the destruction of Maya manuscripts, "We can only add our laments to those of the Maya over this irretrievable loss of a people's literary heritage. Of the many highland Maya hieroglyphic books that must surely have existed in highland Guatemala, not a single one is known to have survived" (Christenson 2007: 34).

We should keep in mind the old adage "absence of evidence is not evidence of absence" when trying to reconstruct Maya thought and beliefs that flourished over twelve centuries before our own time.

REFERENCES CITED

Bardawil, Lawrence W. 1976. "The Principal Bird Deity in Maya Art: An Iconographic Study of Form and Meaning." In *The Art, Iconography, and Dynastic History of Palenque, Part III*, ed. Merle Green Robertson, 195–209. Proceedings of the Segunda Mesa Redonda de Palenque, 1974. Pre-Columbian Art Research, Pebble Beach, CA.

Blom, Frans. 1950. "A Polychrome Maya Plate from Quintana Roo." In *Notes on Middle American Archaeology and Ethnology*, ed. J. Eric S. Thompson, vol. 4, no. 98, 46–47. Carnegie Institution, Washington, DC.

Christenson, Allen J. 2007. *Popol Vuh—the Sacred Book of the Maya*. 2nd revised ed. University of Oklahoma Press, Norman.

Coe, Michael D. 1973. *The Maya Scribe and His World*. Grolier Club, New York.

Coe, Michael D. 1989. "The Hero Twins: Myth and Images." In *The Maya Vase Book*, vol. 1, ed. Justin Kerr, 161–84. Kerr Associates, New York.

Coe, Michael D., and Justin Kerr. 1978. *Lords of the Underworld: Masterpieces of Classic Maya Ceramics*. Princeton University Press, Princeton, NJ.

Hellmuth, Nicholas. 1987. *Monster und Menschen*. Akademische Druck- und Verlagsanstalt, Graz, Austria.

Lowe, Gareth W. 1982. "Izapa Religion, Cosmology, and Ritual." In *Izapa: An Introduction to the Ruins and Monuments*, ed. Gareth W. Lowe, Thomas A. Lee, and Eduardo Martínez Espinosa, 269–306. Brigham Young University, Provo, UT.

Morley, Sylvanus G. 1946. *The Ancient Maya*. Stanford University Press, Stanford, CA.

Norman, V. Garth. 1976. *Izapa Sculpture*, Part II: *Text*. Papers of the New World Archaeological Foundation 30. Brigham Young University, Provo, UT.

Recinos, Adrián, Delia Goetz, and Sylvanus G. Morley. 1950. *Popol Vuh: The Sacred Book of the Ancient Quiché Maya*. [Translation from the Spanish version of Adrián Recinos]. University of Oklahoma Press, Norman.

Robicsek, Francis, and Donald Hales. 1981. *The Maya Book of the Dead: The Ceramic Codex*. University of Virginia Art Museum, Charlottesville.

Stone, Andea J. 1995. *Images from the Underworld: Naj Tunich and the Tradition of Maya Cave Painting*. University of Texas Press, Austin.

Thompson, J. Eric S. 1950. *Maya Hieroglyphic Writing: An Introduction*. Carnegie Institution of Washington, publication 589. Carnegie Institution, Washington, DC.

The Myths of the Popol Vuh
in Cosmology, Art, and Ritual

1

Introduction

The Popol Vuh as a Window into the Mind of the Ancient Maya

ALLEN J. CHRISTENSON AND FRAUKE SACHSE

THE ORIGINS OF THE POPOL VUH

The Popol Vuh was compiled in the mid-sixteenth century by surviving members of the ancient K'iche'-Maya royal court. It is the single most important highland Maya text of its kind, containing a narrative of the creation of the world, the ordering of the cosmos, the nature of the gods, and the historical development of the various highland Maya groups prior to the Spanish Invasion. Since its first publication in the nineteenth century, the Popol Vuh has had a major impact on our understanding of both Precolumbian and present-day Maya culture. The myths found in the Popol Vuh have clear antecedents in the arts as well as textual records that reach well into the Preclassic era. Many of these mythic stories mirror a fundamental worldview that is at the core of present-day Maya oral traditions and ritual practices. Connecting the ancient past with the present, these myths help us understand Maya thought through time. The present edition not only aims to deepen our understanding of the myths contained in the Popol Vuh but also presents the work of some of the leading scholars in the field of Mesoamerican culture that elucidates how Popol Vuh mythology can aid in the analysis and interpretation of the ancient Maya past.

The authors of the Popol Vuh wrote that their work was based on an ancient book that was venerated by the Precolumbian K'iche' kings who consulted it often. They described this older version of the Popol Vuh as an *ilb'al*, literally "an instrument of sight." The word today is used to refer to the clear quartz crystals K'iche' *ajq'ijab'* (traditional highland Maya religious specialists) use in divinatory ceremonies. It is

DOI: 10.5876/9781646421992.c001

also the word used for magnifying glasses or spectacles, by which things may be seen more clearly. The kings are not described as "reading" the text but rather "seeing" its contents:

> They knew if there would be war. It was clear before their faces. They saw if there would be death, if there would be hunger. They surely knew if there would be strife. There was an *ilb'al*—there was a book. Popol Vuh was their name for it. (Popol Vuh, fol. 54r; Christenson 2007: 287)

The authors of the sixteenth-century text of the Popol Vuh wrote that what they compiled was based in some way on the contents of the more ancient version. There has been a great deal of speculation regarding the nature of this Precolumbian Popol Vuh and its relationship to the version we have today. The introductory section of the Popol Vuh includes the following statement:

> We shall bring it [this book] forth because there is no longer the means whereby the Popol Vuh may be seen, the means of seeing clearly that had come from across the sea—the account of our obscurity, and the means of seeing life clearly, as it is said. The original book exists that was written anciently, but its witnesses and those who ponder it hide their faces. (Popol Vuh, fol. 1r; Christenson 2007: 64)

This passage raises some intriguing questions. First, did the Precolumbian version of the Popol Vuh exist in the sixteenth century, and second, was it available to the K'iche' authors of our present version? The text suggests that the answer to both questions may be yes. The first sentence of the passage, which acknowledges that "there is no longer the means whereby the Popol Vuh may be seen," may be interpreted as referring to the destruction or loss of the original book. But the phrase may simply mean that the text is hidden and unavailable for public display. This is certainly in keeping with modern highland Maya usage of the phrase. In traditional Maya communities, sacred objects such as old books, official papers, and ritual paraphernalia are generally kept wrapped in bundles and hidden in chests or kept out of sight in the lofts of houses. They are rarely taken out except under ritually appropriate circumstances. For example, in the Tz'utujil-Maya community of Santiago Atitlán, the town's most precious silver vessels, documents, missals, and other ritual objects are kept in a locked chest. This chest is only opened once a year. When this occurs, the doors are locked and men are posted as guards to ensure privacy. The objects are removed from the chest one by one, checked against a very old inventory, and laid out on the ground on cloths to ensure that they do not touch the ground. The contents of the chest are considered living beings and must be allowed to "breathe" and to be reanimated with prayers and offerings, or they would die. During the year, if anyone were to ask about the contents of this chest or any number of others scattered around the community, the common answer is that *ma kaka'yxi' ta* "they cannot be seen." On the other hand, if something has been stolen or destroyed, the answer is that *ma k'o ta* "it does not exist," or if the person knows the circumstances, he will describe the disappearance. The assertion that the Popol Vuh could not be seen does not therefore necessarily mean that it did not exist anymore.

The next sentence in the passage asserts that "the original exists that was written anciently" and that it is the "witnesses and those who ponder it" who "hide their faces." The text is clear here that the ancient book "exists" rather than "once existed." It is the keepers of the text who are in hiding, implying that the Precolonial version may have still been available to the authors at least by the mid-sixteenth century. The authors of the version of the Popol Vuh available today were anonymous. In the text they refer to themselves as "we," as seen in the passage just quoted. This indicates that more than one contributed to the compilation of the book. The text suggests, however, that they were members of the old K'iche' nobility. Toward the end of the book, the authors declare that the three Nim Ch'okoj (Great Stewards) of the principal K'iche' ruling lineages were "the mothers of the word, and the fathers of the word" (Christenson 2007: 305). *Tzij* (word) is used in the text to describe the Popol Vuh itself (folio 1 recto, in Christenson 2003: 13, 264), suggesting that the Nim Ch'okoj may have been the authors of the book. Nim Ch'okoj was a relatively minor position within the K'iche' nobility, charged with certain duties at royal banquets, perhaps including the recitation of tales dealing with the gods, heroes, and past rulers of the K'iche' nation. In this position they likely would have had access to manuscripts containing such traditions at the K'iche' court (Tedlock 1996: 56–57; Akkeren 2003).

Unlike other documents of the period, the authors of the Popol Vuh chose to remain anonymous, referring to themselves only as "we" (Christenson 2007: 64). The authors' anonymity is unusual since most Early Colonial period highland Maya documents were prepared for some official purpose, such as land titles submitted to the Spanish courts to assert border disputes and claims of privilege. These were all duly signed by their authors as testimony of their veracity. For whatever reason, those who were responsible for compiling the Popol Vuh did not wish their identities to be known. It is likely that those who wrote the Popol Vuh purposely hid their names as it was not intended for the eyes of Spanish ecclesiastical and political authorities. Although the text was compiled after the Spanish Invasion, the authors described the traditional Maya gods as luminous, wise beings who "gave voice to all things and accomplished their purpose in purity of being and in truth" long before the arrival of the European invaders (Christenson 2007: 63). There is certainly no denigration of the Maya gods such as is found in the *Título de Totonicapán*, which was prepared as a legal document and submitted to the Spanish courts. So as not to offend the ecclesiastical and secular Spanish authorities, the K'iche' authors of the Totonicapán document stress that they are the "grandchildren and children of Adam and Eve, Noah, Abraham, Isaac and Jacob" and that they became "lost in Assyria" because of Shalmaneser (Carmack and Mondloch 1983 [1554]: 174), a reference to the lost ten tribes of Israel that was a fairly common explanation for the presence of people in the New World taught by the earliest Christian missionaries. The *Título de Totonicapán* declares that they "fell into lies" and briefly mentions the sun god Junajpu and the moon god Xb'alanke as examples (1983 [1554]: 174).

This stands in marked contrast to the Popol Vuh, which has virtually no intrusive Christian or Spanish cultural influences in the text itself and describes the ancient Maya gods as beneficent and life-giving, as in this prayer:

> Pleasing is the day, you, Juraqan, and you, Heart of Sky and Earth, you who give abundance and new life, and you who give daughters and sons. Be at peace, scatter your abundance and new life. May life and creation be given. May my daughters and my sons be multiplied and created, that they may provide for you, sustain you, and call upon you on the roads, on the cleared pathways, along the courses of the rivers, in the canyons, beneath the trees and the bushes. Give, then, their daughters and their sons. (Popol Vuh, fol. 54r–54v; Christenson 2007: 289)

Such unapologetic reverence for the ancient gods would have been offensive to the Spanish authorities, not to mention the Roman Catholic clergy. During the early decades of the Spanish Invasion, the most obvious expressions of Maya religion and literature were either destroyed or forced into hiding. Precolumbian texts were singled out as particularly dangerous hindrances to the conversion of the people to Christianity and were actively sought out and destroyed. Those who were found in possession of such books were persecuted and even killed. Bartolomé de Las Casas (1958: 346) witnessed the destruction of a number of such books in the early sixteenth century, which were burned to "protect" the Maya from their traditional religion: "These books were seen by our clergy, and even I saw part of those which were burned by the monks, apparently because they thought [they] might harm the Indians in matters concerning religion, since at that time they were at the beginning of their conversion."

As much as 200 years later, Francisco Ximénez (1929–31, I.i.5) wrote that in the K'iche' community of Chichicastenango, many indigenous books were still kept in secret so the Spanish authorities would not learn of them. It was the loss of such precious books as the Precolumbian version of the Popol Vuh that may have prompted K'iche' scribes to preserve what they could of their literature by transcribing the contents into a form that would make it safer from the fiery purges of the Christian authorities. The authors of the Popol Vuh may have recognized the danger in this and cloaked themselves with anonymity to protect themselves.

Regardless of whether the authors of the sixteenth-century manuscript version of the Popol Vuh had direct access to a Precolumbian book, it should not be assumed that they wrote a word-for-word transcription of the original. The few Precolumbian Maya books that survive, as well as the numerous inscriptions found on stelae, altars, architectural wall panels, and the like, all bear texts that are highly formalized and condensed references to dates, persons, and events that briefly outline the stories they wish to tell. These are often accompanied by illustrations to further elucidate the otherwise terse prose. No known Precolumbian text contains the kind of long storytelling devices, descriptive detail, commentary, and extensive passages of dialogue found in the Popol Vuh. Nor is the structure of the written language conducive to such extended narrative. The Popol Vuh, as written in the mid-sixteenth century, is more likely to have been a compilation of oral traditions based to one degree or another on mythic and historical details outlined in a Precolumbian codex with their associated painted illustrations.

THE XIMÉNEZ COPY OF THE POPOL VUH

The fate of the sixteenth-century transcription of the Popol Vuh is unknown for the next 150 years. At some time during this period, it was taken from Santa Cruz del Quiché to the nearby town of Chuwila', now known as Santo Tomás Chichicastenango. Chichicastenango had long since eclipsed Santa Cruz in size and importance, and most members of the K'iche' nobility had transferred their residence there. Between 1701 and 1704, a Dominican friar named Francisco Ximénez, the parish priest of Chichicastenango, came to obtain the manuscript. Since 1694, Ximénez had served in various Maya communities where he learned a number of dialects and studied K'iche' grammar so he could teach it to newly arrived clerics. Ximénez was also interested in the ancient traditions of the K'iche'. He noted that in his parish the people still conserved ancient "errors" they had believed prior to the arrival of the Spaniards (Ximénez 1929–31, I.i.54). His curiosity concerning ancient K'iche' history and religion may have overcome the suspicion of the guardians of the Popol Vuh manuscript, and they allowed him to borrow it, at least long enough to make a copy. In his *proemium*, Ximénez writes that the book had a wide circulation in the town and that the K'iche' knew the myths from the Popol Vuh and other, similar books well:

It was with great reserve that these manuscripts were kept among them, with such secrecy, that none of the ancient ministers knew of it; and investigating this point, while I was in the parish of Santo Tomas Chichicastenango, I found that it was the doctrine which they first imbibed with their mother's milk, and that all of them

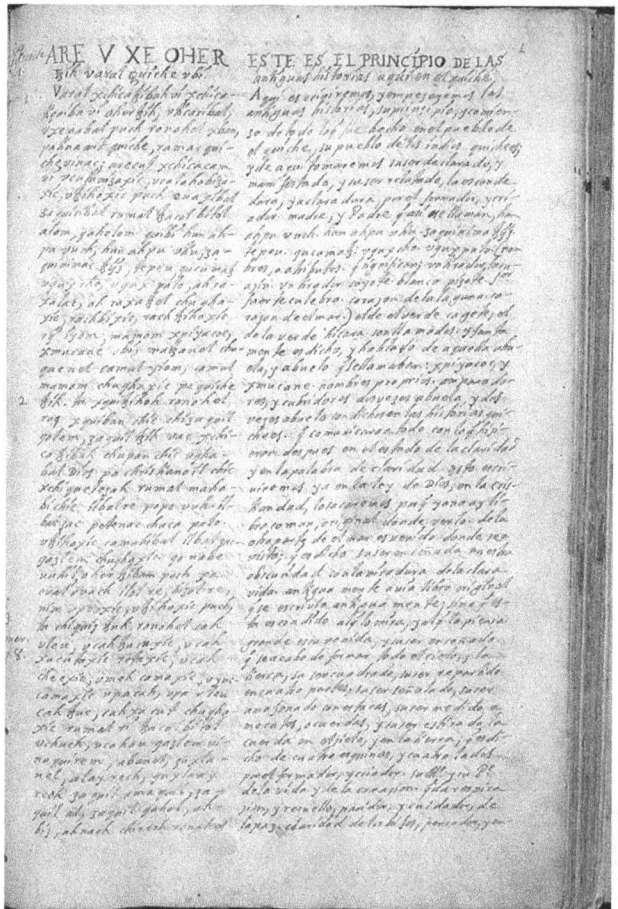

FIGURE 1.1. Folio 1r of the Ximénez manuscript (Ayer MS 1515) of the Popol Vuh. *Courtesy*, Newberry Library, Chicago.

knew it almost by heart; and I found that they had many of these books among them. (Ximénez 1929–31, I.i.5, in Recinos et al. 1950: 6)

Ximénez's copy of the Popol Vuh manuscript comprises a total of fifty-six double-sided folios and is organized in two columns, the original K'iche' text on the left and a Spanish translation on the right (figure 1.1). Ximénez explains that he modified the orthography of the original text that was shown to him in Chichicastenango. We do not know what else Ximénez may have changed or left out in the process of copying, but his manuscript is the oldest version of the K'iche' text we have today. It is unknown what happened to the original sixteenth-century manuscript version, although presumably Ximénez returned it to its K'iche' owners.

After the expulsion of the religious orders from Guatemala and the closing of all convents and monasteries in 1829, Ximénez's papers ended up in the library of the University of San Carlos in Guatemala City, where they were first discovered by Juan Gavarrete. Gavarrete produced a handwritten copy titled *Empiezan las historias del origen de los Indios* (Beginning of the history of the origin of the Indians). However, this copy was not published until 1872 (see Recinos et al. 1950: 45–46).

In 1854, a copy of the original Ximénez manuscript was shown to the Austrian diplomat Karl Scherzer on his travels through Guatemala. Scherzer showed particular interest in the text of the Popol Vuh and commissioned a copy of the Spanish column, which he published on his return to Vienna in 1857 under the title *Las historias del origen de los Indios*. Only a short time later, the French priest, collector, and scholar Charles Étienne Brasseur de Bourbourg obtained Ximénez's papers, including a copy of the Popol Vuh, for his personal collection. In 1861, he published the first translation of the original K'iche' text into French under the title *Popol Vuh: Le livre sacré et les mythes de l'antiquité américaine avec les livres héroïques et historiques des Quichés*. After Brasseur's death, the manuscript was purchased by Alphonso Pinart, who sold it in 1883 to the American collector Edward E. Ayer. In 1911, Ayer donated his collection to the Newberry Library in Chicago, where the Popol Vuh resides today, cataloged as Ayer MS 1515.

Ever since Brasseur's first rendering into French, many scholars have contributed to making the Popol Vuh accessible in European languages. The number of existing editions and translations is too long to be listed here in full, but to give an idea of the scholarship that has been produced on the text over the years, we would like to mention a few.

While most of the early scholarship was based on Brasseur's translation, scholars sometimes produced their own translations, such as that of Eduard Seler, published posthumously by Gerd Kutscher in 1975. The first systematic translation that also reproduced the K'iche' text, however, was the German version made by Leonhard Schultze-Jena in 1944. This translation is rarely used today due to its rather dated linguistic style, although in many instances his translation is remarkably precise. Similarly, José Antonio Villacorta Calderón produced a line-by-line translation of the K'iche' text into Spanish that was published in 1962 and was for a long time the standard Spanish translation.

A more popular translation into Spanish was produced by Adrián Recinos in 1947. Recinos's translation was later rendered into English by Delia Goetz and Silvanus G. Morley (1950), which became one of the most widely distributed editions in the English-speaking world. Munro S. Edmonson (1971) published the entire K'iche' text with parallel English translation, arranged for the first time using parallel couplets, recognizing that the Popol Vuh was composed utilizing Maya poetic forms.

Dennis Tedlock released his translation based on the original K'iche' text in 1985 (republished in a second revised edition in 1996). Allen J. Christenson produced a two-volume critical edition of the Popol Vuh. The first volume contains a grammatic English translation (2003, 2007). The second volume includes the original K'iche' text in both its original modified Latin and modern orthographies, as well as a literal line-by-line literal English translation (2004). The later electronic version also includes a high-resolution scan of the original manuscript, as well as a new Spanish translation of the text (2007).

After releasing a poetic monolingual K'iche' edition of the "Popol Wuj" in 1999, the Guatemalan scholar and native speaker of K'iche' Enrique Sam Colop published a Spanish translation of the text in 2008. There are also translations of the Popol Vuh, in whole or in part, rendered into other Mayan languages. For the most part, these are re-translations of either Scherzer's edition or other Spanish translations (see, e.g., ALMG 2001a, 2001b, 2001c). Several of the aforementioned editions are referenced in the present volume. Each translation reflects a different hermeneutical approach and has its own merits.

THE POPOL VUH IN MAYA STUDIES

Early scholarship recognized the Popol Vuh first and foremost as a source for the mythology of Mesoamerica in general. The first scholars who referred to the Popol Vuh in their research include Hubert Bancroft, Daniel G. Brinton, H. D. Charencey, and Eduard Seler, among others (see Recinos et al. 1950: 45). Brinton (1881, 1882) used the text to reconstruct ancient Maya religion by analyzing the names of the K'iche' gods and their mythic histories. Similarly, the father of Mesoamerican studies in Germany, Eduard Seler (see, e.g., 1894, 1907), used the myths of the Popol Vuh to analyze and interpret indigenous texts from Central Mexico.

More recently, ethnohistorians have attempted to place the Popol Vuh in the context of other written sources composed by K'iche' and Kaqchikel scribes to reconstruct the Precolonial history of the highland Maya (Recinos et al. 1957; Edmonson 1964; Carmack 1968, 1981; Fox 1978, among others). Robert M. Carmack's groundbreaking work in this regard relied heavily on his analysis of the Popol Vuh as the central source against which all other indigenous texts from highland Guatemala were matched and compared.

The value of the mythological narratives from the Popol Vuh for our understanding of ancient Maya culture was again recognized in the 1970s, when Michael D. Coe first identified the characters of the Hero Twins in the iconography of Classic Maya vases (see preface, this volume). Coe's identification established a new paradigm for both iconographers and epigraphers to search for parallels between

Colonial and Classic Maya written records. This includes a growing awareness of the strong Central Mexican influence on Postclassic highland Maya culture that is also reflected in the Popol Vuh narratives, as previously noted by Seler (1913). Building on Coe's foundational work, David Freidel, Linda Schele, and Joy Parker (1993: 43) asserted that the mythic traditions of the Popol Vuh, as well as other Colonial Maya texts, are key to interpreting core elements of ancient Maya religion: "The Popol Vuh is a touchstone and the closest thing to a Maya bible surviving to the present." Scholars working to interpret the material remains of ancient Maya culture, religion, and ritual practices have often taken into account the ancient myths from highland Maya texts such as the Popol Vuh.

The Popol Vuh has also had a significant impact on archaeological research. Our understanding of Popol Vuh mythology has helped identify related ritual practices in the archaeological record, including the cosmological layout of architectural patterns, burial practice, and cave rituals (see, e.g., Moyes and Awe, chapter 7, this volume). For example, the archaeological interpretation of ballcourts and the caches found therein has been helped by the textual understanding of the role of the ballgame in the Popol Vuh and its function in ordering the cosmos. Similarly, Classic Maya burial practices are better understood with reference to the eschatological mythology in the K'iche' text. The mytho-historical sections of the Popol Vuh that describe the arrival of the K'iche' forefathers following a long migration with various settlements along the way have helped identify specific archaeological sites in the highlands. It is again Robert Carmack's (1981) well-published study of the K'iche' capital at Q'umarkaj (Utatlán) that is the best-known example of this approach, which combines archaeological and ethnohistoric research based on the Popol Vuh.

Even more relevant is the role of ethnographic research, or more precisely the cultural knowledge of present-day highland Maya, for our interpretation of the Popol Vuh text. Iyaxel Cojtí Ren's analysis of the *saqarib'al* "dawning places," included in this volume, is just one of many examples (see chapter 4). The scholarship on the Popol Vuh, which interprets not only the text itself but how it assists in reconstructing Ancient Maya culture and thought, is relevant to modern Maya people today. Particularly since the devastating Guatemalan civil war (1960–1996), the Popol Vuh has become a focal point for uniting disparate Maya groups as part of a general resurgence in interest in their ancestral heritage that crosses language and cultural backgrounds. In this context, the Popol Vuh constitutes an important source of modern identity, not only for K'iche' or highland Maya but for all Maya people. Any scholarship that employs the Popol Vuh to reconstruct ancient Maya culture and thought therefore has an ethical dimension inasmuch as it must not only include the voice of the K'iche' but also be aware of being "heard" by all Maya who recognize the Popol Vuh as a marker of their identity.

THE CONTRIBUTIONS IN THIS VOLUME

The chapters in this volume reflect an integrated and comparative approach to the Popol Vuh, by which its myths are analyzed to elucidate the ancient Maya past while recognizing that archaeological and ethnographic information can reciprocally help us better understand the text itself. The chapters are grouped into four thematic parts.

The first part includes chapters that focus on the interpretation of highland Maya worldview and thought through analysis of the Popol Vuh text itself.

Allen J. Christenson's contribution analyzes the *topos* of world and human creation. Christenson discusses the mutual interdependence between deities and humans. Much of the first half of the Popol Vuh text is devoted to the creation of the world and the gods' attempts to order it as a self-sustaining entity. The gods focused their efforts on forming beings who would be able to perpetuate not only the life of the world they established but their own lives as well. Sacred ritual, performed at the proper time and in a manner established by ancient precedent, is necessary to maintain the link between this world and the world of the sacred. This reciprocity is fundamental to Maya thought—humans could not exist without the gods nourishing and sustaining them with food, light, and water. At the same time, the gods require nourishment as well in the form of prayers, offerings, and properly timed rituals of rebirth.

In the following chapter, Frauke Sachse analyzes the textual and cosmological coherence of the Popol Vuh as a source. She argues that the narrative myths of the text are combined to fit the cultural logic of highland Maya eschatological belief, which sees human life as analogous to the growth cycle of maize. Analyzing the account of world and human creation, as well as the migration of the K'iche' people, she shows that this analogy forms a conceptual metaphor that is reflected in the language of the Popol Vuh and creates a window into highland Maya cultural worldview.

Iyaxel Cojtí Ren's contribution complements the preceding two chapters in that it identifies a narrative element from the Popol Vuh as a cultural metaphor. Drawing on analogies between Central Mexican and Maya mythologies, Cojtí Ren interprets the mythic episode in the text that describes the first dawn of the sun (*saqirik*) as a metaphor for the foundation of cultural and political power through ceremony. Cojtí Ren argues that "dawning" rituals were a shared cultural trait among the various major highland Maya groups, particularly the K'iche' and Kaqchikel. She asserts that the existence of *saqarib'al* altars is proof of the continuity of this concept to the present day.

The second part of this volume groups together chapters that focus on understanding the Precolumbian Maya archaeological record as it relates to the myths of the Popol Vuh. The first two chapters deal with the interpretation of architectural arrangements and burials.

Jaime J. Awe shows that Maize God mythology reaches back into the Preclassic era and can be identified in the architectural program at Cahal Pech (Belize). Analyzing the components of a burial within a specific structure of the site, he argues that the cosmological interpretation of this layout is informed by the Popol Vuh narrative and proves the continuity of an eschatological belief in resurrection.

Thomas H. Guderjan and Colin Snider show how the narratives of the Popol Vuh can be used to understand Classic Maya architecture. Based on a case study from Blue Creek in Belize, they argue that architectural arrangements reflect political power that is legitimized by religious ideology. The role of the Hero Twins as ballplayers, as well as the description of the Mountain of Sustenance as the place of human creation in the Popol Vuh, assist in understanding the cosmological layout of Classic Maya sites. This includes the function of monumental architecture, ballcourts, and the positioning of caches.

In their joint chapter, Holley Moyes and Jaime Awe demonstrate the relevance of Popol Vuh mythology for the interpretation of archaeological finds in Classic Maya caves. They provide a detailed analysis of the Main Chamber of the undisturbed cave at Actun Tunichil Muknal in Belize. Drawing on creation mythology from the Popol Vuh, they demonstrate that the artifacts and remains found in this context show that the cave was used to ritually reenact mythological world creation.

Part 3 is devoted to the analysis of ancient Maya iconographic motifs. Barbara MacLeod proposes that the deeds of the Hero Twins in the Popol Vuh were rooted in specific narrative themes also found in Classic Maya mythology. Drawing on evidence from two recently discovered Codex-Style ceramic vessels as well as calendric data from Naj Tunich cave, McLeod links the recurrent motif of the sacrifice of the "Baby Jaguar" and "Snake Lady" with the history of the Hero Twins in the underworld realm of Xibalba. Not only does this elucidate the survival of elements of this major cycle of ancient Maya myth into the sixteenth century, but it broadens our understanding of the richness of the underlying story.

Karen Bassie-Sweet and Nicholas Hopkins compile data drawn from Classic Maya ceramic art as well as textual evidence to explore the nature and role of predatory birds in the Popol Vuh. Birds play key roles in Maya mythology as avatars and messengers of various gods, rulers, and secondary lords. This study focuses on the eagle and the laughing falcon and their relationship to specific Maya deities as well as analogous gods venerated by the Nahua cultures of Central Mexico.

The chapters in the fourth part of this volume are concerned with mythological continuities and change. Oswaldo Chinchilla Mazariegos critically evaluates the methodological approach of using the Popol Vuh as a source for the interpretation of Classic Maya iconography and ancient Maya religion and mythology. He reassesses Michael Coe's original association of the Hero Twins and their father with the images of the Headband Twins and the Maize God on Classic Maya ceramics. Drawing on comparative evidence from other parts of Mesoamerica, Chinchilla Mazariegos proposes an alternative interpretation of Classic Maya imagery with the solar and lunar heroes in Mexica and Oaxacan mythology and cautions against using the Popol Vuh as a sole source for reconstructing Classic Maya mythology.

Julia Guernsey's chapter connects the myths of the Popol Vuh with iconography from Preclassic Izapa. Focusing on the Great Bird imagery, or the Principal Bird Deity and its association with Seven Macaw from the Popol Vuh narrative, she discusses continuity and change in the mythological representations. She argues that the myth evolved over time, based on changes in the principles of social organization.

The last chapter in this part by Jesper Nielsen, Karl Taube, Christophe Helmke, and Héctor Escobedo expands the approach to mythological continuity and change, demonstrating that narratives from the Popol Vuh can be key to understanding mythologies from other parts of Mesoamerica. They likewise focus on the fight with the Great Bird, presenting iconographic evidence from Teotihuacan murals, Central Mexican codices, and Izapan monuments to demonstrate that the slaying of a Great Bird with solar aspects was a common Mesoamerican mythological theme.

FINAL REMARKS

The present volume combines interpretations of myths from the Popol Vuh with analyses of archaeological, iconographic, epigraphic, and ethnographic data that can be elucidated from the narrative found in this important highland Maya text. Several of the contributors reflect on the methodological aspects of their comparative approach. Indeed, appropriate caution must be taken when utilizing the Popol Vuh as a tool for interpreting Mesoamerican religions outside its temporal and geographic origins. The authors of the Popol Vuh did not intend to record a comprehensive theogony that addressed all aspects of their religion, ceremonial practices, or worldview. The text belongs to a very specific area of the Guatemalan highlands that had just recently suffered the trauma of invasion by a foreign power. Their world was far different from that of their own K'iche' ancestors, much less that of the Classic Maya in the distant lowlands of the Peten and Yucatan or the inhabitants of other regions of Mesoamerica. Nevertheless, the Popol Vuh does preserve fundamental aspects of worldview and ancient mythology that often resonate with analogous concepts found in the art and literature of ancient Mesoamerica. Despite all the potential pitfalls, the Popol Vuh has proven to be a rich and reliable source for indigenous beliefs regarding Maya deities and their actions in the mythic past. It is, after all, the singular text in which Maya voices, only recently torn from their Preconquest world, speak of their own myths and history, apparently with their people in mind as the intended listeners. Nearly every scholar in the field of Mesoamerican studies has used it to one degree or another as an aid to interpret the literature and artistic motifs of the region. The list of recent scholars who have relied on passages from the Popol Vuh in their work is far too lengthy to include in a comprehensive way. Many appear in this volume as contributors. Suffice it to say that the importance of the Popol Vuh as a window into the mind of the ancient Maya has only grown with time tempered, as is appropriate, with the understanding that it is just one window and we all wish there were more like it.

A NOTE ON SPELLING CONVENTIONS

The authors of the Popol Vuh utilized a modified Latin script that had been developed by early missionaries and taught to the ruling elite in special monastery schools soon after the Spanish Invasion. In this volume, the K'iche' terms from the Popol Vuh are rendered in the modern orthography for highland Maya languages as published by the Academy for Mayan Languages of Guatemala (1988). Where the etymology of proper names and titles is ambiguous or unclear, the original spelling in the manuscript is retained. This applies also to the title of the book Popol Vuh itself, which is kept in the original spelling out of respect for the orthographic rendering used by the sixteenth-century K'iche' authors of the text.

REFERENCES CITED

Academia de las Lenguas Mayas de Guatemala (ALMG). 1988. *Lenguas Mayas de Guatemala: Documento de referencia para la pronunciación de los nuevos alfabetos oficiales*. Documento 1. Instituto Indigenista Nacional, Guatemala City.

Academia de las Lenguas Mayas de Guatemala (ALMG). 2001a. *Poop Juuj: Lok' q'orb'al poqoman*. ALMG, Guatemala City.

Academia de las Lenguas Mayas de Guatemala (ALMG). 2001b. *Poop wuuj: tujaal tziij sakapulteko*. ALMG, Guatemala City.

Academia de las Lenguas Mayas de Guatemala (ALMG). 2001c. *Pop hum: skohnhob'al ab'xub'al popti'*. ALMG, Guatemala City.

Akkeren, Ruud van. 2003. "Authors of the Popol Vuh." *Ancient Mesoamerica* 14 (2): 237–56.

Brasseur de Bourbourg, Charles Étienne. 1861. *Popol Vuh: Le livre sacré et les mythes de l'antiquité américaine avec les livres héroïques et historiques des Quichés*. A. Bertrand, Paris.

Brinton, Daniel G. 1881. "The Names of the Gods in the Kiche Myths, Central America." *Proceedings of the American Philosophical Society* 19 (109): 613–47.

Brinton, Daniel G. 1882. *American Hero-Myths: A Study in the Native Religions of the Western Continent.* H. C. Watts, Philadelphia.

Carmack, Robert M. 1968. *Toltec Influence on the Postclassic Culture History of Highland Guatemala.* Middle American Research Institute Publications 26, 49–92. Tulane University, Middle American Research Institute, New Orleans.

Carmack, Robert M. 1981. *The Quiché Maya of Utatlán: The Evolution of a Highland Guatemala Kingdom.* University of Oklahoma Press, Norman.

Carmack, Robert M., and James Mondloch. 1983 [1554]. *El Título de Totonicapán: Texto, traducción y comentario.* Instituto de Investigaciones Filológicas, Centro de Estudios Mayas. Fuentes para el Estudio de la Cultura Maya 3. Universidad Nacional Autónoma de México, Mexico City.

Christenson, Allen J. 2003. *Popol Vuh: The Sacred Book of the Maya, the Great Classic of Central American Spirituality.* O Books, Winchester.

Christenson, Allen J. 2004. *Popol Vuh,* vol. 2: *Literal Poetic Version, Translation and Transcription.* O Books, Winchester.

Christenson, Allen J. 2007. *Popol Vuh—the Sacred Book of the Maya.* 2nd revised ed. University of Oklahoma Press, Norman.

Edmonson, Munro S. 1964. "Historia de la tierras altas mayas segun los documentos indígenas." In *Desarrollo cultural de los Maya,* ed. Evon Z. Vogt and Alberto Ruz L., 273–302. Universidad Autónoma de México, Mexico City.

Edmonson, Munro S. 1971. *The Book of Counsel: The Popol Vuh of the Quiche Maya of Guatemala.* Middle American Research Institute, New Orleans.

Fox, John W. 1978. *Quiche Conquest: Centralism and Regionalism in Highland Guatemalan State Development.* University of New Mexico Press, Albuquerque.

Freidel, David, Linda Schele, and Joy Parker. 1993. *Maya Cosmos: Three Thousand Years on the Shaman's Path.* William Morrow, New York.

Las Casas, Bartolomé de. 1958. *Apologética historia de las Indias.* Vol. 13. Biblioteca de Autores Españoles, Madrid.

Recinos Adrián. 1947. *Popol Vuh: Las antiguas historias del Quiché.* Fondo de Cultura Económica, Guatemala City.

Recinos, Adrián, Delia Goetz, and Sylvanus G. Morley. 1950. *Popol Vuh: The Sacred Book of the Ancient Quiché Maya.* [Translation from the Spanish version of Adrián Recinos.] University of Oklahoma Press, Norman.

Recinos, Adrián, Delia Goetz, and Sylvanus G. Morley. 1957. *Crónicas Indígenas.* Editorial Universitaria, Guatemala City.

Sam Colop, Enrique. 1999. *Popol Wuj: Version Poética K'iche'*. PEMBI-GTZ and Cholsamaj, Guatemala City.

Sam Colop, Enrique. 2008. *Popol Wuj: Traducción al español y notas*. Fundación Cholsamaj, Guatemala City.

Scherzer, Karl. 1857. *Las historias del origen de los Indios de esta provincia de Guatemala*. C. Gerold, Vienna.

Schultze-Jena, Leonhard. 1944. *Popol Vuh: Das heilige Buch der Quiché Indianer von Guatemala*. Kohlhammer, Stuttgart.

Seler, Eduard. 1894. "Der Fledermaus-Gott der Mayastämme." *Zeitschrift für Ethnologie* 26: 577–85.

Seler, Eduard. 1907. "Einiges über die natürlichen Grundlagen mexikanischer Mythen." *Zeitschrift für Ethnologie* 34: 1–41.

Seler, Eduard. 1913. "Der Bedeutungswandel in den Mythen des Popol Vuh: Eine Kritik." *Anthropos* 8 (2–3): 382–88.

Seler, Eduard. 1975. *Popol Vuh: Das Heilige Buch der Quiche Guatemalas (Stimmen indianischer Völker)*. Ed. Gerd Kutscher. Gebr. Mann Verlag, Berlin.

Tedlock, Dennis. 1996. *Popol Vuh: The Definite Edition of the Mayan Book of the Dawn of Life and the Glories of Gods and Kings*. 2nd revised ed. Simon and Schuster, New York.

Villacorta Calderón, José Antonio. 1962. *Popol-vuh: crestomatía quiché*. 2 vols. José de Pineda Ibarra and Ministerio de Educación Publica, Guatemala City.

Ximénez, Francisco. 1929–31. *Historia de la provincia de San Vicente de Chiapa y Guatemala*. Biblioteca "Goathemala" de la Sociedad de Geografía e Historia de Guatemala Publication 1. 3 vols. Tipografía Nacional, Guatemala City.

PART I

Understanding Highland Maya Worldviews through the Mythologies of the Popol Vuh

2

"For It Is with Words That We Are Sustained"

The Popol Vuh and the Creation of the First People

ALLEN J. CHRISTENSON

The K'iche'-Maya view of the creation as outlined in the Popol Vuh emphasizes the formation of beings who can provide for and sustain not only the newly created world but the gods themselves. In traditional Maya theology, gods are not immortal, any more than the elements or the living beings of the natural world. The sun dies each evening, maize plants dry up and die at the time of harvest, animals sicken and die, and gods suffer weakness and death in regular cycles. In the worldview of the Maya, human beings stand as mediators between this universal life and universal death. They alone bear the burden of carrying out life-renewing ceremonies so that rebirth can follow death naturally and in its proper time. In the Popol Vuh, the gods themselves declare that they require "providers and sustainers" who will be able to speak the appropriate life-giving words:

> It shall be found; it shall be discovered how we are to create shaped and framed people who will be our providers and sustainers. May we be called upon, and may we be remembered. For it is with words that we are sustained, O Midwife and Patriarch, our Grandmother and our Grandfather, Xpiyacoc and Xmucane. Thus may it be spoken. May it be sown. May it dawn so that we are called upon and supported, so that we are remembered by framed and shaped people. (Christenson 2007: 80)

The original K'iche' word for sustainer is *q'ol*, which refers to one who provides sustenance, primarily in the form of nourishment, but also nurtures in any other way—such as a mother caring for an infant. The wording of this passage implies that

DOI: 10.5876/9781646421992.c002

the authors of the Popol Vuh consider that human beings bear the burden of caring for the gods in much the same way a mother nourishes and cares for her child. In the theology of Roman Catholicism, if a person fails to participate in the sacraments of the church or to pray to God regularly, it may be personally deleterious, but it does not affect God's power or longevity. This is not true of traditional Maya theology. If *ajq'ijab'* (traditional K'iche' ritual specialists) do not carry out the proper ceremonies in season, they believe the world and its gods will simply cease to be.

THE CREATORS OF HUMANKIND

The text makes clear that the "sustainers" are to be framed and shaped by the gods, particularly the grandmother goddess Xmucane and the grandfather god Xpiyacoc (Christenson 2007: 62, 79–80). They bear several titles in the Popol Vuh text, but the most common are Alom (She Who Has Borne Children) and K'ajolom (He Who Has Engendered Sons), emphasizing their role as life bearers (2007: 60, 76). The linguistic structure of these titles is interesting. The root of Alom is *alaj* ("to bear a child" or "to give birth"). The form *alom* is in the perfect aspect of the verb ("to have borne" or "to have given birth"). In K'iche' the same verb is used when referring to the birth of either a male or a female child. The title does not specify the number of children, but because the Popol Vuh mentions that Xmucane bore at least one set of twins (2007: 113), the most accurate translation would be "She Who Has Given Birth to Children" or "She Who Has Borne Children." I suppose this could be translated simply as "Mother," and many have done so in the past. But K'iche' has a perfectly good word for "mother," *chuch*, which is used throughout the text. In this case I prefer to translate it in a form that most closely reflects the original language, despite the unwieldy length.

The male deity of the pair is Xpiyacoc, who bears as one of his major titles K'ajolom, derived from *k'ajolaj* ("to engender" or "to beget" a male child). In K'iche' there are separate words for a father engendering a male child (*k'ajolaj*) and a female child (*mialaj*). The form of the title again is in the perfect, thus the title would most literally be translated "He Who Has Engendered Sons" or "He Who Has Begotten Sons."

Notice that in paired titles, the female comes first—Midwife before Patriarch, Grandmother before Grandfather, She Who Has Borne Children before He Who Has Engendered Sons. This is consistent with modern K'iche' speech in which female terms generally precede male terms when paired. Thus ancestors are referred to as "the ancient mothers and fathers." In ritual processions, women generally walk ahead of the men (figure 2.1). A Maya *ajq'ij* once told me that this is because only women can create and bear life in the form of human flesh. They lead processions

FIGURE 2.1. Women leading procession, Santiago Atitlán. Photo by Allen J. Christenson.

because their life-giving power cleanses and prepares the way for the other participants in the procession and renews the life and power of the gods and saints borne
by the men behind them. Only women have that creative power.

   Another pair of the principal titles for the grandparent deities in the Popol Vuh
text is Tz'aqol (Framer) and B'itol (Shaper). Because it comes first, presumably
Tz'aqol is the title for the Grandmother and B'itol, coming second, would be the
title for the Grandfather, but this is only a supposition based on the usual arrangements of female/male pairing in which the female generally comes first. It does
make sense, however. Framing and shaping are the two principal means of creating things. The root verb of the title Tz'aqol is *tz'aq*, which is to build or construct
something from component parts. For example, *tz'aq* is used to describe the construction of a house—putting together the wood, adobe, thatch, concrete blocks,
glass for the windows, and other elements. It can also be used to describe making
a meal from various ingredients or a woven cloth from individual threads. These
things provide a framework for the created object. Since only women can create
a human body from the component parts of bones, flesh, hair, and other elements,
this would seem to be more appropriate to the role of the mother/grandmother.
When translating the text, I struggled over what English term to use here. Builder,
Constructor, Assembler, and others would all be appropriate but hardly seem ideal

in tone to the nature of this particular goddess as a creator deity. Maker and Creator are too general to reflect the original meaning of the title.

Translation work can be a frustrating endeavor, since there are often no precise equivalents in English for K'iche' terms. It thus becomes a process of choosing from a list of unsatisfying alternatives and compromises. The best solution I know of is to find the closest alternative and then provide a footnote to clarify the original meaning of the K'iche' word with as much of its nuance and subtlety as possible. The result is a flood of footnote entries that at times takes up more space on the page than the text itself. In the case of Tz'aqol, I eventually settled on "Framer," a useful term in that it accurately describes the process of giving a constructed framework to the created being while also being poetic enough to appropriately describe the generation of a significant object (for example, the American founding fathers are described as "framers of the Constitution" or the Christian deity is said to have "framed" the world [Hebrews 11:3]). At the same time, "Framer" is non-specific enough to avoid inappropriate links with Western religious traditions. I use this as just one example among many, not to emphasize the difficulties inherent in translating ancient texts but to lay bare the imperfect nature of the enterprise itself. No translation will ever be perfect or even satisfactory. It is the compromise we make to glean what we can from the great literary works of the world written in languages we do not speak. The Popol Vuh is far more beautiful and rich in its original language. Those who do not speak K'iche' are regrettably consigned to read the book through a dark glass flecked with distortions and imperfections. The effort more than repays the patient reader in the case of the Popol Vuh, but it should be remembered that it can never be the same as reading it in one's mother tongue. As I wrote in the preface to my published translation of the Popol Vuh, "Translation is an art whose cloth is woven from a variety of threads. Any defects are solely the fault of the weaver. Its beauty is solely dependent on the threads themselves" (Christenson 2007: 25). I have to say that the Maya authors of the Popol Vuh composed their work with achingly beautiful threads.

The other creator deity, likely the male counterpart to Tz'aqol, bears the title of B'itol (Shaper). The word is derived from *b'it*, a verb used to describe making something out of an amorphous substance, such as a vessel from a lump of clay or a sculpture from uncut stone. It is given shape rather than constructed from separate pieces. The pairing of Tz'aqol and B'itol is an example of merismus, a common literary practice in the Popol Vuh in which a broad concept (creation, in this case) is expressed by a pair of complementary elements that are narrower in meaning. Other examples of such paired elements include "sky-earth," representing all creation as a whole, "mountain-valley" for the face of the earth, "deer-birds" to describe all wild animals, and "dog-turkeys" to refer to all domesticated animals. The pairing of Tz'aqol-B'itol not only describes the union of female and male creator deities acting in concert but also recognizes the nature of creation as composed of both structural frame and modeled shape.

Together, the gods known as the Framer and the Shaper are seen as the principal deities who organize and give life to the world and all its inhabitants:

> All then was measured and staked out into four divisions, doubling over and stretching the measuring cords of the womb of sky and the womb of earth. Thus were established the four corners, the four sides, as it is said, by the Framer and the Shaper, the Mother and the Father of life and all creation, the giver of breath and the giver of heart, they who give birth and heart to the light everlasting, the child of light born of woman and the son of light born of man, they who are compassionate and wise in all things—all that exists in the sky and on the earth, in the lakes and in the sea. (Christenson 2007: 65–66)

THE POPOL VUH ACCOUNT OF THE CREATION OF THE WORLD

According to the Popol Vuh, the world before the creation consisted of a vast expanse of dark water shrouded by a sun-less darkened sky:

> This is the account of when all is still silent and placid. All is silent and calm. Hushed and empty is the womb of the sky.
>
> These, then, are the first words, the first speech. There is not yet one person, one animal, bird, fish, crab, tree, rock, hollow, canyon, meadow, or forest. All alone the sky exists. The face of the earth has not yet appeared. Alone lies the expanse of the sea, along with the womb of all the sky. There is not yet anything gathered together. All is at rest. Nothing stirs. All is languid, at rest in the sky. There is not yet anything standing erect. Only the expanse of the water, only the tranquil sea lies alone. There is not yet anything that might exist. All lies placid and silent in the darkness, in the night. (Christenson 2007: 67–68)

The authors of the Popol Vuh chose to write this passage describing the primordial world at the beginning of time in present-progressive tense, painting a picture of the stillness that existed prior to the creation as if in vision before their eyes. This is consistent with the practice of storytelling among the Maya today. When I first began working in the Guatemalan highlands in the mid-1970s as a linguist and ethnographer, traditional K'iche' homes in the more remote regions often lacked electricity. Lamps and candles were expensive or difficult to obtain. As a result, evenings were frequently spent without light. Maya families in such circumstances sometimes gathered to tell stories in the darkness before going to bed. These might be humorous tales about talking animals or parents telling their children what it was like when they were young. But a favorite way to spend the evening was for the elderly members of the family to talk about how things began—their village, their traditions, early ancestors, or even the birth of gods or Maya versions of Roman Catholic saints. In the Maya view of the world, how things begin their existence, to a great extent, determines their power and relevance in the present.

This fascination for the origin of things carries over into the more public Maya ritual offerings, processions, and ceremonies. Nearly all their major ceremonies deal with creation and rebirth in one way or another. When such ceremonies are performed, they are not seen by participants as commemorations or reenactments of the creation but as creation itself. In the Tz'utujil-Maya community of Santiago Atitlán, a sacred ceremony of world rebirth is performed in mid-November by a powerful ritual specialist called the *nab'eysil*. As part of the ceremony, the *nab'eysil* extracts a series of tunics from a sacred bundle, believed to be the "clothing" or "skins" of a powerful creator god the Tz'utujil call Martín. The *nab'eysil* wears these tunics in succession as he dances to the four cardinal directions to re-create the limits of the world (figure 2.2). Following the performance of this dance in 1997, the *nab'eysil* sought me out to ask if I had seen "the ancient *nawals* (gods and sacred ancestors) giving birth to the world." He explained that they had filled his soul with their presence as he danced, guiding him in his steps, and now everything was new again. In the eyes of the *nab'eysil*, the dance was not a symbol of the rebirth of the cosmos but a genuine creative act in which time folded inward on itself to replicate the actions of deity at the beginning of time.

The world in which the Maya live is difficult and sometimes cruel. It is a source of great hope that through prayer, sacred ritual, and offerings, the world and its guardians can return to the moment of their first creation to be reborn to new life in a pure, uncorrupted form. It is this periodic renewal that allows life itself to continue. If these rituals are not performed in the proper way and under the proper circumstances, the Maya believe that they and all creation would simply slip back into primordial darkness, chaos, and perpetual death. For the Maya who continue to practice their ancient traditions, storytelling and sacred rituals in the night are not simply the idle retelling or reenactment of events from long ago. Words and movements that follow ancient precedent have the power to make those present witnesses to and participants in the events described. As Stephen Houston and David Stuart (1996: 299) note with regard to the ancient Maya, kings who performed sacred drama clothed in the garments of deity were not merely engaged in mummery but shared in the divinity of those gods. They were not "theatrical illusion but a tangible, physical manifestation of a deity." When the modern Maya storyteller begins his tale with the phrase "let us spend this night with our ancestors," in a sense, he or she means it quite literally. Such experiences have the power to transport those present

FIGURE 2.2. *Nab'eysil* wearing the Martín tunic, Cofradía of San Juan, Santiago Atitlán. Photo by Allen J. Christenson.

back to the moment of first beginnings. The darkness of the room and the silence of the sparsely populated mountain terrain of such communities resonate with the soft sounds of the storyteller's voice—leaving the listeners with the almost palpable sense that they are in an ancient place that once existed before the first dawning of the sun. The description of the creation in the Popol Vuh in present tense reflects the Maya view that the creation of the world is not something exclusively belonging to the distant past but something that is renewed with each telling. Words have power—it is with words that the earth was first created. It is with the repetition of those words that the world is sustained and regenerated in endless cycles.

The speech uttered in prayers and rituals is focused not on praising or even thanking deity but rather on regenerative acts that would sustain the world and the very gods that created it. Human speech has power that mirrors the words of the gods at the beginning of time. The creation of the world itself is described in the text as "the first speech" and is initiated by the utterance of words:

"Then be it so. You are conceived. May the water be taken away, emptied out, so that
the plate of the earth may be created—may it be gathered and become level. Then
may it be sown; then may dawn the sky and the earth. There can be no worship, no
reverence given by what we have framed and what we have shaped, until humanity
has been created, until people have been made," they said.

Then the earth was created by them. Merely their word brought about the creation
of it. In order to create the earth, they said, "Earth," and immediately it was created.
Just like a cloud, like a mist, was the creation and formation of it.

Then they called forth the mountains from the water. Straightaway the great mountains came to be. It was merely their spirit essence, their miraculous power, that brought
about the conception of the mountains and the valleys. (Christenson 2007: 71–72)

THE CREATION OF THE ANIMALS

Maya gods are not infallible, and they make several botched attempts to create beings that can provide for and sustain the world. Their first attempt was the
animals of the mountains and forests, specifically deer, birds, pumas, jaguars, and
various poisonous serpents. Once formed, the gods called on the animals to speak
aloud the names of their creators (Christenson 2007: 76). But the animals proved
incapable of pronouncing the names of the gods. Instead, they just squawked, chat-
tered, and roared. Because of their incapacity to speak properly, their homes were
limited to the forest, and they were condemned to submit their bodies to be eaten
by those who could fulfill the gods' commands more successfully:

"Your calling will merely be to have your flesh eaten. Thus be it so. This must be your
service," they were told. (Christenson 2007: 77)

It may seem odd that the focus of successfully created beings should be their ability to speak the names of the gods intelligibly. When I first started work on a new
translation of the Popol Vuh in 1978, I requested the help of a group of *ajq'ijab'* in
the area of Momostenango with regard to certain esoteric terms in the text related
to traditional Maya ceremonies. They approached this work with a great deal of
caution because to fail to find the right words in translation would be to put *b'anom
tzij* ("lying words") in the mouths of the ancestors, an act they believed could bring
upon themselves illness or even death.

In Maya belief, to speak the name of something in a ritual context is to make it
physically manifest. This is also true of modern Maya ceremonialism. Before our
first session together, one of the *ajq'ijab'* asked me to put together a list of the names
of any gods or ancestors that might be mentioned on that day. When we had all
gathered together, this *ajq'ij* prepared a brazier with hot coals from the fire and

placed a spoonful of copal incense in the brazier. Once there was a good steady cloud of incense smoke, we each prepared ourselves in a cleansing ceremony, commonly done before any major ritual. Each person takes the brazier and waves it under each arm (to purify the actions of our hands), then in front of our chest (to purify our hearts), then finally in front of our faces, breathing the smoke into our lungs (to purify our thoughts). Then the *ajq'ij* took the brazier and waved it over the sheet of paper with the list of names as well as the computer-generated pages with the original K'iche' text I had prepared for that day. Having done so, the *ajq'ij* knelt before the pages and invoked each of the names of the gods and ancestors in turn, inviting them to be present in the room and to help us in the work we were to do that day so our hearts and minds would be pure and we would translate the words properly. At the end of each day of work, one of the *ajq'ijab'* would repeat each of the names again, thanking them individually for being with us. On one occasion, the *ajq'ij* apologized if they had something better to do that day but insisted that their presence was necessary for us "to know their words and their thoughts." Often the *ajq'ijab'* would pause after reading a name and briefly nod in acknowledgment of that person's presence in the room. For the *ajq'ijab'*, this was a physical presence, brought about by the pronunciation of the god's or ancestor's name. When gods are remembered or their names are spoken aloud, they are in a sense given a kind of rebirth. On a number of occasions, the *ajq'ijab'* noted that were it not for the Popol Vuh and for their ability to read and know its contents, the names of their ancestors would be forgotten. They would therefore be truly dead, never able to live again among their descendants. The word they used in the ceremony when reading through the litany of names was *k'astajik* ("to resurrect" or "to give life"). The simple act of speaking aloud the names of deities and ancestors gave them physical presence in the room as if they had been reborn.

THE CREATION OF THE MUD PERSON

After the creation of the animals in the Popol Vuh account, the gods made a second attempt using mud to form the flesh of a being they hoped would be able to sustain them. The resulting "mud person" turned out to be a failure as well:

> Then was the framing, the making of it. Of earth and mud was its flesh composed.
> But they saw that it was still not good. It merely came undone and crumbled. It
> merely became sodden and mushy. It merely fell apart and dissolved. Its head was
> not set apart properly. Its face could only look in one direction. Its face was hidden.
> Neither could it look about. At first it spoke, but without knowledge. Straightaway it
> would merely dissolve in water, for it was not strong. (Christenson 2007: 78)

There are two words for "face" in K'iche'. The first is *palaj*, meaning the front of the head where the eyes, nose, and mouth are. The word used in this passage, however, is *wach*, which not only includes the idea of the face or the front of something but also the "essential nature" of a thing. If a K'iche' wishes to ask how you are, they say *la utz awach*, literally "is your face good?" If you do not like something, you would say *man utz taj kaqaj chnuwach*, "it falls badly on my face." If you wish to say a person is bad by nature, you would say *qas itzel uwach* "truly malevolent is his face." To say that the mud person's face could only look in one direction is to say that he is prideful or incapable of being open-minded because he can only see things one way. Far worse is the passage that says the mud person's face is "hidden." This would mean he is essentially false in his nature. When we came to this passage in the translation, one of my K'iche' colleagues said he knew people like this—"liars and deceivers, people who have two hearts. They never show their true face, preferring to hide who they are."

The mud person was able to speak, but there was no *na'oj* ("knowledge") behind its words. In highland Maya languages, this word also includes the larger concept of the soul, socialization, the capacity to learn, and even conventions of morality (Watanabe 1992: 100). Only human beings have *na'oj*. It is what separates them from animals. Thus the mud person lacked the essential awareness and understanding a human must have to honor the gods properly.

THE CREATION OF THE WOOD PEOPLE

The third attempt by the gods resulted in beings carved of wood. But these "wood people" also turned out to be incapable of fulfilling their purpose as sustainers and providers for the gods:

> They had the appearance of people and spoke like people as well. They populated the whole face of the earth. The effigies of carved wood began to multiply, bearing daughters and sons.
>
> Nevertheless, they still did not possess their hearts nor their minds. They did not remember their Framer or their Shaper. They walked without purpose. They crawled on their hands and knees and did not remember Heart of Sky. Thus they were weighed in the balance. They were merely an experiment, an attempt at people. At first they spoke, but their faces were all dried up. Their legs and arms were not filled out. They had no blood or blood flow within them. They had no sweat or oil. Their cheeks were dry, and their faces were masks. Their legs and arms were stiff. Their bodies were rigid. Thus they were not capable of understanding before their Framer and their Shaper, those who had given them birth and given them hearts. They were the first numerous people who have lived here upon the face of the earth. (Christenson 2007: 83–84)

Although the wood people could speak, they did not *remember* their creators. The word "remember" is derived from *na'*, which also means "to touch" or "to know." For a Maya to remember a deity or ancestor is equivalent to "feeling" them or "knowing" them. When viewing an old photograph taken in the nineteenth century by Alfred P. Maudslay, an *ajq'ij* from Santiago Atitlán pointed to a number of individuals in the photograph and identified them by name. When I asked how he could possibly know them, since they died so long ago, he replied:

> We all know them. They still visit us in dreams and in person. We know their faces, they still are very powerful, the soul of the town. White are their minds, white are their souls. This is our inheritance. These people live because I live, I carry their blood, I remember. They are not forgotten. (2003, author fieldnotes)

In ritual prayers, *ajq'ijab'* often say their memories reside in their flesh and especially in their blood. The wood people in the Popol Vuh account lacked blood, and their flesh was dry and rigid. As a result, though they looked like people and could reproduce, they still lacked the essential memory and intimate knowledge of the gods within their flesh and blood to allow them to make the gods manifest with their words.

Blood for the Maya bears the most powerful essence of their ancestors and, to an extent, the gods who engendered them. Memory and understanding, the *na'b'al* of a person, is seated in the blood. Without blood, there can be no memory and thus no link to the creators. The faces of the wood people are masks because they are false people. A young *ajq'ij* referred to this aspect of blood when he explained to me that the ancestors continue to operate through him during divination ceremonies:

> As the old people say, when the Spaniards came they broke off many of our branches. They even burned the trunk. But we will never die because the roots have power. We draw strength from the ancestors who live in our blood. If we as a people ignore our roots, we will all die. (2003, fieldnotes)

Because of the power of blood to regenerate life, it is the object of ancient Maya sacrifice. Thus in the Popol Vuh, the lords of death—One Death and Seven Death—call upon their owl messengers to sacrifice a mother deity to obtain her blood-laden heart, for "truly delicious was the smell of the blood to them" (Christenson 2007: 134). But the lords of death did not deserve true blood because of their falseness and malignity. Therefore the mother deity tricked the lords of death by having the owls give to them the red-colored sap of the croton tree as a burned offering instead of the blood from her heart:

> The heart will no longer be theirs . . . Only the true fornicator will be subject to One Death and Seven Death. Mere croton tree sap will be theirs henceforth. Thus be it so.

It will be this that you shall burn before their faces. It will not be this, the heart, that you will burn before their faces. Thus be it so. (Christenson 2007: 132–33)

The patron god of the K'iche' people was Tojil, and the offering he demanded was human blood, given by the first ancestors as a means of maintaining the gods who created them. For this reason the principal titles of the ancestors of the K'iche' people, repeated numerous times in the text as a paired couplet, were "bloodletters and sacrificers" (Christenson 2007: 202). This auto-sacrificial blood was then placed in the mouth of the stone images of Tojil and other creator deities. The implication is that the gods were "fed" in this way or that the blood gave the gods the power of regenerative speech:

> Then they pierced their ears and their elbows before the faces of their gods. They scooped up their blood and rubbed it inside the mouths of the stones. Yet they had not truly become stones. Each of them appeared as young boys when they came. They rejoiced for the blood of the bloodletters and sacrificers. (Christenson 2007: 236)

This practice continues in a number of highland Maya communities today, although the blood is generally that of chickens or turkeys. The K'iche' venerate an ancient stone head called Paxcual Ab'aj in the hills above Chichicastenango (figure 2.3). It is regularly given blood offerings, along with flowers, candles, incense, libations of alcohol, and sugar. The sacrificial blood is often smeared into the mouth area of the image. I was told that this gives the god power to speak and give blessings.

The most powerful offering in the Precolumbian era, however, was not just blood but the entire heart, obtained through the sacrifice of captives. This is described in the Popol Vuh as a "rain" of blood:

> Thus the nations gave their breasts beneath their shoulders and beneath their armpits. This, then[,] was the breast-giving spoken of by Tohil—all the nations were to be sacrificed before him. Their hearts were to be carved out from beneath their shoulders and armpits . . . They gave their blood, which flowed from the shoulders and the armpits of all the people . . . Then was given the breast at the place called Pa Zilizib. And behind it came blood, a rain of their blood as an offering for Tohil. (Christenson 2007: 237)

This practice follows ancient Classic Maya precedent as well. Several of the stone lintels from the Classic Maya site of Yaxchilan clearly show the burning of sacrificial blood as a precursor to the manifestation of deified ancestral beings. Lintel 15 in particular depicts such a deity emerging from the maw of a vision serpent with his hand outstretched in the gesture of speaking (figure 2.4).

FIGURE 2.3. Blood offering to Paxcual Ab'aj, Chichicastenango. Photo by Allen J. Christenson.

FIGURE 2.4. Yaxchilan Lintel 15. Photo by Allen J. Christenson.

THE CREATION OF THE MAIZE PEOPLE

According to the Popol Vuh, the first truly successful human beings were created from maize:

> Thus was found the food that would become the flesh of the newly framed and shaped people. Water was their blood. It became the blood of humanity. The ears of maize entered into their flesh by means of She Who Has Borne Children and He Who Has Begotten Sons . . .
>
> The yellow ears of maize and the white ears of maize were then ground fine with nine grindings by Xmucane. Food entered their flesh, along with water to give them strength. Thus was created the fatness of their arms. The yellowness of humanity came to be when they were made by they who are called She Who Has Borne Children and He Who Has Begotten Sons, by Sovereign and Quetzal Serpent. (Christenson 2007: 194–95)

The text asserts that the maize was ground nine times by the grandmother goddess Xmucane. Maize is seldom, if ever, ground dry. The kernels are soaked overnight or boiled with lime to soften the hard outer shell. The softened maize is then ground until it forms a dough, adding water as necessary to keep it moist. The first grinding results in a lumpy mass with numerous bits of partially ground kernels. This is gathered up and then ground again. Most women will grind it a third time to give the maize dough an even consistency. When preparing maize for ritual meals, this dough may be ground four or five times to make it as fine as possible. I have asked women if they would ever grind the maize nine times, and they respond that that would be foolish—it would take far too much time to be practical. No doubt the intent of this passage of the text is that human flesh is composed of the most refined, perfect maize dough possible. Xmucane is the principal female creator deity, also known as Alom (She Who Has Borne Children). This is the first and only time she appears in the text without her male consort Xpiyacoc, or K'ajolom (He Who Has Engendered Sons). This is likely because only women can create human flesh through childbirth. Among modern Maya, it is considered highly unlucky if a man even touches a woman's grinding stones once they have been used to grind maize, since this taints their ability to create the food that restores human flesh—an exclusively female prerogative, since only they can create human flesh in the womb. Only they have the power to transform maize kernels into living flesh.

In addition, Xmucane is referred to as the grandmother goddess, the goddess of midwives, a goddess of medicine, and a goddess of divination. These attributes link her to the lowland Maya goddess of the moon, Ixchel/Chakchel, who shares all these traits with Xmucane. In Santiago Atitlán, the principal goddess of midwives and medicine is Yaxper, also a moon goddess who bears the title of grandmother

FIGURE 2.5. Yaxper, Cofradía of San Juan, Santiago Atitlán. Photo by Allen J. Christenson.

(figure 2.5) (Carlsen and Prechtel 1994: 101; Christenson 2001: 120–22). It is likely that the grandmother creator goddess Xmucane is also linked with the moon, although nowhere is it specifically stated in the text. If so, the nine grindings would logically be associated with the nine moons/months of human gestation.

There is no such thing as wild maize. It is a wholly domesticated creation, genetically altered in ancient Mesoamerica over thousands of years by cross-breeding until it cannot reproduce itself without human intervention. Over the millennia, ears of maize have developed a tough husk that must be physically shucked for the seeds to be released. Maize fields require nearly constant attention between planting and harvesting. Fully grown maize grows to a height of about 7 or 8 feet in the Guatemalan highlands. But its root system is remarkably shallow to anchor a

FIGURE 2.6. Maize stalk with soil support. Photo by Allen J. Christenson.

plant of such height. To compensate, Maya farmers regularly use a hoe to build up a mound of earth around the base of growing maize plants to support them. If they did not do this, the plants would easily topple over in a stiff wind or driving rain (figure 2.6). The Maya are dependent on maize, but maize is equally dependent on the Maya to live and reproduce. It is this reciprocity that intertwines the needs of both man and maize. One cannot live without the other.

The cultivation of maize represents the basic metaphor for the creation of the cosmos and its spatial orientation. In the account of the creation in the Popol Vuh, the gods came together in the Primordial Sea to determine how the world was to be made. This creative act is described most frequently as a couplet pairing the verbs *awaxoq* ("to be sown") with *saqiroq* ("to dawn"):

> How shall it be sown? How shall there be a dawn for anyone? Who shall be a provider? Who shall be a sustainer? (Christenson 2007: 71)

To sow and to dawn are not considered independent actions but equivalent expressions for the same generative event, linked with childbirth. Among modern

K'iche', when a woman becomes pregnant, the event is announced by a respected elder of the community at certain lineage shrines. This ceremony is referred to as "the sowing" of the future child (Tedlock 1982: 80). This connection between maize and human flesh has influenced birth rituals in highland Guatemala since remote antiquity. Francisco de Fuentes y Guzmán wrote in the seventeenth century that when a male child was born, the Maya of Guatemala burned blood shed from the severed umbilical cord and passed an ear of maize through the smoke. The father then planted the seeds from this ear in the child's name in a specific area of the maize field. Parents used the maize from this small patch of land to feed the child "until he reached the age when he could plant for himself, saying that thus he not only ate by the sweat of his brow but of his own blood as well" (Fuentes y Guzmán 1932–33, I: 281).

Mothers in Santiago Atitlán place an ear of maize into the palm of their newborns and eat only dishes made from maize while breast-feeding to ensure that the child grows "true flesh." Once the child is weaned, it is given only food prepared with maize for several months, and parents avoid giving it maize grown anywhere but in their own community. For the Maya, the maturation of the child must take place by means of locally grown maize or it will not grow to become a legitimate member of the community. Nicolás Chávez Sojuel, a traditionalist from Santiago Atitlán, explained to me that a child must also eat maize to learn to speak Maya properly:

> When a woman prepares maize dough for making tortillas, she repeatedly dips her hands into a bowl of water in order to keep the dough moist. Mothers give this water mixed with maize to their young children to drink so that they will learn how to speak and learn the customs of their ancestors. This mixture of water and maize we call "blood," and it is what makes the blood of the growing child. If an older child can't speak well the mother will also give this same mixture of maize and water. One must be careful, however, because if a child receives too much of this at an early age, he will never shut up. For a child who is powerful, and remembers well the ancestors, a mother will give the same watery maize with cacao mixed in. Cacao and maize are the same food, but cacao is more powerful. It is also our flesh. (1997, fieldnotes)

Fray Gerónimo de Mendieta (1993: 232) wrote in the sixteenth century that rituals and beliefs concerning maize were the most persistent ancient Maya elements to survive the Spanish Invasion because they were so heavily tied to their everyday way of life: "They continue to worship their devils by night, especially at the time of planting and harvesting of maize, such rites having been performed since time immemorial by their ancestors and thus understandably difficult to abandon." Fuentes y Guzmán (1932–33, I.12.3) noted that this tendency continued in Guatemala more than a century after the Conquest: "Everything they did and said so concerned maize that they almost regarded it as a god. The enchantment and rapture with which they look upon their maize fields is such that on their account they forget children, wife, and any other pleasure, as though the maize fields were their final purpose in life and the source of their happiness."

DESCENDANTS OF THE FIRST MAIZE PEOPLE AND BLOOD MEMORY

In much the same way maize depends on humans to maintain their life cycle, traditionalist Maya believe the world itself is dependent on them. Ceremonies and ritual prayers have life-regenerating efficacy. If they are not carried out properly, the world could not hope to negotiate the perils of sunsets, dry seasons, and the annual death of its gods, including Christian deities and saints that have been adopted into their communities. In the Maya view of the world, gods, saints, and ancestors have great power, but they depend on humans to help them to carry out their labors.

Because of the divine nature of their maize flesh, the first men formed by Xmucane had the gift of extraordinary vision whereby they could see all things:

> Perfect was their sight, and perfect was their knowledge of everything beneath the sky. If they gazed about them, looking intently, they beheld that which was in the sky and that which was upon the earth. Instantly, they were able to behold everything. They did not have to walk to see all that existed beneath the sky. They merely saw it from wherever they were. Thus their knowledge became full. Their vision passed beyond the trees and rocks, beyond the lakes and the seas, beyond the mountains and the valleys. (Christenson 2007: 197–98)

The ancestors of the K'iche' people are also described in the *Título de Totonicapán* as magical and wise, whose "sight reached far into the sky and the earth; there was nothing to equal all that they could see beneath the sky" (Carmack and Mondloch 1983 [1554]: 71; English translation from K'iche' by author). Although the creator gods eventually clouded this vision so the first men could only see those things that were "nearby" (Christenson 2007: 201), the descendants of these progenitors nevertheless believe they bear within their blood the potential for divine sight, inherited from their first ancestors. Present-day *ajq'ijab'* believe these ancestors continue to operate through them as conduits at appropriate times and under appropriate circumstances. It is their ancestral vision that allows the *ajq'ijab* to "see" beyond the limits of time and distance, as the first men once did. Evon Z. Vogt noted that the Tzotzil-Maya of Zinacantan believe that anciently, their people could see inside sacred mountains where the ancestors live. Today, only shamans are recognized to have this ability. Thus the Tzotzil term *h'ilol* means "seer," in the sense of one who can "see" things on a supernatural level (Vogt 1993: 205).

Among the Maya, there is no institutional religion to sanction the qualification of a person to become an *ajq'ij*. Every Maya woman and man potentially has this ability because it is inherent in their blood. *Ajq'ijab'* are chosen by the ancestors to serve as mediators between this world and that of the spirit, not because they are qualitatively different from anyone else in this regard but because they are called by the spirit world to do so as an obligatory service to the community. Once called, generally through dreams or the discovery of a sign interpreted as an invitation to serve from the ancestors, the prospective *ajq'ij* often enters a period of apprenticeship. The approach experienced *ajq'ijab'* take in training their apprentices is to teach them how to interpret signs and spirit communication, often described as lightning in the blood, that they had always received since young childhood but lacked the experience to understand properly.

For this reason, not all *ajq'ijab'* go through a process of apprenticeship. A well-respected *ajq'ij* named Diego, living in Santiago Atitlán, told me that although he had watched a number of elderly *ajq'ijab'* carry out prayers and ceremonies in his youth, he did not learn how to do his work from them:

> When I was born, I already knew how to do these things. I had no teacher. I speak with the ancestors and ancient kings and they speak with me. They help me to know how to heal and solve problems for people. I ask the ancestors these things in places that are sacred where I can be touched by them. (2006, fieldnotes)

Apprenticeships and learning by example are undoubtedly important methods of passing along knowledge from one generation to another; however, the perception among Maya *ajq'ijab'* is that this is not the principal means by which sacred knowledge is gained. This must come directly from within oneself, directly from the person's own blood, or it is powerless (figure 2.7). Non-Maya do not necessarily have this kind of ability because their blood does not originate from the same visionary ancestral source. In my own experience working with *ajq'ijab'* in Momostenango in the 1970s, my frequent displays at ineptitude in learning divinatory and calendric skills were interpreted as the lack of Maya blood in my veins. I was not able to see with ancestral vision in the same way because I had a different lineage, likely not a very divine one.

MAIZE PEOPLE AND SACRED SPEECH

In their various languages, the Maya generally refer to themselves as some variant of *qas winaq* ("true people"). One reason they consider themselves to be the only "true people" is because they eat maize and therefore their flesh is composed of divine substance, something people who eat other foods as the principal part of their diet

FIGURE 2.7. K'iche' *ajq'ij*, Chichicastenango. Photo by Allen J. Christenson.

lack. Foreigners may be perfectly fine people and admirable in many ways, but in a very real sense they are a different species because they do not eat maize. Because they eat bread rather than tortillas, they are "wheat people." Maya language is intimately bound with this concept that "true people" are composed of the flesh of maize. To be a *qas winaq* and to speak the Maya language properly, a person must first eat maize. This notion implies that the power of human speech is not merely a means of communication that can be imitated by memorizing grammar and vocabulary but a function of the physical essence of the Maya as a people. Vogt (1993: 50) noted the belief among the Tzotzil-Maya of Chiapas that "unless people eat maize tortillas, they are never fully socialized, nor can they ever speak BAZ'IK'OP ('the real word,' or the Tzotzil language)."

I am reminded of Zuñi feasting rituals as described by Frank Hamilton Cushing in the nineteenth century. He reported that the Zuñi saw feasting as a way to make the physical bodies of those who participate like in kind and thus establish bonds similar to kinship ties. They even invited enemy groups like Navajos and Apaches to their feasts on special occasions to prevent future conflict. This was not conceived by the participants simply as a process of mollifying hostilities by means of a pleasant banquet but as a physical bonding through shared flesh-forming maize that made the participants (albeit temporarily) of the same body.

It is well documented in highland Maya records that the ancient K'iche' conducted elaborate feasting rituals at their capital city of Q'umarkaj prior to the Spanish Invasion. All the major polities of highland Guatemala participated in these ceremonies, including the Kaqchikel and Tz'utujil, who were otherwise rival states that often engaged in bloody conflict. Fr. Bartolomé de Las Casas (1967 [1550], III.clxxviii: 218–22) and Fr. Jerónimo Román y Zamora (Ximénez 1929–31 [1722], I.xxix–xxx: 81–86) described these festivals as including huge banquets as well as ritual dances and sacrifices in honor of their titular gods. Such banquets served to establish mutually beneficial ties among adversarial polities.

When Cushing moved in with the Zuñi governor in 1879 (uninvited, of course) and the latter realized that he could not persuade him to go away, the governor insisted that Cushing eat only local food, particularly maize. He explained that this would make him a Zuñi, and he could then learn the language and customs of his people. The implication is that this would have been impossible otherwise. The governor cautioned him in this way:

> "You must never go to Dust-eye's house [the Mission], or to Black-beard's [the trader's] to eat; for I want to make a Zuñi of you. How can I do that if you eat American food?" With this he left me for the night. (Cushing 1979: 90)

Once he had remained in Zuñi for an extended period of time, he became accepted as a member of the pueblo community, even by an aged priest who had previously been wary of him. Again, this acceptance was associated with eating local maize:

> Now that I wore the head-band and moccasins of his people, his attentions were redoubled, and he insisted constantly that I should dress entirely in the native costume, and have my ears pierced. That would make a complete Zuñi of me, for had I not eaten Zuñi food long enough to make a complete Zuñi of me, for had I not eaten Zuñi food long enough to have starved four times, and was not my flesh, therefore, of the soil of Zuñi? (Cushing 1979: 91)

I find this intriguing with regard to the highland Maya. When I first began working as an ethnographer in K'iche' communities in Guatemala, I found it curious that when I struck up a conversation in K'iche' with someone I did not know, that person would sometimes interrupt me in mid-sentence and ask me what I ate, specifically if I ate tortillas or wheat bread. When I affirmed that I ate what they ate, including tortillas, they would nod as if that explained a great deal. After a number of such experiences, I asked a friend why people were curious about what I ate. He laughed and said, "It's probably because you can speak our language. I wondered if it was because you ate maize from here. If so then you have the flesh of the ancients in your flesh and therefore can speak what they spoke."

This is apparently a very old Mesoamerican concept. In the *Historia Tolteca-Chichimeca*, barbarian Chichimec messengers from the north arriving at the court of the Nahuatl-speaking court of the Mexica were given a grain of local maize to eat so they could speak intelligibly in Nahuatl (Kirchoff et al. 1976: 169 [211–13]; fol. 19v, n. 4).

Ruth Leah Bunzel (1952: 232, 238) noted that the K'iche' of Chichicastenango claimed that their formalized speech and ceremonies were attributed to ancient ancestral precedent: "And now this rite and custom belongs to the first people, our mothers and fathers ... This belongs to them; we are the embodiment of their rites and ceremonies." To alter the actions of the ancestors would be to change the very fabric of their existence in potentially destructive ways. As mediators between this world and that of the sacred, it is the Mayas' obligation to continue the actions of their divine ancestors in as authentic a manner as possible: "It is our name and destiny to repeat and perpetuate these ceremonies before the world" (1952: 242). When asking Tz'utujils when certain rituals began, a common response is that they are as old as the world and were first performed by their ancestors who had divine power (Mendelson 1965: 91).

At Momostenango, a prominent *ajq'ij* told me that when he sits at his table, he becomes a living representation of the organization of the world:

> When I am seated at the table, I am *aj nawal mesa* (of or pertaining to the ancestral spirit essence table). My body is in the form of a cross just like the four sides of the world. This is why I face to the east and behind me is the west. My left arm extends out toward the north, and my right arm points to the south. My heart is the center of myself just as the arms of the cross come together to form its heart. My head extends upward above the horizon so that I can see far away. Because I am seated this way I can speak to *Mundo* (World). (1979, fieldnotes)

When the *ajq'ij* performs a ceremony, he places himself in a transcendent role that bridges the three layers of the cosmos (figure 2.8). His legs extend beneath the surface of the sacred table he sits at, conceptually reaching into the underworld; his arms manipulate its sacred geography, while his upper body rises into the upperworld. In so doing, the *ajq'ij* is able to "see" all places where the spirit beings live and converse with them. Maude Oakes (1951: 138) noted that shamanic tables at Todos Santos bear a cross addressed as *Santo Mundo* (Holy World), which represents the first shaman-priest of the world. The *ajq'ij* who sits at this table thus acts as the representative of the first ancestor who set the precedent for such ceremonies. In

FIGURE 2.8. K'iche' ceremonial table, Momostenango. Photo by Allen J. Christenson.

a similar way, the *ajq'ijab'* of the Tz'utujil-Maya are believed to carry within their blood the power by which they are able to pray "according to the ancient words of god" (Mendelson 1957: 281).

When a living *ajq'ij* repeats the actions of an ancestor through ceremony or prayer, he or she becomes a substitute or vessel for sacred power. One of the highest titles held by the traditionalist priests of Momostenango is *chuch-qajaw* ("mother-father"), as he represents the living embodiment of his lineage. As such, he is able to act in the name of his ancestors, whose blood he possesses. It is essential, therefore, that he approach the duties of his office with great seriousness and in a state of ritual purity. Prior to laying out the contents of his bundle on the table, the *ajq'ij* calls on the essential powers of the world as well as his own ancestors to be present for the ceremony. He begins by pleading for them to take away any sin or error that might taint his ability to act in their name and reveal their will. The following is a divinatory prayer I recorded in Momostenango in 1979, given by an *ajq'ij* when he first seated himself at his table on behalf of a sick client:

> We call upon you Earth, we ask you Lord of the day 11 No'j, we ask you Lord 5 No'j, and to you secretary 11 K'at, and you secretary 5 K'at; we ask a favor of you; we ask you a favor because there is sickness among us, there is a sick little girl. Take away

my error, King of the World, Savior of the World, so that you may speak—the Seven Skies, the Seven Earths. Take away my error that there may be light, that there may be clarity. Take away my error I ask you, the great mountains, the small mountains; the great plains and the small plains; the great animals who are lords of the mountains and you small animals who are in the mountains. Take away my error you, our people, our mothers and fathers, our grandmothers and our grandfathers. Take away my error and witness us here today at this table. It has its service, to bring out the transformation, to bring out the mother fathers. This is its service. Take away my error. (1979, fieldnotes)

In this litany, the *ajq'ij* asked the powers he wished to have present at the ceremony to take away any flaws in his body or character that would taint the results. Among these powers are, first, the representatives of time in the form of the two principal Day Lords (11 No'j and 5 No'j), who presided over that period of the year, as well as their two secretaries (11 K'at and 5 K'at); second, space or sacred geography as described by the mountains, the plains, as well as their animal inhabitants; and finally, lineage, represented by the mothers and fathers, the grandmothers and grandfathers. The Seven Skies and the Seven Earths refer to the organization of the sky and the earth into seven major divisions—the four cardinal directions plus up, down, and center. Thus the *ajq'ij* positions himself at the center of the cosmos, surrounded on all sides by sacred power (figure 2.9).

The first attribute ascribed to the newly-created maize people was the power of speech:

Their frame and shape were merely brought about by the miraculous power and the spirit essence of the Framer and the Shaper, of She Who Has Borne Children and He Who Has Begotten Sons, of Sovereign and Quetzal Serpent. Thus their countenances appeared like people. People they came to be. They were able to speak and converse. They were able to look and listen. They were able to walk and hold things with their hands. They were excellent and chosen people. (Christenson 2007: 197)

Once created, the first human beings successfully addressed the gods that formed them, calling them by name and thanking them for their existence. Again, the first attribute they gave thanks for was the power of speech:

Truly we thank you doubly, triply that we were created, that we were given our mouths and our faces. We are able to speak and to listen. We are able to ponder and to move about. We know much, for we have learned that which is far and near. We have seen the great and the small, all that exists in the sky and on the earth. We thank you, therefore, that we were created, that we were given frame and shape. We became because of you, our Grandmother, and you, our Grandfather. (Christenson 2007: 199)

FIGURE 2.9. *Ajq'ij* conducting divinatory ceremony, Chutinamit, Santiago Atitlán. Photo by Allen J. Christenson.

Subsequent passages from the text describe these first ancestral progenitors as persons of "good speech" (Christenson 2007: 199); they "remembered the word of the Framer and Shaper" and used "esteemed words" in calling on the gods (2007: 206). The god Tojil is described as "one before whom we may speak" (2007: 208). The Popol Vuh states that a primary responsibility of the lords of the K'iche' people was to name the gods in their prayers and offerings. By so doing, they were able to give them power to manifest themselves and bestow their life-generating influence. For the K'iche', to remember a god is not only to recall an image in the mind—it is to feel and make manifest the presence of that divine being in the blood. If the blood is then offered in sacrifice, the god is brought tangibly into this world. A portion of the prayer offered by the ancient lords of the K'iche' refers to this responsibility to sustain the gods through the utterance of remembered divine names. In turn, the gods are thus given regenerative power to create new generations of maize people to continue the cycle:

Alas, you, Framer, and you, Shaper: Behold us! Hear us! Do not abandon us. Do not allow us to be overthrown. You are the god in the sky and on the earth, you, Heart of Sky, Heart of Earth. May our sign, our word, be given for as long as there is sun and light. Then may it be sown, may it dawn. May there be true life-giving roads and pathways. Give us steadfast light that our nation be made steadfast. May the light be favorable that our nation may be favored. May our lives be favored so that all creation may be favored as well. (Christenson 2007: 206)

I had the opportunity to read through the creation story of the Popol Vuh with a group of traditional Maya priests in Canquixaja, a small community near Momostenango. When we had finished the passage that recounted the gratitude of the first maize people and their extraordinary vision, one of the priests stood and said he had a word to say. He was the eldest of the group and normally sat quietly and listened as the others spoke, so on the few occasions when he did speak up, the others immediately paid close attention. I think his comments perfectly encapsulate the essence of the K'iche' view of humankind's responsibility to sustain the world. He should have the last word:

I wonder if these words belong only to the ancient past. I think all of us pass through the various stages of creation. When we were born we were like the animals. We could only squawk and make animal sounds. Later we learned to say a few words, but they were words without any understanding behind them—like the Mud Person. I think Wood People are like teenagers. They can speak, they can reproduce, but they forget who they are. They do not remember their mothers and fathers or the ancient people. They don't know their purpose in life. *Wachalal* ("brothers"), we bear a heavy sweet burden on our backs, because we remember. And because we remember we must bear the burden of carrying out our work so that the ancestors may speak to us through our blood and our flesh. This is often very hard. But if we didn't do this, who would? Everything would be finished. (1979, fieldnotes)

REFERENCES CITED

Bunzel, Ruth Leah. 1952. *Chichicastenango*. American Ethnological Society, Publication 22. University of Washington Press, Seattle.

Carlsen, Robert S., and Martin Prechtel. 1994. "Walking on Two Legs: Shamanism in Santiago Atitlán, Guatemala." In *Ancient Traditions: Culture and Shamanism in Central Asia and the Americas*, ed. Gary Seaman and Jane Day, 77–111. University Press of Colorado, Niwot.

Carmack, Robert M., and James Mondloch. 1983 [1554]. *El Título de Totonicapán: Texto, traducción y comentario*. Instituto de Investigaciones Filológicas; Centro de Estudios Mayas. Fuentes para el Estudio de la Cultura Maya 3. Universidad Nacional Autónoma de México, Mexico City.

Christenson, Allen J. n.d. Fieldnotes, Momostenango and Santiago Atitlán, 1978–2005. Manuscript in possession of the author.

Christenson, Allen J. 2001. *Art and Society in a Highland Maya Community: The Altarpiece of Santiago Atitlán*. University of Texas Press, Austin.

Christenson, Allen J. 2004. *Popol Vuh*, vol. 2: *Literal Poetic Version, Translation and Transcription*. O Books, Winchester.

Christenson, Allen J. 2007. *Popol Vuh—the Sacred Book of the Maya*. 2nd revised ed. University of Oklahoma Press, Norman.

Cushing, Frank Hamilton. 1979. *Zuñi: Selected Writings of Frank Hamilton Cushing*. Ed. Jesse Green. University of Nebraska Press, Lincoln.

Fuentes y Guzmán, Francisco de. 1932–33. *Recordación Florida*. Vols. 6–8. Biblioteca Goathemala, Guatemala City.

Houston, Stephen, and David Stuart. 1996. "Of Gods, Glyphs, and Kings: Divinity and Rulership among the Classic Maya." *Antiquity* 70: 289–312.

Kirchoff, Paul, Lina Odena Güemes, and Luís Reyes García, eds. 1976. *Historia Tolteca-Chichimeca*. Instituto Nacional de Antropología e Historia, Mexico City.

Las Casas, Bartolomé de. 1967 [1550]. *Apologética historia sumaria de las Indias*. 2 vols. Universidad Nacional Autónoma de México, Mexico City.

Mendelson, E. Michael. 1957. "Religion and World-View in Santiago Atitlán." PhD dissertation, University of Chicago, IL.

Mendelson, E. Michael. 1965. *Las escándolas de Maximon*. Publication 19. Seminario de Integración Social Guatemalteca, Guatemala City.

Mendieta, Fr. Gerónimo de. 1993. *Historia Eclesiástica Indiana*. Editorial Porrua, Mexico City.

Oakes, Maud. 1951. *The Two Crosses of Todos Santos*. Bollingen Series 27. Princeton University Press, Princeton, NJ.

Tedlock, Barbara. 1982. *Time and the Highland Maya*. University of New Mexico Press, Albuquerque.

Vogt, Evon Z. 1993. *Tortillas for the Gods: A Symbolic Analysis of Zinacanteco Rituals*. 2nd ed. University of Oklahoma Press, Norman.

Watanabe, John M. 1992. *Maya Saints and Souls in a Changing World*. University of Texas Press, Austin.

Ximénez, Fr. Francisco. 1929–31 [1722]. *Historia de la provincia de San Vicente de Chiapa y Guatemala*. Biblioteca "Goathemala" de la Sociedad de Georgrafía e Historia de Guatemala Publication 1. 3 vols. Tipografía Nacional, Guatemala City.

3

Metaphors of Maize

Otherworld Conceptualizations and the Cultural Logic of Human Existence in the Popol Vuh

FRAUKE SACHSE

The Popol Vuh has been a pivotal source for our understanding of Prehispanic religious traditions and the perception of history in Maya culture. The mythological account of the creation of the world and the origin of the K'iche' people is habitually drawn on to inform and corroborate the reconstructions of ancient Maya cosmology and worldview. However, the text is rarely analyzed in terms of its own internal coherence of the picture it creates of the Maya universe. The present chapter explores aspects of K'iche' eschatology through the language of the Popol Vuh, focusing on conceptualizations of otherworld places and the transformative processes that connect them.

An analysis of theological coherence in the Popol Vuh can help us achieve a better understanding of the nature of the text and the purpose of its compilation. The origin of the Popol Vuh has been a point of debate throughout the history of its scholarship. While the actual manuscript we have is an eighteenth-century copy from the hand of Francisco Ximénez, the text itself was composed about thirty years after the Invasion by members of the K'iche' elite—likely the lineage of the Nim Ch'okoj—near the former capital of Q'umarkaj (Tedlock 1996: 56–57; Akkeren 2003; Christenson 2007: 37). The authors are referring to an "original Popol Vuh" (*nab'e popol wuj*) that served as an "instrument of sight" (*ilb'al*) (fol. 1r; 54r), which may be an allusion to a Preconquest pictographic book in the style of almanacs or annals as we know them from Central Mexico (cf. Tedlock 1996: 23–25; Christenson 2007: 32–35). In fact, the *Título de Yax* mentions the *pop vuh* as a book of prophecy

DOI: 10.5876/9781646421992.c003

in the possession of the K'iche' kings (fol. 9v; Carmack and Mondloch 1989: 86). There is no evidence, however, that the Colonial version of the Popol Vuh was actually transcribed from such a codex, and the statement in the text that *maja b'i chik ilb'al re popo[l] wuj, ilb'al saq* "there is not anymore a means of seeing the Popol Vuh, a means of seeing the light" and that *xa ewal uwach ilol re, b'isol re* "just hidden is the face of its seer, its ponderer" (fol. 1r) rather suggests that this version may not have been available to the authors. The structure and complexity of the text indicate that we are not dealing with a mere transcription of a hieroglyphic text but rather with a pictographic source that may have served as a mnemonic device for the reciting of oral traditions or prognostics (see Akkeren 2003: 237; Christenson 2012: 314–16).

The mythological narratives of the Popol Vuh likely stem from a canon of common oral literature. The *Theologia Indorum* [1552–54] that was written by Domingo de Vico several years earlier contains references to various deities and episodes known from the Popol Vuh (see Acuña 1985). Several of the narrative *topoi* in the text seem to have been originally adapted from Central Mexican traditions. These include the concept of multiple human creations, the Mexica migrations, the descriptions of the Chichimeca, and the heroic deeds of the legendary ruler Topiltzin Quetzalcoatl. A structural comparison of the Popol Vuh and the *Anales de Cuauhtitlán* shows furthermore that both accounts follow the same narrative pattern, starting with the creation of the world, followed by episodes involving the deeds of culture heroes (i.e., Hero Twins, Topiltzin Quetzalcoatl) and the description of human and ethnic origin (i.e., K'iche', Mexica). There was considerable cultural influence from Central Mexico in the Guatemalan highlands throughout the Postclassic, and it is not at all surprising to find this reflected in the mythology.

With respect to the question of theological coherence, we can assume that the authors intentionally composed the text from existing narrative traditions. In his recent work on Domingo de Vico's *Theologia Indorum*, Garry Sparks (2019: 322–373; 2014: 108–16; Sparks et al. 2017) offers an interpretation of the Popol Vuh as a direct indigenous response to Christianity, in particular to the existence of a central dogmatic text. He argues that Vico's theological treatise, the *Título de Totonicapán*, and the Popol Vuh are intertextually related and reflect the dialogue between Dominican missionaries and highland Maya religious specialists (Sparks et al. 2017: 209). In this understanding, the Popol Vuh is more than just a text that was written to preserve ancient religious traditions; it was written to refute the new belief system (see Dürr 1989; Tedlock 1996: 30; cf. Sparks 2019: 370–373). Rather than a mere transcription of a Preconquest written or oral tradition, the text reflects deliberate choices of the authors, who answered biblical narratives by masterfully spinning various threads of religious mythology into the fabric of a single account that is coherent within the logical framework of K'iche' theology and eschatology.

The narrative of creation, hero lore, and the origin of the K'iche' in the Popol Vuh manifests a coherent system of highland Maya conceptualizations of cosmology. I will argue that the various otherworld locations mentioned in the text are systematically interrelated through a conceptual metaphor that defines the essence of Maya cultural thinking, religion, and eschatology: that human life is perceived in analogy to the growth cycle of a maize plant.

CONCEPTUAL METAPHORS

Conceptual metaphors are straight avenues into systems of cultural logic. Metaphors are figures of speech that express one concept in terms of another and can be words, phrases, or entire narratives. Cognitive linguistics fundamentally changed our view of metaphors as primarily poetic tools to metaphors as devices that structure daily discourse and reflect our conceptualization of the world. "Conceptual metaphors" are "ontological mapping[s] across conceptual domains" (Lakoff 1993: 208). In conceptual metaphors, the terminology of a source domain is applied to activities and participants in a target domain. George Lakoff and Mark Johnson's (1980: 4) famous example of ARGUMENT IS WAR illustrates that in English, a wide range of terms and expressions from the source domain of WAR can be used to refer to instances or results of ARGUMENTS (e.g., "Your claims are *indefensible*" or "He *attacked every weak* point in my argument"). Such conceptual metaphors are understood as being systematic, inasmuch as not only the lexical meaning of one term but the logical structure of the source domain is projected onto the target domain (Lakoff 1990: 54). While these systematic mappings are generally grounded on an experiential basis and are therefore manifestations of the universal human conceptual system (Lakoff and Johnson 1980), they also reflect cultural idiosyncrasies and are key to understanding culture-specific concepts. The conceptual metaphor TIME IS MONEY (1980: 7–8) would, for instance, not be meaningful outside the cultural system of Western capitalism.

Ethnographic and linguistic research has brought forth a range of conceptualizations that enhance our understanding of Maya and Mesoamerican cultural ideology. The majority of these studies focus on the analysis of individual terms and their metaphorical applications. The analysis of the *jaloj-k'exoj* principle by Robert S. Carlsen and Martin Prechtel (1991) and the unraveling of the cultural meaning of the concept of HEART by Edward F. Fischer (1999) may suffice here as examples. Studies on metaphor in Mesoamerican languages comprise discussions of conceptual mappings by source domain—for example, the metaphorical applications of color terms (Maxwell 2004) or the term for ROAD (Wichmann 2004)—as well as by target domain, such as the analysis of the various expressions and euphemisms used to refer to the human body (Laughlin 2004). Other studies concentrate on particular conceptual metaphors, such as COMMUNITY IS FAMILY or AGREEMENT IS REPETITION (Brody 2004).

The potential conceptual metaphor theory has for our understanding of Colonial K'iche' semantics is not duly appreciated. Indigenous texts from Early Colonial times are rich in metaphorical language, which is often not well understood. In 500 years of colonialism, K'iche' underwent considerable changes in lexical meanings and grammatical forms, although present-day speakers may still retain knowledge of hitherto undocumented semantic concepts. Colonial dictionaries supply meanings for many terms and metaphors that are lost in modern K'iche'. However, these lexicons were primarily compiled for the project of evangelization, and their entries may thus reflect lexical innovations as well as semantic reinterpretations. As metaphorical meanings have been lost, Colonial K'iche' texts can often only be understood literally. In other cases, metaphorical mappings may be known, but the context does not clarify whether the literal or the metaphorical meaning of a term applies—an issue that is reflected not the least in the deviations of the various translations of the Popol Vuh that have been produced in the course of the past decades (cf. Schultze-Jena 1944; Recinos et al. 1950; Tedlock 1996; Christenson 2007; Sam Colop 2008).

The most apparent metaphorical devices in Mayan speech and literature are diphrastic kennings. Diphrastic kennings are a typical feature of the Mesoamerican linguistic area and can be defined as lexical parallelisms that consist of either partially synonymous or complementary word pairs that express a third, metaphorical meaning (Garibay K. 1968; Hull 2003: 137; Christenson 2007: 48; Montes de Oca Vega 2004). The text of the Popol Vuh shows a particular degree of poetic complexity and figurative speech (see Christenson 2007, 2012; Sam Colop 1999). Diphrastic kennings occur in the text as lexical pairs as well as distributed over lines into couplets and chiasms, which can make them difficult to distinguish from other forms of parallelisms that do not carry any metaphorical meaning. Parallelisms and couplet structure are stylistic devices of ritual speech still used in K'iche' and other highland Mayan languages today. Without entering the debate as to whether diphrastic kennings have historically developed from such parallelisms, it needs to be recognized that various parallelisms in the Colonial sources that suggest literal meanings may in fact be lost metaphors. This is even more of an issue for lexical pairs that are exclusively attested in the Popol Vuh.

The remainder of this chapter illustrates that the metaphorical meanings of some lexical pairs can be unraveled from their relationship with the semantic properties of conceptual metaphors. Conceptual metaphors form webs of meaning and cultural logic that may be rather time-stable and as such can serve as tools for comprehending the underlying principles of figurative speech.

The metaphor most characteristic of Maya culture is the conceptualization of human life in analogy to the life cycle of maize, the essential Mesoamerican staple crop. The cultural concept has been the subject of various studies (see, e.g., Vogt 1976; Haly 2004; Christenson 2006; Stross 2007); and the analysis of other key concepts, such as the aforementioned *jaloj-k'exoj* principle (Carlsen and Prechtel 1991, see further below), is founded on the basic understanding that (HUMAN) LIFE IS A MAIZE PLANT. The conceptual metaphor constitutes the organizing principle for indigenous theology and cosmology as it is related in the Popol Vuh. We will see that terminology from the source domain of "maize agriculture" is applied to refer to aspects of human origin, life, and afterlife. The semantic properties and semantic fields associated with these terms are projected onto the target domain and thus shape the perception of human existence in this world and in the otherworld.

WORLD CREATION

The starting point for our exploration here is the figurative language used in the Popol Vuh in the context of world creation. The K'iche' refer to the concept of the "world" metaphorically as *kaj ulew* "sky-earth." In its extended form, the expression occurs in the Popol Vuh with another diphrastic kenning *cho palow* "lake-sea." Together, the four terms *kaj, ulew, cho, palow* describe the elements that define the human cosmos: the four-cornered sky and land with its (fresh)waters and the (salt)waters surrounding it. According to the Popol Vuh, this four-dimensional Maya cosmos had no eternal prior existence but was physically formed and shaped by the divine. First the earth with its mountains, valleys, and waterways was created; then the sky was set apart from the earth and the earth was set apart in the water (fol. 2r). Before this creation, only sky and sea existed, imbued with the spiritual essences of the creator deities: Tepew Q'ukumatz "Sovereign Quetzal Serpent" in the water and *Uk'u'x Kaj* "Heart of Sky" in the sky. In the text, the creation of the earth is characterized as a process of birth that results from the interaction of these creator deities inside the sky, which appears to be conceptualized as a pre-world womb, filled with the amniotic fluids of the Primordial Sea.

K'a katz'ininoq, k'a kachamamoq,	Still be it silent, still be it placid,
katz'inonik, k'a kasilanik, k'a kalolinik,	it is silent, still it is calm, still it is hushed
katolona' puch upa kaj	and empty is the womb of the sky.
(Popol Vuh, fol. 1v)[1]	

Xa utukel kaj k'olik,	Just alone the sky exists,
mawi q'alaj uwach ulew,	the face of the earth is not clear yet,
xa utukel remanik palow,	just alone the calm sea,
upa kaj ronojel.	all is in the womb of the sky.
(Popol Vuh, fol. 1v)	

In his translation of the Popol Vuh, Allen J. Christenson renders the expression *upam kaj* as "womb of the sky" (see, e.g., 2007: 67). The choice of "womb" over "stomach" or "inside of the sky" is supported by the contextual terminology and internal logic of the text. Before creation, everything is described as silent and calm and the "inside of the sky" is empty, like a womb before conception. The creator deities Tepew Q'ukumatz and "Heart of Sky" initiate the conception of earth and life by means of contemplation and speech and are literally referred to in the text as "giving birth" (*alaj*).

Ta xena'ojinik, ta xeb'isonik,	Then they thought, then they pondered,
xeriqow kib',	they found themselves,
xkikuch kitzij, kina'oj.	they gathered their words, their thoughts.
Ta xkalaj,	Then they gave birth,
ta xkik'u'xlaj kib'.	Then they remembered themselves.
Xewi saq	(There was) just light
Ta xkalaj puch winaq.	when they gave also birth to people.
(Popol Vuh, fol. 1v)	

The creation of "sky-earth" is furthermore described with terms from the semantic domain of "agriculture." At the onset is the measuring and outlining of the *kaj tz'uk, kaj xukut* "four corners, four angles," which pictures the divine planning of the world in analogy to laying out the maize field, or *milpa* (see Tedlock 1996: 220; Christenson 2007: 65).

Ukaj tz'ukuxik, ukaj xukutaxik,	Four cornerings, four anglings,
retaxik, ukaj che'xik,	measurings, four stakings,
umej k'a'amaxik,	doubling over cord measurement,
uyuq k'a'amaxik,	stretching cord measurement,
upa kaj, upa ulew.	of the inside of the sky, the inside of the earth.
(Popol Vuh, fol. 1r)	

The creation of "sky and earth" is the beginning of a world that bears life. This notion of "beginning (of life)" is conceptualized in the Popol Vuh with a set of metaphors from the domain of agriculture and plant growth. The verbs *tikarik* "become planted" and *awaxik* "become sown" refer to the start of a new growth cycle that commences with the placing of the seed or seedling into the earth and usually involves humans as agents. This metaphor is used in K'iche' generally to refer to any form of beginning. After being "sown," the Popol Vuh describes that sky-earth "germinates" or "sprouts" (*tz'uk*) (fol. 1r), which further alludes to the conceptualization of the beginning of the world in terms of plant growth.

The terms *tikarik* and *awaxik* recur in the text in a lexical pair with the verb *saqirik* "to become light" or "to dawn." I discuss further below that both terms, "sowing/planting" and "dawning," form a diphrastic kenning that is part of the semantic complex of the conceptual metaphor of LIFE IS A MAIZE PLANT and refer to the beginning and completion of creation.

Ta chawaxoq,	Then may be sown,
ta saqiroq kaj ulew.	Then may dawn sky and earth.
(Popol Vuh, fol. 2r)	

The creation of the Maya cosmos is thus conceptualized as a process of "conception and birth" as well as "sowing and growing," both of which imply the involvement of an instigating agent and suggest that the world is perceived as a living thing. This idea largely determines the form of human interaction with this cosmos and is reproduced in the eschatological belief system.

K'ICHE' ESCHATOLOGY

Conceptualizations of life and afterlife are intrinsically connected to notions of otherworld places. The K'iche' cosmos as it is described in the Popol Vuh encompasses two supernatural spheres: the underworld and the sky. The sky existed even before creation and is clearly identified as the non-human abode of the deity "Heart of Sky," who is also identified as the storm deity *Juraqan* and the bearer of wisdom. When the creation of the first humans from maize turned out too perfectly and the first men could see everything beneath the sky and beyond the horizon, the deities blurred their vision, as supernatural knowledge was confined to the gods.

Xk'is keta'maj	Completed was their knowledge
ronojel xkimuquj:	of everything they saw:
Kaj tz'uk, kaj xukut,	(The) four corners, four angles,
upam kaj, upam ulew.	of the inside of the sky, the inside of the earth.
(Popol Vuh, fol. 33v)	

The other non-human domain of the Maya cosmos is the underworld, which Colonial sources from highland Guatemala refer to as *xib'alb'a(l)* "place of fear."

Most of our understanding of this underworld derives from the Popol Vuh. In the record of hieroglyphic texts, the concept has not been identified so far (Fitzsimmons 2009: 15), and what is known about the Classic Maya concept of the underworld is based largely on interpretations of iconography analyzed within the context of the narratives from highland Maya mythology (see, e.g., Freidel et al. 1993).

The Popol Vuh and other indigenous sources from the highlands clearly specify that Xibalba is located beneath the surface of the earth. With the Hero Twins and their father explicitly "descending" (*qajik*) to and "ascending" (*aq'anik*) from Xibalba, the "realm of fear" can confidently be identified as an underworld location. The account of the creation of the world and the ordering of the Maya cosmos does not specifically mention the formation of this underworld, which may suggest that it was perceived as a part of the earth. Early sixteenth-century missionaries employed the term *Xibalba* to refer to the Christian concept of "Hell." The inherent properties of the Maya underworld were quite different from the notion of eternal human suffering, though, and the decision to reuse this term may eventually have had a counterproductive effect on the objective of evangelization (see Bredt-Kriszat 1999: 192–94; Fitzsimmons 2009: 13).

The Popol Vuh itself does not mention Xibalba or the sky as abodes for the spirit essences of the deceased. All episodes involving either of these non-human spheres take place in the deep mythic past before the creation of humankind. These myths, however, can be seen to set the parameters for the human relationship to these otherworld locations. In particular, the account of the underworld bears a clear relation to human life and death.

The narrative of the Hero Twins Junajpu and Xb'alanke, who descend to Xibalba to avenge their father's death, constitutes a central element of the Popol Vuh creation mythology. It is the last of three mythological episodes involving the Hero Twins. In the first section, the Twins act as culture heroes who by the order of Uk'u'x Kaj (Heart of Sky) overthrow Wuqub' Kaqix (Seven Macaw), the false sun and ruler of the third creation. The following episodes go back in time and tell the story of the father of the Hero Twins, Jun Junajpu, and his brother Wuqub' Junajpu, who were defeated and beheaded in Xibalba. Placed into a calabash tree, Jun Junajpu's head magically impregnates a young lady from Xibalba, who escapes to the surface of the earth, where she gives birth to the Hero Twins. The third episode tells of the birth of the Hero Twins and their descent to the underworld to defeat the Lords of Death and "limit" their control over the people on the surface of the earth. With their deeds, the Twins balance the cosmos, define the present world order, and prepare the surface of the earth for the life of humankind.

The Hero Twins narratives have been widely recognized as related to maize mythology (see, among others, Taube 1985; Stross 2006, 2007; Braakhuis 2009).

The extent to which the account helps us understand the mythological scenes in the iconography of the Classic Maya Maize God is still an issue of debate. Karl A. Taube (1985) has argued for an identification of the Hero Twins' father, Jun Junajpu, as the Popol Vuh version of the Classic Maya Maize God Ajan, based on his association with the Central Mexican deity Xochipilli and representations of the Classic version of the Hero Twins, Jun Ajaw and Yax B'alam, accompanying an image of Ajan sprouting from a turtle shell. Referring to the different stages of the Maize God narrative that were identified in the iconographic record by Michel Quenon and Geneviève LeFort (1997), Edwin Braakhuis (2009) suggested that these images were more in accord with Totonac and Tepehua maize hero mythology from the Gulf Coast. He described the concept of a "dead maize baby" that is buried and then grows into a maize stalk, from which a cob is taken and ground. The maize flour is thrown into water where the "child is reconstituted by the fish of the river" (2009: 5–6).

Braakhuis links this oral tradition to the self-sacrifice of the Hero Twins, who throw themselves into the fires of the pit oven, then have their bones ground and strewn into the rivers of Xibalba, where they come back to life as people-fish (*winaq kar*) (fol. 29r). This Popol Vuh episode of sacrificial death and rebirth has been associated with the present-day Tz'utujil practice of preparing the ceremonial drink *maatz'*, an *atole* produced from maize that is toasted, ground, and mixed with ashes (see Carlsen and Prechtel 1991: 32; Carlsen 1997: 57–59; Christenson 2001: 123–24). *Maatz'* is consumed at the time of sowing and represents semen (Carlsen and Prechtel 1991: 31). In terms of its eschatological significance, the consumption of *maatz'* is symbolic of the concept of divine sacrifice and rebirth and is celebrated in contexts analogical to the Catholic holy communion (cf. Christenson 2001: 196).

The eschatological connection of the Hero Twins and maize is also apparent in another tale from the Popol Vuh. Before descending to Xibalba, Junajpu and Xb'alanke leave two ears of maize buried in their grandmother's house. Depending on whether they survive or die in the underworld, the ears would sprout or wither. When the Twins are defeated, the ears first dry up but then sprout again when they are reborn in Xibalba and trick the lords into their own defeat. The relationship between the Twins and the maize is analogical. What is important here is that the Twins bury unripe ears of maize (*aj*) and not ripe ears of maize (*jal*) (see Tedlock 1996: 284–85). This detail of the Popol Vuh story is best understood through the conceptual metaphor of LIFE IS A MAIZE PLANT. Based on observations in the growth cycle of maize, which begins with the planting of a dried seed of ripe maize into the ground, highland Maya religious ideology sees life as generated out of death. Just like the seed that, if sufficiently watered, will sprout and develop into a new plant, dead humans are buried and regenerate new life. This concept is reflected in the Tz'utujil reference to maize seeds as *muq* "interred ones" and *jolomaa* "skulls" (Carlsen and Prechtel 1991: 26). While humans enter the underworld only after death, the Hero Twins descend alive to confront the lords of Xibalba. The unripe ears of maize they plant before their departure are therefore tokens of the fate of their souls.

The eschatological concept of intergenerational exchange has been described by Carlsen and Prechtel (1991) for traditional Tz'utujil society and been coined as the *jaloj-k'exoj* principle. The metaphor refers to exterior and interior change of the maize plant, which corresponds to the changes experienced in the growth and decay of human life. The cultural concept is also found in the Classic Maya record. The famous sarcophagus of Pakal from Palenque depicts the upper bodies of the deceased ancestral kings of the dynasty as seeds with plant shoots of fruit trees sprouting from their heads (1991: 34; Schele and Freidel 1990: 221). A similar image on the well-discussed "death vase" in the collection of the Ethnologisches Museum in Berlin (K6547) depicts the dead body of a ruler from which three anthropo-morphic fruit trees emerge (Schele and Mathews 1998; Taube 2004: 79–81). Both Classic representations have been identified as scenes relating to the mythical decomposition and rebirth of the Maize God in a paradisiacal otherworld place of creation, also called the "Mountain of Sustenance" (Martin 2006). The idea of rebirth as a transformation into fruit is also the theme of a vessel in the Dumbarton Oaks collection. Here, the Maize God is depicted as an "anthropomorphic cacao tree" that is referred to in the text as *iximte'* "maize tree" (2006: 156). Simon Martin (2006: 162) links these images with the Central Mexican dema deity Centeotl, who "buries himself in . . . a cavern and from his body grows maize, as well as the fruits and seeds of other useful plants."

The idea of divine transformation into primordial fruit is represented in the Popol Vuh in the form of the Hero Twins' father, Jun Junajpu, whose decapitated head becomes the fruit of a calabash tree that generates the life of his saviors. The Late Classic Maya vase K5616 may depict an image of the deity's head in a fruit tree—in this case a cacao tree (Reents-Budet 1994: 277; Martin 2006: 164–65), which has been interpreted as an image of the *iximte'*, the origin of all food, with cacao consid-ered "primordial maize" (see Miller and Martin 2004: 63; Martin 2006: 165). The primeval, life-giving tree at the center of the world that engendered all life is a rec-ognized concept in present-day Tz'utujil religious belief (see Carlsen and Prechtel 1991: 27). Interpreted in this context, the role of Jun Junajpu in the Popol Vuh may be that of primordial maize, which would also explain why the Hero Twins, who restore their father's head after defeating Xibalba, fail in the end to bring him back to life. Jun Junajpu stays in Xibalba, just like Centeotl.

The narrative of Jun Junajpu defines the human relationship to maize and the underworld: the dead turn into food for the living. Just like a maize seed that is planted in the ground in order to sprout, the deceased need to be buried in order to be reborn. This rebirth is indirect, in the sense that the bones of the deceased fertilize the ground, which yields the crops that give sustenance to future generations. Xibalba is therefore a place of both death and rebirth.

Thus the Hero Twin stories in the Popol Vuh define the basic cultural principles of human existence and regeneration. Humans' fate is to be buried and regenerate in the underworld to give life to their descendants. Only those who are able to defeat the Lords of Death can rise up to the sky, just like Junajpu and Xb'alanke, who do not produce offspring and therefore do not partake in the cycle of life. Their triumph over death is preceded by defeat in the sacrificial fires and the grinding up of their bones. The myth may be conceptually connected to the shift toward cremation that emerged in the burial practices of highland Guatemala during the Postclassic (see, e.g., Carmack 1968: 62–63; Braswell 2003: 301). This general understanding of afterlife and rebirth also plays a role in the mythologization of human origin as it is told in the Popol Vuh.

JOURNEY OF CREATION

The Popol Vuh describes the story of K'iche' origin as a mythical journey that starts with the creation of humankind at the place of Paxil K'ayala' and ends with the foundation of Q'umarkaj. The account begins with the creation of the first four people from maize, who become the founding fathers of the K'iche' nation. They are given wives and produce offspring to create other nations. According to the text, this dark place of human creation and original procreation is located *chi relib'al q'ij* "at the place where the sun emerges," which is the common K'iche' term for the cardinal direction of East. Yearning to see their first sunrise and in search of a divine protector, the ancestors of the K'iche' embark on a mythical journey to a citadel (*tinamit*) called Tulan Suywa and *wuqub' pek, wuqub' siwan* "Seven Caves, Seven Canyons." At Tulan, the K'iche' along with the other nations receive their gods. Ultimately, their languages change and the nations separate. The K'iche' move on to find a place where they can see their first sunrise. Crossing the sea, they arrive at Chi Pixab', where the K'iche'-speaking groups and subdivisions receive their individual names. In the dark and without food, they hide their gods in ravines and climb the mountain Jaq'awitz to see the sunrise. When dawn arises, their gods turn to stone. In the narrative structure, this sunrise marks a new beginning. The K'iche' stay for a while at Jaq'awitz, where they increase in numbers and subdue other local nations. Then they relocate again, first to a place called Chi K'ix and then to Chismachi', before the final foundation of their capital at Q'umarkaj.

The migration account is found in similar form, with deviations in the particular stages of the journey, in other highland Maya sources, including the *Título de Totonicapán*, the *Título Tamub*, and the Kaqchikel *Memorial de Sololá*. It has been previously discussed that these narratives from highland Guatemala show a strong resemblance to the Mexica migrations in the Central Mexican sources (see, e.g., Graulich 1997: 207–47; Braswell 2001). Described in a large number of written and pictorial documents, the Mexica migrations have been the subject of investigation from the early years of Mesoamerican studies until today (see, among others, Seler 1894; Davies 1973; Smith 1984). Although the precise time depth is still debated, the expansion of Uto-Aztecan speakers southward into the Central Mexican highlands (see Kaufmann 2001 [1991]) likely created the historical precedent for this mythological narrative that became such a prominent feature of Postclassic Mesoamerican historiography and seems to have coincided with a cultural *topos* of claiming legitimacy through foreign descent, which can be traced back at least to the Early Classic Teotihuacan entradas (Stuart 2004).

Despite the great variation the Central Mexican migration accounts show with respect to particular migration stages and ethnic belonging of the migrants, most sources mention the legendary origin places of Aztlan "place of herons," Chicomoztoc "Seven Caves," Tamoanchan, Tollan, and Colhuacan. The narratives that match these individual places are often conflated with each other or with other places mentioned in the accounts. The Popol Vuh and other highland Maya sources replicate these narratives and locations and even the precise place names. The concept of Tulan Suywa, *wuqub' pek, wuqub' siwan* "Seven Caves, Seven Canyons," is a clear reference to the distinct mytho-locations of Chicomoztoc and Tollan. The concept of Tulan in the Popol Vuh absorbs further narrative events associated with other places in the Mexican sources, such as Colhuacan, where the Mexica receive their patron god Huitzilopochtli, and the legendary Tamoanchan, where they split apart from the other nations (see *Historia Tolteca-Chichimeca*).

The Mesoamerican migration accounts constitute an excellent case study for the transpositioning of narrative elements. Notwithstanding, the highland narratives have often been understood as mytho-historical accounts, and the references to Tulan and Seven Caves have been interpreted as an indication for an actual Central Mexican origin of K'iche' noble ancestry (see Carmack 1981; Akkeren 2000). Places mentioned in the later stages of the K'iche' migrations account (e.g., Chikix, Chismachi') are likely real toponyms of towns that played a role in highland Maya political history and were plotted onto the general outline of the Central Mexican origin myth. But we should be cautious about using the names of mythological places of origin (e.g., Paxil, Tulan, Seven Caves) as a basis for reconstructing prehistoric migration routes. I have argued before that certain stages in the high-land Maya traditions of origin and migration refer metaphorically to otherworld places of creation rather than to actual toponyms (see Sachse and Christenson 2005; Sachse 2008).

The tale of human origin can be read as a metaphor and reflects K'iche' under-standing of the purpose of life in general and of social groups in particular. While originally adapted from Central Mexican mythology, the migration narrative has been reinterpreted and modified to map onto the conceptual metaphor of LIFE IS A MAIZE PLANT. Metaphorical expressions and diphrastic kennings in the text can be shown to refer to the consecutive stages of the "sowing" and the "dawning" of plant life.

SOWING

Maize in its cultivated form cannot naturally reproduce itself but needs to be sown out by humans, who then tend the plant so the stalk will not break and bear the fruit that will sustain them. This symbiotic relationship is reproduced in the rela-tionship between humans and deities. While humans are created by the gods, gods need humans to sustain them so the cosmos—and hence, life—can persist (see Monaghan 2000: 36–38; Christenson, this volume).

The account of K'iche' origin begins with the description of human creation in a place called Pan Paxil Pan Cayala. The term *paxil* literally reads "splittedness" or "Split Place" and has been associated with a common *topos* in Mesoamerican mythology—the discovery of maize by splitting the Mountain of Sustenance (see Christenson 2007: 193). The term *pax* can also refer to the splitting of the earth by means of a digging stick at the time of planting, which may be the basic agricultural idea underlying the mythological concept. The meaning of the term *cayala* is less straightforward. Dennis Tedlock (1996: 288) reads it as *k'ayala'* or *k'ay-al (j)a'* "bit-ter water," which Christenson (2007: 193) understands as an allusion to primordial water. According to Ruud van Akkeren, in modern K'iche' the term *k'ayala'* refers to the lime water that is added to ground maize dough (cited in Christenson 2007: 193).

The Popol Vuh describes Paxil K'ayala' as a Garden of Eden, full of delicious foods and fruits, referred to in the text as *ch'uti echa', nima echa'* "small foods, large foods" as well as *ch'uti tiko'n, nima tiko'n* "small plantings, large plantings." The par-allelism of *ch'uti, nima* is used by Vico (n.d.: 75–77) in the *Theologia Indorum* to describe the abundance of the Christian concept of the earthly paradise. It is not entirely clear whether the use of these terms needs to be understood as an immedi-ate reference to Vico's theology or whether the Dominican friar reused a concept from K'iche' ritual discourse.

The creator deities involved with the creation of humankind are named Alom K'ajolom, Tz'aqol B'itol, and Tepew Q'ukumatz. They conceive humankind in the darkness and in the night, before the sun, moon, and stars existed. To create human flesh they use yellow and white maize. The authors of the Popol Vuh make the literal statement that *xa echa' okinaq kiti'ojil* "only food entered their flesh," which can be read as a direct and critical response to the biblical creation of Adam from earth. The analogy of the creation of humankind with the processing of maize for food has been widely noted and discussed. The deity Xmucane grinds the yellow and white ears of maize nine times to create particularly fine maize dough (Tedlock 1996: 288; Christenson 2007: 195). She adds water for the blood and then forms the first four humans, just like tamales or tortillas.

Four men are created, who become the ancestral fathers of the K'iche' nation. Their names are B'alam Kitze (Jaguar of ?), B'alam Aq'ab' (Jaguar of Night), Majukutaj (?), and Ik'i B'alam (Black Jaguar). In Maya culture, the number four is associated with completeness and perfection, and these first four people were indeed perfect. They could see everything beneath the sky and beyond the horizon. So the deities had to blur their vision to ensure that the first people would reproduce, grow, and become true sustainers of the gods. In the text they ask:

We mawi kepoq'otajik, kek'iritajik,	If they are not increased, not multiplied,
ta chawaxoq, ta saqiroq?	when would it be sown, when would it dawn?
We mawi chik'iyarik,	If it does not multiply,
ta chuxoq?	when would it come to be?
(Popol Vuh, fol. 34r)	

As Christenson (this volume) points out, humans are needed to sustain the cosmos and the gods. Unless they reproduce, they cannot fulfill this task. The deities therefore diminish the men and make them incomplete so they would multiply. This implies that reproduction is considered a human trait. Divine beings are perfect and eternal; they have no need to multiply. The deities create wives, and the first humans reproduce as intended.

The terms used in the Popol Vuh for the concept of human procreation are completive passive forms of the versive verbs *k'irik* "to become many" and *poq'ik* "to burst, break (like an egg in hatching)." Both verbs have apparent metaphorical connections to maize agriculture. The verb used in modern K'iche' to refer to the concept of growing maize plants is *k'iyisaj* "to make (sth.) many." While *k'iyisaj* is a causative verb expressing the involvement of human agency in maize agriculture, the conceptualization of multiplication for humans and maize is essentially expressed by the same term. The verb *poq'ik* seems at first to refer to a simple concept of birth and fertility but may also have a metaphorical connotation relating to the maize complex. In Gulf Coast mythology we find the tale of an egg that floats in the sea or in a river, arrives at a shore, and turns itself into a maize field (see Braakhuis 2009: 6). We can therefore argue that the verbs *k'iritaj* and *poq'otaj* are used in the Popol Vuh not in their literal sense but in a metaphorical sense by referring to the original procreation of humankind in terms of the growth of a maize field, with many individual plants that form a whole.

Within the logic of the metaphor LIFE IS A MAIZE PLANT, this initial stage of human existence is portrayed in analogy to the planting and germination of the maize seed. Maya farmers prefer to place four seeds into each hole they create with the digging stick. In the same way, the creator deities conceive four ancestral fathers of the K'iche'. Like the maize seeds in the *milpa*, they germinate and grow. The Popol Vuh specifies that this multiplication takes place in darkness, before the existence of the sun, and in a place that is located in the East, "where the sun emerges." The apparent contradiction that is posed by location and the nonexistence of the sun may be resolved if the following statement is read metaphorically rather than literally and the place "where the sun emerges" is understood as a mythical "place of creation" rather than an actual place or direction.

Xpoq'otaj wi uloq releb'al q'ij.	It was multiplied from where the sun emerges.
K'iya winaq xuxik chi q'equ'mal,	Many people became in the darkness,
ta xk'iyarik.	when they became many.
Maja chalaxoq q'ij, saq,	Not had been born sun and light,
ta xek'iyarik.	when they became many.
Xa jun xek'oje' wi konojel.	Only as one all of them existed.
E tzatz chi kik'oje'ik,	They were densely packed in their existence,
kib'inowik chila' releb'al q'ij.	their origin, where the sun emerges.
(Popol Vuh, fol. 34v)	

The next stage in the journey of human origin is the departure of the forefathers and their offspring to the place called Tulan in search of the sun and a divine protector. At Tulan the K'iche' forefathers receive their patron gods Tojil, Awilix, and Jaq'awitz. Tojil gives them fire, which legitimates K'iche' dominance over the other K'iche'an nations. The Popol Vuh describes that it was at Tulan where the languages of the K'iche', Kaqchikel, Rab'inaleb', and Tz'utujil changed and where the nations split apart:

Ta xepetik chi Tulan.	When they came from Tulan.
Chiri' k'ut xkipaxij wi kib'.	There they split themselves apart.
(Popol Vuh, fol. 36r)	

In Colonial dictionaries, the verb *paxij* is given with the meaning "to break sth." in terms of breaking a ceramic vessel, as well as "to escape, get away" with respect to people and animals (Ximénez 1985 [~1710]). The Anonymous Franciscan Dictionary (1787) translates the reflexive expression *paxin-ib'* as "to depopulate a settlement" (*despoblar un pueblo*) (fol. 90r). In the context of plant growth, the process of "breaking" may refer to the actual sprouting of the planted seed, which grows in both directions: toward the surface of the earth as well as into the ground to form roots.

Akarok, mawi waral xchiqil wi usaqirik,	Alas, not here shall we see the dawn,
ta chalaxoq ri q'ij,	when the sun will be born,
saqirisay uwach ulew.	the illuminator of the face of the earth.
(Popol Vuh, fol. 38r)	

The forefathers leave Tulan and move on toward the dawn, crossing the sea. I have argued that the phrase *ch'aqa palow* that is found in the Popol Vuh and other sources refers to an otherworld place of creation and rebirth rather than to a geographical location, which had been the prime understanding of the narrative (Sachse and Christenson 2005; Sachse 2008). Water is the element that is needed for the seed to germinate and sprout. The same catalytic function can be attributed to the sea as a narrative element: it is the medium through which the K'iche' "sprout" and cross over from the mythical otherworld into the present physical world.

DAWNING

The other aspect of K'iche' origin that needs to be understood in analogy to plant growth is the concept of the dawn. The Popol Vuh describes that the K'iche' and the other nations are constantly on the move until they reach their mountain Jaq'awitz, where they await the *saqirik* "becoming light" or "dawn." The first sunrise is described as *ralaxik q'ij* "birth of sun/light" and *aq'anoq ri q'ij* "has risen the sun/light." The text says the sun was extremely hot and immediately dried up the predawn surface of the earth, which was wet and soggy. The concept of the creation of the sun seems to originate from the Central Mexican mythological tradition, although the overthrow of the false sun Seven Macaw by the Hero Twins who rise up to the sky as sun and moon appear to constitute the more likely parallel to the Nahua legend of the suns (see Bierhorst 1992).

As a narrative element, the human dawn and the dichotomy of darkness and light in the Popol Vuh separate events that occur in mythical otherworld locations from those in the real, historical world. The creation of the world and of humankind occurs in darkness, in the cold. It is the search for light and warmth that instigates the first humans' journey. This image is again consistent with the conceptualization of human origin in terms of plant growth. The first humans search for light like the sprouts of the (maize) seed that grow upward toward the surface of the ground to find light. It is within this metaphorical reading that we need to understand the forefathers' plea to the creator deities before they leave Tulan:

"Xa ta kojb'ek,	"Only then we go,
xa ta pu kojyakatajik.	and only then we arise.
Ma ta waral kojk'oje' wi chi ewal taj	Not here shall we exist in hiding,
kojiya' wi.	where you place us.
Mixyopij usaqirik?	Has not approached the dawn?
Ma pa toq'ob' iwach	Do you not pity,
we kojkanab'ixik rumal ajlab'al?	if we become spoils by enemies?
Chi tz'aq wa' oj k'o wi iwumal,	In this framing we exist because of you,
ix ajk'ixb', ajk'ajb'.	you bloodletters and sacrificers.
Jujun ta k'ut kojiya' wi,"	Then place each one of us,"
xecha' k'ut, ta xech'awik.	they said then, when they spoke.
"Utz b'a la', xa kojb'oqotajik	"It is good that we are just pulled up
qatzukuj taq ri k'eche'laj"	to search the forests,"
xecha' k'ut konojel.	said therefore all of them.
(Popol Vuh, fol. 38v)	

The verbs *yakatajik* "arise" and *b'oqotajik* "become pulled up" refer to plants or shoots growing upward. The forefathers do not want to stay *chi ewal* "in hiding" in the ground, where they were sown and where they could become the spoils of "enemies," such as insects and other vermin. This interpretation is supported by the repeated statement in the text that the forefathers had to fast and did not eat before the dawn while they were still in darkness. In Maya culture, the concept of fasting is imminently connected to otherworld locations and the spiritual transition between the worlds (see Sachse 2008). The statement that the first humans were fasting can therefore be seen as an indication for the otherworldliness of the pre-dawn locations of K'iche' origin. We may, however, also interpret the journey without sustenance in analogy to sprouts that develop in the ground, or underworld, and start taking in energy in the form of sunlight only after shooting through the surface of the earth. This idea may be reflected in a statement from the Popol Vuh that explicitly refers to the dawn as the completion of human creation: only a plant that has grown out of the ground is a true plant.

Mi xyopijik usaqirik,	Approached has the dawn,
mi xtz'aq utzinik	it has been framed the completion
mi pu xq'ale'ik	and it has been revealed
tzuqul q'ò'l,	the provider and sustainer,
saqil al, saqil k'ajol.	the daughter of light, the son of light.
Mi xq'ale' winaq,	It has appeared (the) human,
uwinaqil uwach ulew.	the population for the face of the earth.
(Popol Vuh, fol. 32v)	

The role of light as a provider of life is expressed in the plea of the first humans to the creator god Tz'aqol B'itol to give them offspring. The prayer is full of intricate metaphors. The forefathers implore their deities for calm and steady *saq* "light" and *amaq'* "nation," for "good life and creation":

"Akarok, at Tz'aqol, at B'itol.	"Alas, you Framer, you Shaper.
Kojawila', kojata',	See us, hear us,
mojatzaqo, mojapisk'alij,	do not abandon us, do not displace us,
at k'ab'awil chi kaj, chi ulew,	you god of sky, of earth,
Uk'u'x Kaj, Uk'u'x Ulew.	Heart of Sky, Heart of Earth.
Chaya'taj qetal, qatzijel,	It shall be given our sign, our word,
chib'e q'ij, chib'e saq,	as long as there is sun, as long as there is light,
ta chawaxoq, ta saqiroq.	may it be sown, may it dawn.
Qi ta raxal b'e, raxal jok.	Truly may there be green roads, green paths.
Kojaya' wi	Give us
li'anik saq, li'anik amaq' taj,	calm light, calm settlement,
utzilaj saq, utzilaj amaq' taj.	good light, good settlement,
utzilaj k'aslem, winaqirem ta puch	good life and creation
kojaya' wi.	may you give to us.
At Juraqan,	You Juraqan,
Ch'ipi Kaqulja, Raxa Kaqulja,	Young Thunderbolt, Sudden Thunderbolt,
Ch'ipi Nanawak, Raxa Nanawak,	Young Nanavac, Sudden Nanavac,
Wok, Junajpu,	Falcon, Junajpu,
Tepew, Q'ukumatz,	Sovereign, Quetzal Serpent;
Alom, K'ajolom,	Bearer, Begetter,
Xpiyacoc, Xmucane,	Xpiyacoc, Xumqane,
Rati't Q'ij, Rati't Saq.	Grandmother of Sun/Day, Grandmother of Light.
Ta chawaxoq, ta saqiroq," xecha'.	Then may be sown, may it dawn," they said.
(Popol Vuh, fol. 35r)	

The interpretation of the couplet *saq amaq'* is not straightforward, as the meaning of the second noun *amaq'* is not particularly well understood. The term refers to the second highest level of highland Maya social organization. The Popol Vuh indicates that the K'iche' *winaq* "people" fall into various *amaq'*, which again are divided into multiple *chinamit* "lineages." The Colonial dictionaries translate *amaq'* as "pueblo" (see *Vocabulario otlatecas* 2017 [n.d.]; Basseta 2005 [1690]) or "ciudad" (see Basseta 2005 [1690]; Anonymous Franciscan Dictionary 1787), with connotations of both a social group and a place. The territorial meaning is particularly clear in the expression *ruq'a' amaq'* (lit. arm of the *amaq'*), which refers to "*lugares o pueblos pequeños que están sujetos a otros* [places or small towns that are subject to others]" (Coto 1983 [~1650]) and "*estancia, pueblo sujeto a otro* [estate, town that is subject of another]" (*Vocabulario otlatecas* 2017 [n.d.]), that is, subordinate outskirts of central places. The Popol Vuh and other sources refer to the ethnically distinct social groups that were subjected by the K'iche' and their allies as *wuqub' amaq'*, which has been variously translated as "seven tribes" (Tedlock 1996) or "seven nations" (Christenson 2007) and seems to refer to the provinces occupied by the K'iche' in their first territorial expansion. The term *amaq'* is the root of the adverb *amaq'el* "forever, always," which may suggest that the noun also has the semantic connotation of "permanence" of a human group in a specific territory. "Settlement" may therefore be a close, although still inadequate, translation. As a metaphor, the pair *saq* "light" and *amaq'* "permanence" appears to refer to the two conditions essential for successful plant growth: sunlight and local stability.

In the K'iche'an sources, the concept of "light" occurs in various diphrastic kennings that refer to human life. The Popol Vuh mentions the K'iche' pleading for (*tz'ononik*) (fol. 54r) as well as venerating (*loqb'al*) (fol. 54v) *saq* "light" and *k'aslem* "life." The couplet is extended in another context, where the first five generations of K'iche' lords are referred to as the *uxe' saq, uxe' amaq', uxe' k'aslem* "root of light, root of nation, root of life" (fol. 50v).

In the *Rabinal Achi* the metaphor *saqil al, saqil k'ajol* "daughters of light, sons of light" refers to the local vassals of King Job' Toj; and the Popol Vuh mentions the triplet *saqil amaq'il, saqil al, saqil k'ajol* "nations/settlements of light, daughters of light, sons of light" to refer to the birth of humankind in the context of world creation (fol. 1r). Further evidence for the association of light and human life is provided by the diphrastic kenning of *q'ij* "sun/day" and *saq* "light." The pair occurs in the Popol Vuh and other indigenous sources in three basic semantic contexts, which suggests that it functions as a metaphor referring to the thriving and prosperity of human progeny. The plea for "sun" and "light" is used in petition prayers for offspring and food, as is illustrated by the following appeal to the gods from the

Título de Totonicapán:

"At Kaj Ulew, at pu Tz'aqol B'itol chaya' ta qami'al qak'ajol, chaya' uxer web'al uch'ab'al chiqe, at pu chaq'a cho, chaq'a palo, at upam kaj, at relib'al q'ij, at raq'anib'al q'ij, chaya' ta **qaq'ij qasaq**" xecha' . . .

"You Sky Earth and You Framer Shaper, give us daughters and sons, give us plates and cups, You across the lake, across the sea, You Inside of the sky, You Sunrise, You Path of the sun, give us our sun and our light," they said . . .

(*Título de Totonicapán*, fol. 22v–23r)

Descendants and subsistence are qualified as the essence of human life and prosperity, and the elements of "sun" and "light" are the necessary prerequisites. Accordingly, indigenous authors refer to founders of lineages and descent groups as the "roots of sun, roots of light." Such is B'alam Aq'ab', the "first grandfather, father" (*nab'e mamaxel qajawixel*) of the Nija'ib' K'iche', who is mentioned in the Popol Vuh as the *uxe' q'ij uxe' saq chi winaq* "root of sun, root of light of the people" (fol. 56r).

Consistent with this view, the Popol Vuh labels the creator deities Xmucane and Xpiyacoc as "Grandmother of sun and light" (*rati't q'ij, rati't saq*) (fol. 3v) and thus associates them with those very elements that provide nourishment and sustenance for the sprouts that break through the surface of the earth and develop into full-grown plants, branch out, and reproduce. This image is mapped onto the concept of human life, which prospers in its offspring. It is particularly relevant that the metaphor refers to human progeny not in individual terms but in terms of the social group. *Q'ij* and *saq* denote the life-giving elements that assure future continuity of one's lineage or ethnic group. This idea is also reflected in the expression *chib'e q'ij chib'e saq* "as long as there is sun, as long as there is light," which has been employed by Colonial missionary authors to refer to the Christian concept of "eternity." The metaphor may be best translated as "forever," although the K'iche' concept clearly implies the dependence of future human life on the existence of sun and light.

Bearing the above in mind, the narrative element of the "dawn" in the Popol Vuh marks the beginning of K'iche' proliferation and dominance in the Maya highlands. *Saqirik* literally means "to become white/bright" and not only refers to the concept of the rising of the sun but also refers to the movement of the K'iche' plant breaking through the surface of mythology into the light of history. The Popol Vuh states that the other K'iche'an nations (*amaq'*) went through the same process. They all had their own individual dawn on their own individual mountain, which suggests that all these groups are perceived historically as separate plants:

Jarub' pa chi amaq'	However many of the nations
k'o wakamik,	there are today,
mawi ajilan chi winaq,	uncountable people,
xa jun xsaqir wi ronojel amaq'.	only once became light/dawned all nations.
(Popol Vuh, fol. 40r)	

This takes us back to the abovementioned interpretation of *amaq'* as a term for the permanent human settlement that—in analogy to a plant—cannot be displaced once rooted. The idea that kingdoms and communities are trees is corroborated by other sources. The *Rabinal Achi* draws the image of a king as a tree whose roots and trunk can be cut, which would result in the perishing of the polity:

. . . [wi] kanuk'iso	. . . that I complete
uch'ayik uwixal ukutamil	the striking of the root, the trunk
la ajaw chakachib', tzamanib'.	of Your Lord of the Chakachib', Tzamanib'.
(Rabinal Achi, fols. 12–13)	

The Tz'utujil of Santiago Atitlán perceive their town as a tree, in which the people are the fruits and flowers, the *cofradías* constitute the branches, the *principales* form the trunk, and the ancestors are the roots (Carlsen and Prechtel 1991: 29). An opening in the church floor that is used every year in Good Friday ceremonies to place the large wooden cross with the crucified Christ is referred to as the *r'muxux ruchiliew* "navel of the face of the earth" (Christenson 2001: 77). Traditionalists in Atitlán understand the erection of the cross analogically to the planting of a seed, with Christ "reborn" on the cross "like a new maize plant" (2001: 77). The cross is furthermore symbolic of the world tree, "or *axis mundi*, which stands at the center of all things and passes through each of the three major layers of existence—underworld, earth's surface, and sky" (2001: 105). The concept of the "navel of the world" is known from other Maya communities (2001: 80). Christenson points out that in Tz'utujil ideology, every town with its populace has its own navel, its own *axis mundi* (personal communication, 2009), which would be consistent with the statement in the Popol Vuh that every *amaq'* had its own place of dawning, where it sprouted, stabilized, and prospered. The journey of human creation is epitomized in the terms *sowing* and *dawning*, which form a well-cited couplet first identified by Dennis Tedlock (1996: 225) as a metaphorical reference to the sowing and sprouting of plants. In their prayer for human offspring, the K'iche' forefathers ask the creator deities for sun and light so that *ta chawaxoq, ta saqiroq* "it may be sown, it may dawn." In this context, the couplet may be understood as a reference to human creation, from the initiation of life in the seed that is placed into the earth to the completion of creation by breaking through the surface of the earth and nourishing on the light of the sun. This process instigates the cycle of human life, in which the sowing and dawning is repeated within each generation "as long as there is light." The text specifies further that the K'iche' ancestors were "sown and dawned" in the same locations, where their patron deities Tojil, Awilix, and Jaq'awitz turned into stone at the time of the first dawn:

Are' saqirib'al	It is the place of dawning
Pa Tojil, Pa Awilix, Pa Jaq'awitz,	at Tojil, at Awilix, at Jaq'awitz,
kuchaxik wakamik,	it is called today,
are' k'ut xechawax wi, xesaqir wi	where they were sown, where they dawned,
qamam, qaqajaw.	our grandfathers, our fathers.
(Popol Vuh, fol. 39v)	

The concept of associating specific religious locations with origin places of descent lines is still found in present-day Momostenango, where patrilineage shrines are referred to as *awexib'al tikb'al* "places of sowing, places of planting" (Tedlock 1996: 225). Such shrines are the location of ceremonies called *awex tiko'n* "sowing and planting," which are held to announce the pregnancy of a woman who will give birth to a new member of the lineage (Tedlock 1992: 113). The birth of the child itself is referred to as *kuya ri saq* "to give light" (Tedlock 1996: 225), which confirms that the metaphor of "sowing" and "dawning" refers to human gestation from the conception in the womb to the delivery. Tedlock (1996: 225–26), moreover, sees another eschatological semantic dimension that denotes the "sowing" of the deceased human body into the earth and the "dawning" of the soul rising to the sky. The diphrastic kenning of "sowing and dawning" projects the stages of plant development from the seed to the shoot onto the origin of life in individual as well as social terms. In the Popol Vuh, it particularly refers to the origin of human descent lines and the rooting and settling of the K'iche' in their ancestral territory.

THEOLOGICAL COHERENCE

The narrative of human origin as it is told in the Popol Vuh is understood best in terms of the conceptual metaphor of LIFE IS A MAIZE PLANT. Just like maize seeds, the first humans are sown into the watery otherworld, where they burst into germination. The K'iche' ancestors separate and diversify in Tulan, just like the sprouts of seeds that grow into the ground to form the roots and then grow toward the surface of the earth. Pushing through the soil, they experience their dawn and develop into a stalk that forms leaves. Ideal maize plants have twenty leaves, just like humans have twenty fingers and toes. The association of maize plants as persons and persons as maize plants thus seems logical in a society whose entire subsistence is based on maize agriculture. And it is not surprising that "maize in one form or another colors almost every waking thought of those whose ancestors domesticated it" (Stross 2006: 578).

In the Popol Vuh, the conceptual metaphor is expressed in a range of analogical expressions and diphrastic kennings, as well as narrative images. Humans are defined as beings of maize, and the terminology of maize agriculture with its various semantic frames is systematically projected onto the perception and purpose of human life. The view that all life begins in a seed and grows toward the light is codified in the kenning of the "sowing and dawning" that expresses the beginning and completion of human creation. A complete human matures, procreates, and eventually has to die. The mature maize plant forms ears and tassels, with the pollen from the tassels fertilizing the silks in the ears, which are ready to harvest twenty days later. The seeds from the cob will dry up and die before they can be placed into the earth to start a new cycle of life. In the same way, it is the logical fate of humans to be buried in the earth and give life to new generations. The experienced cyclicality of the life of maize created the template for the origin of humankind and human existence within the cosmos.

The world is a living thing, and the perception of world creation therefore follows the same parameters of cyclicality as that of all life within it. Human life is intimately connected with the underworld as the place of origin and the final abode. Only those with superhuman abilities can escape this eternity of "sowing," "dawning," "multiplying," and "dying." In traditional highland Maya communities, influential ancestors are referred to as *nawal*, people who never actually died but simply left to stay in the mountains or caves and watch over and control the fate of the town (Cook 1986: 152; Christenson 2001: 84, 87; 2009: 106–7). In the same way, the venerated founding fathers in the Popol Vuh never died or were buried but merely disappeared (*sachik*) on the mountain Jaq'awitz (fol. 47v).

For the Classic Maya, it has been suggested that the deceased divine kings, following the maize cycle, were reborn and ascended to the celestial upperworlds (Fitzsimmons 2009: 52–60), a place the Popol Vuh also reserves for deities and deified ancestors. Humans did not share that privilege. From Central Mexican Nahuatl sources, we know that the otherworldly abodes of the deceased were determined by the date of their birth and the cause of their death rather than by their moral conduct in life (Burkhart 1989: 50). Warriors who died in battle and women who died in childbirth with the baby still in the womb were considered "social failures," and their souls dwelled in different parts of the sky (1989: 50–51). This moral validation makes sense within the logic of the conceptual metaphor LIFE IS A MAIZE PLANT, as these humans are withdrawn from the eternal cycle of death and rebirth.

We can entertain the idea that Postclassic and Early Colonial highland Maya culture may have shared this moral perception.

The concept of a calm and balanced human life that evolves and terminates like that of a maize plant seems to constitute a fundamental principle of Maya theology. Analyzed within the context of the conceptual metaphor, the narratives and episodes in the Popol Vuh form a coherent system of thought and belief. Although they may originally come from various Mesoamerican traditions, they reflect the common principles of highland Maya religious mythology. To respond to Christianity, the authors drew from this well of narratives and metaphors to create the alternative theology of the sixteenth-century maize people, which defines the cultural logic of human existence within the Maya universe until the present day.

ACKNOWLEDGMENTS

I am grateful to the Dumbarton Oaks Research Library and Collections for awarding me a research fellowship in the academic year 2012–13, during which time this chapter was written.

NOTE

1. All transcriptions of the Popol Vuh text into modernized spelling as well as translations are based on Christenson (2003, 2004, 2007), with modifications and changes by the author of this chapter.

REFERENCES CITED

Acuña, Rene. 1985. "La Theologia Indorum de Fray Domingo de Vico." *Tlalocan* 10: 281–307.

Akkeren, Ruud van. 2000. *Place of the Lord's Daughter: Rab'inal, Its History, Its Dance-Drama.* Center for Non-Western Studies Publications 91. Center for Non-Western Studies, Leiden.

Akkeren, Ruud van. 2003. "Authors of the Popol Vuh." *Ancient Mesoamerica* 14 (2): 237–56.

Anonymous Franciscan Dictionary (AFD). 1787. *Vocabulario de lengua kiché compuesto por el apostólico zelo de los m.r.p. Franciscanos de esta Santa Provincia del Dulcíssimo Nombre de Jesús del Arzobispado de Guatemala.* Copiado por d. Fermín Joseph Tirado. Special Collections manuscript C.A.6 V 85. Tozzer Library, Harvard University, Cambridge, MA.

Basseta, Domingo de. 2005 [1698]. *Vocabulario en lengua quiché.* Ed. René Acuña. Universidad Nacional Autónoma de México/Instituto de Investigaciones Filológicas/Centro de Estudios Mayas, Mexico City.

Bierhorst, John, ed. 1992. *History and Mythology of the Aztecs: The Codex Chimalpopoca.* University of Arizona Press, Tucson.

Braakhuis, H. Edwin M. 2009. "The Tonsured Maize God and Chichome-Xochitl as Maize Bringers and Culture Heroes: A Gulf Coast Perspective." *Wayeb Notes* 32, http://www.wayeb.org/notes/wayeb_notes0032.pdf.

Braswell, Geoffrey. 2001. "Ethnogenesis, Social Structure, and Survival: The Nahuaization of K'iche'an Culture, 1450–1550." In *Maya Survivalism*, ed. Ueli Hoestettler and Matthew Restall, 51–58. Acta Mesoamericana 12. Verlag Anton Saurwein, Markt Schwaben.

Braswell, Geoffrey. 2003. "K'iche'an Origins, Symbolic Emulation, and Ethnogenesis in the Maya Highlands: A.D. 1400–1524." In *The Postclassic Mesoamerican World*, ed. Michael Smith and Frances Berdan, 297–303. University of Utah Press, Salt Lake City.

Bredt-Kriszat, Cristina. 1999. "La Theologia Indorum y la respuesta indígena en las crónicas de Guatemala." In *La lengua de la cristianización en Latinoamérica: Catequización e instrucción en lenguas amerindias; The Language of Christianization in Latin America: Catechization and Instruction in Amerindian Languages*, ed. Lindsey Crickmay and Sabine Dedenbach-Salazar Sáenz, 183–203. Bonner Amerikanistische Studien 32, Centre for Indigenous American Studies and Exchange, Occasional Papers 29. Verlag Anton Saurwein, Markt Schwaben.

Brody, Jill. 2004. "Comunidad es familia, acuerdo es repetición: relación entre dos metáforas clave en tojolab'al." In *La metáfora en mesoamérica*, ed. Mercedes Montes de Oca Vega, 63–80. Estudios sobre Lenguas Americanas 3. Universidad Nacional Autónoma de México, Mexico City.

Burkhart, Louise M. 1989. *The Slippery Earth: Nahua-Christian Moral Dialogue in Sixteenth-Century Mexico*. University of Arizona Press, Tucson.

Carlsen, Robert S. 1997. *The War for the Heart and Soul of a Highland Maya Town*. University of Texas Press, Austin.

Carlsen, Robert S., and Martin Prechtel. 1991. "The Flowering of the Dead: An Interpretation of Highland Maya Culture." *Man* 26: 23–42.

Carmack, Robert M. 1968. *Toltec Influence on the Postclassic Culture History of Highland Guatemala*. Middle American Research Institute Publications 26. Tulane University, Middle American Research Institute, New Orleans.

Carmack, Robert M. 1981. *The Quiché Maya of Utatlán: The Evolution of a Highland Guatemala Kingdom*. University of Oklahoma Press, Norman.

Carmack, Robert M., and James Mondloch. 1983 [1554]. *El Título de Totonicapán: Texto, traducción y comentario*. Instituto de Investigaciones Filológicas, Centro de Estudios Mayas. Fuentes para el Estudio de la Cultura Maya 3. Universidad Autónoma de México, Mexico City.

Carmack, Robert M., and James Mondloch. 1989. *El Título de Yax y otros documentos qui-chés de Totonicapán, Guatemala*. Universidad Autónoma de México, Mexico City.

Christenson, Allen J. 2001. *Art and Society in a Highland Maya Community: The Altarpiece of Santiago Atitlán*. University of Texas Press, Austin.

Christenson, Allen J. 2004. *Popol Vuh*, vol. 2: *Literal Poetic Version, Translation and Transcription*. O Books, Winchester.

Christenson, Allen J. 2006. "You Are What You Speak: Maya as the Language of Maize." In *Maya Ethnicity: The Construction of Ethnic Identity from Preclassic to Modern Times*, ed. Frauke Sachse, 209–16. Acta Mesoamericana 19. Verlag Anton Saurwein, Markt Schwaben.

Christenson, Allen J. 2007. *Popol Vuh—the Sacred Book of the Maya*. 2nd revised ed. University of Oklahoma Press, Norman.

Christenson, Allen J. 2009. "Ancestral Presence at the Navel of the World: Francisco Sojuel and Santiago Atitlán." In *Landscapes of Origin in the Americas: Creation Narratives Linking Ancient Places and Present Communities*, ed. Jessica J. Christie, 98–119. University of Alabama Press, Tuscaloosa.

Christenson, Allen J. 2012. "The Use of Chiasmus by the Ancient K'iche' Maya." In *Parallel Worlds: Genre, Discourse, and Poetics in Contemporary, Colonial, and Classic Period Maya Literature*, ed. Kerry M. Hull and Michael D. Carrasco, 311–36. University Press of Colorado, Boulder.

Cook, Garreth W. 1986. "Quichean Folk Theology and Southern Maya Supernaturalism." In *Symbol and Meaning beyond the Closed Community: Essays in Mesoamerican Ideas*, ed. Gary H. Gossen, 139–53. Studies on Culture and Society 1. Institute for Mesoamerican Studies, State University of New York, Albany.

Coto, Thomas. 1983 [~1650]. *Thesavrvs Verborvm: Vocabularia de la Lengua Cakchiquel V(el) Guatemalteca*. Ed. René Acuña. Universidad Autónoma de México, Mexico City.

Davies, Nigel. 1973. *The Aztecs: A History*. University of Oklahoma Press, Norman.

Dürr, Michael. 1989. "Strategien indianischer Herrschaftslegitimierung im kolonialzeitlichen Mesoamerika: ein Vergleich der Argumentation im Popol Vuh und im Título von Totonicapán." *Sociologus* 39: 172–81.

Fischer, Edward F. 1999. "Cultural Logic and Maya Identity: Rethinking Constructivism and Essentialism." *Current Anthropology* 40 (4): 473–99.

Fitzsimmons, James L. 2009. *Death and the Classic Maya Kings*. University of Texas Press, Austin.

Freidel, David, Linda Schele, and Joy Parker. 1993. *Maya Cosmos: Three Thousand Years on the Shaman's Path*. William Morrow, New York.

Garibay K., Angel María. 1968. *Poesía náhuatl III*. Universidad Autónoma de México, Mexico City.

Graulich, Michel. 1997. *Myths of Ancient Mexico*. University of Oklahoma Press, Norman.

Haly, Richard. 2004. "Of Maize and Men: Some Articulations of a Mesoamerican Metaphor." In *La metáfora en mesoamérica*, ed. Mercedes Montes de Oca Vega, 123–70. Estudios sobre Lenguas Americanas 3. Universidad Autónoma de México, Mexico City.

Hull, Kerry M. 2003. "Verbal Art and Performance in Ch'orti' and Maya Hieroglyphic Writing." PhD dissertation, Department of Anthropology, University of Texas, Austin.

Kaufman, Terrence. 2001 [1991]. "The History of the Nawa Language Group from the Earliest Times to the Sixteenth Century: Some Initial Results." Revised version of unpublished manuscript.

Lakoff, George. 1990. "The Invariance Hypothesis: Is Abstract Reason Based on Image-Schemas?" *Cognitive Linguistics* 1 (1): 39–74.

Lakoff, George. 1993. "The Contemporary Theory of Metaphor." In *Metaphor and Thought*, ed. Andrew Ortony. 2nd ed. Cambridge University Press, Cambridge.

Lakoff, George, and Mark Johnson. 1980. *Metaphors We Live By*. University of Chicago Press, Chicago.

Laughlin, Robert M. 2004. "De cabo a rabo: las expresiones metafóricas de la anatomía tzotzil de Zinacantán." In *La metáfora en mesoamérica*, ed. Mercedes Montes de Oca Vega, 51–62. Estudios sobre Lenguas Americanas 3. Universidad Autónoma de México, Mexico City.

Martin, Simon. 2006. "Cacao in Ancient Maya Religion: First Fruit from the Maize Tree and Other Tales from the Underworld." In *Chocolate in Mesoamerica: A Cultural History of Cacao*, ed. Cameron L. McNeil, 154–83. University Press of Florida, Gainesville.

Maxwell, Judith. 2004. "Säq, räx, qän, blanco, verde, amarilla: metáforas kaqchikeles de los siglos xvi y xx." In *La metáfora en mesoamérica*, ed. Mercedes Montes de Oca Vega, 33–50. Estudios sobre Lenguas Americanas 3. Universidad Autónoma de México, Mexico City.

Miller, Mary Ellen, and Simon Martin. 2004. *Courtly Art of the Ancient Maya*. Thames and Hudson, London.

Monaghan, John. 2000. "Theology and History in the Study of Mesoamerican Religions." In *Handbook of Mesoamerican Indians, Supplement 6—Ethnology*, ed. John W. Monaghan and Robert Wauchope, 24–49. University of Texas Press, Austin.

Montes de Oca Vega, Mercedes. 2004. "Los difrasismos: ¿Núcleos conceptuales meso-americanos?" In *La metáfora en mesoamérica*, ed. Mercedes Montes de Oca Vega, 225–51. Estudios sobre Lenguas Americanas 3. Universidad Autónoma de México, Mexico City.

Quenon, Michel, and Geneviève Le Fort. 1997. "Rebirth and Resurrection in Maize God Iconography." In *The Maya Vase Book*, vol. 5, 884–902. Kerr Associates, New York.

Recinos, Adrián, Delia Goetz, and Sylvanus G. Morley. 1950. *Popol Vuh: The Sacred Book of the Ancient Quiché Maya.* [Translation from the Spanish version of Adrián Recinos.] University of Oklahoma Press, Norman.

Reents-Budet, Dorie. 1994. *Painting the Maya Universe: Royal Ceramics of the Classic Period.* Duke University Press, Durham, NC.

Sachse, Frauke. 2008. "Over Distant Waters: Places of Origin and Creation in Colonial K'iche'an Sources." In *Pre-Columbian Landscapes of Creation and Origin*, ed. John E. Staller, 123–60. Springer, New York.

Sachse, Frauke, and Allen J. Christenson. 2005. *Tulan and the Other Side of the Sea: Unraveling a Metaphorical Concept from Colonial Guatemalan Highland Sources.* Mesoweb, http://www.mesoweb.com/articles/tulan/Tulan.pdf.

Sam Colop, Enrique. 1999. *Popol Wuj: Version Poética K'iche'.* PEMBI-GTZ/Cholsamaj, Guatemala City.

Sam Colop, Enrique. 2008. *Popol Wuj: Biblioteca Guatemala 1.* F&G Editores, Guatemala City.

Schele, Linda, and David Freidel. 1990. *A Forest of Kings: The Untold Story of the Ancient Maya.* William Morrow, New York.

Schele, Linda, and Peter Mathews. 1998. *The Code of Kings: The Language of Seven Sacred Maya Temples and Tombs.* Scribner, New York.

Schultze-Jena, Leonhard. 1944. *Popol Vuh: Das heilige Buch der Quiché Indianer von Guatemala.* Kohlhammer, Stuttgart.

Seler, Eduard. 1894. "Wo lag Aztlan, die Heimath der Azteken?" *Globus* 65: 317–24.

Smith, Michael E. 1984. "The Aztlan Migrations of the Nahuatl Chronicles: Myth or History?" *Ethnohistory* 31: 153–86.

Sparks, Garry. 2019. *Rewriting Maya Religion: Domingo de Vico, K'iche' Maya Intellectuals, and the* Theologia Indorum. Louisville: University of Press of Colorado.

Sparks, Garry. 2014. "Primeros folios, folios primeros: Una breve aclaración acerca de la Theologia Indorum y su relación intertexual con el Popol Wuj." *Voces: Revista semestral del Instituto de Lingüística e Interculturalidad* 9 (2): 91–142.

Sparks, Garry, with Frauke Sachse and Sergio Romero. 2017. *The Americas' First Theologies: Early Sources of Post-Contact Indigenous Religion.* Religion in Translation Series of the American Academy of Religion. Oxford University Press, New York.

Stross, Brian. 2006. "Maize in Word and Image in Southeastern Mesoamerica." In *Histories of Maize: Multidisciplinary Approaches to the Prehistory, Linguistics, Biogeography, Domestication, and Evolution of Maize*, ed. John E. Staller, Robert H. Tykot, and Bruce F. Benz, 578–99. Elsevier-Academic Press, Boston.

Stross, Brian. 2007. "Eight Reinterpretations of Submerged Symbolism in the Mayan Popol Wuj." *Anthropological Linguistics* 49 (3–4): 388–423.

Stuart, David. 2004. "The Beginnings of the Copan Dynasty: A Review of the Hieroglyphic and Historical Evidence." In *Understanding Early Classic Copan*, ed. Ellen E. Bell, Marcello A. Canuto, and Robert J. Sharer, 215–47. University of Pennsylvania Museum of Archaeology and Anthropology, Philadelphia.

Taube, Karl A. 1985. "The Classic Maya Maize God: A Reappraisal." In *Fifth Palenque Round Table (1983)*, vol. 7, ed. Merle Greene Robertson and Virginia Fields, 171–81. Pre-Columbian Art Research Institute, San Francisco.

Taube, Karl A. 2004. "Flower Mountain: Concepts of Life, Beauty, and Paradise among the Classic Maya." *RES—Anthropology and Aesthetics* 45: 69–98.

Tedlock, Barbara. 1992. *Time and the Highland Maya*. 2nd revised ed. University of New Mexico Press, Albuquerque.

Tedlock, Dennis. 1996. *Popol Vuh: The Definite Edition of the Mayan Book of the Dawn of Life and the Glories of Gods and Kings*. 2nd revised ed. Simon and Schuster, New York.

Título de Totonicapán. See Carmack and Mondloch 1983.

Vico, Domingo de. n.d. [1554]. *Theologia Indorum en lengua 4iche*. Garrett-Gates Collection of Mesoamerican Manuscripts 175. Princeton University Library, Princeton, NJ.

Vocabulario otlatecas. 2017. *Diccionario k'iche' de Berlin: El Vocabulario en lengua 4iche otlatecas, edición crítica e introducción*. Ed. Michael Dürr and Frauke Sachse. Estudios Indiana. Ibero-Amerikanisches Institut and Reimer Verlag, Berlin.

Vogt, Evon Z. 1976. *Tortillas for the Gods: A Symbolic Analysis of Zinacanteco Rituals*. University of Oklahoma Press, Norman.

Wichmann, Søren. 2004. "El concepto de camino entre los mayas a partir de la fuentes epigráficas, iconográficas y etnográficas." In *La metáfora en mesoamérica*, ed. Mercedes Montes de Oca Vega, 13–32. Estudios sobre Lenguas Americanas 3. Universidad Autónoma de México, Mexico City.

Ximénez, Francisco de. 1985 [~1710]. *Primera parte del Tesoro de las lenguas Cakchiquel, Quiché y Zutuhil, en que las dichas lenguas se traducen a la nuestra, española*. Ed. Carmelo Sáenz de Santa María. Academia de Geografía e Historia de Guatemala, Guatemala City.

4

The *Saqirik* (Dawn) and Foundation Rituals among the Ancient K'iche'an Peoples

IYAXEL COJTÍ REN

This chapter proposes that the *saqirik*, or the dawn episode, described in ethnohistoric documents from Guatemala, was a tradition that represented stages in the sociopolitical development of Postclassic polities and was performed to take possession of new territories. The dawn was a widespread tradition in Mesoamerica that was closely linked to foundation rituals (Boone 2000; Jansen 1997). Foundation rituals are ceremonial activities carried out to establish new polities or dynastic rules at a specific place (Boone 2000: 99). Among K'iche'an groups (K'iche', Kaqchikel, Rab'inaleb', and Tz'utujil), foundation rituals relating to the sunrise are performed on altars oriented toward the four corners of the universe. These altars are usually built around new settlements and are used for fire ceremonies or incense burning to receive the dawn. Altars of this type are dedicated to *k'ab'awil*, "protector deities," and are generally called *saqarib'al*, "dawning place," in K'iche', although they sometimes have individual names. This chapter explores the worldview of the dawn tradition among the K'iche'an peoples, as well as the political implications of its reenactment. I will also address how the concept of *saqirik* is understood among K'iche' people today.[1]

The ethnohistorical sources of the K'iche'an, Mixtec, and Nahua people attest a consistent tradition of dividing the history of humankind into successive creations marked by different suns. Maarten Jansen (1997) argues that the history of the various ethnolinguistic groups, empires, and reigns in Mesoamerica was organized stratigraphically into epochs or suns. Taking into account the history narrated in

DOI: 10.5876/9781646421992.c004

their ancient books, the contemporary Mixtec, for example, divided the human past into three periods: (1) recent history, or the history of their deceased grandparents, corresponding to the Viceroyalty-Republican period dominated by Christianity and Spanish rule; (2) the Precontact epoch, in which the ancestors constructed the ancient cities and archaeological sites known today; and (3) the primordial epoch, when the first sun had not yet risen and darkness prevailed. This period ended with the dawn, which marked the time of foundation when the earth as well as human culture were organized. More specifically, the dawn is tied to the birth of the founding fathers and their division according to the four directions. Newly acquired lands occupied by the founders are established by reenacting the first dawn through ceremonies of New Fire (Jansen 1997: 12–15).

In the same line of interpretation, Alfredo López Austin and Leonardo López Luján (1999) explain that the origin myths of the Postclassic Mesoamerican peoples (900–1524 CE) have a similar structure that can be divided into three phases: *nocturnal, auroral,* and *sunrise.* The nocturnal phase consists of the creation of humans by the creator deities. During this stage, all human beings are united as one group, speak the same language, and do not yet know their particular protector deities. The authors indicate that this phase can be compared to life in utero, from gestation to the moment before birth. In the next phase, auroral, the people leave their places of origin (Chicomoztoc, Seven Caves, Seven Ravines, Tulan, Apoala, or Tamoanchan) in search of their lands. These people are described as semi-conscious, drunk, possessed by the forces of the night. In many traditions, they may also be seen as impoverished, ignorant, or savage. As they proceed on their journey, they do not reach the state of civilization until they witness the sunrise, find their settlements, and start a new sociopolitical organization. These last two phases can be likened to the cultural classifications of *Chichimecayotl* and *Toltecayotl.* The *Chichimecayotl* condition corresponds to nomadic life, where people have no possessions, are ignorant, and lack knowledge about cultivating maize. However, this situation changes when they end their mythical journey, establish their settlements, and adopt a sedentary and civilized lifestyle. Therefore, it is during this sunrise phase that the way of life changes from *Chichimecayotl* to *Toltecayotl* (López Austin and López Luján 1999: 51–78). It is important to be familiar with Central Mexican origin myths, as K'iche'an groups may have adopted elements of this tradition to explain their own origin.

ANTICIPATION OF THE DAWN BY THE K'ICHE' FOUNDING FATHERS

The authors of the Popol Wuj write that in the time of darkness, before the birth of the sun and the moon, the creator deities Alom, K'ajolom, Tz'aqol, B'itol, Tepew, and Q'ukumatz fashioned the first humans out of ground white and yellow maize. These humans were the founding fathers, named B'alam Kitze', B'alam Aq'ab', Majukutaj, and Ik'i B'alam, who along with their wives gave origin to the K'iche' groups. The creation of the founder couples and the multiplication of different peoples occurred in the East, but they were wary because they lacked patron deities (carved of wood and stone) to venerate, which means they had no one to protect them or their descendants. The Popol Wuj describes this grief:

Maja b'i k'u jab'i'oq che'-ab'aj	There was not therefore in existence wood/stone [gods]
Chichajin e qanab'e chuch, qajaw.	To protect our first mothers, our first fathers.
E xa k'u xkos kik'ux chiri'	But their hearts were tired here
Chi royob'ejxik q'ij.	As they awaited the sun.
E k'i chik ronojel amaq',	The people were already very numerous,
Ruk' Yaqi winaq, ajk'ix, ajk'aj.	Including the Yaqui people, and the bloodletters and sacrificers.
"Xa jo', Oj qatzukuj,	"Merely let us go, we shall search,
Oj pu qila' we k'o chi chajin qetala.	We shall look to see if there is one who will guard us.
Chi qarik ri kojtzijon ta chuwach!	We may find one that we can speak before his face!
Xaki K'eje oj k'olik,	It is as if we did not exist,
Maja b'i chajal qe!" Xecha k'ut	For there is no guardian for us!" said
E B'alam Kitze', B'alam Aq'ab',	B'alam K'iche', B'alam Aq'ab',
Majukutaj, Ik'i B'alam.	Majukutaj and Ik'i B'alam.
(modified from Christenson 2003: lines 5340–50)	

It was then that the K'iche' fathers heard of the existence of a city called Tulan Suywa, Seven Caves and Seven Ravines, and they journeyed toward it. In Tulan, many important events occurred: The reception of the protector deities, the differentiation of languages, and the configuration of a political hierarchy among the polities in the highlands. It was in this place that B'alam Kitze' received his deity, Tojil; B'alam Aq'ab' was assigned to the deity Awilix; Q'aq'awitz appeared to Majukutaj; and finally, Ik'i B'alam received the deity Nik'aqaj Taq'aj. However, their hearts were still troubled because they had yet to witness the dawn, so they left Tulan (Sam Colop 2008: 141–42).

According to the Popol Wuj, the first fathers needed to prepare themselves to witness the dawn. This preparation consisted of placing their protector deities in safe places, where they would not be stolen but would still be within reach of their followers. The founding fathers followed their protector deities' instructions, and each one placed the image of his deity in a specific location. B'alam Aq'ab' deposited the deity Awilix in a place called Ewab'al Siwan (Hidden Ravine), and Majukutaj set the deity Q'aq'awitz in a site called Kaqja (Red House); this phrase was also used anciently to refer to mounds.[2] Immediately thereafter, B'alam Kitze' placed Tojil on a mountain called Pa Tojil. Ik'i B'alam is no longer mentioned after this point, possibly because he perished and was replaced by Saqik Tsutuja' (Carmack and Mondlock 1983: 189). After the dawn, the names of the places where the protector deities were deposited were changed to *saqirib'al*:

Xawi k'u chiri' xek'oje' wi	Only, there they were
Pa k'echelaj,	In the forest,
Are Saqirib'al,	In the dawning places,
Pa Tojil,	At Tojil,
Pa Awilix,	At Awilix,
Pa Jaq'awitz, kucha'xik wakamik.	At Jaq'awitz, as they are called today.
Are k'ut xechawax wi,	There therefore they were sown,
Xesaqir wi, qamam, qaqajaw.	They dawned, our grandfathers, our fathers.

(modified from Christenson 2003: lines 6030–40)

There is a direct relationship between the dawn and the placement of the deities on their respective mountains. It is said in the *Título de Totonicapán* that after the dawn occured, the mountains where the deities had been deposited were renamed as follows: Saqirib'al Tohil, or "dawning place of Tojil"; Saqirib'al Awilix, or "dawning place of Awilix"; and Saqirib'al Q'aq'awitz, or "dawning place of Q'aq'awitz" (Carmack and Mondloch 1983 [1554]: 109). Of these three mountains, it was on Q'aq'awitz where the K'iche' founding fathers remained for some time and gave origin to several generations. The anthropologist Robert M. Carmack (2001) identified these three *saqirib'al* in what is now the village of Santa Rosa Chujuyub in the Department of Quiché (see figure 4.1). Carmack (2001: 138) indicates that while the hills Pa Tojil and Pa Awilix still have the same names, the hill Q'aq'awitz could be the one that is now called Chi Tinamit, where there are still remnants of occupation.

Although there was only a primordial dawn for all peoples in the highlands, this event was reproduced several times and in different places for other social groups within the K'iche' polity, as well as for other political communities. For example, in the *Título de Totonicapán* it is said that the K'iche' groups named Tamub', Kakoj, and Ek'omak' had their mountain called Saqirib'al Amaq' Tam, whereas the mountain of the Ilokab' and Juanija' was called Saqirib'al Ajuk'in (Carmack and Mondloch 1983 [1554]: 186). In addition, the Xajil Chronicle mentioned that other political communities from the highlands, such as the Kaqchikel, Rab'inaleb', and Tz'utujil, were also witnesses to the daybreak:

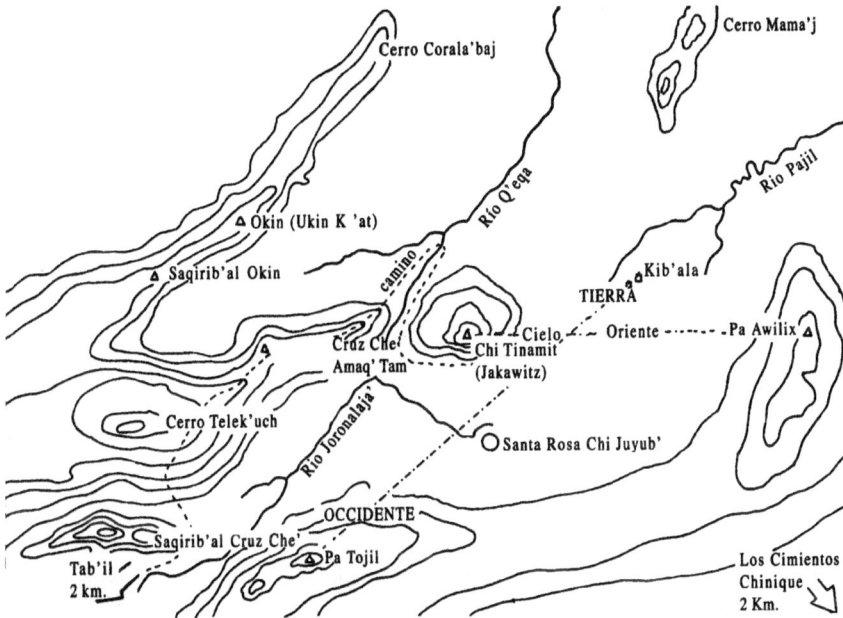

FIGURE 4.1. Location of the K'iche' *saqirib'al* (Carmack 2001: 138)

Chwi k'a juyu' Tojojil xsaqer wi K'eche' winaq	Atop the hill Tojojil dawned the K'iche' winaq
Chuwi' k'a juyu' Samaneb' xsaqer wi Rabinaleb'	The Rab'inal dawned atop the hill Samaneb'
Chi ri' k'a xrajsaqer wi Tz'utujile Pa Tz'ala',	The Tz'utujil almost dawned there at Pa Tz'ala',
Xa maja tutzin rutz'aq	but their buildings were not yet completed
toq xsaqer kuma ruchinamit.	when it dawned, on account of his chinamït.
(Maxwell and Hill 2006: 120)	

Although various political communities experienced the dawn, only those who enjoyed power and autonomy received protective deities in Tulan. This differentiation reconfigured the power relations between the different polities in the highlands. During the Late Postclassic (1200–1524 CE), the Nima' K'iche' Amaq' and its main *chinamit* (Kaweq, Nija'ib', Ajaw K'iche', and Saqik) dominated the political and military fields of the region under the direction of their deity Tojil. Tojil was not only their protector deity and guide but was also a symbol of identity and unity among the three K'iche' confederations (Nima K'iche', Tamub', and Ilokab'). In the Popol Wuj, Tojil instructed his followers to exert their control over the small and big towns, as described in the next paragraph:

"Xa wi waral qa juyub'al,	"Only here our mountains,
Qa taq'ajal chuxik.	Our plains shall come to be.
Oj iwech chik, Mi xuxik.	We have now come to be yours.
Nim qaq'ij, Nim pu qalaxik	Great is our day, great as well is our birth
Rumal ronojel winaq iwech,	Because of all the people that are yours,
Ri ronojel amaq' ...	All the nations ...
Chich'ak ri ronojel amaq'.	You will conquer all the nations.
Chikuk'aj	They shall bring to you
Ukik'el,	Their blood,
U komajil chiqawach.	Their gore before our faces.
Chul wi, kojkiq'aluj.	They shall come, they shall embrace us.
E qech chik,"	They are ours now,"
Xcha' k'u ri Tojil.	Said therefore Tojil.

(modified from Christenson 2003: lines 6320–62)

K'iche' expansionism was facilitated by the support of other groups who played the role of allies during war, especially the Kaqchikel confederation. This alliance began during the reign of the K'iche' ruler Q'uq'umatz (1400–1425 CE) and continued with K'iq'ab' (1425–75 CE). During K'iq'ab's reign, he ordered the protection of his territories from enemy attack by deploying military outposts on the mountaintops surrounding the K'iche' basin and the nearby newly conquered territories. These small settlements were named *calpul*, and their main purpose was to alert K'iche' rulers to enemy incursions and to gather military forces in time of war (Ximénez 1999: 132). The authority of the K'iche' over the *calpul* was reinforced by sending K'iche' captains to lead these small settlements and by imposing several rules that had to be obeyed. Some of the rules explicitly prohibited the veneration of other deities different from those of the K'iche' and denied the *calpul* the right to build temples or altars to those deities. Other rules prohibited local authorities from governing without K'iche' elite authorization or conducting ceremonial witnessing of the dawn due to its political implications (Sam Colop 2008: 202–3; Ximénez 1965: 48–50). In this context, the Kaqchikel lacked autonomy and the possibility of having their own protector deity to protect and guide them, thus limiting their sense of unity and identity. Maarten Jansen further observed that the periodization of history can be used for purposes of legitimization. For example, a current government can be connected to the prevailing sun, while a subjugated population can be condemned to a previous era, relegating all their rights to the past (Jansen 1997: 16). Even though it is said in the Popol Wuj that all peoples experienced the primordial dawn, its ceremonial reenactment was restricted among subjugated groups as a potential act of self-determination, cultural development, and geographic expansion.

The Kaqchikel, who gained a considerable level of autonomy and status after supporting the K'iche' expansionist campaigns, describe in their documents how they experienced the dawn. The following passage describes how this event was closely related to the construction of new settlements or important buildings in newly obtained territories. It is said in the Xajil Chronicle that when the Kaqchikel founding fathers Q'aq'awitz and Saqtekaw arrived at Lake Atitlán[3] to divide up the territory, they ordered their followers to build their edifices because the dawn was about to break:

Nab'ey k'a xepe Q'eqak'uch, Bak'ajol,	First then came the Q'eqak'uch, the Bak'ajol,
Sib'akijay, Kaweq;	the Sib'aqijay, and the Kaweq;
xetaq pe.	they were sent forth.
"Kixnab'eyaj, ix nujay, nu chinamit.	"You go first, you my house, my chinamit.
Tib'ana' apon qatz'aq, qib'aj.	Make our buildings, our house foundations.
Xa jala chik tisaqer.	In just a little while, it will dawn.
Ujix" xe'uche'ex.	Go forth!" They were told.
Xepe k'a, xe'ul	They came then, they arrived
chi ri pa seqerib'al.	there at the place of dawning.
Pan Tzik, Pa Roxone', Sinajijay,	Pan Tzik, Pa Roxone', Sinajijay,
Pa Sub'aqul (y) Pa Kaweq Kejil	Pa Sub'aqul (and) Pa Kaweq Kejil
Rub'i juyu' xesaqer wi.	were the names of the hills where they dawned.
Xtiker k'a rub'anik tz'aq kuma.	The construction of the buildings was begun for them.
K'ulb'al richin kajpop,	The meeting place of their Ajpops,
nimajay rub'i,	(which was) named Nimajay,
nab'ey kitz'aq.	was their first building.
(Maxwell and Hill 2006: 112–13)	

This tradition survived in some communities in the highlands, according to the French anthropologist Alain Breton, who gathered stories among the Achi people from the town of Rabinal. The people of this town, the Rabinaleb', also appear in the ethnohistoric documents as having witnessed the primordial dawn along with the K'iche' and the Kaqchikel:

At the beginning of the world, our forefathers lived on the mountaintops that surround the village, there where the ruins of Kaqyub are found. In those days the valley was covered by water and the world was dark.

When the lagoon dried up, some of our ancestors came down and began to build the church. Only when construction was finished did the sun appear and all became illuminated. Their work finished, our ancestors buried themselves at the foot of the church. (Breton 2013: 305)

In this story, the church has replaced the altars where the protector deities were located, but it still preserved the same function as a place of worship that prompted the sunrise that illuminated all human beings. Currently, among K'iche' peoples, the concept of *saqirik* and *saqarib'al* is still alive. In the next section, I explore how these concepts are understood among the K'iche' *ajq'ijab'* (Maya spiritual guides and daykeepers).

THE *SAQARIB'AL* ALTARS IN CHICHICASTENANGO AND LEMOA

The word *saqirik*, which means "to dawn, illuminate, or clarify," is used daily in K'iche' towns as an expression of greeting in the morning. Formerly, the youth used to kneel in front of the elders or grandparents, who put one hand over their heads to bless them. The phrase used to greet someone with respect was *saqarib'al uwach ulew*, or "clarity on the earth's surface," which is less commonly used among the new generations. During my interviews with *ajq'ijab'* in Chichicastenango in 2014, I was told that the word *saqarib'al* is the generic term for all Maya altars in Chichicastenango, though most of them are better known by their specific names. According to *ajq'ij* José María Tol, all Maya altars are *saqarib'al* because the *ajq'ijab'* ask for clarity, that the truth or the issue may be revealed clearly to help the person who comes to him or her. For the *ajq'ij* Juana Xiloj, Maya altars are *saqarib'al* because that is where the awakening happens and where people assume the responsibility they have in life.

When I asked the *ajq'ijab'* which are the main altars of Chichicastenango, four of thirteen told me that although all of them are important, four to five altars stand out. These were established when Chichicastenango was founded, and they surround the communities at its four cardinal points, with an additional one in the center. In Chichicastenango, the altar located in the east is called Chuoj "among the avocados trees"; the altar in the west is located in the cemetery and is named Chu Kumsanto "among the holy yard" or Chu Kaminaq "among the deceased." In the north, the altar of Don Martin (former name unknown) is found (figure 4.2). The altar of the south is called Chuwi' la Turk'a, and the central altar is the one located at the Calvary in the town's main plaza.

According to *tat* Tomás Calvo, the former indigenous mayor of Chichicastenango, these altars were once connected, but due to the closure of access to one of them at

FIGURE 4.2. View from San Martín altar. Photograph by Iyaxel Cojtí Ren.

some point in time, the connection between them was severed. In December 2012, in commemoration of the completion of Bak'tun 13,[4] permission was requested from the owner of the land to carry out a ceremony at the altar that had been isolated. After the ceremony, the altars were "tied" (*kiximom kib'*) into one unified group (figure 4.3).

When I asked *tat* Tomás whether he knew of any place called *saqarib'al*, he said that each town has its own *saqarib'al* mountain, such as in the town of Lemoa:

Lemoa k'o kajib' juyub' chila' re. (Chu)chi t'uytaq juyub' b'anom. K'o ja juyub' cha'. Kajib' ub'anom. T'uytaq juyub', (chu)chi k'o mes puwi'.

(In) Lemoa there are four hills there. They are like mounds. Mounds shaped like a granary (with four legs), they say. There are four. They are shaped like mounds, where there are altars on top.

Ronojel tinamit k'o usaqarib'al, machit xew Chichicastenango. Quiché, Lemoa, Patzite, Chiché ko kisaqarib'al chila'. K'o releb'al q'ij, kajb'al q'ij, xukut kaj, xukut ulew.

Every town has its saqarib'al, not just Chichicastenango. Quiché, Lemoa, Patzite, Chiché they have their saqarib'al there. They are (the saqarib'al hills) in the east, west, north and south. (*tat* Tomás Calvo, personal communication, 2014)

Lemoa is the abbreviated name for the town called San Sebastián Lemoa, which is located 6 km from the Department of Santa Cruz del Quiché. Carmack describes

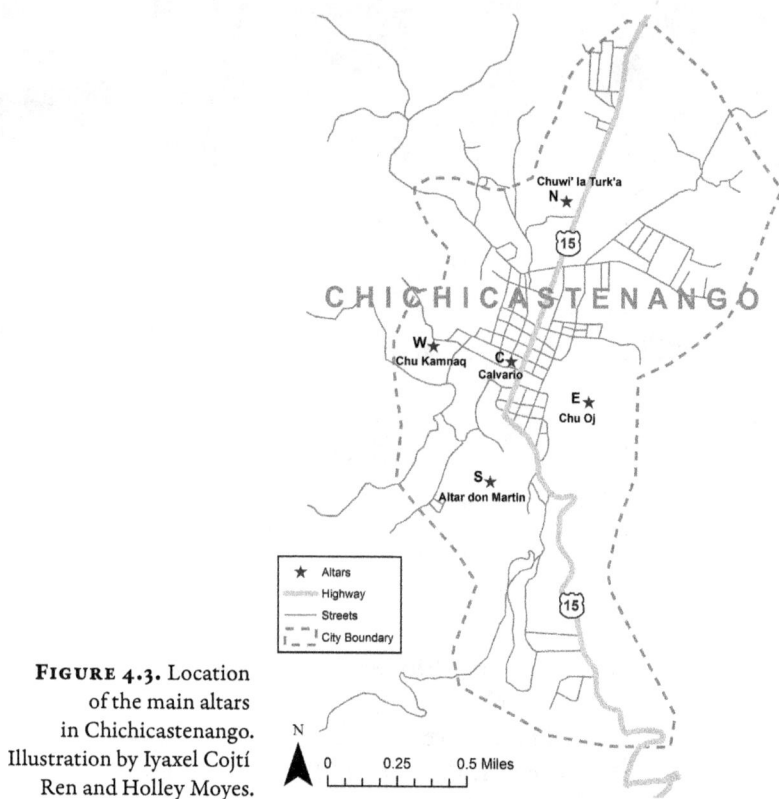

FIGURE 4.3. Location
of the main altars
in Chichicastenango.
Illustration by Iyaxel Cojtí
Ren and Holley Moyes.

how the archaeologist Russell Stewart found pre-K'iche' sites in this town. The largest of these sites is called Pakaja' Lemoa and is made up of eight buildings, thus revealing a very simple pattern of settlement. He also notes that sites with a single mound have ritual altars dedicated to lineages (*chinamit*). The most important of these are four altars that form a cross, since they are oriented toward the cardinal points (Carmack 2001: 124). In figure 4.4, the four altars are identified: in the north, the Kukab'aj Julumuy altar can be seen; in the south, Chisis; in the east, Q'alel; and in the west, Chikroy. This quadripartite model is also replicated on a smaller scale in Chisis, which is named K'oja among the *ajq'ijab'* from Chichicastenango (figure 4.5). K'oja is a granary where corn is stored and usually has four supports. The analogy between the K'oja, or granary, and the altars at Chisis possibly resulted from the idea that both are sources of sustenance and have a quadripartite shape. Furthermore, as *ajq'ij* Juana Xiloj explained, these foundation altars, or energy places, serve to protect the town (figure 4.6).

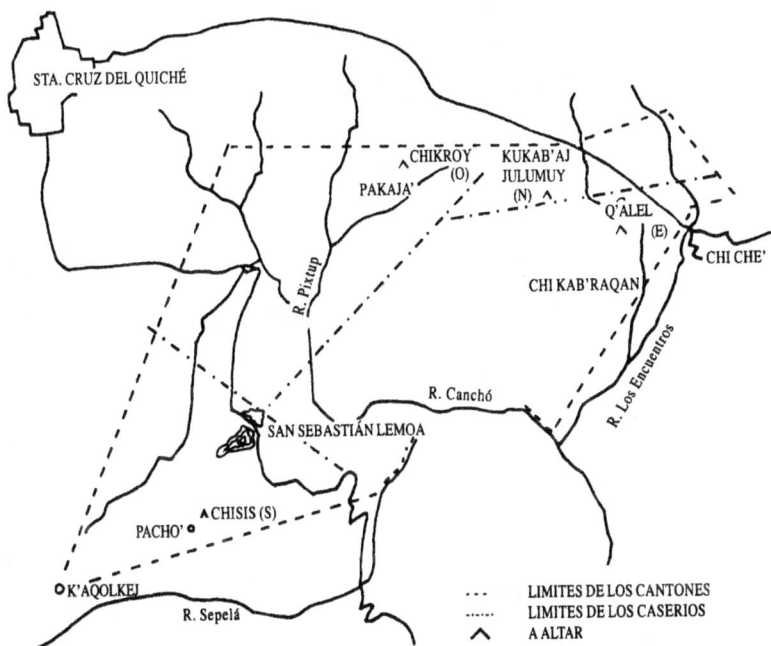

FIGURE 4.4. Location of the main altars in San Sebastián Lemoa (Carmack 2001: 125)

FIGURE 4.5. Chusis's four altars atop small mounds. Photograph by Juan Vidal Luis.

FIGURE 4.6. Traditional K'oja, or granary. Photograph by Juan Vidal Luis.

CONCLUSION

The *saqirik* "dawn" was a tradition described by K'iche'an groups in their origin stories to mark a significant change in the unfolding of their history and cultural development. This change corresponds to the beginning of a more sedentary life, as well as the inception of a new political organization led by the *k'ab'awil*, or protector deities. As a tradition, this primordial dawn was replicated, usually through ceremonies of New Fire, in altars or similar places such as the church in Rabinal. The construction of cult areas or altars to venerate the protector deities, the ancestors, and other energies was necessary to ensure the dawn, since without them people were left unprotected, without a guide, and without a source of sustenance. Today, only the *ajq'ijab'* or *chuch-qajaw* keeps this knowledge, and it seems that the continued observance of this tradition is facing many difficulties. Since Maya people practice diverse religions, it is difficult to keep all main altars of specific towns active because they sometimes belong to particular families or individuals who practice other religions and deny their usage. Despite this situation, K'iche' people still wish their neighbors and family clarity in their thoughts and deeds by simply saying *saqirik* every morning.

NOTES

1 . The concept referred to as *saqirik* in the Popol Wuj and other colonial texts is pronounced *saqirik* in the modern K'iche' variant of Chichicastenango. Accordingly, altars are called *saqarib'al* instead of *saqirib'al*.

2. The researcher Enrique Sam Colop comments that in Colonial dictionaries such as the Calepino en lengua Kaqchikel, the word *kaqjay* means "montecillo redondos de piedra y tierra seca que hacían los antiguos" (small mounds of stone and dry earth the ancients constructed). In Francisco Ximénez's dictionary, the term *caqhai* is translated as "cerros hechos a mano, a manera de cuestas" (manmade mounds that take the shape of hills). This indicates that they were artificially made hillocks (Sam Colop 2008: 152).

3. Lake Atitlán is located in the Department of Sololá in western Guatemala.

4. On December 21, 2012, the completion of thirteen Bak'tun cycles was celebrated throughout the Maya territory. Each Bak'tun is made up of 144,000 days. This cycle is associated with the beginning of a new cycle or era, which is the 14 Bak'tun; however, another trend of interpretation claims the start of a new set of 13 Bak'tun cycles.

REFERENCES CITED

Boone, Elizabeth Hill. 2000. *Stories in Red and Black: Pictorial Histories of the Aztecs and Mixtecs*. 1st ed. University of Texas Press, Austin.

Breton, Alain. 2013. "Mam/Ajaw: tiempo largo, coyunturas y resiliencia en las sociedades mayas actuales." In *Millenary Maya Societies: Past Crises and Resilience*, ed. M. Charlotte Arauld and Alain Breton, 304–12. Mesoweb, www.mesoweb.com/publications/MMS/20_Breton.pdf.

Carmack, Robert M. 2001. *Evolución del reino K'iche'*. Cholsamaj Fundacion, Guatemala City.

Carmack, Robert M., and James Mondloch. 1983 [1554]. *El Título de Totonicapán: Texto, traducción y comentario*. Instituto de Investigaciones Filológicas, Centro de Estudios Mayas. Fuentes para el Estudio de la Cultura Maya 3. Universidad Nacional Autónoma de México, Mexico City.

Christenson, Allen J. 2003. *Popol Vuh: The Sacred Book of the Maya, the Great Classic of Central American Spirituality*, vol. 2. O Books, Winchester.

Jansen, Maarten. 1997. "La Serpiente Emplumada y el Amanecer de la Historia." In *Códices, Caciques y Comunidades*, ed. Maarten Jansen and Luis Reyes García, 11–63. AHILA, Cuadernos de Historia Latinoamericana 5. Ridderprint, Ridderkerk, The Netherlands.

López Austin, Alfredo, and Leonardo López Luján. 1999. *Mito y realidad de Zuyuá : Serpiente Emplumada y las transformaciones mesoamericanas del clásico al posclásico*. Fondo de Cultura Económica, Mexico City.

Maxwell, Judith M., and Robert Hill II. 2006. *Kaqchikel Chronicles: The Definitive Edition.* Bilingual edition. University of Texas Press, Austin.

Sam Colop, Enrique. 2008. *Popol Wuj: Traducción al español y notas.* Fundación Cholsamaj, Guatemala City.

Ximénez, Francisco. 1965. *Historia de La Provincia de San Vicente de Chiapa y Guatemala.* Editorial José de Pineda Ibarra, Guatemala City.

Ximénez, Francisco. 1999. *Historia de La Provincia de San Vicente de Chiapa y Guatemala de La Orden de Predicadores.* Conaculta, Mexico City.

PART 2

The Popol Vuh in Understanding the
Archaeological Record

5

Archaeological Evidence for the Preclassic Origins of the Maya Creation
Story and the Resurrection of the Maize God at Cahal Pech, Belize

JAIME J. AWE

In the *Code of Kings*, Linda Schele and Peter Mathews (1998: 36) commented:

> The Maya and other Mesoamericans often designed their sacred centers to reproduce the structures from the myths that were central to their ideology. For the Maya, two of these myths were of particular importance: the story of Creation, which explained how the world came to have its present form, and the story of the origin of civilized life and the birth of their patron gods.

Schele and Mathews (1998: 36) further noted that "our knowledge of the Maya story of Creation comes from two sources: the Popol Vuh, a seventeenth-century book recording the history of the K'iche' Maya, and inscriptions and imagery from the Classic period." Twenty-five years prior to publication of the Schele and Mathews volume, Michael D. Coe (1973) had also convincingly demonstrated that the myth of the Hero Twins, their trials and tribulations in the underworld, and their subsequent resurrection of their father, the Maize God, were "the subject of a significant number of the scenes depicted on [Classic period] Maya ceramics" (Coe 1978: 12). The more recent discovery of the San Bartolo murals served to extend the antiquity of both the myth of the Hero Twins and the rebirth of the Maize God well beyond the Classic period (Saturno et al. 2005). In this chapter, I present archaeological data from Cahal Pech that provide additional support for the formative manifestation of this ideology and suggest that these myths and concepts were unquestionably "products" of the Preclassic period. I further

DOI: 10.5876/9781646421992.c005

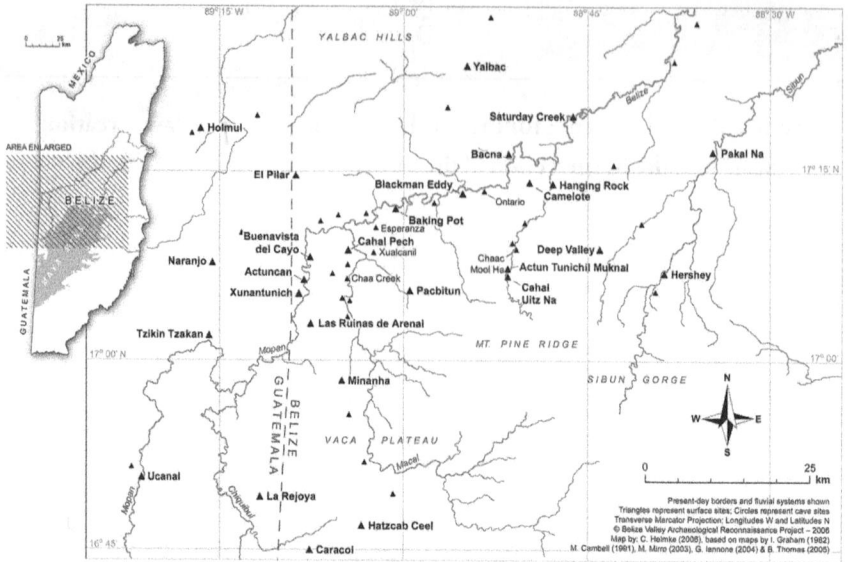

FIGURE 5.1. Map of Belize Valley indicating location of Cahal Pech.

suggest that there are two main reasons why we often fail to recognize the antiquity of these ideological concepts in the archaeological record. The first is simply a result of previous research biases that focused limited archaeological attention on Preclassic contexts. The second, more salient reason stems from our failure to interpret the ideological significance of particular types of archaeological deposits and data.

PRECLASSIC MAYA DEVELOPMENT AT CAHAL PECH

Archaeological investigations during more than thirty consecutive years at Cahal Pech established that this Belize Valley site (figure 5.1) was initially settled at the end of the Early Preclassic (ca. 1200–900 BCE) period (Awe 1992, 2013; Brown et al. 2018; Ebert et al. 2016; Garber and Awe 2008, 2009; Peniche May 2016; Sullivan and Awe 2013; Sullivan et al. 2018). In the ensuing six centuries of the Middle Preclassic period, Cahal Pech developed into one of the primary centers of the upper Belize River Valley, likely a result of its successful exploitation of its rich agricultural environs, as well as its strategic location at the confluence of the two major tributaries of the Belize River (Awe 1992).

During the Cunil phase, dated between 1200 and 900 BCE (Awe 1992; Ebert et al. 2016; Healy and Awe 1995), the precocious Maya at Cahal Pech, like their

Mesoamerican contemporaries, began acquiring exotic goods from across the Maya lowlands, and they produced a variety of fine ceramic vessels (Sullivan and Awe 2013) and artifacts. Many of their ceramic and non-ceramic artifacts were also decorated with regional versions of various motifs that reflect their knowledge and use of a nascent and complex symbol system (Garber and Awe 2009; Brown et al. 2018). The most common iconographic motifs used by the Cunil phase Maya at Cahal Pech included representations of the Avian Serpent, the Quatrefoil (aka. Cave Monster Maw), Crocodilian imagery, Flame Brow, and Kan Cross. As Garber and Awe (2009: 151) previously noted, the use of regional variants of these motifs provides compelling evidence that the Belize Valley Maya were employing their own regional version of a complex symbol system by the Terminal Early Formative period and that this observation was contrary to the "traditional view that the lowland Maya were 'latecomers' as far as their participation in and/or contributions to" what was clearly a pan-Mesoamerican symbol system.

By the start of the Late Preclassic period, Cahal Pech had become one of the primary centers along the upper reaches of the Belize River. The site's elite rulers had begun erecting carved monuments that depicted either deified ancestors or the founder of the Late Preclassic Cahal Pech lineage (Awe et al. 2009), and they were also constructing and modifying monumental buildings that served residential and ritual purposes. One of these special function buildings, Structure B4 (figure 5.2), has a series of architectural modifications that spans the entire Preclassic sequence at Cahal Pech. Deep penetrating excavations in Structure B4 (figure 5.3) also recovered several caches and burials that reflect the Preclassic origin of many ideological concepts that are typically associated with Classic period Maya development. For example, the earliest cache in Structure B4 contained fragments of a crocodile skull along the central axis of a small, Cunil phase platform (Awe 1992). In later construction phases, dating from ca. 900–400 BCE, Structure B4 was transformed from a building that originally served domestic purposes into one of the earliest ancestor shrines at the site. Thereafter, Structure B4 became an important locus for public community rituals and for evoking the community's deified ancestors. This function is suggested by the fact that the building contained more than half of the approximately 1,000 Middle Preclassic figurines found at the site (Awe 1992: tables 3–4). Given its long and continuous history as a special function structure associated with deified ancestors, it also comes as no surprise that the Maya at Cahal Pech would have chosen Structure B4 as the location for the placement of Burial B4-3, a Late Preclassic burial or cache that attests to the ceremonial significance of Structure B4 and forms the primary focus of this chapter.

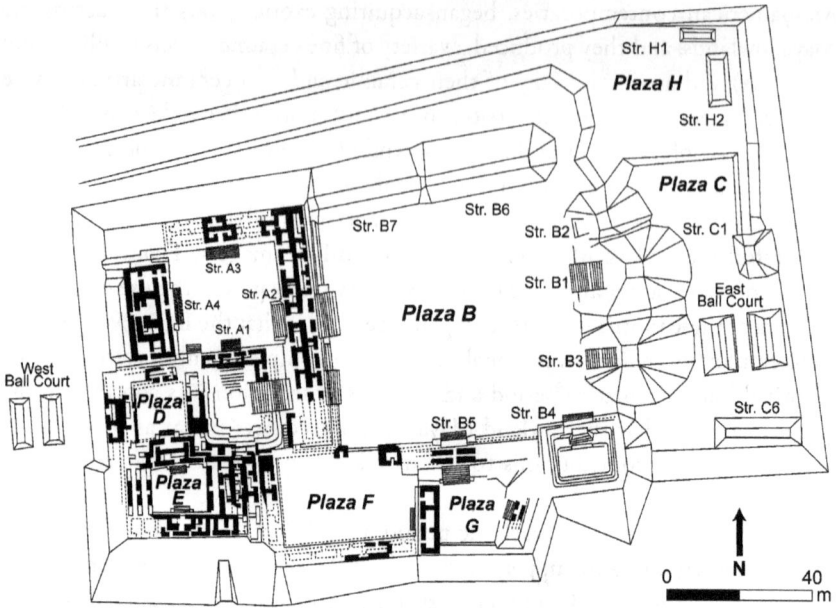

FIGURE 5.2. Map of Cahal Pech indicating the location of Structure B4.

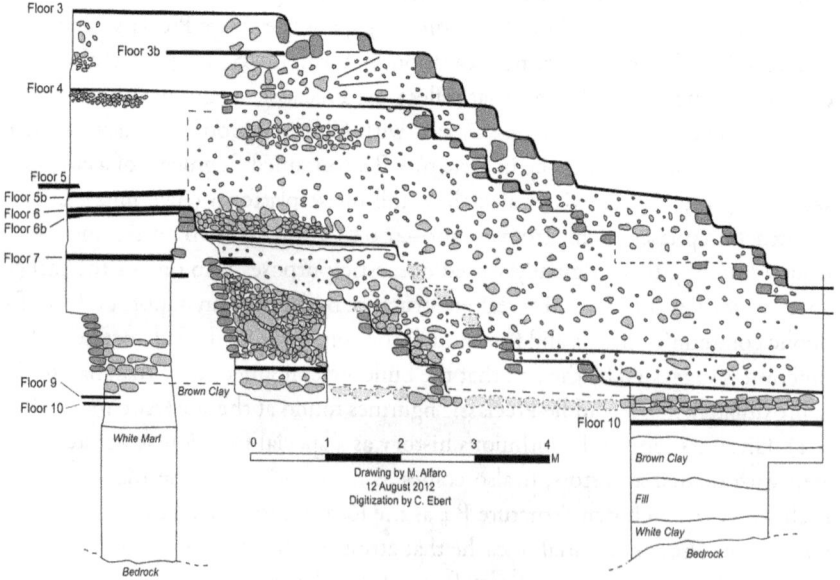

FIGURE 5.3. Section plan of Structure B4, Cahal Pech.

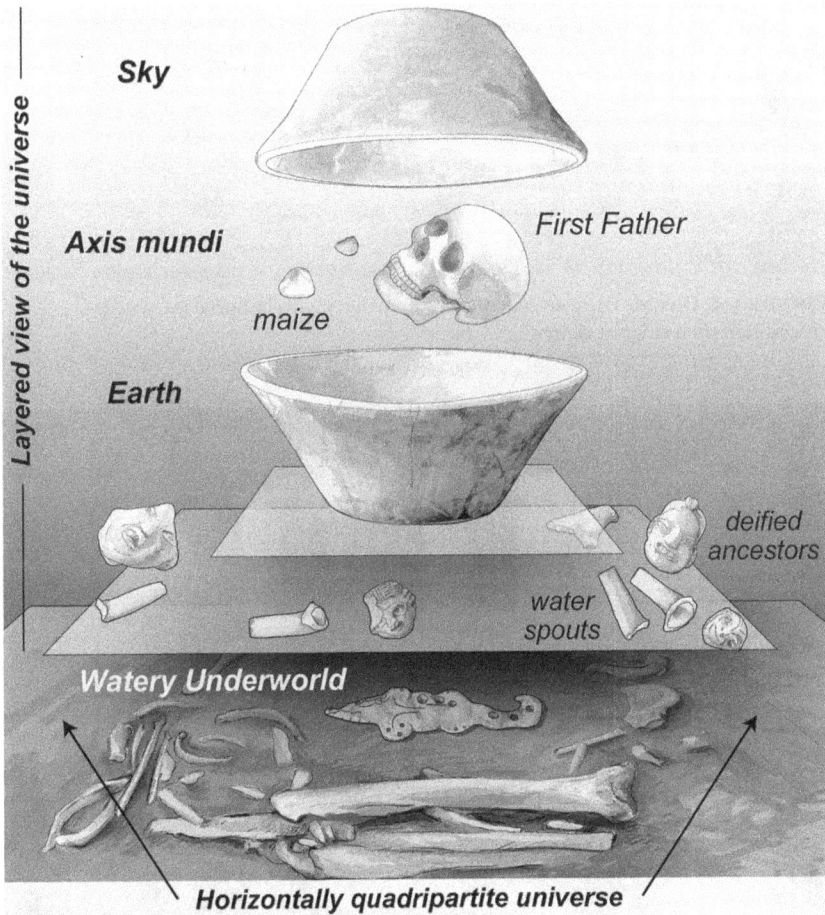

FIGURE 5.4. Artistic reconstruction of Burial B4-3 from Cahal Pech.

CAHAL PECH BURIAL B4-3

We discovered Burial B4-3 approximately 1 meter below the summit of Structure B4/3rd, in a large axial trench that penetrated the north face of the building (figure 5.3). The burial contained several fragments of a human skeleton that were purposely arranged in a quadrangular pattern (figure 5.4). Along the northern and southern border of the quadrangle were a number of long bones and a sacrum (figure 5.5). The pelvis and part of a clavicle formed the eastern border of the quadrangle. To the west were a calcaneus, a clavicle, and several ribs. Along the four sides of the bone quadrangle, on each cardinal direction, were the head of a Middle Preclassic

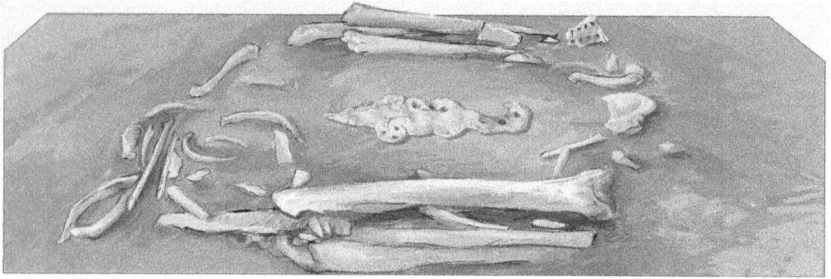

FIGURE 5.5. Quadripartite arrangement of human remains in Burial B4-3 with crocodilian shell effigy at center.

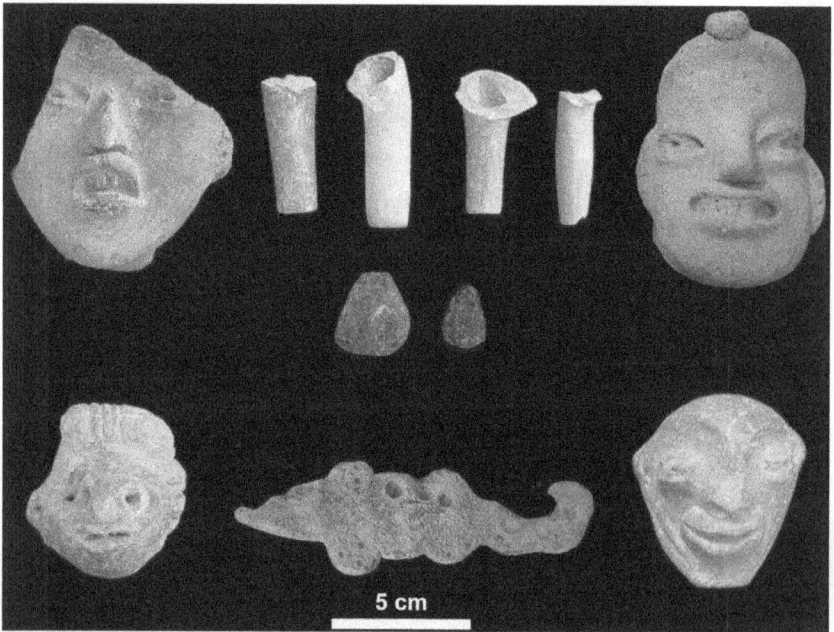

5 cm

FIGURE 5.6. Artifacts associated with Burial B4-3 at Cahal Pech (four ceramic figurines, four chocolate pot spouts, two greenstone triangulates, and crocodilian shell effigy).

ceramic figurine and the spout of a ceramic chocolate pot. At the center of the quadrangle of human bones were two large, lip-to-lip Sierra Red ceramic vessels. Within the vessels were large fragments of a human skull and two jade beads. Beneath the bottom vessel and at the center of the quadripartite bone arrangement was a carved conch shell zoomorphic figure in the form of a crocodile (figures 5.5 and 5.6).

During analysis of the human remains framing the Late Preclassic Sierra Red vessels, we noted that the skeleton was incomplete. Conspicuously absent were most of the smaller and more fragile bony remains. The skull fragments enclosed within the lip-to-lip vessels were also missing all the teeth, the maxilla, and the mandible. The absence of teeth, fragile remains, and small bony elements is a pattern that is consistent with burials that have been exhumed from their original place of interment and then reburied in new contexts. The quadripartite arrangement of the bones, the Middle Preclassic date of the four figurines and four chocolate pot spouts, and the Late Preclassic date of both the Sierra Red vessels and the Structure B4 context where Burial B4-3 was discovered indicate that the skeletal remains in Burial B4-3 were likely exhumed from a Middle Preclassic context long after their original deposition and that they were subsequently reburied in Structure B4. Equally important and as I argue below, the vertical and horizontal patterning of the burial, plus the selection and well-planned arrangement of the associated grave goods imbued with symbolism, are clear manifestations of a well-established ideological system and reflect cognition of the myth of the Hero Twins and the resurrection of the Maize God.

THE IDEOLOGICAL SIGNIFICANCE OF BURIAL B4-3 AT CAHAL PECH

In an effort to demonstrate the symbolic and ideological significance of Burial B4-3, I will examine and discuss each of the individual components that frame and form the burial.

QUADRIPARTITE ARRANGEMENT OF HUMAN REMAINS

As noted above, the human remains recovered in Burial B4-3 clearly indicate that the interment represents a secondary burial. The absence of several skeletal remains, particularly the teeth and small fragile elements, is also consistent with burials where skeletal remains have been exhumed and subsequently reburied in new contexts. According to Patricia A. McAnany (1998: 276), the exhumation and reburial of revered ancestors was not an uncommon practice among the ancient Maya. In some cases, she argues, "The dead may have been held in temporary storage (or displayed) while their final crypt was constructed" (McAnany 1998: 276). Given that quite a number of postcranial bones, the mandible, and teeth are missing from Burial B4-3, it appears that in the Cahal Pech case, a considerable period of time had elapsed between the original interment and subsequent exhumation and reburial of the remains in Structure B4. Andrea Stone and Marc Zender (2011: 55) note that "in Mesoamerica, it was not customary to leave the bones of the departed in eternal peace," for bones—especially those of revered ancestors—"were viewed as the seeds of future life." This type of reverential treatment of the bones of important ancestors is particularly evident on Altar 5 from Tikal, which depicts two elite males venerating the skull and long bones of a noble woman.

In regard to the quadrangular arrangement of the human remains in Burial B4-3, I suggest that they were purposely deposited in this pattern to reflect the quadripartite Maya view of the universe, while the layered sequence of grave goods and human remains—beginning with the crocodilian shell effigy at the bottom, followed by the lip-to-lip ceramic vessels above it—undoubtedly represents the vertical divisions of the universe. This patterned arrangement of the human remains and grave goods in Burial B4-3 parallels, at least conceptually, other early representations of Mesoamerican cosmograms, such as those depicted on several Preclassic Olmec artifacts of known and unknown provenance (Riley 1995). For example, the incised decoration on a greenstone tablet from Guerrero depicts a (vertical) maize plant/world tree at the center of a (horizontal) plaza bordered by four platforms (figure 5.7). It is also well-known that Mesoamericans regarded earth "as a four-sided field, with the four directions corresponding to each of the sides. For the Maya, this model is metaphorically compared to the quadrangular maize field" (Miller and Taube 1993: 83–84).

FIGURE 5.7. Incised decorations depicting cosmograms on greenstone tablet from Guerrero, Mexico, and on the Humboldt Axe.

THE CROCODILIAN SHELL EFFIGY

The crocodilian shell effigy was positioned at the center of the bone quadrangle and directly beneath the two lip-to-lip Sierra Red ceramic vessels. In Mesoamerican ideology, the crocodile (or caiman) represents one of the most revered earth creatures.

"Because of its aquatic habitat, great size, and spiny back, the caiman was a common metaphor for the mountainous earth floating upon the sea" (Miller and Taube 1993: 48; also Taube 1992, 1998), a concept I believe is emphasized by the marine shell used in the production of the crocodilian effigy at Cahal Pech. In Late Preclassic Izapan art, crocodiles are also "depicted as the trunks of trees, presumably to represent the *axis mundi*" (Miller and Taube 1993: 48). Stone and Zender (2011: 183) further note that because of its aquatic habitat and characteristics, the crocodile "made an ideal analog of the primordial earth" floating in the sea. In addition, "The crocodile was a potent symbol of cosmic order because it stood for both earth's surface when in a horizontal position and, in a vertical position, the axis of the universe, much like a World Tree" (Stone and Zender 2011: 183).

Stephen Houston and Karl A. Taube (2011: 29) suggest that "in Mesoamerican thought, the sea is commonly identified with a primordial crocodilian being that symbolizes the earth." Known as Itzam Cab Ain (Itzam Earth Caiman) by the Yukatek Maya, crocodilians were creatures "of chaos and destruction that must be slain for the ordered world to be created." Houston and Taube (2011: 29) propose: "It is likely that through the mythic act of slaying the cosmic crocodile, the world tree and sky were created out of the Primordial Sea. According to the Colonial Yukatek Chilam Balam books of Mani and Tizimin, the directional world trees were fashioned to raise the heavens after [the] slaying of Itzam Cab Ain." Houston and Taube (2011: 30) also add that "the Maize God is connected, in some fashion, to primordial crocodiles in bodies of water" and note that there are polychrome ceramic vessels that depict the emergence and death of the Rain God and refer to crocodiles immediately after naming the Maize God. Given these ideological connections, I suggest that the Cahal Pech Maya purposely chose to place the crocodilian shell effigy beneath the lip-to-lip vessels and at the center of the quadrangle of human bones because of the crocodile's symbolic representation of earth, because of its association with the *axis mundi*, and, as Houston and Taube (2011: 30) note, because of the connection between primordial crocodiles and the Maize God.

THE CERAMIC FIGURINES IN BURIAL B4-3

A ceramic figurine was positioned on each of the four sides of the bone quadrangle, along each cardinal direction. I propose that the four figurines in the Cahal Pech cache were purposely arranged in this manner to represent the original four human ancestors who were formed at the time of creation (Christenson 2007: 184; Tedlock 1985: 164–65). In reference to these four humans, the Popol Vuh mentions that "they were simply made and modeled, it is said; they had no mother and no father" (Tedlock 1985: 165). In Allen Christenson's (2007: 187) more recent translation of the Popol Vuh and in reference to these original four human ancestors, he adds that "their knowledge of everything that they saw was complete—the four corners and the four sides, that which is within the sky and that which is within the earth." Interestingly, this association with deified ancestors concurs with the function of figurines proposed by David C. Grove and Susan B. Gillespie (1984: 32) and Joyce Marcus (1993), who suggest that Preclassic ceramic figurines either represented ruler portraits or were used in divination rituals and in early cults of the ancestor.

Another alternative is that the figurines could represent Pauahtuns. These "Maya mythological earth-bearers of the four cardinal points" (Fash 1991: 163) are common in Classic period Maya iconography. At Copan, for example, they are depicted on carved benches in Structure 9N-82 C 1st of the Sepulturas Group, as well as in Structure 66C (Fash 1991: 161; Webster et al. 2000: 54–55). Yet another example can be found at the entrance to Temple 22 at Copan (Fash 1991: 163). Taube (1998: 429–32) and others (cf. Coe and Kerr 1997: 187) have also argued that Pauahtuns are quadripartite and that they represent "four aged beings supporting the corners of the universe" or "cosmic house." If we accept this premise, it can be argued that the skull in the lip-to-lip vessels in Burial B4-3 was symbolically associated with the *axis mundi* from which the four cardinal directions radiate and that the figurines, like aged ancestral Pauahtuns, were used to demarcate the four cardinal boundaries of the quadripartite earth (represented by the human remains that encased the crocodilian effigy and lip-to-lip ceramic vessels).

THE CERAMIC SPOUTS IN BURIAL B4-3

Like the four figurines, the four chocolate pot spouts were located on each cardinal direction alongside the human bone quadrangle. In the case of the four chocolate pot spouts, I would argue that they are symbolically associated with the pouring of precious fluids—in this case water, not cacao. In their analysis of spouted pots, for example, Terry G. Powis and his colleagues (2002: 96) noted that "spouted vessels or *pichingas*, as they are called by modern Maya groups living in highland Guatemala, are used as water bottles . . . In the town of Merida, Yucatan spouted jars also occur, but the modern Maya use them as water containers or coolers." The four spouts in Burial 4-3 at Cahal Pech may therefore represent the concept of *pars pro toto*, where one part of the pot (the spout, in this case) represents the whole spouted ceramic vessel.

The spouts in Burial B4-3 are thus representing whole vessels that, symbolically, would have been used to pour water on the skull inside the lip-to-lip bowls. This would further suggest that the fragmented skull within the lip-to-lip-vessels was associated with or accorded qualities of the Maize God. As noted above, the appropriation of the Maize God persona appears to have been standard practice among

FIGURE 5.8. Late Classic polychrome dish depicting the resurrection of the Maize God.

Classic period Maya rulers and is commonly depicted on art executed on poly-chrome ceramics in the lowlands. The scene painted on the so-called Resurrection Plate provides one of the most vivid depictions of the Hero Twins pouring water through a cleft on the earth and onto the skull of their father (figure 5.8). It is through this act that they revive first father's skull and by which he subsequently rises out of the underworld as the Maize God. The fragmented skull in the lip-to-lip vessels and the four spouts around the sides of the vessels may therefore be synony-mous with this same act.

THE JADE TRIANGULATES

The two jade triangulates (cf. Powis et al. 2010, 2016) that accompanied the skull fragments enclosed within the lip-to-lip vessels are almost certainly symbolic repre-sentations of kernels of corn and are associated with fertility and preciousness. The association of jade with corn is a long-established concept in Maya archaeology. Indeed, Adrian Digby (1964: 25–26, plate xivb), almost sixty years ago, identified a "plaque pendant of unidentified provenience as a depiction of the maize god and based the assertion on a comparison with a stone sculpture of the maize deity from Structure 22 at Copan" (Ishihara-Brito and Taube 2012: 246). Reiko Ishihara-Brito and Karl Taube further note that Late Classic depictions of the "dead" Maize God on triangular-shaped jade plaque-pendants are a common Late Classic Maya tradition. They (Ishihara-Brito and Taube 2012: 246) suggest that "given the central importance of maize to Maya subsistence and cosmology, the portrayal of the maize deity in precious green jade was apt, fusing concepts of growth and wealth." They (2012: 244–47) also contend that

> a Middle Preclassic ceramic object from highland Guatemala that shows a human head with bifurcated scrolls falling from the neck portrays an early form of the Maya maize god. Here, his head also incorporates the turtle carapace, which symbolizes the earth (figure 144). Like the two Dumbarton Oaks pendants, this ceramic pendant also appears to depict the severed head of the maize deity and, at the same time, his rebirth.

During the Early Historic period in the Yucatan, it was common practice to place a jade bead in the mouth of the deceased. Mary Ellen Miller and Simon Martin (2004: 57) note that this practice served to symbolically plant "the germ of the Maize God" in the deceased "in preparation for rebirth." The Preclassic date of Burial B4-3 at Cahal Pech suggests that this tradition was of considerably greater antiquity than indicated by the more recent Historic practice in the Yucatan.

It is also possible that the two jade triangulates may have been placed in the vessels along with the skull as part of what Brian Stross (1998) calls animation rituals. This tradition, Stross (1998: 31) argues, would ensure that the skull could be "animated or imbued with life." R. Jon McGee (1998: 45) describes a similar ritual for animating god pots among the Lacandon. According to McGee (1998: 45), the Lacandon originally placed rubber anthropomorphic figurines in god pots so the gods could be animated. More recently, they have substituted the figurines with stones from Yaxchilan or Bonampak. In both cases, the objects served to "awaken" the god pots.

CACHES CONTAINING LIP-TO-LIP CERAMIC VESSELS

The two large ceramic vessels were placed at the center of the bone quadrangle, directly over the crocodilian effigy. Cached lip-to-lip ceramic vessels have been found in Preclassic to Late Classic contexts at almost all lowland Maya sites that have ever been excavated. Late Preclassic examples, often containing human skulls, are a particularly common deposit in eastern shrines, or "E-Groups," at Uaxactun, Tikal, and Cerros and at sites in the Belize Valley (Awe et al. 2017; Freidel and Schele 1989; Freidel et al. 1993: 241; Laporte and Fialko 1990).

In one Uaxactun cache, excavated by Oliver G. Ricketson and Edith B. Ricketson (1937: 49–58), the lip-to-lip vessels encased a skull and a greenstone artifact. The latter example reflects a pattern akin to that of Burial 4-3 at Cahal Pech; but, as with almost all of the central Peten cases, archaeologists interpreted the skull in this Uaxactun cache as the severed head of a sacrificial victim (Freidel et al. 1993: 241). Rather than representing the decapitated heads of victims, I propose that human skulls in lip-to-lip caches more likely represent the remains of exhumed ancestors (see Awe 2013: 38–40). This perspective concurs with McAnany's (1998) research at Kaxob, where she argued that these types of interments generally incorporate the remains of exhumed ancestors. I further contend that the interment of exhumed ancestor skulls in these types of burials/caches is linked with concepts of the resurrection of the severed head of the Maize God, the primary ancestral deity whose persona, as noted previously, was commonly appropriated by Classic period Maya rulers.

Maya art is rife with depictions of the decapitated head of the Maize God within ceramic vessels and other containers. For example, Justin Kerr's rollout photograph 1183 portrays the Hero Twins meeting with Itzamna, who shows them their father's skull held in a ceramic jar (figure 5.9a). In yet another of Kerr's rollouts, Kerr 8468, the scene on the polychrome vase depicts Itzamnaaj looking down at the head of the Maize God contained in a vessel (figure 5.9b). On a stucco facade from Tonina, a rabbit or gopher (Stone and Zender 2011: 192–93) is shown carrying the head of Jun Junajpu in a jar (figure 5.10), and on other ceramic vessels, the decapitated head of the Maize God is actually painted or carved at the center of the vessels (figure 5.11a, b). Miller and Martin (2004: plates 28, 29) also illustrate a jade head effigy of the Maize God in a limestone box, likely from Tonina, and an image of a dancing Maize God that is painted at the center of a polychrome dish of unknown provenience.

In *Maya Cosmos*, David Freidel and his coauthors (1993: 240–41) suggested that lip-to-lip vessels represent earth ovens known as *pib* and that *pib na's*, or underground houses, were places where kings could "magically transform into sustenance fit for the gods." Rather than sweat baths, I suggest that the placement of ancestor skulls within lip-to-lip ceramic vessels is more likely a symbolic representation of the Maize God's skull lying in the underworld. The placing of skulls within lip-to-lip vessels and their deposition in ancestral shrines (funerary temples) may thus be synonymous with the severed head of the Maize God lying in a cave within the sacred mountain. In the Popol Vuh, the Hero Twins retrieve the severed head of their father after they defeat the Lords of Death; following his resurrection, they

FIGURE 5.9. Late Classic polychrome vases depicting the decapitated head of the Maize God.

FIGURE 5.10. Tonina stucco facade depicting a rabbit (or gopher) carrying decapitated head of Jun Junajpu in a jar.

FIGURE 5.11. Late Classic ceramic dishes depicting severed head of the Maize God.

ascend to the Three-Stone-Hearth-Place of creation where the Maize God then creates the first four human ancestors. By placing the skulls of ancestors within lip-to-lip vessels, the ancient Maya were therefore metaphorically suggesting that, like the Maize God, the revered ancestor would resurrect and ascend to the heavens.

COMPARISON OF LIP-TO-LIP CACHES

The published literature contains descriptions of caches and burials from sites across the Maya lowlands that share many parallels with Burial B4-3. At Cahal Pech, for example, Platform B, a Preclassic platform located more than a meter below the surface of Plaza B, contained early caches on all four corners of the structure (figure 5.12). The offering on the southeast corner of the platform included a cache and a burial. The cache had two lip-to-lip Sampopero Red ceramic vessels that encased a fragmented human skull and six greenstone beads. To the north of this cache was a small cist containing the poorly preserved remains of a headless skeleton. The cache in the northeast corner of Platform B contained three slate bars beneath a Middle Preclassic headless ceramic figurine, which, in turn, was overlain by a cluster of thirteen polished greenstones (figure 5.13). Garber and Awe (2008: 187) previously suggested that this cache was symbolic of a layered cosmogram and that the deposit represented "the created universe which took place at the Three Stone Place of creation." They further suggested that the thirteen greenstones in the cache likely represented the headless body of the Maize God. The cache at the northwestern corner of Platform B included another layered cosmogram but appears to be the "reciprocal opposite" of the northeastern deposit. This northwestern cache contained three

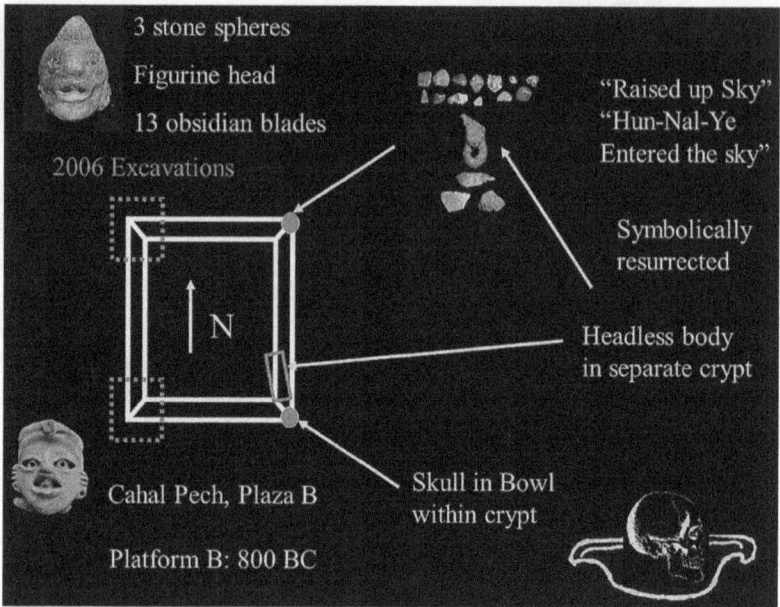

FIGURE 5.12. Plan of Platform B at Cahal Pech with Middle Preclassic caches on the four corners of the building.

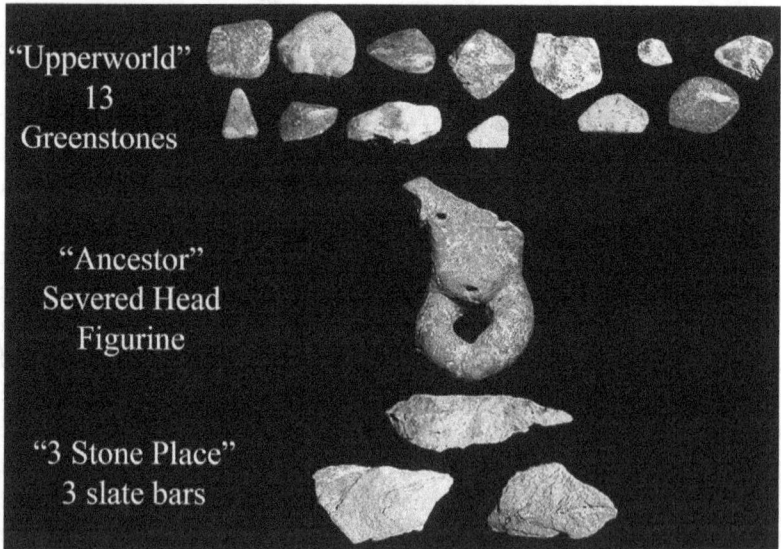

FIGURE 5.13. Middle Preclassic cache from the northeast corner of Platform B at Cahal Pech.

river-rolled pebbles that were placed above a ceramic figurine head that, in turn, overlaid thirteen obsidian chips. The fourth cache, located at the southwestern corner of Platform B, contained a single Middle Preclassic ceramic figurine head. The contextual distribution of the four caches and their layered contents led Garber and Awe (2008: 189) to suggest that the Preclassic caches represented "the remains of a ritual circuit associated with the death of an important individual. The purpose of this ritual was to symbolically resurrect that individual and place him in the sky—the place of revered ancestors."

At Copan's Group 10J-45, archaeologists uncovered a lidded stone vessel containing an Early Classic cache that provides another excellent example of directional symbolism and shares many parallels with Burial B4-3 from Cahal Pech (see Fields and Reents-Budet 2005: 114; Finamore and Houston 2010: 266). The lidded container in the Copan cache "held a quincunx-patterned offering of spondylus shells and carved jades oriented to the cardinal directions [figure 5.14]. The centerpiece is a jadeite figure of an Early Classic king wearing a maize plant on his royal headband, signifying his role in centering the cosmos" (Fields and Reents-Budet 2005: 114). The centerpiece figurine had been placed within a large spondylus shell. Bordering the latter were four smaller jade figures and four other shells, each containing a single jade bead. According to Daniel Finamore and Stephen D. Houston (2010: 266), "The cache is a cosmic diagram portraying the Maize God as the pivotal *axis mundi* in the center of the cardinal and intercardinal points," and "the stone lid probably symbolized the overarching sky." I would add that the lidded container is akin to lip-to-lip ceramic vessels and that its interior symbolically represents the cave in the sacred mountain. The spondylus shells reflect the watery underworld, while the carved jades at the four cardinal directions frame the quadripartite earth. The centerpiece jadeite figure of the king may also be equivalent to the skull of a revered ancestor and is likely associated with the Maize God.

Another quincunx-patterned offering, almost coeval in date with the Cahal Pech burial, is the well-known Structure 6B cache from Cerros in northern Belize (figure 5.15). As at Copan, the Cerros cache contained five "headband jewels," or greenstone figurines, that had been placed in a quincunx pattern "within a vessel layered with spondylus shells and mosaic mirrors" (Fields and Reents-Budet 2005: 114; Schele and Freidel 1990: 120–21, figure 3.9). Here again, it is likely that the greenstone figurine at the center of the cache represents the Maize God as the *axis mundi*, while the other four figures are either framing the quadripartite earth at cardinal directions or represent the first four ancestors created by the Maize God following his resurrection.

In Structure A6 at Caracol, Diane Z. Chase and Arlen F. Chase (1998: 314–15, figure 11) discovered a Late Preclassic cache that also shares many parallels with

FIGURE 5.14. Early Classic quincunx-patterned dedicatory cache from Group 10J-45 at Copan, Honduras.

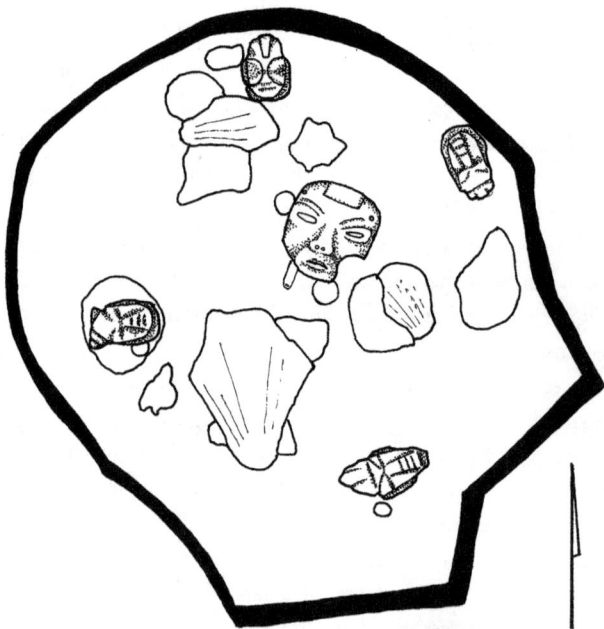

FIGURE 5.15. Late Preclassic Quincunx-patterned cache from Structure 6B at Cerros, Belize.

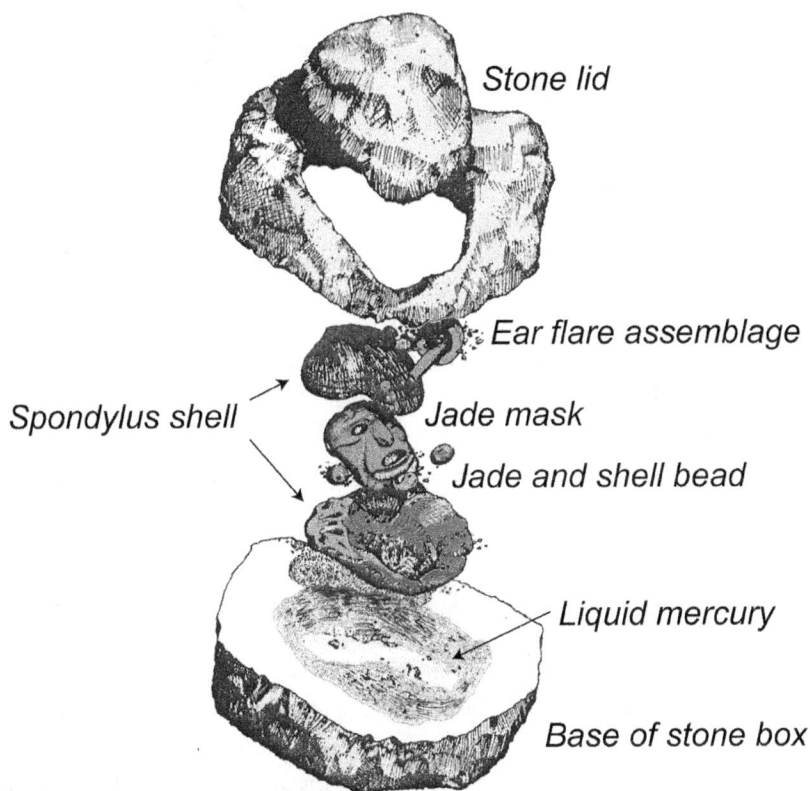

FIGURE 5.16. Exploded view of Late Preclassic cache from Structure A6, Caracol, Belize. *Courtesy*, Arlen Chase.

Cahal Pech Burial B4-3. The cache (figure 5.16) consisted of a geode, or stone box, with a lid that contained a small jadeite mask and two greenstone beads within two lip-to-lip spondylus shells. The latter sat in a pool of liquid mercury. Above the shells were several malachite pebbles plus a jadeite earflare assemblage. The Chases (1998: 314) noted that this and other early Caracol caches generally have "contents that are layered and/or ordered in such a way as to suggest an intentional plan or design reflecting both directional order and placement." They (1998: 303) further suggested that the Caracol cache "evince[s] an ordered layout that appears to reflect the Maya view of the cosmos. Lower layers of mercury, jadeite, malachite, coral, or shells distinctly reflect the watery underworld," while the "groupings of four versions of the same kinds of artifacts around a central unit . . . may indicate the sacred landscape of the present world."

CONCLUSION

In this chapter, I noted that Burial B4-3 at Cahal Pech contained the incomplete skeleton of a male individual whose remains were exhumed from its original place of interment and subsequently reburied in Structure B4, one of the most important Preclassic temples at the site. I contend that the careful horizontal and quadripartite arrangement of the human remains, the four figurine heads, the four chocolate pot spouts along with the vertically arranged crocodilian shell effigy and lip-to-lip vessels containing skull fragments and greenstone triangulates clearly reflect that the Preclassic Maya at Cahal Pech were cognizant of concepts such as the vertical and horizontal partitioning of their cosmos.

The purposeful patterned arrangement of the burial also suggests that the person interred in Burial B4-3 likely represents one of the Preclassic rulers at the site and that those who exhumed and arranged his remains in the pattern described above were likely associating him with the Maize God. As previously noted, the four chocolate pot spouts around the lip-to-lip vessels convey the idea that the pots would or could have been used to pour water on the skull inside the vessels and that, like the Maize God, this revered ancestor would also resurrect and become a deified persona in the heavens.

The spatial arrangement of the human and cultural remains in Burial B4-3 clearly reflects knowledge of a complex ideology and symbol system that included concepts of the Maya creation story, the myth of the Hero Twins, and the resurrection of the Maize God. Schele and Miller (1986: 32) previously argued that "the Popol Vuh stories are not illustrated word for word in the art of the Classic period, but many elements of the story line have compelling parallels in Classic imagery created seven hundred years before" the Popol Vuh was written. I suggest that the caches discovered on Platform B and those from Burial B4-3 at Cahal Pech confirm and extend the presence of this ideology well into the Preclassic period.

Cahal Pech Burial B4-3 is also an excellent example of what McAnany (1998: 271) refers to as the "incorporation of ancestors into monumental architecture to establish a political and ritual *axis mundi*." The burial undoubtedly represents another early lowland Maya example of the tangible and symbolic expression of an ideology that, over time, became more embellished and institutionalized. The Cahal Pech offering further suggests that caches and burials, which symbolically associate elite males in the community with the Maize God, became prevalent at that point in time when Maya leaders began to appropriate religious ideology to legitimize their power, authority, and right to rule. Data from the Maya lowlands—particularly at sites such as Cahal Pech, Cival (Estrada-Belli 2011: 82–83), and San Bartolo (Saturno et al. 2005), to name a few—suggest that this practice began to be manifested in the Middle Preclassic period, coeval with similar expressions of ideological concepts elsewhere in Mesoamerica. In time, "The imaging and placement of ancestors in the built environment of the lowland Maya changed significantly" (McAnany 1998: 281–92), and by Classic period times, "royal ancestor veneration became an overtly political institution couched within a grand cosmological scheme."

REFERENCES CITED

Awe, Jaime J. 1992. "Dawn in the Land between the Rivers: Formative Occupation at Cahal Pech, Belize and Its Implication for Preclassic Developments in the Maya Lowlands." PhD dissertation, Institute of Archaeology, University of London, England.

Awe, Jaime J. 2013. "Journey on the Cahal Pech Time Machine: An Archaeological Reconstruction of the Dynastic Sequence at a Belize Valley Polity." *Research Reports in Belizean Archaelogy* 10: 33–50.

Awe, Jaime J., Nikolai Grube, and David Cheetham. 2009. "Cahal Pech Stela 9: A Preclassic Monument from the Belize Valley." *Research Reports in Belizean Archaeology* 6: 179–90.

Awe, Jaime J., Julie A. Hoggarth, and James J. Aimers. 2017. "Of Apples and Oranges: The Case of E-Groups and Eastern Triadic Architectural Assemblages in the Belize River Valley." In *Early Maya E-Groups, Solar Calendars, and the Role of Astronomy in the Rise of Lowland Maya Urbanism*, ed. David A. Freidel, Arlen F. Chase, Anne Dowd, and Jerry F. Murdock, 412–49. University Press of Florida, Gainesville.

Brown, M. Kathryn, Jaime J. Awe, and James F. Garber. 2018. "The Role of Ritual in the Rise of Social Complexity in the Belize River Valley." In *Pathways to Complexity: A View from the Maya Lowlands*, ed. M. Kathryn Brown and George Bey III, 87–116. University of Florida Press, Gainesville.

Chase, Diane Z., and Arlen F. Chase. 1998. "The Architectural Context of Caches, Burials, and Other Ritual Activities for the Classic Period Maya (as Reflected at Caracol, Belize)." In *Function and Meaning in Classic Maya Architecture*, ed. Stephen D. Houston, 299–332. Dumbarton Oaks Research Library and Collection, Washington, DC.

Christenson, Allen. 2007. *Popol Vuh: Sacred Book of the Quiché Maya People*. Electronic version of original 2003 publication. Mesoweb, http://www.mesoweb.com/publications/Christenson/PopolVuh.pdf.

Coe, Michael D. 1973. *The Maya Scribe and His World*. Grolier Club, New York.

Coe, Michael D. 1978. *Lords of the Underworld: Masterpieces of Classic Maya Ceramics*. Art Museum, Princeton University Press, Princeton, NJ.

Coe, Michael D., and Justin Kerr. 1997. *The Art of the Maya Scribe*. Harry N. Abrams, New York.

Digby, Adrian. 1964. *Maya Jades*. Trustees of the British Museum, London.

Ebert, Claire E., Brendan J. Culleton, Jaime J. Awe, and Douglas J. Kennett. 2016. "AMS ¹⁴C Dating of Preclassic to Classic Period Household Construction in the Ancient Maya Community of Cahal Pech, Belize." *Radiocarbon* 2016: 1–19.

Estrada-Belli, Francisco. 2011. *The First Maya Civilization: Ritual and Power before the Classic Period*. Routledge, London.

Fash, William L. 1991. *Scribes, Warriors, and Kings: The City of Copan and the Ancient Maya*. Thames and Hudson, London.

Fields, Virginia, and Dorie Reents-Budet. 2005. *Lords of Creation: The Origins of Sacred Maya Kingship*. Los Angeles County Museum of Art, Los Angeles.

Finamore, Daniel, and Stephen D. Houston, eds. 2010. *The Fiery Pool: The Maya and the Mythic Sea*. Peabody Essex Museum and Yale University Press, London and New Haven.

Freidel, David, and Linda Schele. 1989. "Dead Kings and Living Temples: Dedication and Termination Rituals among the Ancient Maya." In *Word and Image in Maya Culture: Explorations in Language, Writing, and Representation*, ed. William F. Hanks and Don S. Rice, 233–43. University of Utah Press, Salt Lake City.

Freidel, David, Linda Schele, and Joy Parker. 1993. *Maya Cosmos: Three Thousand Years on the Shaman's Path*. William Morrow, New York.

Garber, James G., and Jaime J. Awe. 2008. "Middle Formative Architecture and Ritual at Cahal Pech." *Research Reports in Belizean Archaeology* 5: 185–90.

Garber, James G., and Jaime J. Awe. 2009. "A Terminal Early Formative Symbol System in the Maya Lowlands: The Iconography of the Cunil Phase (1100–900 BC) at Cahal Pech." *Research Reports in Belizean Archaeology* 6: 151–60.

Grove, David C., and Susan B. Gillespie. 1984. "Chalcatzingo's Portrait Figurines and the Cult of the Ruler." *Archaeology* 37 (4): 27–33.

Healy, Paul F., and Jaime J. Awe. 1995. "Radiocarbon Dates from Cahal Pech, Belize: Results from the 1994 Field Season." In *Belize Valley Preclassic Maya Project: Report on the 1994 Field Season*, ed. Paul F. Healy and Jaime J. Awe, 198–215. Department of Anthropology, Trent University, Peterborough, Ontario, Canada.

Houston, Stephen, and Karl A. Taube. 2011. "The Fiery Pool: Water and Sea among the Classic Maya." In *Ecology, Power, and Maya Landscapes*, ed. Christian Isendahl and Bodil Liljefors Persson, 17–38. Acta Mesoamericana 23. Verlag Anton Saurwein, Markt Schwaben.

Ishihara-Brito, Reiko, and Karl A. Taube. 2012. "Plaque Pendants." In *Ancient Maya Art at Dumbarton Oaks*, ed. Joanne Pilsbury, Miriam Doutriaux, Reiko Ishihara-Brito, and Alexander Tokovinine, 244–47. Precolombian Art at Dumbarton Oaks 4. Dumbarton Oaks Research Library and Collection, Washington, DC.

Laporte, Juan Pedro, and Vilma Fialko. 1990. "New Perspectives on Old Problems: Dynastic References for the Early Classic at Tikal." In *Vision and Revision in Maya*

Studies, ed. Flora S. Clancy and Peter D. Harrison, 33–66. University of New Mexico Press, Albuquerque.

Marcus, Joyce. 1993. "Men's and Women's Ritual in Formative Oaxaca." Paper presented at the Dumbarton Oaks Conference on Ritual Behavior, Social Identity, and Cosmology in Preclassic Mesoamerica, Washington, DC, October 9–10, 1993.

McAnany, Patricia A. 1998. "Ancestors and the Classic Maya Built Environment." In *Function and Meaning in Classic Maya Architecture*, ed. Stephen D. Houston, 271–98. Dumbarton Oaks Research Library and Collection, Washington, DC.

McGee, R. Jon. 1998. "The Lacandon Incense Burner Renewal Ceremony: Termination and Dedication Ritual among the Contemporary Maya." In *The Sowing and the Dawning: Termination, Dedication, and Transformation in the Archaeological and Ethnographic Record of Mesoamerica*, ed. Shirley B. Mock, 41–46. University of New Mexico Press, Albuquerque.

Miller, Mary Ellen, and Simon Martin. 2004. *Courtly Art of the Ancient Maya*. Thames and Hudson, London.

Miller, Mary Ellen, and Karl A. Taube. 1993. *The Gods and Symbols of Ancient Mexico and the Maya: An Illustrated Dictionary of Mesoamerican Religion*. Thames and Hudson, London.

Peniche May, Nancy. 2016. "Building Power: Political Dynamics in Cahal Pech, Belize during the Middle Preclassic." PhD dissertation, University of California, San Diego, CA.

Powis, Terry G., Paul Healy, Jaime J. Awe, and Gyles Iannone. 2010. "The Function of Middle Preclassic Maya Green Stone Triangulates: A Unique Mesoamerican Groundstone Artifact Type." Paper presented at the 75th meeting of the Society for American Archaeology, April 14–18, St. Louis, MO.

Powis, Terry G., Sherman Horn, Gyles Iannone, Paul F. Healy, James F. Garber, Jaime J. Awe, Linda Howie, and Sheldon Skaggs. 2016. "Middle Preclassic Period Maya Greenstone 'Triangulates': Forms, Contexts, and Geology of a Unique Mesoamerican Groundstone Artifact Type." *Journal of Archaeological Science: Reports* 10: 59–73.

Powis, Terry G., Fred Valdez Jr., Thomas R. Hester, W. Jeffrey Hurst, and Stanley M. Tarka Jr. 2002. "Spouted Vessels and Cacao Use among the Preclassic Maya." *Latin American Antiquity* 13 (1): 85–106.

Ricketson, Oliver G., and Edith B. Ricketson. 1937. *Uaxactun, Guatemala, Group E, 1926–1931, Part I: The Excavations; Part II: The Artifacts*. Publication 477. Carnegie Institution of Washington, Washington, DC.

Riley, Kent, III. 1995. "Art, Ritual, and Rulership in the Olmec World." In *The Olmec World: Ritual and Rulership*, ed. Michael D. Coe, 27–45. Art Museum, Princeton University, Princeton, NJ.

Saturno, William A., Karl A. Taube, and David Stuart. 2005. *The Murals of San Bartolo, Peten, Guatemala, Part 1: The North Wall*. Ancient America 7. Center for Ancient American Studies, Barnardsville, NC.

Schele, Linda, and David Freidel. 1990. *A Forest of Kings: The Untold Story of the Ancient Maya*. William Morrow, New York.

Schele, Linda, and Peter Mathews. 1998. *The Code of Kings: The Language of Seven Sacred Maya Temples and Tombs*. Scribner, New York.

Schele, Linda, and Mary Ellen Miller. 1986. *The Blood of Kings: Dynasty and Ritual in Maya Art*. Kimbell Art Museum, Fort Worth, TX.

Stone, Andrea, and Marc Zender. 2011. *Reading Maya Art: A Hieroglyphic Guide to Ancient Maya Painting and Sculpture*. Thames and Hudson, London.

Stross, Brian. 1998. "Seven Ingredients in Mesoamerican Ensoulment: Dedication and Termination in Tenejapa." In *The Sowing and the Dawning: Termination, Dedication, and Transformation in the Archaeological and Ethnographic Record of Mesoamerica*, ed. Shirley B. Mock, 31–40. University of New Mexico Press, Albuquerque.

Sullivan, Lauren A., and Jaime J. Awe. 2013. "Establishing the Cunil Ceramic Complex at Cahal Pech, Belize." In *Ancient Maya Pottery: Classification, Analysis, and Interpretation*, ed. James John Aimers, 107–20, University of Florida Press, Gainesville.

Sullivan, Lauren, Jaime J. Awe, and M. Kathryn Brown. 2018. "The Cunil Complex: Early Villages in the Maya Lowlands." In *Pathways to Complexity: A View from the Maya Lowlands*, ed. M. Kathryn Brown and George Bey, 35–48. University of Florida Press, Orlando.

Taube, Karl A. 1992. *The Major Gods of Ancient Yucatan*. Studies in Pre-Columbian Art and Archaeology 32. Dumbarton Oaks, Washington, DC.

Taube, Karl A. 1998. "The Jade Hearth: Centrality, Rulership, and the Classic Maya Temple." In *Function and Meaning in Classic Maya Architecture*, ed. Stephen D. Houston, 427–78. Dumbarton Oaks, Washington, DC.

Tedlock, Dennis. 1985. *Popol Vuh: The Mayan Book of the Dawn of Life*. Simon and Schuster, New York.

Webster, David, Anne Corinne Freter, and Nancy Gonlin. 2000. *Copan: The Rise and Fall of an Ancient Maya Kingdom*. Harcourt Brace, Orlando.

6

The Dynamics of Dynasty, Power, and Creation Myths Embedded in Architecture

A Case Study from Blue Creek, Belize

THOMAS H. GUDERJAN AND COLIN SNIDER

Archaeologists have recognized that Maya public and residential architectures are physical manifestations of broad patterns of Mesoamerican religious ideas and principles and that these are discoverable. The ancient Maya city of Blue Creek provides insight into the dynamics of the ancient Maya past, including the dynastic institution of *ajaw*, in the absence of traditional iconographic and artistic sources of information. In this chapter, we review the data from Blue Creek to demonstrate that patterns of the rise and fall of ruling lineages can be seen through architectural events and changes. Further, we can show that such ruling lineages utilized their relationship to religion as a validating principle for their power and that they did so by embedding concepts passed to us through the Popol Vuh.

Maya monumental architecture can be seen as a symbolic, physical representation of Maya religion, specifically their understanding of creation. The Maya view of the cosmos reflects elements of the creation story told in the Popol Vuh. The creators, Xpiyacoc and Xmucane, had already made and destroyed the world three times before the present and fourth creation. The creation was made possible "with the utterance of a word and the appearance of the thing embodied by the word" (Freidel et al. 1993: 59). During the third creation, the Lords of the Underworld killed the uncle and father of the Hero Twins because they had angered the Xibalbans by playing the ballgame too loudly. So the Xibalbans killed them and buried them under the ballcourt and hung the father's decapitated head on a tree. The skull then magically impregnated the daughter of one of the lords. She sought refuge in the

DOI: 10.5876/9781646421992.c006

world of people and gave birth to the Hero Twins, Junajpu and Xb'alanke. They eventually went to Xibalba and defeated the murderer of their father and resurrected their father and uncle.

When the creators began again with the fourth creation, they knew that maize and water would make up humanity but did not know where to find maize. They heard of a place full of food named the "Witz Mountain" or "First-True Mountain" or "Split Mountain," which rose from the Primordial Sea. The maize there was molded into the first four humans, and the water became their blood.

Almost everything in Maya life is linked to this creation story and symbolic recreations of the Maya cosmos. David Freidel, Linda Schele, and Joy Parker (1993) have demonstrated that Classic Maya public architecture is, in fact, a reenactment of the landscape of creation. Maya temples are the symbolic Witz Mountains rising from the plazas, which themselves are symbolically the Primordial Sea. Further, Kent Reilly (1994) has shown that this arrangement dates to the origins of complex society in Mesoamerica. The Olmecs at La Venta originated this symbolic re-creation by making the Witz Mountain a volcano and "painting the Primordial Sea green" with large serpentine mosaics. Mathews and Garber (2004) correctly point out that these motifs, particularly the quadripartite directional symbolism, exist at a multiplicity of scales and are seen on single small artifacts as well as at the macro-level in site planning.

BLUE CREEK

The senior author directed annual excavations at Blue Creek, a medium-sized Maya center in northwestern Belize, from 1992 through 2013 with the exception of a four-year hiatus (Guderjan 2007, 2009, among others). Much of the effort was focused on the *kawik*, or central precinct, yielding detailed architectural data (Driver 2008; Guderjan 2004, 2005, 2007). Blue Creek was occupied from approximately 600 BCE until approximately 1000 CE (Guderjan 2004, 2007). Spatially, the "greater" Blue Creek area covers approximately 100–150 square kilometers (Guderjan 2007; Lichtenstein 2000). More than 500 ancient buildings have been documented and approximately 100 excavated in the 20 percent of this area that has been intensively surveyed. Excavations have been undertaken throughout this area and across all contextual zones.

The central precinct of Blue Creek included two large, open plazas, surrounded by graceful yet massive temples and two stelae (one carved, one uncarved; unfortunately, the carved stela was stolen from the site approximately forty years ago) that proclaimed the accomplishments of their kings. The Maya origin myth was ritually reenacted in ballcourts. Aside from such public functions, the central precinct also included the private residences of the ruling elite.

THE POPOL VUH

As the archaeological, historical, and linguistic records all demonstrate, broad networks of interregional contacts between indigenous peoples existed throughout Mesoamerica, and the Maya were far from exempt from these networks. Even in the Postclassic (900–1500 CE), when the K'iche' of the southern highlands were a dominant group, cultural artifacts and linguistic threads reveal the ties among Maya, Toltecs, and even the Nahuas of the 1400s. The evidence of such contacts is visible not only in goods found at archaeological sites of the Classic and Postclassic or in linguistic similarities but even in the very face of indigenous ruins. In this regard, the ceremonial ballgame, a key element of K'iche' culture (as evident in the Popol Vuh), is a particularly strong example of these interregional contacts. While the exact cultural or religious importance or even the rules of the game varied from one culture to another, ballcourts appear throughout Mesoamerica, ranging as far north as Arizona, south to Nicaragua, and into the Caribbean. This proliferation is important in understanding the depth and range of indigenous exchange networks through which not only goods but also languages and cultures influenced one another and spread throughout Mesoamerica across thousands of years.

This interregional contact likely had a central role in the production of the Popol Vuh. The text of the K'iche' creation story describes itself as "The Light That Came from Beside the Sea" or as having its origins "from across the sea," depending on the translation (Tedlock 1996; Christenson 2007). While the prepositional difference between translations is not insignificant, Dennis Tedlock argues that "beside" may be the more accurate translation of the Mayan word *ch'aqa*, which, in turn, suggests that the Popol Vuh had its origins in coastal Yucatan, possibly on a pilgrimage from the Guatemalan highlands to the lowlands (Tedlock 1996). However, either "across" or "beside" points to a Yucatec origin here. The spelling used by the author, *ch'aqa*, is straightforward "across" and cannot mean "beside." However, whether "across" or "beside" is a more correct translation is in some ways irrelevant; either word indicates that the Popol Vuh's origins rest in K'iche' contact with peoples in other regions in Mesoamerica.

Yet the Popol Vuh itself was very much a K'iche' story. The Late Classic period witnessed not just a territorial shift in centers of power into the northern Yucatan and the Guatemalan highlands; it also witnessed a transformation in mediums of writing and recording history. In the Late Classic, glyphic representations of Mayan culture and history moved away from carvings on monuments toward painting on walls and in books. In these new books, phonetic glyphs gained a growing importance in Mayan writing, even as they maintained a dialectic relationship with images that would have been included in such books (Tedlock 1996). Such a relationship is lost in modern translations that depend on Father Francisco Ximénez's transcription of the Popol Vuh from the early 1700s. However, it is still visible in the way the Popol Vuh is translated; for example, the portion of the story telling of Seven Macaw comments "this is Seven Macaw and a great nance tree. This, then, is the food of Seven Macaw" (Christenson 2007: 97). This narrative structure appears throughout multiple translations of the Popol Vuh and suggests the ways images and text would have interacted not only in the Late Classic period but even after the arrival of the Spanish in the sixteenth century. Indeed, the Popol Vuh provides just a small amount of insight into a more common practice, in which texts were not so much read as they were performed for communities (Clendinnen 1987).

As for the Popol Vuh itself, it is a mytho-history that simultaneously serves as the creation story of the K'iche' people, the explanation of the origins of the universe, a descriptor of the creation and role of different plants and animals, a guide to some ceremonial and ritual origins, and a history of K'iche' dynasties up to the 1500s. While the K'iche' kingdom only came to power in the 1200s, the K'iche' Maya were in the highlands of Guatemala for several hundred years before; only when outside conquerors arrived and founded new lineages did the K'iche' kingdom begin to exert regional power (Carmack 1981). Thus while the Popol Vuh is often associated with the K'iche' kingdom itself during the Postclassic, like many Maya tales and histories since lost, the Popol Vuh likely dates back hundreds of years. Indeed, colonial Spanish authorities themselves suggested that Mayan stories dated back hundreds of years and across the histories of the Mayan peoples (Zorita 1994), something the lineages in surviving accounts like the Popol Vuh reinforce. Thus while the K'iche' kingdom was a relatively "late" arrival, the earlier K'iche' presence in the Guatemalan highlands went back much further, making the Popol Vuh one of the few surviving mytho-historical documents of Mayan culture that has roots in the Classic and even the Early Classic era.

Throughout the text, the book provides insights into and justifications of practices such as the need for human sacrifice, the centrality of maize to Mayan life and the universe, and the relation between peoples and the gods. At the same time, the text provides invaluable insights into K'iche' understandings and perceptions of the world around them, including the quadrilateral vision of the world, with four as a recurring number throughout the text—be it in the 400 boys who try to defeat Sipakna and end up being put in the sky (explaining the Pleiades), the four attempts to create humans, or the four first humans themselves. Thus, as a whole, the Popol Vuh itself uses the origins of humans and of the universe to reveal "the triumph of the ancestral humans over the forces of death, decay, and disease through cunning and trickery" (Freidel et al. 1993: 43). At the same time, these loosely woven-together threads reflect a broader understanding of time in Mayan culture, in which "history was simultaneously prophecy, prophecy becoming history again with the next swing of the cycle" (Clendinnen 1987: 146).

While the narrative arc of the Popol Vuh has its origins in pre-contact K'iche' culture, the version that exists today likely does not. To date, in a tragic irony given the importance of the number four to K'iche' cosmology, only four pre-contact Mayan texts appear to have survived contact. The Popol Vuh is likely based on a pre-contact text that is no longer extant. As Allen J. Christenson has noted, based on scholarly understanding of those texts and of subsequent Mayan narrative practices, there is no evidence of the narrative devices and flourishes found in the Popol Vuh. Rather, he suggests that the version that exists today "is more likely to have been a compilation of oral traditions" that drew on Precolumbian texts long since lost to conquest or time (Christenson 2007: 35).

This scarcity is due to the effects of conquest itself. In an effort to conquer the indigenous peoples of the Americas, the Spanish relied on conquest methods that dated back to the *Reconquista* of the Iberian Peninsula from the 700s up to 1492. These methods, when adapted to the Americas, included the destruction of indigenous religious practices and sites of worship, as well as the texts that contained knowledge of indigenous religious practices, culture, and histories. While these efforts to completely destroy all vestiges of indigenous cultures could never be total, many indigenous texts and artifacts from throughout the Americas were lost to the Spanish Invasion. Mayan texts and books suffered a particularly acute attack, as in the 1560s when the zealous Franciscan friar Diego de Landa set out to completely eradicate all traces of Mayan culture and identity through repressive and brutal means. This included the destruction of dozens of Mayan texts and thousands of images. It is possible that other texts may have originally survived Landa's and others' eager destruction, secreted away in homes or hiding places where they could be safe, but those that were not consumed by flame have since been lost to the vagaries of time, leaving only the four extant texts for scholars to work with.

It was in this context of persecution, conquest, and the prospect of cultural annihilation that the version of the Popol Vuh we have today was first recorded. The text itself points to its post-contact production, as it refers to the Mayan leaders who were tortured after Spanish arrival (Tedlock 1993). Current estimates place its reproduction as somewhere between 1554 and 1558, based not only on the reference to torture but also to the names of the leaders of the communities mentioned in the last portion of the book; the periods the documentary records place them as alive and in positions of leadership. Given the timing of the Popol Vuh's production, it was likely written by semi-anonymous nobility who would have been part of the pre- and post-contact Mayan social matrix built on "the relationship between piety, social status, and economic activity" (Restall 1997: 154). In the face of this onslaught, this nobility may have been making an effort to save both its culture and its status within K'iche' society.

Transcribing the performance of the Popol Vuh was not only an attempt toward cultural preservation, however; it also was likely a political statement of cultural autonomy. The K'iche', like other indigenous peoples throughout Mesoamerica, were accustomed to adopting new gods in the face of military or political defeat. Conversion was a natural part of these cultural and political relations. However, the Spanish mission was a fundamentally different one; whereas indigenous cultures would incorporate the new gods into the pantheon alongside the old deities, the Spanish wanted a divine monopoly on the cosmological universe in a religious setting where the Christian god was the only god rather than one among others. The efforts to force this religious monopolization, particularly visible in (though certainly not limited to) Landa's campaign, caused no small amount of unrest and anger among indigenous communities.

As Matthew Restall (1997: 149) put it, "It is the coming of Christianity, not Christianity itself (the timing and nature of its arrival, not its spiritual implications) that is associated with these catastrophes" in the Mayan world. In this context, the Popol Vuh can also be read as an assertion of the legitimacy of Mayan gods and religious practices in the face of the Christian onslaught. However, the timing and context of its production also means that while it provides insights into pre-contact beliefs, its narrative form is not likely a "pure" representation of pre-contact K'iche' society.

Yet this is not the only modification the Popol Vuh has undergone. Indeed, the text scholars work with today is not that of the mid-1550s but of the early 1700s. In another wave of proselytization in the Guatemalan highlands, Ximénez dedicated himself to contesting and suppressing K'iche' beliefs (in turn demonstrating their durability through the first century-plus of conquest). As a result, he set out to translate K'iche' texts, including the Popol Vuh, in an effort to fully know and thus be able to thoroughly refute K'iche' religious beliefs. Ximénez's translation did place his translated Spanish alongside the original K'iche' language, providing insight into the language itself, but his translation was bereft of any of the images that might have accompanied the text and that would have been a part of the performative dialectic between phonetic glyph and image. In addition, the very nature of Ximénez's project made his a project not of religious preservation, as in the 1550s version of the text, but of religious destruction (Quiroa 2011). Whatever version (or versions) Ximénez may have worked with has long been lost to scholars, leaving us only with the early 1700s transcription.

Obviously, this is not to suggest that the Popol Vuh is historically dubious, even in spite of the different contexts, moments, and agendas of its production. In addition, when placed alongside those carved ruins throughout Mesoamerica, we are able to better understand both the figures on the glyphs and the figures and themes of materials like the Popol Vuh.

THE RISE OF A DYNASTIC LINEAGE AT BLUE CREEK

If the Popol Vuh can be seen as a local representation of pan-Mesoamerican religious beliefs, then Maya public architecture can be viewed as the materialization of those beliefs and their employment in validating the power and authority of a polity's *ajaw*. The first event in our archaeological docu-drama is the installation of the first *ajaw*, marked by the placement of Cache 21 in front and at the base of Structure 4-I, the earliest building constructed on Plaza A (figure 6.1). This cache is also the source of controversy. Cache 21 consists of a large number of artifacts (494 or 544, depending on which count is correct) that were apparently wrapped in a textile (or, more correctly, processed fabric) and buried under a rock with three or four chert bifaces buried on top of the rock in front of Structure 4-I. Cache 21 was placed under the plaster floor, just in front of the building along the medial axis, and is dated and calibrated to 80–220 CE (Beta–82949); it consisted of 7 chert bifaces; 5 pieces of coral; 10 shells, mostly riverine bivalves; 17 jade artifacts; and 458 pieces of obsidian. The obsidian included 425 blades, 27 cores, and 6 fragments, all from El Chayal (Haines 2000). These materials were found bundled together as though they had been wrapped in a cloth, a fragment of which was recovered but identification is not certain.

As at many sites, Cerros, for example, such caches mark the instatement of the royal lineage and first king, or *ajaw*, and this seems to also be the case at Blue Creek. Cache 21 can be seen as the material remains of a massive bloodletting ceremony related to the dedication of this building and perhaps the installation of Blue Creek's first king in a ceremony during which hundreds of people used the obsidian blades for bloodletting. Then the bloodletting tools were buried in Cache 21, at the symbolic location of creation. Such a ritual would validate a ruler's blood lineage and establish his authority and rule.

The controversy regarding Cache 21 relates to the departure from the project of the excavator (who did work under the senior author's direction) without a full report having been completed. For example, table 6.1 lists the contents of the cache according to the original excavator (Weiss 1996) and W. David Driver, who later became the field director of the central precinct excavations. There is also a difference of opinion about the cache's stratigraphic location. Driver (2008) believes the cache was placed under Structure 4-IIA to dedicate that building, and I believe it was located in front of the earlier Structure 4-I and then buried by Structure 4-II.

As the original excavator stated, the cached artifacts were in a generally spherical bundle on top of a small, well-preserved fragment of woven, processed fiber with one fiber dyed blue (Blair Mills, personal communication, 2014), leading us to believe the artifacts were tied into a cloth in a bundle and placed in a hole in

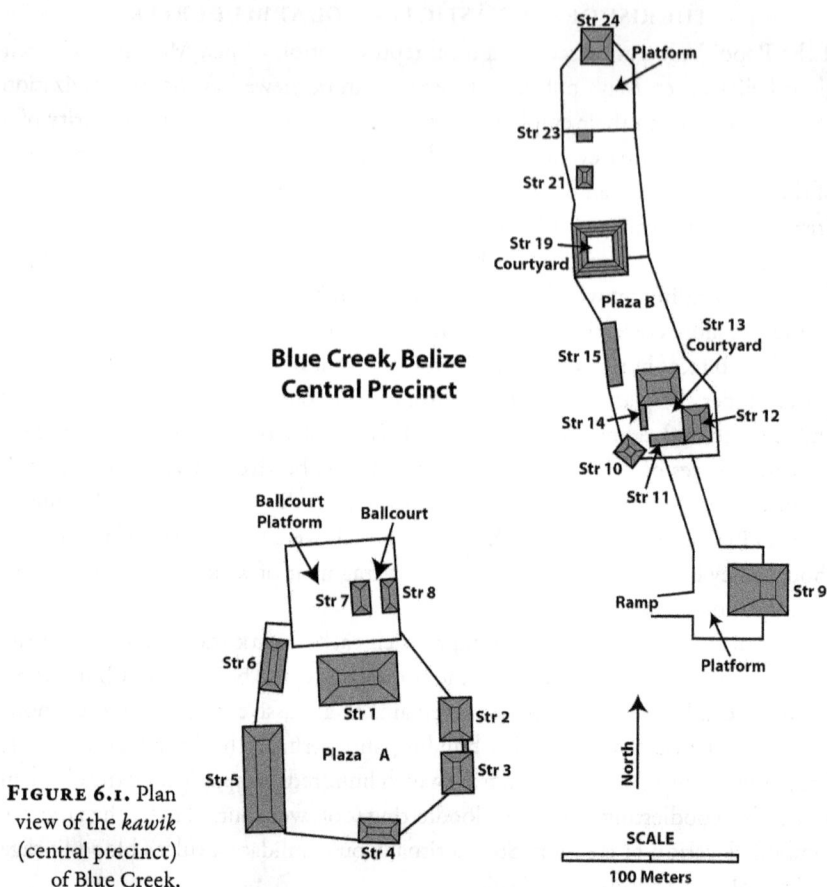

FIGURE 6.1. Plan view of the *kawik* (central precinct) of Blue Creek.

front of Structure 4-I, then covered with both a circular stone and other material. This would be a very unusual departure from the pattern seen in traditional dedicatory caches of the period (Bozarth and Guderjan 2004), so we disagree with Driver regarding the function as well as the placement setting of Cache 21.

Consequently, we interpret the event as the material residue of a large-scale bloodletting event marking the installation of the first king and the initiation of a royal dynasty that ruled Blue Creek for several hundred years. The purpose of Maya bloodletting rituals was in part to give birth to the gods and materialize them into the world (Furst 1976; Schele and Freidel 1990; Stuart 1984, 1988), and important events in dynastic life were marked by bloodletting (Schele and Miller 1986)—especially ascension to the *mat*, or throne, of an *ajaw* (Freidel et al. 1993).

TABLE 6.1. Contents of Cache 21

Artifact Form	Weiss 1996	Driver 2008
Chert bifaces	7	8
Chert flakes	na	2
Coral red	2	na
Coral "small branch" fragments	2	na
Coral	na	6
Jade ear flares	2	3
Jade beads	5	13
Jade fragments	10	13
Obsidian blades	425	441
Obsidian cores	27	28
Obsidian fragments	4	na
Shell Florida worm	2	na
Shell unidentified bivalve 1	2	na
Shell unidentified bivalve 2	2	na
Shell unidentified bivalve 3	2	na
Shell unidentified bivalve 4	2	na
Marine shell	na	27
Freshwater bivalve	1	na
Bone fragment	na	8
Bone bead	1	na
Total	494	544

EARLY CLASSIC CONTINUITY: CONSTRUCTION OF THE *KA'WIK*

Throughout the Early Classic period, public architecture at Blue Creek showed both change and fundamental continuity. While there were remodelings and alterations, there were no radical changes in function and orientation of buildings. We interpret this as leadership remaining in the royal lineage of the founder whose installation was marked by Cache 21. Soon after the placement of Cache 21, the *ajaw* of Blue Creek began to commission significant architectural projects, including Structure 4-IIA and subsequent work at Structure 4 but especially Structure 4-III. Several of these are relevant to our understanding of aggrandizing the lineage of the *ajaw* and connecting the *ajaw* to religious concepts in the Early Classic period.

In the Early Classic, Structure 4-III was the largest expansion of the building. After the initial construction, a large area was removed from the front and summit of

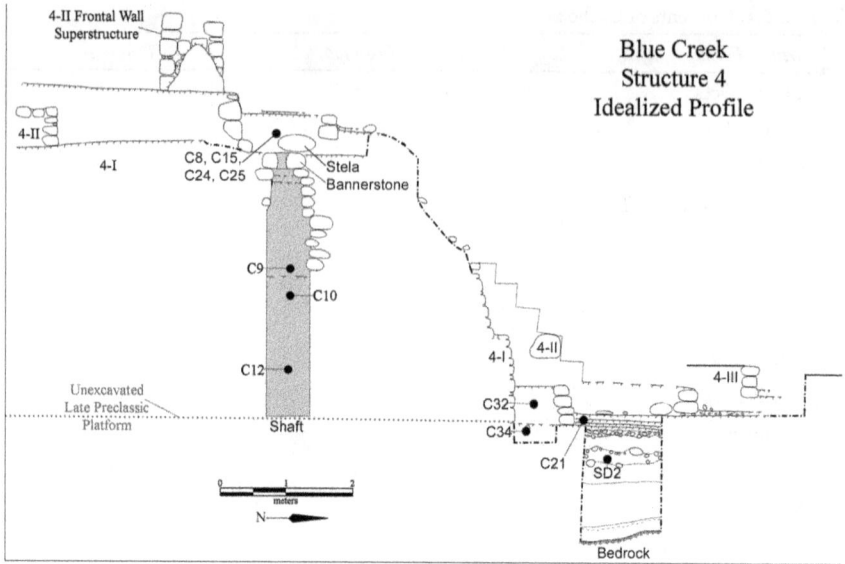

FIGURE 6.2. Conceptual rendering of the Structure 4 world tree shaft and caches.

Structure 4-II (figure 6.2). Then the shaft was built, and the fill was replaced around it (Guderjan 2004, 2007; *contra* Guderjan 1998 and *contra* Driver 2008). Radiocarbon dates from this material suggest that Structure 4-I was impacted as well and that material from that building was recycled into the newly modified Structure 4-II. The shaft was then capped with a bannerstone, a large circular limestone disk with a 50-cm-diameter hole in the center that was the opening of the shaft. It is clear that the shaft was open and empty for perhaps a century prior to the shaft-filling event.

At the base of the shaft was a four-point eccentric chert oriented to the cardinal directions. Near the upper part of the shaft, four Early Classic ceramic vessels were cached, one in each of the cardinal directions. Two were lidded and contained pre-natal or neonatal human sacrifices. The vessels were placed at the cardinal directions approximately 1 meter from the shaft. This shaft clearly marked Structure 4 as a symbolic *axis mundi*, or center of the world, and may have supported a banner on a pole in front of the superstructure (Guderjan 1998, 2005, 2007).

In earlier discussions, the senior author has speculated that the shaft and its associated components functioned on one scale as an *axis mundi*—marking the place where the first king ascended to the throne, connecting the *ajaw* and his lineage forever to the center of the universe, and validating his lineage's rule through its connection with the supernatural. A more emic function may have been to support a pole with a banner (Reese-Taylor 2002).

However, in recent discussions with Kent Reilly, we came to realize that we may not have yet fully and correctly interpreted the importance of the shaft. Like the "airtubes" leading to the staircase into Pakal's tomb at Palenque, the shaft may have actually been psycho-tubes that allowed the spirit of the deceased ruler to come and go from the spiritual world to the material world. Our excavation was terminated after we could no longer determine that additional materials were associated with the shaft. However, it was unclear whether we had actually emptied the entire section of the building that had been excavated and re-filled to construct the shaft. We may have failed to do so, and it is possible that a tomb underlies the shaft—possibly that of the first *ajaw* who commissioned the construction of Structure 4-III.

While Structure 4 became the defining building for the south side of Plaza A, Structure 5 was constructed as the defining building on the west side of the plaza. Structure 5 is 52 m long and relatively narrow, 16–18 m at the base, and it rises about 6 m above the plaza floor. It was excavated in 1993–94 by Dale Pastrana (1995).

We expected to find a series of complex construction events contributing to the building's final form and were surprised to find only two. Structure 5-I was built in the Early Classic period and is by and large the final form of the building. The second construction phase, Structure 5-II, consists of the razing of the previous superstructure and the construction of a single vaulted room using Structure 5-I as the substructure. The interior of the room was about 45 m long and about 2.5 m wide. It had a central doorway flanked by three more on each side, and there were doorways at the end of the building, for a total of nine entrances.

Pastrana (1995) argues that this is a viewing gallery from which nobles could observe activities in the plaza. While determining the function of buildings in public areas is difficult, her point is certainly important. First, the building provides a full view of all activities in the plaza, and an individual can move from point to point to see activities from differing perspectives. Second, this building would provide extraordinary views of sunrises (and sunsets from the back side) and any ritual activity associated with the solstices and equinoxes.

Aside from such material functions, the nine doors of the viewing gallery are a clear reference to the nine lords of the underworld, the lords of death and disease. These deities are, in modern K'iche', still used to "describe an underground hell inhabited by demons who cause sickness" (Christenson 2007: 114).

Another striking aspect of Early Classic architecture at Blue Creek is that the *ajaw* was commissioning architectural innovations such as Structure 1, the largest building on Plaza A, which defines the plaza's northern boundary. Structure 1 rises 12.7 m above the plaza, measures 46 m across the base, and is 26 m wide. There are six known construction phases: Structure 1-I through Structure 1-VI (Driver 2008). The earliest of these buildings, Structures 1-I and 1-II, were built during the Late

Preclassic period as low platforms, and Structure 1-III was an Early Classic construction. In many senses, though, the most important phase was Structure 1-IV, an Early Classic–period tiered pyramid with a central staircase and a columned superstructure. We are uncertain how tall it was in its final form, as the columns were truncated for later construction. However, the superstructure's floor is about 10 m above the plaza level, and remnants of the columns extend at least 2 m higher and are approximately 1.5 m in diameter. As they are made of a stone and marl conglomerate, they would not have been able to support a stone roof. There are two rows of columns, with eight in both the front and back rows. This remarkable building is the earliest known columned building in the southern lowlands (Driver 2002). Only Aké in northern Yucatan (Roys and Shook 1966) may be as old.

Also relevant to this discussion is Structure 9, the Temple of the Masks, built atop a large ramped dance platform and rising more than 11 m above the platform. At the escarpment's edge, it presents an impressive view to visitors coming from the east, and it defines the southern end of the Plaza B complex. Structure 9 had been severely looted, with a massive trench dug into the east side and other large trenches on the north and south sides. Consequently, we have lost some important information—notably, through the destruction of two tombs. However, several profitable years of excavation were supervised by Helen R. Haines (Grube et al. 1995; Guderjan 2004, 2007). Relatively little is known about the first three construction phases, and Structure 9-IV holds the most interest for this discussion.

Structures 9-III and 9-IV were both fairly standard Peten-style temples, with a central staircase leading up to a single-room superstructural temple. Near the top of each staircase was an outset that could be used for overviewing the assembled public who were on the platform in front of the building. The front of the staircase outset on Structure 9-IV was decorated with five panels of medium-relief stucco masks that date to the early part of the Early Classic period, roughly 300–400 CE. Looting damaged these, and only two panels and part of a third survive.

The two preserved masks have bib motifs under their chins, generally an Early Classic trait. The left head has scrolls and a central bracket under the chin strap or bib, a feature that also occurs in Late Preclassic masks in the North Acropolis of Tikal (Coe 1990: 4, figure 123b) and at Structure 5C-2nd at Cerros (Freidel 1985). The headdress of the left head is shaped as an Early Classic *ajaw* glyph. The volutes above the cartouche may represent smoke or foliation, like the "smoke" superfix that distinguishes the simple T533 *nik'* (flower) glyph from the glyph "smoking flower" (T535), used as a metaphor for "man's child." The "smoking flower" sign most often appears on the headgear of Early Classic nobles and can also be a reference to maize.

So clearly, the individual represented is most likely the *ajaw* of Blue Creek. Another view of the bib, though, is also relevant. Kent Reilly has noted that the bib could also be the bloody bowl of creation, and the *ajaw* then may be portraying himself as emerging from the bloody bowl as the materialization of the Maize God, Jun Junajpu of the Popol Vuh—an important god linked to the life-regenerating power inherent in the agricultural cycle of maize as well as to all life cycles, including those of humans.

Between the two remaining heads is an inset panel that once was also stuccoed. Above it remains a kind of sky or earth band. This is an early form of Thompson's T103 (1962), generally accepted as having the value *ki*. *Ki* probably refers to "heart" or "center" (Freidel et al. 1993: 74–75). It suggests not only that the building is the geographic center of the site but also that it was seen as a second place of the *axis mundi*, the center of the cosmos.

Tied less directly to the idea of a ruling lineage but clearly reflective of principals are other architectural elements in the *kawik*. For example, the ballcourt consists of Structures 7 and 8 and rests on top of an oversized platform. Its construction was commissioned by an Early Classic *ajaw*. There is a strong correlation between the presence of ballcourts and that of royal elites or nobility (Scarborough and Wilcox 1991, among others). Further, there is clearly a power-based connection between the ritual playing out of Maya creation through the ballgame and those who would have been able to commission formal ballcourts. Like most southern Maya ballcourts, Blue Creek's is positioned between the two major units of public architecture, possibly with the game functioning as a mediating force involving factions of leadership (Ashmore 1981; Scarborough and Wilcox 1991).

Further, as discussed earlier, pyramid-plaza complexes are themselves cosmograms. There is also a redundancy in the expression of these complexes in architecture. Plazas represent the Primordial Sea, and pyramids represent the First Mountain. Therefore, the base of a pyramid's central axis is the location where the Maize God created Maya from twisted maize. It is at this location where archaeologists commonly find "lip-to-lip" dedicatory caches. In all Terminal Late Preclassic and Early Classic caches at Blue Creek, we found elements of the sea (e.g., sponges, coral) and elements of the terrestrial world (e.g., jade, other stones) covered by the inverted upper pot that represents the Maya cosmos (Bozarth and Guderjan 2004). So as Mathews and Garber (2004) demonstrate for quincunx arrangements, these materializations of origin myth concepts appear redundantly and on multiple scales. Also, since we see such caches in contexts ranging from the most humble through royal settings, it is clear that they were shared across social strata and that religion was an encompassing and integrative mechanism that could be used by the royal lineage as a means of validating its power and authority.

From the founding of the *ajaw* system at Blue Creek and throughout the Early Classic, we see the same themes expressed in architecture and repeated use of the religious concepts to validate the power and authority of the multigenerational lineage of the *ajaw*.

THE END OF A DYNASTY: EARLY TO LATE CLASSIC TRANSFORMATIONS

As the Early Classic drew to a close, dramatic architectural shifts occurred at Blue Creek. Some can be best understood as reflections of the dynamics of changing leadership, including the end of a dynasty.

The shaft in Structure 4 was filled in a dramatic ritual at approximately 500 CE. We obtained two corrected radiocarbon dates from the interior fill of the shaft. One was from the upper portion of the shaft dated to 400–620 CE (Beta-75432) and the other from the lower portion dating to 400–600 CE (Beta-75433) or, for present purposes, approximately 500 CE (Guderjan 1998). As the shaft was filled, nearly 1,000 jade artifacts were deposited in it along with numerous non-jade artifacts, Candelario Appliqued censor ring stands (each a depiction of the ceiba tree in the same manner as done by Lacandon Maya people today), smoking and burning wood and incense, and a human phalange. These were dropped sequentially into the shaft. Twice as the shaft was filling, the process was paused to construct a plaster floor within it. Confirming that the filling was a single event and not a protracted process, we found sherds of the Candelario Incised ring bases in contexts separated by these floors. On top of the final floor, approximately 30 cm below the opening of the shaft, two pairs of lip-to-lip Aguila Orange ceramic vessels (Caches 9B and 9C) were placed. Cache 9B contained 341 jade artifacts and 21 non-jade artifacts in the 2 Aguila Orange bowls. Notable among these are 33 earflares, 4 anthropomorphic pendants, and 5 zoomorphic pendants. One of the jade pendants (505 BCE) is an Olmecoid Bib-and-Helmet face. One of the zoomorphic pendants (513 BCE) depicts a monkey's face. Cache 9C contained four jade artifacts in two Aguila Orange bowls. One jade artifact is a large anthropomorphic bead, and another is a unique bib-head pendant. The other two artifacts are subspherical jade beads. Finally, with the shaft filled, the opening of the bannerstone was covered with the uncarved stela and then buried.

This massive and opulent ritual sacrifice terminated the *axis mundi* and the royal lineage that created it. Perhaps it even ended access to the material world for the deceased lineage founding *ajaw* whose tomb is yet undiscovered under Structure 4. Regardless of whether that was the case, the pattern of continuity in architectural expression at Blue Creek had been broken, as, we believe, was the pattern of leadership that had been unbroken for 400 years.

Across the plaza, the summit of Structure 1 was dramatically reconfigured to accommodate a royal tomb. At around 500–550 CE, the columns of Structure 1-IV were razed and Structure 1-V was built. The summit was elevated about 2 m and reconfigured into a platform approximately 12 m above the plaza level to accommodate Tomb 4. This was the interment of an important, probably royal, young adult male (Guderjan 2007) and contained a pair of jade earspools, three ceramic vessels dating to the end of the Early Classic (Williams-Beck 1997), and a possible blood-letting kit composed of two obsidian blades, two bone skewers, and a shell plaque.

Each of two sets of associated caches, Cache 4 and Cache 6, consisted of two sets of small Aguilla Orange vessels placed lip to lip. They collectively contained a pair of jade plaques, a pair of jade earflares, six jade beads, unworked greenstone fragments, one piece of hematite, a marine shell (*Crepidula aculeta*), other marine-shell fragments, numerous sponge spicules, possible cacao phytoliths, and a platanillo (*Heliconia*) phytolith (Bozarth and Guderjan 2004; Driver 2008).

While temporally close, it is admittedly a stretch to argue that the filling of the shaft at Structure 4 and the entombment of the royal elite at Structure 1 were contemporaneous. Nevertheless, it is enticing to think that these events were connected. If so, the royal burial can be seen as the material remains of an *ajaw* of Blue Creek placed in the singular most important location possible. If he was the last of his lineage, the concurrent termination of his royal lineage's *axis mundi* and possibly the psycho-tube connecting the burial of his lineage's ancestral founding *ajaw* mark his death as the end of his lineage's rule. Further, events of the Late Classic period would soon indicate that there had been a significant shift in power and authority at Blue Creek.

THE NEW ORDER IN THE LATE CLASSIC PERIOD

Despite the apparent prominence suggested by the columned Structure 1 and the presence of an Early Classic ballcourt, Blue Creek lacked an important element that had become increasingly common at Peten centers since about 250 CE: an E-group. E-Groups, named after Group E at Uaxactun, were architectural assemblages that marked the rising sun on the solstices and equinoxes. Generally, they consisted of two or three buildings on the east side of a plaza oriented in such a way with a west-side building that the sun would rise over fixed points on the mornings of the solstices and equinoxes. Early E-groups were generally very precise and functional, while many later ones were less so.

Until the early part of the Late Classic, the east side of Plaza A remained open to the east and surely was the staging area for magnificent sunrises, as the open plaza overlooked miles of the Belize coastal plain. At this time, though, the plaza was extended to the east by 10 or more meters; and two new buildings, Structures 2 and 3, both about 8 m tall, were built on a shared platform. I have termed this a Pseudo-E-Group (Guderjan 2006), as it had no corresponding western building;

though we excavated a large plaza area in search of a marker in mid-plaza, we did not find one. Further, since it was atop a 100-m-tall escarpment, it would have been late morning before the sun rose above the buildings from any viewable point. By that time, the sun's perceived size in the sky would have been so large that correlation with any single point would not have been possible. I have argued that functionality is not necessary for Pseudo-E-Groups (Guderjan 2006). Instead, they had become embedded into the Maya conception of necessary elements in public architecture.

At about the same time, Structure 9 was also dramatically reconfigured. Earlier, it faced west toward Plaza A, with a ramp leading to the dance platform in front of it. In the largest single construction of the Late Classic period, it was massively expanded and reoriented toward Plaza B to the north, indicating that Plaza A, established by the first *ajaw*, no longer held the central importance it once had and that Plaza B was of increasing importance.

Tied to the increasing importance of Plaza B were functional shifts in the Structure 13 Courtyard, adjacent to Plaza B and between it and Structure 9. In the Early Classic, the Structure 13 Courtyard had actually been a small public plaza, with Structure 13 on the north and Structure 12 on the east. Early in the Late Classic period, the plaza platform was extended west and Structure 10, a 6-m-tall shrine-pyramid, was added. At what appears to have been the same time, the northeast quadrant was converted into secular residential space. We interpret these changes as responses to a need for additional residential space for a new ruling lineage—yet another indication that the changes from the Early Classic included a change in the royal lineage.

CONCLUSION

The Popol Vuh documents religious and creation concepts that are pan-Mesoamerican and that were likely viewed and implemented differently at different times and places. These concepts were used by *ajaws* and ruling lineages. Given the fact that the historical and narrative roots of the Popol Vuh likely stretched across hundreds of years into the Classic and Early Classic period, along with the cultural and political structures explained in the Popol Vuh, it serves as a useful tool for interpreting the dynamics of public architecture as ways to validate the legitimacy of Maya power and authority. Consequently, we can use the same concepts to decode and better understand the political meaning of architectural dynamics. At Blue Creek, we can use these tools to understand the continuities of the Early Classic period and the discontinuities of the Early Classic/Late Classic transition as a mirror for the dynamics of ruling lineages and the beginning, middle, and end of an Early Classic ruling lineage replaced with at least one other in the Late Classic period.

REFERENCES CITED

Ashmore, Wendy, ed. 1981. Lowland Maya Settlement Patterns. University of New Mexico Press, Albuquerque.

Bozarth, Steven, and Thomas H. Guderjan. 2004. "Biosilicate Analysis of Residue in Maya Dedicatory Cache Vessels from Blue Creek, Belize." *Journal of Archaeological Science* 31 (2): 205–15.

Carmack, Robert M. 1981. *The Quiché Maya of Utatlán: The Evolution of a Highland Guatemala Kingdom.* University of Oklahoma Press, Norman.

Christenson, Allen J. 2007. *Popol Vuh—the Sacred Book of the Maya.* 2nd revised ed. University of Oklahoma Press, Norman.

Coe, Michael D. 2011. *The Maya.* 8th ed. Thames and Hudson, New York.

Coe, William B. 1990. *Excavations in the Great Plaza, North Terrace, and North Acropolis of Tikal.* Tikal Reports 14. 5 vols. University Museum Monographs 61. University Museum, University of Pennsylvania, Philadelphia.

Driver, W. David. 2002. "An Early Classic Colonnaded Building at the Maya Site of Blue Creek, Belize." *Latin American Antiquity* 13 (1): 63–84.

Driver, W. David. 2008. "The Construction of Intrapolity Sociopolitical Identity through Architecture at the Ancient Maya Site of Blue Creek, Belize." PhD dissertation, Department of Anthropology, Southern Illinois University, Carbondale.

Freidel, David A. 1985. "Polychrome Facades of the Lowland Preclassic." In *Painted Architecture and Polychrome Monumental Sculpture in Mesoamerica*, ed. Elizabeth Boone, 5–30. Dumbarton Oaks Research Library and Collections, Washington, DC.

Freidel, David, Linda Schele, and Joy Parker. 1993. *Maya Cosmos: Three Thousand Years on the Shaman's Path.* William Morrow, New York.

Furst, Peter. 1976. *Hallucogens and Culture.* Chandler and Sharp, San Francisco.

Grube, Nikolai, Thomas H. Guderjan, and Helen R. Haines. 1995. "Late Classic Architecture and Iconography at the Blue Creek Ruin, Belize." *Mexicon* 17 (3): 51–57.

Guderjan, Thomas H. 1998. "The Blue Creek Jade Cache: Early Classic Maya Ritual and Architecture." In *The Sowing and the Dawning: Dedication and Termination Ritual Events in the Archaeology and Ethnology of Mesoamerica*, ed. Shirley Mock, 101–12. University of New Mexico Press, Albuquerque.

Guderjan, Thomas H. 2004. "Public Architecture, Ritual, and Temporal Dynamics at the Maya Center of Blue Creek." *Ancient Mesoamerica* 15 (2): 1–17.

Guderjan, Thomas H. 2005. "The Early Classic at Blue Creek." *Research Reports in Belizean Archaeology* 2: 131–42.

Guderjan, Thomas H. 2006. "E-Groups, Pseudo-E-Groups, and the Development of the Classic Maya Identity in the Eastern Petén." *Ancient Mesoamerica* 17 (1): 1–8.

Guderjan, Thomas H. 2007. *The Nature of an Ancient Maya City: Resources, Interaction, and Power at Blue Creek, Belize*. University of Alabama Press, Tuscaloosa.

Guderjan, Thomas H. 2009. "Power and Authority at the Classic Maya City of Blue Creek." *Research Reports in Belizean Archaeology* 6: 119–36.

Haines, Helen R. 2000. "Intra-Site Obsidian Distribution and Consumption Patterns in Northern Belize and the North-Eastern Peten." PhD dissertation, University College, London, England.

Lichtenstein, Robert J. 2000. *Settlement Zone Communities of the Greater Blue Creek Area*. Occasional Paper 2. Maya Research Program, Fort Worth, TX.

Mathews, Jennifer P., and James F. Garber. 2004 "Models of Cosmic Order: Physical Expression of Sacred Space among the Ancient Maya." *Ancient Mesoamerica* 15 (1): 49–59.

Pastrana, Dale. 1995. "Excavations of Structures 5 and 6 on the Main Plaza." In *Archaeological Research at Blue Creek, Belize: Progress Report of the Third (1994) Field Season*, ed. Thomas H. Guderjan and W. David Driver, 43–57. Maya Research Program. St. Mary's University, San Antonio, TX.

Quiroa, Nestor. 2011. "The *Popol Vuh* and the Dominican Religious Extirpation in Highland Guatemala: Prologues and Annotations of Fr. Francisco Ximénez." *The Americas* 67 (4): 467–94.

Reese-Taylor, Kathryn. 2002. "Ritual Circuits as Key Elements in Maya Civic Center Design." In *Heart of Creation: The Mesoamerican World and the Legacy of Linda Schele*, ed. Andrea Stone, 143–66. University of Alabama Press, Tuscaloosa.

Reilly, Kent. 1994. "Visions to Another World: Art, Shamanism, and Political Power in Middle Formative Mesoamerica." PhD dissertation, University of Texas, Austin.

Restall, Matthew. 1997. *The Maya World: Yucatec Culture and Society, 1550–1850*. Stanford University Press, Stanford, CA.

Roys, Ralph, and Edwin Shook. 1966. *Preliminary Report on the Ruins of Ake, Yucatan*. Memoirs of the Society for American Archaeology 20. Society for American Archaeology, Salt Lake City.

Scarborough, Vernon L., and David Wilcox. 1991. *The Mesoamerican Ball Game*. Tucson: University of Arizona Press.

Schele, Linda, and David Freidel. 1990. *A Forest of Kings: The Untold Story of the Ancient Maya*. William Morrow, New York.

Schele, Linda, and Mary Ellen Miller. 1986. *The Blood of Kings: Dynasty and Ritual in Maya Art*. Kimbell Art Museum, Fort Worth, TX.

Stuart, David. 1984. "Blood Symbolism in Maya Iconography." *RES* 7–8: 6–20.

Stuart, David. 1988. "Blood Symbolism in Maya Iconography." In *Maya Iconography*, ed. Elizabeth P. Benson and Gillett G. Griffin, 175–221. Princeton University Press, Princeton, NJ.

Tedlock, Dennis. 1993. "Torture in the Archives: Mayans Meet Europeans." *American Anthropologist* 95 (1): 139–52.

Tedlock, Dennis. 1996. *Popol Vuh: The Definite Edition of the Mayan Book of the Dawn of Life and the Glories of Gods and Kings*. 2nd revised ed. Simon and Schuster, New York.

Thompson, J. Eric S. 1962. *A Catalog of Maya Hieroglyphs*. University of Oklahoma Press, Norman.

Weiss, Pamela. 1996. "The Continuation of Excavations at Structure 4." In *Archaeological Research at Blue Creek, Belize: Progress Report of the Fourth (1995) Field Season*, ed. Thomas H. Guderjan, W. David Driver, and Helen Haines, 37–42. Maya Research Program. St. Mary's University, San Antonio, TX.

Williams-Beck, Lorraine. 1997. "Blue Creek Whole Vessels." Manuscript on file. Maya Research Program. St. Mary's University, San Antonio, TX.

Zorita, Alonso de. 1994. *Life and Labor in Ancient Mexico: The Brief and Summary Relation of the Lords of New Spain*. Trans. Benjamin Keen. University of Oklahoma Press, Norman.

7

Sacrifice of the Maize God

Re-creating Creation in the Main Chamber of Actun Tunichil Muknal, Belize

HOLLEY MOYES AND JAIME J. AWE

Research conducted on ancient Maya cave sites has been effective in establishing that caves were ritual spaces that provide scholars with an unambiguous context to study ritual and religion in the deep past based on ethnographic, ethnohistoric, and iconographic sources (Brady 1989; Brady and Ashmore 1999: 124; Brady and Prufer 2005; Christenson 2008; Moyes and Brady 2005, 2012; Schávelzon 1980; Stone 1995; Taube 2004; Thompson 1975; Vogt and Stuart 2005). However, it has been much more difficult for archaeologists to ascertain what exactly occurred in the Classic period deep within caves. There is little epigraphic documentation describing cave rites (Helmke 2009: 523), and among the modern Maya, cave rituals have traditionally been considered highly esoteric; therefore, there are few descriptions of what occurred in their inner sanctums. For instance, ethnographer Oliver LaFarge (1947: 127) was warned "emphatically and many times" not to approach the cave of Yalan Na', which clearly had significant ritual importance to the local Maya. Alfred M. Tozzer (1907: 148–49) reported that while studying the Lacandon, he accompanied a family on a visit to a cave shrine. Upon arrival, the father and eldest son went to the cave while Tozzer and the rest of the family waited behind in a canoe. This sort of report led Von Jarslaw Theodore Petryshyn (2005: 329) to believe he was the first researcher to eye-witness a Lacandon cave ceremony. Native attitudes regarding their religion led Martin Prechtel and Robert Carlsen (1988: 123) to note that "it is customary for the Maya to refuse to divulge the most basic of their sacred beliefs." In light of indigenous beliefs regarding the

36

DOI: 10.5876/9781646421992.c007

most sacred aspects of the religion, the lack of ethnographic data regarding caves seems hardly surprising.

In addition, many modern rites occur in front of caves rather than in their interiors. Yet, as borne out in the archaeological record by the extensive architectural modifications and artifact assemblages found in caves, it is apparent that throughout the Classic period, caves not only functioned as metaphors for cosmological beliefs but were ceremonial venues that reified cosmologies and provided potent venues for ritual performance. We know that despite continuities in meaning, there are some fundamental differences in the form of rites occurring in and around caves, and it follows that changes in ritual practice accompany changes in the rituals themselves. This can occur without changes in meaning or conceptualizations of the cave itself as a sacred space for contacting and propitiating deities. For instance, in Moyes's 2006 diachronic study of Chechem Ha cave, she found that the cave was used from the time of the earliest local settlements (1200–800 BCE) to the Late Classic period (700–900 CE). Through a rigorous dating program, detailed recording of features and artifacts, and excavations, she was able to demonstrate that over time, the cave was used in different ways and there was variation in ritual practices even though the caves remained a ritual site—suggesting that the rituals themselves were dynamic over time, although meaning remained constant. Hence, we should expect disjunctions and changes in ritual practices among the Classic period rituals, ethnohistoric accounts, and modern cave rites—creating a situation in which cave archaeologists are highly dependent on the archaeological record to infer the types of rites or specific rituals that occurred in the past in the depths of caves. As Andrea J. Stone (2005: 135–36) noted, "The difficulty of reconstituting the motivation of cave ritual from archaeological remains . . . means we have only the vaguest notion of the specialized rituals that may have been practiced by the elite in caves."

Researchers have proposed a number of rites, including the Cuch or Deer Ceremony (Pohl 1981; Pohl and Pohl 1983), hunting (Brown 2005), period ending (Bassie-Sweet 1991), accession (Bassie Sweet 1991; Helmke and Awe 1998; Helmke et al. 2003), foundational (Moyes and Prufer 2013), scribal (Stone 2005), sweatbathing (Moyes 2005), New Year's (Taube 1988), bloodletting (Awe et al. 2005), and scaffold sacrifice (Reents-Budet and MacLeod 1997). The few surviving modern cave rites are primarily agricultural and rain related, motivating a number of archaeologists to argue that related rites occurred in the past. These include rites such as rain rituals (Brady 1989; MacLeod and Puleston 1978; Moyes et al. 2009; Rissolo 2005), fertility rites (Brady 1988; Nielsen and Brady 2006), and first fruit rites (Morehart 2002a, 2002b, 2005). Good arguments can be advanced for the occurrence of all these types of rituals, and different types of rites likely occurred over a long temporal period, though they may all be somewhat related. Variation in morphological cave settings may have also helped to determine which rites may have been practiced within particular caves. At the same time, we know nothing about why some caves were utilized and some were not.

There has been little discussion of the relationship between Classic period rites and myth or mythic reenactments. One of the few works to connect caves with mythology was Barbara MacLeod and Dennis E. Puleston's *Pathways into Darkness: The Search for the Road to Xibalba* (1978). The authors argued that caves were considered entrances to the underworld as told in the Popol Vuh story, an ethnohistoric rendition of the Maya creation myth, thus connecting caves to Maya cosmology and a three-tiered universe. Further, they suggested that the trials related in the Hero Twins story may have been part of actual rites conducted within caves. Based on the traditional relationship between myth and ritual, it seems plausible that myth could be played out in cave rites, given the purportedly strong connections between the two. This goes back to pioneering anthropologist E. B. Tylor, who understood myth to be the most important facet of ancient religion because it explained the physical world and, he argued, functioned as the ancient counterpart to modern science (Segal 2008: 103–4). He considered mythic stories to be creeds, independent of and antecedent to ritual. Thus myth explained the world and ritual was its enactment, therefore dependent on myth.

The myth-ritualist theory (Ackerman 1975, 1991; Segal 2006, 2010: 384) was a major research focus for early anthropologists and religious scholars that is still somewhat debated today. According to this theory, first advanced by William Robertson Smith and Sir James George Frazer, in its strongest incarnation myth is *always* tied to ritual and the function of myth is to justify the ritual enactment. According to Smith's (1969 [1889]) evolutionary framework of the emergence of religion, ritual exists in the first stage. The second is the myth-ritualist stage, in which myth arises to explain ritual. In Frazer's evolutionary model, based on his comparative approach, agricultural people replaced the magic of nature with a myth that described the life of the god of vegetation. Rituals enacted the death and rebirth of the deity in order to control agricultural fertility. He explains:

> For although men now attributed the annual cycle of change primarily to corresponding changes in their deities, they still thought that by performing certain magical rites they could aid the god who was the principle of life, in his struggle with the opposing principle of death. They imagined that they could recruit his failing energies and even raise him from the dead. The ceremonies which they observed for this purpose were in substance a dramatic representation of the natural processes which they wished to facilitate; for it is a familiar tenet of magic that you can produce any desired effect by

merely imitating it. And as they now explained the fluctuations of growth and decay, of reproduction and dissolution, by the marriage, the death, and the rebirth or revival of the gods, their religious or rather magical dramas turned in great measure on these themes. (Frazer 2003: 436 [1890, 2 vols.; 1900, 3 vols.; 1911–15, 12 vols.])

Frazer inspired a group known as the Cambridge Ritualists that included Jane Ellen Harrison (1850–1928), F. M. Cornford (1874–1943), and A. B. Cook (1868–1952), who accepted the close association of ritual and myth and begged the question, which came first—ritual or myth? Their aim was to show that prehistoric Dionysian fertility rites were the structural models for later Greek drama. The heart of the ritual-theorist's argument was not that all rituals were tied to myth but that all myths were tied to rituals because ritual was thought to temporally precede myth (Segal 2008: 107–10).

Over the years, the theory has been revised and it survives in weaker or altered forms (Segal 2008: 111–21). For example, Bronislaw Malinowski (1992 [1948]) adopted a weak version of the theory, arguing that myth shapes rituals and imparts the mystique of an ancient origin to them, but he also observed that some myths flourished without rituals and some rituals did so without myths. For Mircea Eliade (1968 [1963]), myths were not only concerned with rituals but provided sanctioning for various phenomena. Rituals fulfilled the function of myth because when enacted, myths carried the participants back in time and closer to God.

Others see closer ties. Edmund Leach (1965: 11–12) argued that "myth implies ritual and ritual implies myth," and Clyde Kluckholm (1942: 78) noted that because they fulfill similar psychological needs, the two tend universally to be associated, although the relative importance of myth and of ritual varies greatly. In the more recent anthropological functionalist view, myth is regarded as a charter, justification, or rationalization for ritual action for the sake of the security or solidarity of the social structure (Penner 1968). Recently, classicist Gregory Nagy (2002) argued that once myth is spoken, it becomes an oral performance and therefore a verbal aspect of ritual. Though very few scholars now adhere to the strong version of the myth-ritualist theory, most would agree that some myths are indeed related to ritual activity. The long history of research in this area and years of debate attest to the strength of the relationship between the two.

Here, we argue for a connection between cave rites and the Maya creation myth as it is related in the Popol Vuh and epigraphic texts. This chapter proposes a mythic theme based on artifacts and their contexts in the Main Chamber of the unlooted site of Actun Tunichil Muknal (ATM), a Late Classic ritual cave in western Belize (figure 7.1). One of the problems typically encountered in attempting detailed ritual reconstructions is that most caves have been looted and the spatial contexts and

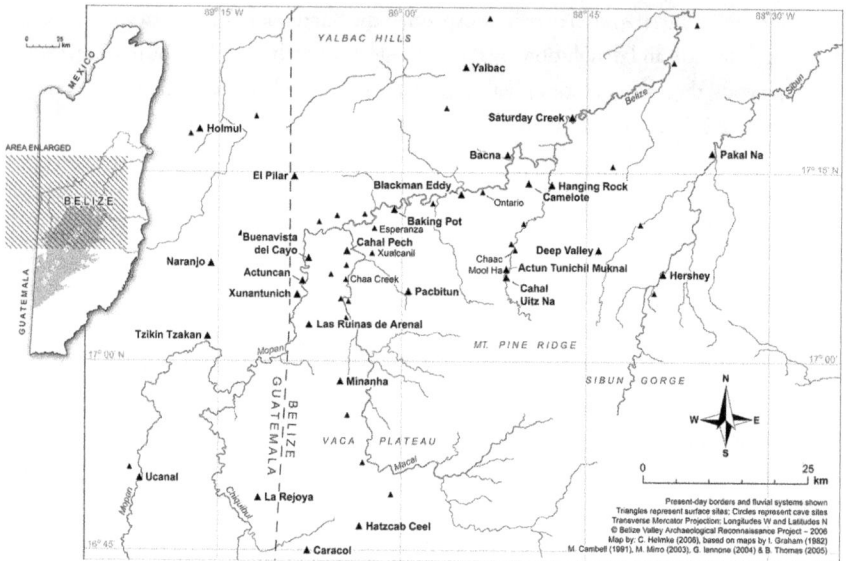

FIGURE 7.1. Location of Actun Tunichil Muknal on a tributary of the Roaring Creek River in western Belize. *Courtesy,* Western Belize Regional Cave Project.

artifact assemblages have been severely disrupted or lost. This makes it difficult to "read" archaeological remains as "texts" to be explored and interpreted. ATM is one of the few cave sites in the Maya lowlands that upon its discovery was undisturbed by humans; therefore, it is one of the most important finds in cave archaeology. The site, affected only by natural taphonomic processes, provided us with the rare opportunity to study the remains of ancient Maya ceremonies in situ.

In this chapter, we describe the cave and its artifact assemblage and propose a methodology for thinking about how to link artifact assemblages with ritual practices. Based on the context, artifacts, and their spatial distributions, we argue that a ritual reenactment of elements of the ancient Maya creation myth, including the sacrifice of the Maize God, occurred in the cave at the end of the Late Classic period.

INFERRING THE RITUAL THEME

Victor Turner (1982: 81) argued that rituals are integrated wholes, often ordered by a dramatic structure or plot involving a rich symbolic system that engages all of the participants' sensory systems. For Turner, ritual is an "artwork," a social drama that is an "interweaving" of the mind and senses. Therefore, rituals may be thought of as possessing thematic characteristics. The theme serves to integrate the whole and is referenced in terms of the spatial setting, the actions of the participants, ritual language, and the objects employed. Attention is devoted to the symbolic details involving virtually every aspect of the ritual enactment, including the location, costume, and behavior of participants as well as the special nature of ritual objects. Symbolism becomes instantiated in the posture, movement, and speech of the performers and in the decorative motifs of ritual objects and their placement in the performance space.

In understanding cave rites, context plays an important interpretive role, as does the cave's morphology, artifact assemblage, and the use of space. When present, architectural features provide structure to natural caves and may aid in reconstructing ritual performances (Moyes 2012, 2020.). Despite the fact that most archaeological cave sites are heavily looted, artifact assemblages in caves produce a rich corpus of remains of ancient ritual activity. This includes ceramics, lithics, unmodified stones, plant and animal remains, speleothems, incense, wood, charcoal, and human remains. As ritual deposits, artifacts may acquire polyvalent meanings. Utilitarian objects used in rituals may take on a symbolic value that transcends their function as household objects (Brady and Peterson 2008). Their symbolic expression is communicated by the individual object or as a collection of objects. These items may have functioned as props in the ritual itself that were left in the cave as "ritual trash," or they may have functioned as votive objects or gifts for deities. These uses are not mutually exclusive. It is unclear how objects were chosen for ritual use, and, in fact, ethnographic evidence suggests that some ceramics were collected from middens (Hayden and Cannon 1984), while other accounts indicate that unusual or special objects were carefully curated for ritual purposes (Brown 2000). Therefore, it is unlikely that objects used in cave rites were randomly selected, though some may have been. Particularly in the case of special finds such as pyrite mirrors, jewelry, decorated ceramics, jade objects, and other valuable commodities, it is probable that they were carefully chosen personal items or possessions required for specific rites or imbued with special meaning.

Contextualized spatial data patterns and the artifacts associated with them are potentially capable of producing archaeological "signatures" or "unambiguous indicators of a behavioral process" (Aldenderfer 1987: 95). Signatures are typically employed to establish the types of rituals that may have occurred in caves. In proposing that cave rites included in the Cuch (burden or cargo) Ceremony, John and Mary Pohl (Pohl 1981, 1983; Pohl and Pohl 1983) consulted modern ethnography and prehistoric art to establish material signatures that could be compared to the archaeological record for concordance. They argued that the presence of deer bones was evidence for the rite and argued that deer bones found in caves and cenotes supported this interpretation. Later research demonstrated that deer bones are found in hunting shrines not tied to cargo rites (Brown 2005). Clearly, the problem with this method is that one has to be certain that the signature is unambiguous. In addition, it is imprudent to rely on a single artifact to infer a particular ritual without drawing from many other data sources, including contextual information.

If we begin to think of artifacts or elements of ritual as symbols, we may be better able to infer what art historian Christopher B. Donnan refers to as ritual "themes." Donnan (1975) developed a "thematic approach" to the study of Moche art, in which he suggests that it is possible to identify a ritual theme based on a specific set of characteristic symbolic elements. Donnan used a basic theme from Christ's birth to illustrate his method. He argued that in its depiction, the associated symbolic elements might include individuals such as the infant, the Virgin Mary, Joseph, the wise men, the innkeeper, and objects such as the manger, the inn, barnyard animals, or a star. Any or all of the elements could be used to identify the theme, and combinations of elements might vary (Donnan 1975: 147–48). We add that taken out of context, unless a symbol is demonstrated to be unambiguous, a single element is not sufficient to identify even a familiar theme, but contextualization of the element can constrain its interpretive possibilities. For instance, a star may have a number of meanings, but a star on a Christmas card is recognized as the Star of Bethlehem.

While no single artifact or element is apt to explain events that occurred in cave interiors, by considering clusters of elements and their contexts, it becomes increasingly possible to formulate a ritual theme. Henry B. Nicholson (1976: 171) addressed this issue in his studies of Olmec art. He argued that clusters were of greater significance than the occurrence of any single element in the interpretation of meaning when moving back through time. This method of studying ancient iconography and art can be applied to the study of artifacts in ritual contexts if we consider each artifact as a contextualized symbolic element that articulates with other artifact symbols functioning within a narrative framework. While we may not always be able to infer a specific ritual and, in fact, some cave rites may not exist in the ethnographic corpus or have been completely lost, determining the ritual theme is an important step in understanding ancient cave use.

In this study, we examine the elements at the center of the Main Chamber at Actun Tunichil Muknal. The center of the chamber was chosen for analysis because of its spatial importance in Maya ritual. In addition, artifacts and human remains in the area are in close spatial proximity to one another and are located on or near the surface. A major difference between cave and surface archaeology is that in most cases, caves lack stratigraphy. At some cave sites, surface deposits may form a palimpsest in which artifacts from different temporal periods co-occur, but this is not the case in the Main Chamber. Here, similarly dated artifacts are strewn throughout the site, forming clusters (Moyes 2001, 2005). This suggests that a variety of rituals or a number of similar or related rituals were likely to have occurred in the space over a limited temporal period, within 100 to 150 years. Based on the law of association, clustering is expected to be a significant factor in postulating synchronic events, and a best-fit model will be used to postulate the ritual theme operating in this delimited spatial area. Examining the artifact assemblage and its spatial context makes it possible to propose a model of events that took place at the center of the chamber and relate them to ancient Maya creation events described in ethnohistoric mythic narratives and epigraphic texts.

MYTHS OF CREATION

Accounts of the Maya creation are derived from a number of ethnohistoric and ethnographic sources as well as ancient hieroglyphic texts (Freidel et al. 1993; Knowlton 2010). The most thorough treatment of the creation is from the Popol Vuh, the most important example of Maya Precolumbian literature to have survived the Spanish Invasion. Over the past 300 years, there have been over thirty translations in seven languages and, most recently, two in English (Tedlock [1996 (1985)]; Christenson [2007]) translated from the original K'iche' Maya text. It is thought that the Popol Vuh stories were originally oral histories that were written in hieroglyphic form, then translated to the European alphabet no later than 1558 CE (Akkeren 2003; Christenson 2007: 37; Tedlock 1996 [1985]: 56–57). Between 1701 and 1703, a copy came into the hands of Francisco Ximénez, a Spanish priest who copied the K'iche' text and added a Spanish translation. Tedlock described the document as a "myth-history" that follows Maya history from creation to the Historic period. Changes may have occurred to parts of the text for political reasons (Akkeren 2003: 238–39), but the myths were of ancient origin. Characters and depictions of narratives from the saga of the Hero Twins appear in iconography dating to the Preclassic period on the Izapa stelae (Guernsey 2006, this volume; Freidel et al. 1993) and in Classic period Maya vase paintings (Coe 1989; Freidel et al. 1993).

According to the Popol Vuh, in the beginning the world was dark because there was no sun and the cosmos consisted of a Primordial Sea. In this dark primordial time, gods of the earth and sky created a vision of the emergence of the earth from water and its subsequent population by plants, animals, and people. This is expressed in terms of "sowing" and "dawning," which, according to Tedlock (1996 [1985]: 31–32), has a threefold meaning. In agricultural terms, "sowing" is the planting of seeds and their sprouting is the "dawning." The "sowing" also refers to the sun, moon, and stars that will have their "dawning." The third meaning refers to humans who have their "sowing" in the womb and "dawning" at birth, followed by the "sowing" of their souls at death that "dawn" as sparks of light. These concepts are ideally expressed metaphorically in the birth of the Maize God, who is sacrificed ("sown") in the underworld or under the earth and reborn ("dawns") as the maize plant (Tedlock n.d.).

Before humans could occupy the earth, the way had to be prepared. This became the task of two sets of Hero Twins. The Twins, as proponents of human life, were set in direct opposition to the underworld denizens of death. The first pair of Twins, One Junajpu and Seven Junajpu, were great ballplayers. The noise from their game offended the underworld gods, who summoned the Twins to the underworld (Xibalba) to play ball with the evil lords that dwelled therein. The Twins made the long and twisted path down into the underworld where they underwent a series of tests, were defeated, and were summarily sacrificed. Their bodies were buried in the ballcourt, and the head of One Junajpu was placed in a barren calabash tree, which began to bear fruit. The people of Xibalba were amazed but were forbidden to approach the tree or pick the fruit. The daughter of one of the lords disobeyed the taboo, approached the tree, and was impregnated by spittle from the skull of One Junajpu. Once her father became aware of her pregnancy, he ordered her to be sacrificed, but she was able to trick the evil lords and escape to the surface where she sought out her mother-in-law. She managed to convince the old woman that she carried the twin sons of One Junajpu and stayed in her home, giving birth to Junajpu and Xb'alanke, the second pair of Hero Twins. In their youth, the Twins performed deeds that prepared the earth for the coming of humans and the dawning of the sky.

Junajpu and Xb'alanke acquired their father's ballgame equipment and began to play the game. Again, the Lords of the Underworld were perturbed and summoned the boys to Xibalba. Before taking leave, they planted ears of corn in the center of their house in a dry place. The maize was to be kept as a sign to alert their grandmother as to whether they had died in the underworld.

Like their father and uncle, the Twins set off on the road to Xibalba, but unlike their predecessors, they were not so easily defeated by the evil lords. By using their wits and recruiting animals to help them, the Twins survived their underworld ordeals. But despite their success, they discovered that they would be sacrificed anyway, so they accepted a challenge to jump over a fire pit. Instead of jumping over the pit, the Twins hopped into it and were consumed by the fire. With knowledge of their impending certain death, the Twins had the foresight to consult two seers to request that upon their death, the seers would carry out a divination and suggest that their bones be ground and scattered into the river.

Following their immolation, the evil lords, believing they had triumphed, did as the seers suggested. In the river, the Twins were reconstituted and reappeared as catfish men that turned into humans and traveled the country disguised as performers who did magical acts. One of their tricks was to perform a sacrifice without killing the victim. The lords of Xibalba heard of this and invited them to their palace to perform the trick. During the performance the Twins sacrificed a dog, then Junajpu, and all were brought back to life. The lords of Xibalba were so delighted that they, too, asked to be sacrificed. The Twins obliged but did not restore the evil lords to life, thus defeating them. Following their victory, the Twins proceeded to the ballcourt and attempted to restore their father, One Junajpu, who became the Maize God. But because he could not speak properly, One Junajpu (First Father) was left to dwell in the ballcourt and was given a promise that he would be worshipped. The boys then ascended to the heavens, Junajpu becoming the sun and Xb'alanke the moon.

Here, Classic period texts provide further insight into other events that help piece together facets of the ancient myth and cosmological accounts (Freidel et al. 1993). Drawing heavily on the Tablet of the Cross texts and images from the Cross Group at Palenque (1993: 68–93), these texts note that as in the Popol Vuh, prior to the formation of the cosmos, the sky is "lying down" on the Primordial Sea and must be raised. One Junajpu (the Maize God or First Father) centers the cosmos by setting the first three hearthstones at a place called "Lying-down-Sky, First-Three-Stone-Hearth-Place" (1993: 75). David Freidel and his colleagues (1993: 71) note that in order to raise the sky, First Father must plant the World Tree (named in the central panel of the Temple of the Cross imagery at Palenque as "Raised Up Sky," or *Wakah-Chan*) at the Three-Stone-Hearth-Place. The tree rises out of a sacrificial plate in the Palenque image. This action separates the earth from the sky and establishes the eight cardinal and inter-cardinal directions of the cosmos. As his final action, First Father "turned the Raised-up-Sky Heart," which Freidel and his colleagues interpret as setting the stars and planets in motion and completing the layout of the cosmos, allowing the sun to rise upon the earth. This is the dawn of creation and occurs at the Long Count date of 13.0.0.0.0, 4 Ajaw 8 Kumk'u (which correlates to 3114 BCE). The date is recorded by the ancient Maya on the Tablet of the Cross at Palenque, Quirigua Stela C, and Coba Stela 1 (1993: 59–74).

Ethnographic evidence from the K'iche' links this event to caves. Duncan M. Earle (1989, 2008) suggested that the "dawning place" of Hacauitz, mentioned in the Popol Vuh, serves as an important mountain shrine today and has reported the presence of two caves on the mountain. These caves, also reported by A. Ledyard Smith (1955: 43) in 1949, are used as pilgrimage sites for the entire region. Earle argues for a reading of "Hacauitz" as "mountain-with-an-opening" or "Cave Mountain" based on the verb *jal*, which has numerous meanings but usually refers to "opening," or *jakal*, meaning "opened" or "excavated." The two caves are stations used today in ritual routes made by priest-shaman initiates at the end of their 260-day training. At present, on the east side of the mountain on a ridge called

Saqirib'al, various groups conduct all-night vigils to await the dawn. These vigils can be thought of as cosmological renewal events commemorating the first dawning of the sky (Earle 1989, 2008).

THE SETTING

Actun Tunichil Muknal was discovered by Thomas Miller, a geomorphologist who was the first human to visit the cave since the Late to Terminal Classic period (700–900 CE). He produced a map and reported that there were artifacts and human remains deep within the tunnel system in an area he called the Main Chamber (1989, 1990). The Western Belize Regional Cave Project (WBRCP), under the direction of Jaime Awe, conducted investigations at the site from 1996 through 1998. In the summer of 1996, Moyes visited ATM with the WBRCP to assist in mapping the Main Chamber and recording human remains. In 1997, she returned as a staff member to supervise the mapping and recording of artifacts and conduct spatial analyses (Moyes 2001, 2005; Moyes and Awe 1998, 1999).

The site is located on a tributary of the Roaring Creek River near Teakettle Village in western Belize (Awe et al. 2005; Moyes 2006; see figure 7.1). It is classified as a "wet cave" because a perennial stream flows through the tunnel system before emerging from the main east-facing cave entrance. The opening is a keyhole-shaped archway approximately 8 m in height that towers over a blue-green pool. Artifacts were located in several areas of the system, including the Entrance Chambers, the Sinkhole Tunnels, the Stela Chamber, and the Main Chamber. The Stela Chamber, best described as a shelf or alcove overlooking the stream, contains an altar-like construction with two modified slate monuments or stelae (Awe et al. 2005). The Main Chamber is a high-level passage that splits off from the tunnel system 500 m from the cave entrance (figure 7.2). It is oriented on an east-west axis and is entered through a squeeze located in the easternmost section of the chamber. The chamber is cavernous with a total area of approximately 4,450 m², measuring 183 m in length, 35 m at its widest point, and 5 m at its narrowest point. It is composed of a number of rooms and passageways partitioned by large areas of breakdown, stalagmitic columns, and large boulders. The most heavily utilized area of the Main Chamber was the Burial Chamber located in the geographic center of the cave (Moyes 2001, 2005; Moyes and Awe 1998, 1999).

Much of the floor of the Main Chamber consists of a series of rimstone or travertine dams (formed by precipitation of calcium during water evaporation), a few patches of mud, and sandy loam that occurs sporadically along the cave walls. The dams create a honeycomb of gour pools formed by connecting rimstone dams that fill with water intermittently when there are very heavy rains. They cover the central

FIGURE 7.2. Map of the tunnel system of Actun Tunichil Muknal showing location of the Main Chamber. Courtesy, Western Belize Regional Cave Project (after Miller 1990: 36).

portion of the floor area and descend gradually toward the eastern entrance, indicating that in the past, the chamber experienced wetting and drying events. Having witnessed the flooding of the chamber in 1997, we can attest that the pools filled with water that dripped from the ceiling and slowly drained over a three-week period. This explained why so many of the artifacts on the surface of the chamber were encrusted in calcite, literally cemented to the floor. The pools functioned essentially as containers for these objects.

Typical of most cave sites, almost all of the artifacts deposited in the chamber were broken, some in situ but others imported into the cave as fragments. There were 1,408 fragmented objects representing a minimum number of 718 artifacts and ecofacts. Of these, 77 percent were ceramics, and other classes included speleothems (broken or shaped stalactites), groundstone objects (*manos*, *metates*, greenstone celts, and pyrite mirror fragments), animal teeth and bones, obsidian blades, crystals, slate, and a few ornaments. The chamber also contained several hearths and a number of human remains. In 1997, Sheryl A. Gibbs (2000) recorded fourteen individuals both male and female ranging in age from infants to middle-aged adults. Of these, six were infants under three years of age, one was a child of approximately seven years, and seven were adults ranging from twenty to forty years old. Only the adults could be sexed. Two were likely female and three were male; the remaining two were heavily encrusted in calcite and could not be determined. Recently, the remains of four additional individuals were located in the chamber, bringing the total minimum number to eighteen. One was the disarticulated skeleton of an infant found in the western section of the chamber tucked away in a gour pool behind a stalagmitic column. Another was a partially visible infant covered by flowstone, increasing the total number of infants to eight. The remains of the other two individuals were fragmentary. None of the individuals in the chamber were "buried," and all were deposited on the cave floor, cached in niches, or deposited in gour pools.

Due to their poor condition, it was impossible to determine anatomical positioning in most cases, but interment #13, the best-preserved individual (known to tourists as "the Crystal Maiden"), was clearly placed in a gour pool, the person's arm landing akimbo extended overhead (see Moyes 2001: 26–27; Gibbs 2000: 121; Lucero and Gibbs 2007: 61, figure 3.6). The cave context, number of children present, evidence of trauma in some instances, and few grave goods accompanying the remains suggested to both Gibbs and Moyes that these were sacrificial victims (Gibbs 2000; Moyes and Gibbs 2000; Moyes 2001). Lisa J. Lucero and Gibbs (2007) have argued elsewhere that some of these individuals may have been witches that were sacrificially dispatched in the cave.

Temporal use of the chamber was initially determined by relative dating of the ceramic assemblage using the type-variety-mode method of analysis (Moyes 2001). The ceramic types identified were subsequently cross-referenced with James C. Gifford's Barton Ramie ceramic report (1976), and the dates were corroborated by the results of three AMS assays from charcoal recovered from a hearth and beneath the flowstone in the chamber confirmed these results. All diagnostic sherds, as well as whole and partial vessels, dated to the late part of the Late Classic or Spanish Lookout phase (700–900 CE). With the exception of a red molded-carved vase, a jar with an appliqued anthropomorphic figure, and fragments of Daylight Orange/Darknight Variety bowls, there were no other decorated vessels in the chamber. All other vessels were represented by unslipped or monochrome red and black slipped types. Ringed vases with high pedestals were present, and there were no ash-tempered wares. Gordon Willey (1973) observed that for Belize Valley ceramics, there is a change in ceramic patterning during the second half of the Spanish Lookout phase, beginning around 830 CE and ending between 890 CE and 950 CE. He noted the following changes for these terminal phase assemblages: (1) ash-tempered wares disappear, (2) calcite-tempered wares are reasserted, (3) polychrome painting is gone, and (4) there is very little decoration (1973: 105–6). Based on Willey's model, utilization of the chamber can be narrowed to between 830 and 950 CE. This overlaps with all three AMS assays from the Main Chamber calibrated using OxCal v. 4.3 (Bronk Ramsey 2009) and the IntCal13 Northern Hemisphere atmospheric curve (Reimer et al. 2013). At the 2 sigma range, they yielded dates of (AA57315) 695–945 CE, (AA57316) 720–945 CE, and (UCIAMS 177189) 710–885 CE.

CREATION AT THE CENTER

THE MAIN CHAMBER AS COSMOLOGICAL SPACE

In our analyses of the Main Chamber, we have suggested elsewhere that the spatial distributions of artifacts within the cave reflect the quincuncial model pervasive in the structure of Maya cosmology that is essential to ritual practice (Moyes and Awe 1998, 1999; Moyes 2001, 2005). We were able to identify four ritual pathways corresponding to the cardinal directions delineated by artifact scatters along cave walls and the cosmic center, or *axis mundi*, located in the geographic center of the chamber, marked by a cluster of three speleothems that we have argued elsewhere constitute a representation of the Classic period Three-Stone-Hearth-Place. This is hardly surprising when we consider that the creation of a ritually enclosed and secure space is one of the hallmarks of modern Maya ritual practice. William F. Hanks (1990: 336–37) refers to this aspect of Maya ritual as "binding" because it creates a mini-cosmos in which the ritual can be safely conducted. This is accomplished through shamanic discourse that invokes the cardinal directions in which spirits are brought down from their celestial realm and are returned at the end of the ceremony. John R. Sosa (1985: 470–71) also noted that the "tying" or binding of ritual space is modeled after the Maya understanding of the cosmological order and references the sun delimiting the boundaries of the cosmos in its daily circuit around the earth.

Designation of a bounded ritual space occurs at various scales, from the altar to the household to the community level. It is employed in laying out *milpas* and house protection rites (Hanks 1990: 345) as well as dedication ceremonies (Vogt 1998: 24–26). In house dedications, offerings are deposited at the corners (intercardinal points), at the centers of the four walls (cardinal points), and in the center of the floor, which are the most susceptible places for demons to enter. Evon Z. Vogt (1998: 27) reports that when someone dies, the corpse is laid out with the head placed toward the setting sun, and the area is "fenced off" within the house by household articles to prevent the spirit from wandering.

In the *loh* (meaning "redeem" or "free") ceremony, a community rite in Yucatan, the participants traverse a ritual circuit to each of the four entrances of the village and at each point bury crosses, obsidian, and salt in the road to prevent evil winds (Redfield and Villa Rojas 1962 [1934]: 176). Barbara Tedlock (1992: 82) reported that at Los Cipréses in highland Guatemala, the priest-shaman makes a four-part pilgrimage to the mountains surrounding the town. This ritual circuit is referred to as either the "sowing and the planting" or the "stabilization" of the community. By studying ethnohistoric documents, Angel García-Zambrano (1994) found that throughout Mesoamerica, in establishing communities there existed a complex set of rituals that bound the territory, creating a mini-cosmos. These began with the identification of five mountains. Four were considered the periphery of the community and the fifth, which contained a water source, became the center. From the central mountain, a group carrying ropes constructed of boughs and grasses beat the boundaries of the new community, establishing borders along community perimeters. This binding of space echoes our findings in the Main Chamber, where offerings placed along walls and in remote areas established ritual boundaries as an important means of defining a safe social space within the cave.

Centrality is equally important in understanding Maya ritual frameworks. In Maya cosmological models, the center is the zenith and nadir of the sun's path as it travels through the sky during the day and the night sky in the underworld. In myth, the Three-Stone-Hearth-Place is the center of the cosmos where the Maize deity erects the World Tree for the first time, which raises the sky from the watery earth and sets the stars in motion (Freidel et al. 1993: 71). Karl A. Taube (1998: 430) reminds us of the analogy among household architecture, sacred architecture, and the Maya cosmos. He argues that temples were configured as "god houses" whose roofs were supported by four posts and whose center was the Three-Stone Hearth that represented both a place of creation and the *axis mundi* that connected the sky, earth, and underworld.

This feature is clearly marked in the center of the Burial Chamber with three modified stacked stalactites. They were carved from their natural cone shape to a more rounded appearance, more closely resembling a round hearthstone. The cluster is notable due to its odd configuration in which one stone is stacked on top of the other two and is the only instance in the cave that this particular configuration occurs. The specific arrangement was identified by Taube (1998: 433) in epigraphic representations of the Three-Stone Hearth (figure 7.3). The speleothem cluster was central not only to the Burial Chamber where it is located but to the larger Main Chamber as well. This element completes the quincuncial frame delineated by the linear scatters found in the four cardinal directions and the speleothem cluster marking the center (figure 7.4).

ARTIFACTS AT THE CENTER

There are a number of artifacts as well as human remains clustered in the 5 m × 5 m central area of the Main Chamber surrounding the three stacked speleothems that suggest a literal reenactment of the Popol Vuh story (figure 7.5). The floor in this area of the chamber is composed of a honeycomb of rimstone dams with a number of artifacts placed on crests or in pools surrounding the three-speleothem cluster, which is situated on a crest. Lying in a gour pool adjacent to the feature is Individual #1, a calcite-encrusted skeleton of an adult male estimated to be thirty to forty years old. The bones are not well-articulated and appear to have floated around within the pool before becoming encased in calcite and cemented to the chamber floor. They are commingled with six partially intact medium-sized jars. The cranium rests face-up on the east edge of the crest of the dam apart from the

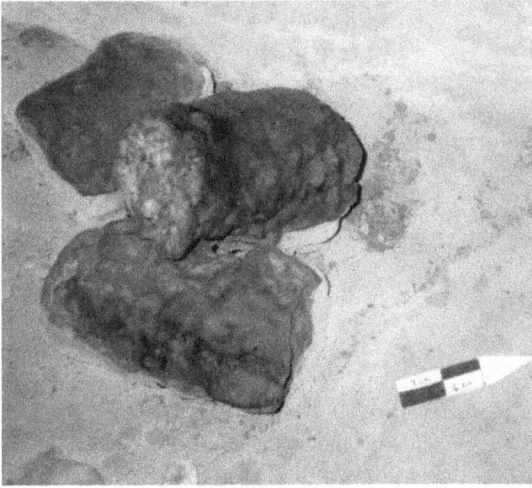

FIGURE 7.3. Top: Photograph of the three-speleothem cluster located in the center of the Main Chamber of Actun Tunichil Muknal. *Courtesy*, West Belize Regional Cave Project. Photograph by Holley Moyes, 1997. Bottom: Drawings of epigraphic depictions of the Three-Stone Hearth (Taube 1998: 433) (a) the green hearthstone place, Quirigua; (b) the Seibal emblem glyph, Tablet 4 of hieroglyphic stairway, Seibal; (c) three smoking hearthstones, Monument 74, Tonina; (d) one of a series of smoking hearthstones on headdress of ruler, detail of recently excavated stela, Tonina; (e) three stones with burning wood, Naranjo Stela 30; (f) smoking sky hearthstones with glyphs for Tikal Paddlers, Stela 16, Copan; (g) smoking hearthstones with sky ahau glyph, Stela 1, Salinas de los Nueve Cerros.

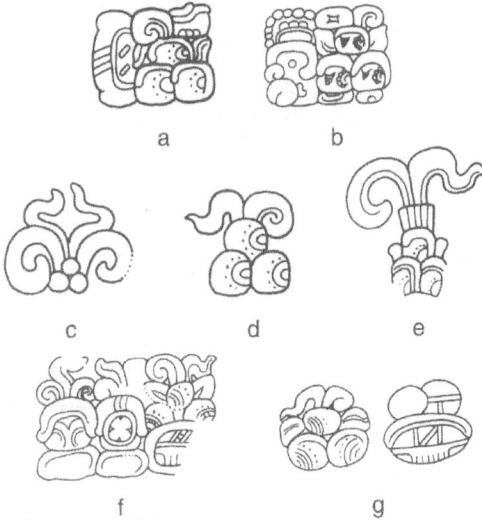

rest of the body (figure 7.6). The cranium exhibits modifications that consist of elongation and flattening of the forehead and tooth filing in the Romero-type A-2 style (Gibbs 2000: 105, figure 7). Because the skull could not possibly have rolled or been washed into this position, we tentatively suggest that the person may have been decapitated.

A large stalagmitic column dominates the central area approximately 3 m to the west of the three-speleothem cluster. Adjacent to the column is a dry calcite

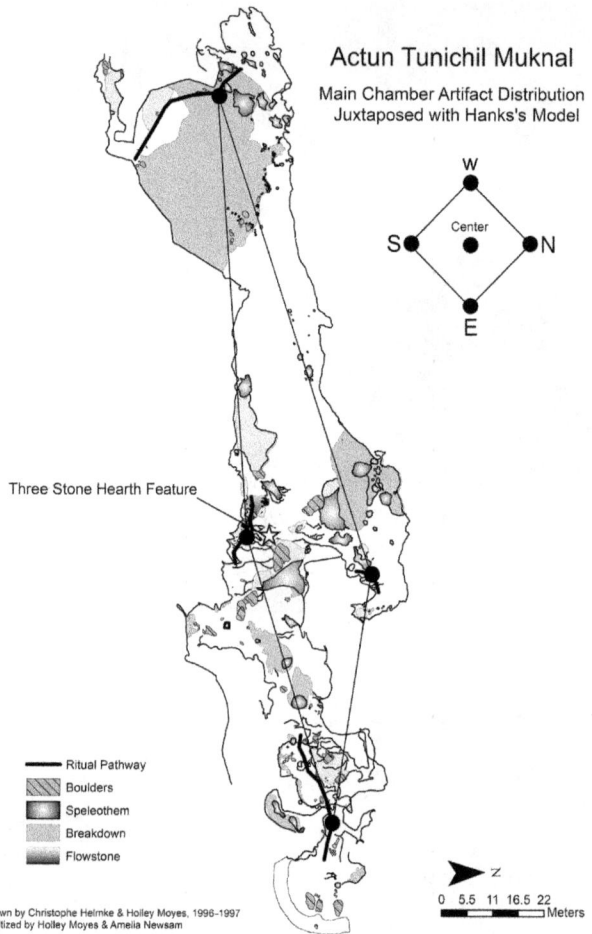

FIGURE 7.4. Ritual pathways juxtaposed with Hanks's model illustrate artifact pathways and Three-Stone Hearth feature (after Moyes 2001).

waterfall that cascades into a gour pool below as if frozen in time. Individual #2 and Individual #3 lie beneath the column in the intermittent pool, which fills with water during heavy rains. The two calcite-encrusted adult skeletons are identified as a male and a possible male (Gibbs 2000: 105; Lucero and Gibbs 2007: 57–58, table 3.3), though they were both originally thought to be male (Gibbs 1998: 76). The individuals were likely thirty to forty years old. One cranium exhibited modification and the other has tooth decoration in the Romero A-2 style, similar to Individual #1. The presence of an intact spinal column, the identification of most of the bones under the calcite, and their relative positions suggest that these were primary interments.

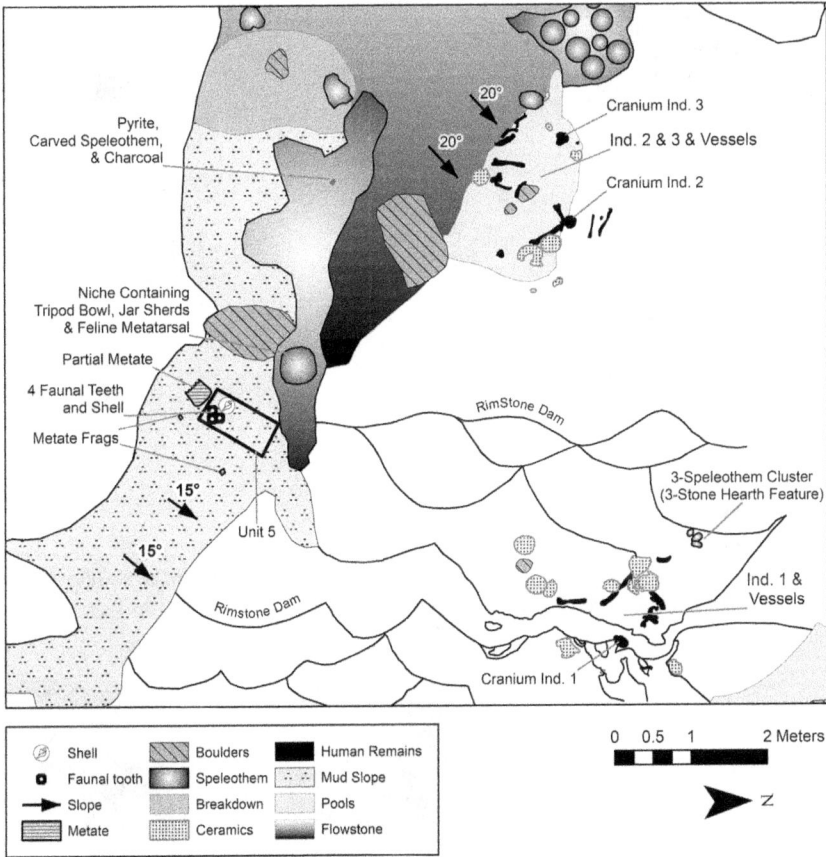

FIGURE 7.5. Close-up map of the central area of the Main Chamber of Actun Tunichil Muknal. *Courtesy*, Western Belize Regional Cave Project, digitized by Holley Moyes and Amelia Newsam.

Stalagmitic and stalacto-stalagmitic formations line the southern wall to the west. Sitting on a flattop rock in this area are a small carved unidentified speleothem object, a pyrite tessera from a mirror, a few small sherds, and a scatter of charcoal. The carved speleothem is rather odd but is similar to an object found at Petroglyph Cave, tentatively identified as a "labret" by Doris Jane Reents-Budet and Barbara MacLeod (1997: 67), though this is somewhat doubtful because the ornament is more common to Central Mexico. The Petroglyph Cave example was also found in association with a pyrite mirror. While the evidence is sparse, it is possible that

FIGURE 7.6. Photo of pool containing Individual #1, the remains of adult male located in the center of the Burial Chamber. The cranium lies on the rimstone dam on the east side. *Courtesy*, Western Belize Regional Cave Project. Photograph by Holley Moyes, 1997.

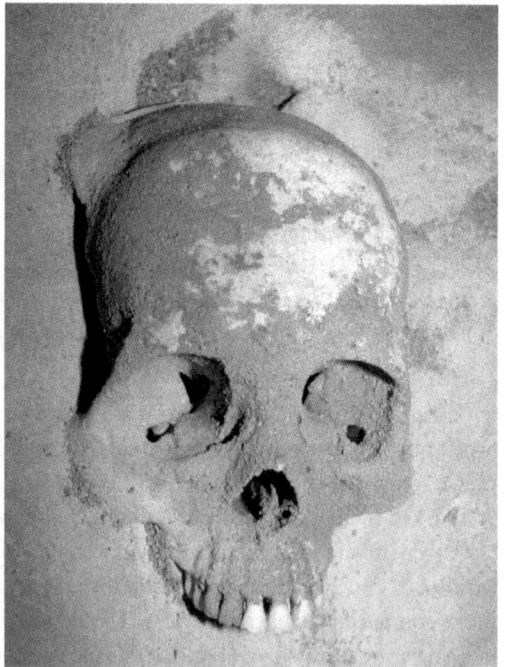

FIGURE 7.7. Close-up photograph of the cranium of Individual #1 showing tooth decoration and cranial modification. *Courtesy*, Western Belize Regional Cave Project. Photograph by Holley Moyes, 1997.

the objects were part of the mirror or in some way related to it. In his study of mirrors at Teotihuacan, Taube (1992a: 197) proposed that, among other things, mirrors were recognized as symbolic caves that represented passageways from which deities or ancestors communicated with the living. Mary Ellen Miller and Taube (1993: 114–15) later generalized that throughout Mesoamerica, mirrors or other reflective surfaces such as pools of water were used for divinatory scrying.

Cached within a niche in the same speleothem configuration were sherds from five vessels, including slipped and unslipped jars, as well as a jaguar metatarsal (Norbert Stanchley, personal communication, 1998). On top of the stack were the sherds from a large Late Classic Roaring Creek Red bowl with a highly polished orange/red slip, one of the most elaborate pieces found in the Main Chamber ceramic assemblage (figure 7.8). The bowl was missing three hollow feet, two of which were located on the floor of the niche underneath the stacked sherds. Decorating the hollow feet were air holes in the shape of crosses surrounded by an incised border. The feet could easily be refitted, so it was likely that the bowl was smashed in situ as part of a ritual.

Abutting the south wall of the cave is a pile of alluvium or mud that slopes from the cave wall to the floor at approximately 15 degrees. A concentration of charcoal was observed in the mud matrix, and artifacts were located on the floor along the edge of the mud/flowstone juncture. Located on the surface of the slope were half of a granite turtle-back *metate* and two broken feet from a basalt *metate*. Although the presence of *metates* could be suggestive of ritual food preparation, because they were broken and fragments were from different vessels, it is more likely that their function was strictly symbolic.

A 1 m × 0.5 m unit placed on the slope produced four animal teeth stuck into the surface of the mud along with a perforated oyster shell tinkler that may have been attached to an article of clothing and fifteen to twenty "soda straws" (incipient stalactites). The mud matrix also produced fifty Late Classic sherds (Griffith 1998; Moyes 2001: 22). The four teeth included two incisors and two molars. A root was missing from each molar and there were no perforations to suggest that they functioned as ornaments. Although it is not unusual to find animal teeth in cave deposits (for example, see Brady 1989: 383–91; Pendergast 1971: 85–109, 1974: 58, 72), there has been little analysis of their function or meaning. At Actun Polbiche (Pendergast 1974: 58, 72), one cache contained 466 dog teeth, many of which were perforated—indicating that they were used as adornments—but some were not. At Petroglyph Cave, twelve shells were carved into the shape of teeth (Reents-Budet and MacLeod 1997: 74–76). Caches of animal teeth were also found at Actun Koh in the Mountain Pine Ridge area of Belize. Animal and human teeth were found in Ofrendas Cave on the eastern drainage of the Macal River.

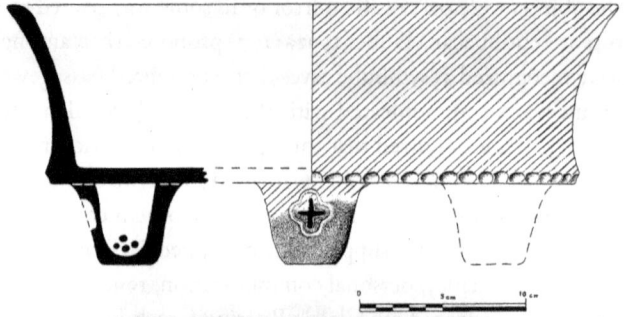

Orange/red tripod
bowl found cached
in a stalagmitic
formation on south
wall. *Courtesy*,
Western Belize
Regional Cave
Project. Drawing by
Christophe Helmke.

RE-CREATING CREATION

When viewed collectively, the artifacts and their contexts support a best-fit model
that suggests a ritual theme of the Maya creation events as reported in myth, Classic
period iconography, and texts. When we consider the context of the Main Chamber,
we can envision a group of ritual participants moving through the watery underworld on the long and sinuous walk to reach the entrance of the chamber deep
within the earth. This watery theme is sustained in the chamber itself, whose pools
fill during heavy rains, leaving crystalline calcite formations on the objects placed
within them as the water drains out. This is not the only cave in the Maya area to
exhibit these morphological features, but it is the best example of a watery entrance
and underground river leading to a wet chamber. This calls to mind the primordial
world when the sky lay in darkness on the waters, as well as the journey of the Hero
Twins into the depths of Xibalba. One could not ask for a more salient backdrop
for rites invoking creation events.

We argue that within the Main Chamber ritual, participants created a safe
space by demarking the boundaries of the chamber and identifying the center or
Three-Stone-Hearth-Place with three stacked speleothems. The central location of
Individual #1 adjacent to the Three-Stone Hearth feature suggests that the sacrifice

was intended to invoke the Maize God and his journey through the watery under-world to erect the World Tree. Individual #1 is likely to be a god impersonator, as evidenced by the physical characteristics, especially the elongation of the cranium. Taube (1985: 172–73) argued that the most striking physical feature of the Maize God was his elongated head and tonsured coiffure, suggestive of the maize cob. Although two other deities, God K and God D, possessed similar characteristics, God D was often paired with the Maize God and God K was identified with maize as well. In addition, because decapitation of the Maize God was a pervasive and well-known theme in ancient Maya mythology (Taube 1992b: 41–50; Miller and Taube 1993: 108–10; Miller and Martin 2004: 54–58, 72), if the victim was decapi-tated as we suspect, this would further bolster our argument.

In the same chamber only a few meters away are two individuals whose bones are commingled within a single gour pool, suggesting that they were dispatched together. Individuals #2 and #3 were arguably god impersonators representing Junajpu and Xb'alanke that were literally sacrificed in the underworld in a reenact-ment of the creation myth. One of these individuals has the elongated cranium of the Maize deity, and the other displays tooth filing in the same pattern as Individual #1. The sacrificial victims may have been chosen for this rite based on these superfi-cial body adornments, suggesting a symbolic familial relationship. All three of the individuals were accompanied by jar sherds and partially intact vessels placed adja-cent to their bodies within the same gour pools. Moyes, Awe, and their colleagues (2009) suggested elsewhere that jars found in caves were offerings for rain gods based on iconographic evidence that illustrate these deities pouring water from sim-ilar vessels. In this context, they were likely to have been employed symbolically to invoke rain as well as to refer to mythological concepts illustrated in Classic Maya iconography. For instance, on Kerr vessel 1892, the Maize deity is depicted as an anthropomorphic maize plant emerging from a cleft in the turtle eath. He is flanked by his sons Junajpu and Xb'alanke, who pour water on the scene in this agricultural metaphor (figure 7.9).

Recall that in the Popol Vuh story, following their immolation the Twins requested a divination by two seers as to the disposal of their bones. This is well represented by the pyrite mirror tersera cached within the speleothem niche. The presence of the *metate* fragments on the mud slope likely alludes to the grinding of the bones of the Hero Twins in the Popol Vuh. In the story, following their death in the fire pit, the bones of Junajpu and Xb'alanke are ground and cast into a river so they can be reborn. The story makes sense in terms of creation, birth, and rebirth when we consider that the grinding stone is considered to be the archetypal image of the female sexual organs (Tarn and Prechtel 1986: 177). This is also reported by Victoria Bricker (1973: 74), who noted that "grinding" not only refers to the making

FIGURE 7.9. Late Classic plate illustrating the emergence of the Maize deity from the turtle earth (Kerr vessel 1892). *Courtesy*, Justin Kerr.

of bread or tortillas but also means "to have sexual intercourse," which ties in well with the agricultural metaphor in the Hero Twins saga. When we consider that grinding stones are a sexual metaphor for conception (or in this case rebirth), it is easy to see why the ground bones should be cast into a river. The water is analogous to the womb, and the river may symbolize the water breaking before birth. It is hardly surprising that fertility and the woman's role in creation should be referenced as a symbol of cosmic renewal. As an agricultural metaphor, the Twins may be simultaneously viewed as analogs for the life cycle of corn, whose fate is to be ground. The story helps explain Landa's report that during Wayeb renewal rites, the drink given to the participants is made of burned maize that is ground and mixed with water (in Tozzer 1941: 141).

To begin to understand the presence of teeth on the mud slope, we turn to linguistics. In Yucatec Maya (Barrera Vásquez 2007: 323), the word for grain or tooth is *ko* or *koh*. It is used to describe corn kernels as in *koh ixi'im*, therefore teeth and corn grains are cognates for each other. This helps explain the story in the Popol Vuh saga in which the Hero Twins replace the missing teeth of the Principal Bird Deity, Wuqub' Kaqix (Seven Macaw), with corn kernels. The context of the teeth in the Burial Chamber may also be somewhat telling because they were placed in mud, suggesting that they were literally "planted," likely referring to the "planting" or underworld experience of Junajpu and Xb'alanke. This may even reference the ritual the Twins conduct before their descent into the underworld (Tedlock 1996: 116). Ears of corn are sown in their grandmother's house, and the health of the plants was to be a sign that the Twins were dead or alive. The sowing is done in a very special way, with the ears not planted under the ground but sown above the earth rather than in it. The context of the teeth placed on the ground on a mud slope suggests that what is being referenced is the "sowing" before the "dawning," a phrase often repeated in the Popol Vuh as an agricultural metaphor for the creation of the cosmos literally enacted in the ritual. Among the Mixe, "sowing" is also a metaphor for the act of sexual intercourse (Monaghan 1995: 115), which agrees well with the theme of creation, particularly that of humans. The use of *metate* fragments and teeth in the ritual was likely to have referenced elements from the Popol Vuh narrative in which the sacrificed Twins are reborn.

The large red dish cached on the south wall supports the theme of creation as well. The folk classification for this type of vessel is *hawa(n)te*, or wide dish (Houston et al. 1989: 722–23), and can be seen on Classic Maya vessels containing maize products (Taube 1989). In one vessel scene, a dish is used to carry the regalia of the Maize God and his decapitated head (Robicsek and Hales 1981: 201, plate 186). In addition to being used to contain maize products, these vessels may have also functioned as containers for implements of sacrifice or could have been used to carry blood-soaked paper resulting from bloodletting. Often emerging from the dish is the World Tree, which suggests to Freidel and his colleagues (1993: 215–18) that these types of vessels functioned as *ol*, or portals, to other worlds. The Tunichil vessel contained no discernible residue, which suggests that its function may have been primarily symbolic. The cross design of the feet is reminiscent of motifs from ceremonial *noh wah* tamales and Ch'orti' copal balls denoting the four cardinal directions (Taube 1988: 167; 1989: 45). The overall significance of the artifact suggests that it references the World Tree and cardinal directions radiating from the center of the cosmos, as well as the blood sacrifice necessary to create and maintain it. In light of Dennis Tedlock's (1996: 216) suggestion that bowls or plates may refer to the earth and sky, the Tunichil dish likely represents a miniature cosmos referencing the sacrifice of the Maize deity necessary for raising the World Tree and setting the cosmos in order.

DISCUSSION

Viewed as an integrated whole, the context and artifacts found at the center of the Main Chamber suggest a ritual theme of sacrifice and world renewal as elaborated in the Popol Vuh narrative supplemented by Classic period texts. We might imagine that this type of ritual was altogether lost. However, although we do not have direct evidence for the sacrifice of Maize God impersonators during the Classic period, both Fray Bartolomé de Las Casas (1967 [1550s]: II.clxxvii.149) and Ximénez (1929–30 [1722]: I.81–101) report a festival held by highland people prior to the Spanish Invasion in which the Maya creation myth as recounted in the Popol Vuh was reenacted. The great festival took place in a ballcourt and involved the king in the role of the Maize deity. The reenactment was the symbolic death of the gods and their confrontation of the Lords of the Underworld. In the rite, the king disappears and is considered to be symbolically in the underworld, leaving the earthly realm to be governed by the underworld gods who reign over the community during his absence, much like the present-day Mam or Maximon during Easter ceremonies in Santiago Atitlán. The king ultimately returns to the community, emerging out of the ballcourt with great glory, having defeated the death gods and restored order as a form of ritual renewal (Ximénez 1929–30 [1722]: I.85).

One must also consider the timing and ponder why such dramatic renewal rites occurred in the Late Classic period, most likely between 830 and 950 CE. We would be remiss not to note that an important period ending occurred during this narrow window. March 15, 830 CE, was the occasion of the ending of the ninth Bak'tun 10.0.0.0.0. 7 Ajaw 18 Sip, a calendrical event that would only occur every 400 years. The theme of creation would be an obvious choice for rituals concerned with the renewal of time, so rites conducted in the Main Chamber would have been good candidates for celebrating such an important period-ending rite.

CONCLUSION

Although we will never be able to venture back in time and witness the events that unfolded in the Main Chamber of Actun Tunichil Muknal, by considering multiple lines of evidence we can infer the ritual theme that is referenced in rites that remain obscure. The thematic approach in the analysis of cave data considers not only the artifacts themselves and their spatial contexts but also the morphology of the cave itself. Calendrical rites or rituals of renewal were certainly not the only

ceremonial activities conducted in caves, but when the evidence is viewed holisti-
cally, this body of rituals is the best fit for those carried out at the center of the
Main Chamber of Actun Tunichil Muknal, whose dark, watery environment was a
near-perfect underworld setting for reenactments of mythological creation events.
Our example from the Main Chamber also demonstrates that cave morphology
invited the opportunistic use of space and that natural venues served as real-world
stages for specialized ritual productions, enhancing the embodied experience for
participants and reifying the narrative enactment. In such a ritual performance,
myth emerges from its murky past to become a living, vibrant, and powerful force
that reasserts itself in the present.

ACKNOWLEDGMENTS

The Western Belize Regional Cave Project was funded by a grant from the Social
Science and Humanities Research Council of Canada to Dr. Jaime Awe. This chapter is based on work supported by National Science Foundation Grant no. DGE
9870668, Integrative Graduate Education and Research Training in Geographic
Information Science, awarded to Holley Moyes by the University at Buffalo. Moyes
also received personal support from the Ann Adams Scholarship Fund at Florida
Atlantic University. The permit for the project was provided to Dr. Jaime Awe by
the Belize Institute of Archaeology, and thanks go to Dr. John Morris, Dr. Allan
Moore, Brian Woodeye, George Thompson, and the institute's hardworking
staff. Special acknowledgment to the 1997 staff of the WBRCP—Sherry Gibbs,
Cameron Griffith, Christophe Helmke, Mike Mirro, Caitlin O'Grady, Vanessa
Owens, Rhanju Song, Jeff Ransom, and Kay Sunahara—as well as to our field sup-
port staff: Don Valentin Cu, Don Josè Mai, Don Ventura (El Tigre) Chi, Alfredo
Puc, Feliz Uck, and Albert Bradley.

REFERENCES CITED

Ackerman, Robert. 1975. "Frazer on Myth and Ritual." *Journal of the History of Ideas* 36:
115–34.

Ackerman, Robert. 1991. *The Myth and Ritual School: J. G. Frazer and the Cambridge
Ritualists*. Garland, New York.

Akkeren, Ruud van. 2003. "Authors of the Popol Vuh." *Ancient Mesoamerica* 14 (2): 237–56.

Aldenderfer, Mark S. 1987. "On the Structure of Archaeological Data." In *Quantitative
Research in Archaeology: Progress and Prospects*, ed. Mark S. Aldenderfer, 89–113. Sage,
Newberry Park, CA.

Awe, Jaime, Cameron S. Griffith, and Sherry A. Gibbs. 2005. "Stelae and Megalithic Monuments in the Caves of Western Belize." In *In the Maw of the Earth Monster: Mesoamerican Ritual Cave Use*, ed. James E. Brady and Keith M. Prufer, 403–11. University of Texas Press, Austin.

Barrera Vásquez, Alfredo. 2007. *Diccionario Maya Cordemex: Maya-Español, Español-Maya*. Quinta ed. Editorial Porrúa, Mérida, Yucatan, Mexico.

Bassie-Sweet, Karen. 1991. *From the Mouth of the Dark Cave: Commemorative Sculpture of the Late Classic Maya*. University of Oklahoma Press, Norman.

Brady, James E. 1988. "The Sexual Connotation of Caves in Mesoamerican Ideology." *Mexicon* 10 (3): 51–55.

Brady, James E. 1989. "Investigation of Maya Ritual Cave Use with Special Reference to Naj Tunich, Peten, Guatemala." PhD dissertation, University of California, Los Angeles.

Brady, James E., and Wendy Ashmore. 1999. "Mountains, Caves, Water: Ideational Landscapes of the Ancient Maya." In *Archaeologies of Landscapes: Contemporary Perspectives*, ed. Wendy Ashmore and A. Bernard Knapp, 124–45. Blackwell, Oxford.

Brady, James E., and Polly A. Peterson. 2008. "Re-envisioning Ancient Maya Ritual Assemblages." In *Religion, Archaeology, and the Material World*, ed. Lars Fogelin, 78–96. Center for Archaeological Investigations, Carbondale, IL.

Brady, James E., and Keith Prufer. 2005. "Maya Cave Archaeology: A New Look at Religion and Cosmology." In *Stone Houses and Earth Lords: Maya Religion in the Cave Context*, ed. Keith Prufer and James E. Brady, 365–80. University Press of Colorado, Boulder.

Bricker, Victoria Reifler. 1973. *Ritual Humor in Highland Chiapas*. University of Texas Press, Austin.

Bronk Ramsey, Christopher. 2009. "Bayesian Analysis of Radiocarbon Dates." *Radiocarbon* 51: 337–60.

Brown, Linda. 2000. "From Discard to Divination: Demarcating the Sacred through the Collection and Curation of Discarded Objects." *Latin American Antiquity* 11 (4): 319–33.

Brown, Linda. 2005. "Planting Bones: Hunting Ceremonialism at Contemporary and Nineteenth-Century Shrines in the Guatemalan Highlands." *Latin American Antiquity* 16 (2): 131–46.

Christenson, Allen J. 2007. *Popol Vuh—the Sacred Book of the Maya*. 2nd revised ed. University of Oklahoma Press, Norman.

Christenson, Allen J. 2008. "Places of Emergence: Sacred Mountains and Cofradía Ceremonies." In *Pre-Columbian Landscapes of Creation and Origin*, ed. John Edward Staller, 95–121. Springer, New York.

Coe, Michael D. 1989. "The Hero Twins: Myth and Images." In *The Maya Vase Book*, vol. 1, by Justin Kerr, 161–84. Kerr Associates, New York.

Donnan, Christopher B. 1975. "The Thematic Approach to Moche Iconography." *Journal of Latin American Lore* 1 (2): 147–62.

Earle, Duncan M. 1989. "The Dawning Place: Sacred Places from the 16th Century Documents and Their Use Today." Paper presented at the Annual Meetings of the American Society for Ethnohistory, November 2–5, Chicago, IL.

Earle, Duncan M. 2008. "Caves across Time and Space: Reading Related Landscapes in K'iche' Maya Text, Ritual, and History." In *Pre-Columbian Landscapes of Creation and Origin*, ed. John Edward Staller, 67–93. Springer, New York.

Eliade, Mircea. 1968 [1963]. *Myth and Reality*. 2nd ed. Harper and Row, New York.

Frazer, James George. 2003 [1st edition: 1890, 2 vols.; 1900, 3 vols.; 1911–15, 12 vols.]. *The Golden Bough*. Project Gutenberg. https://www.gutenberg.org/ebooks/3623, accessed June 7, 2021.

Freidel, David, Linda Schele, and Joy Parker. 1993. *Maya Cosmos: Three Thousand Years on the Shaman's Path*. William Morrow, New York.

García-Zambrano, Angel J. 1994. "Early Colonial Evidence of Pre-Columbian Rituals of Foundations." In *Seventh Palenque Round Table, 1989*, ed. Merle Greene Robertson and Virginia Fields, 217–27. Pre-Columbian Art Research Institute, San Francisco.

Gibbs, Sheryl A. 1998. "Skeletal Remains from Actun Tunichil Muknal and Actun Uayazba Kab, Cayo District, Belize." In *The Western Belize Regional Cave Project: A Report of the 1997 Field Season*, ed. Jaime J. Awe, 71–96. Department of Anthropology Occasional Paper 1. University of New Hampshire, Durham.

Gibbs, Sheryl A. 2000. "An Interpretation of Human Remains from the Caves of the Southern Maya Lowlands." MA thesis, Department of Anthropology, Trent University, Peterborough, Ontario, Canada.

Gifford, James C. 1976. *Prehistoric Pottery Analysis and the Ceramics of Barton Ramie in the Belize Valley*. Memoirs of the Peabody Museum of Archaeology and Ethnology 18. Harvard University, Cambridge, MA.

Griffith, Cameron S. 1998. "Excavations and Salvage Operations in Actun Tunichil Muknal and Actun Uayazba Kab, Roaring Creek Valley, Belize." In *The Western Belize Regional Cave Project: A Report of the 1997 Field Season*, ed. Jaime J. Awe, 39–70. Department of Anthropology Occasional Paper 1. University of New Hampshire, Durham.

Guernsey, Julia. 2006. *Ritual and Power in Stone: The Performance of Rulership in Mesoamerican Izapan Style Art*. University of Texas Press, Austin.

Hanks, William F. 1990. *Referential Practice: Language and Lived Space among the Maya*. University of Chicago Press, Chicago.

Hayden, Brian, and Aubrey Cannon. 1984. *The Structure of Material Systems: Ethnoarchaeology in the Maya Highlands*. Society for American Archaeology Occasional Papers 3. Society for American Archaeology, Washington, DC.

Helmke, Christophe G.B. 2009. "Ancient Maya Cave Use as Attested in the Glyphic Corpus of the Maya Lowlands and the Caves of the Roaring Creek Valley, Belize." PhD dissertation, University College of London, UK.

Helmke, Christophe G.B., and Jaime J. Awe. 1998. "Preliminary Analysis of the Pictographs, Petroglyphs, and Sculptures of Actun Uayazba Kab, Cayo District, Belize." In *The Western Belize Regional Cave Project: A Report of the 1997 Field Season*, ed. Jaime Awe, 141–99. Deptartment of Anthropology Occasional Paper 1. University of New Hampshire, Durham.

Helmke, Christophe G.B., Jaime J. Awe, and Cameron S. Griffith. 2003. "El arte rupestre de Belice." In *Arte rupestre de México oriental y Centro América*, ed. Martin Künne and Matthias Strecker, 97–117. Indiana Beihefte 16. Gebr. Mann Verlag, Berlin.

Houston, Stephen, David Stuart, and Karl A. Taube. 1989. "Folk Classifications of Classic Maya Pottery." *American Anthropologist* 91: 720–26.

Kluckholm, Clyde. 1942. "Myths and Rituals: A General Theory." *Harvard Theological Review* 35 (1): 45–79.

Knowlton, Timothy W. 2010. *Maya Creations Myths: Words and Worlds of the Chilam Balam*. University Press of Colorado, Boulder.

LaFarge, Oliver. 1947. *Santa Eulalia: The Religion of a Cuchumatan Indian Town*. University of Chicago Press, Chicago.

Las Casas, Fray Bartolomé de. 1967 [1550s]. *Apologética historia sumaria de las Indias*. 2 vols. Universidad National Autónoma de Mexico, Mexico City.

Leach, Edmond R. 1965. *Political Systems of Highland Burma*. Beacon, Boston.

Lucero, Lisa J., and Sheryl A. Gibbs. 2007. "The Creation and Sacrifice of Witches in Classic Maya Society." In *New Perspectives on Human Sacrifice and Ritual Body Treatments in Ancient Maya Society*, ed. Vera Tiesler and Andrea Cucina, 45–73. Springer, New York.

MacLeod, Barbara, and Dennis E. Puleston. 1978. "Pathways into Darkness: The Search for the Road to Xibalba." In *Tercera Mesa Redonda de Palenque*, vol. 4, ed. Merle Greene Robertson and Donnan Call Jeffers, 71–77. Hearld Peters, Monterey. Mesoweb, http://www.mesoweb.com/pari/publications/RT04/Pathways.html, accessed June 9, 2021.

Malinowski, Bronislaw. 1992 [1948]. *Magic, Science, and Religion and Other Essays*. Waveland, Prospect Heights, IL.

Miller, Mary Ellen, and Simon Martin. 2004. *Courtly Art of the Ancient Maya*. Thames and Hudson, London.

Miller, Mary Ellen, and Karl A. Taube. 1993. *The Gods and Symbols of Ancient Mexico and the Maya: An Illustrated Dictionary of Mesoamerican Religion*. Thames and Hudson, London.

Miller, Thomas. 1989. "Tunichil Muknal." *Caves and Caving* 46: 2–7.

Miller, Thomas. 1990. "Tunichil Muknal." *National Speleological Society News* 48 (2): 32–35.

Monaghan, John. 1995. *The Covenants with Earth and Rain*. University of Oklahoma Press, Norman.

Morehart, Christopher T. 2002a. "Ancient Maya Ritual Cave Utilization: A Paleoethnobotanical Perspective." Master's thesis, Florida State University, Gainesville.

Morehart, Christopher T. 2002b. "Plants of the Underworld: Ritual Plant Use in Ancient Maya Cave Ceremonies." Report submitted to the Foundation for the Advancement of Mesoamerican Studies, Inc.

Morehart, Christopher T. 2005. "Plants and Caves in Ancient Maya Society." In *Stone Houses and Earth Lords: Maya Religion in the Cave Context*, ed. Keith M. Prufer and James E. Brady, 167–86. University Press of Colorado, Boulder.

Moyes, Holley. 2001. "The Cave as a Cosmogram: A Spatial Analysis of Artifacts from Actun Tunichil Muknal Using GIS." MA thesis, Florida Atlantic University, Boca Raton.

Moyes, Holley. 2005. "Cluster Concentrations, Boundary Markers, and Ritual Pathways: A GIS Analysis of Artifact Cluster Patterns at Actun Tunichil Muknal, Belize." In *In the Maw of the Earth Monster: Mesoamerican Ritual Cave Use*, ed. James Brady and Keith Prufer, 269–300. University Press of Colorado, Boulder.

Moyes, Holley. 2006. "The Sacred Landscape as a Political Resource: A Case Study of Ancient Maya Cave Use at Chechem Ha Cave, Belize, Central America." PhD dissertation, State University of New York at Buffalo.

Moyes, Holley. 2012. "Constructing the Underworld: The Built Environment in Ancient Mesoamerican Caves." In *Heart of Earth: Studies in Maya Ritual Cave Use*, ed. James E. Brady, 95–110. Bulletin Series 23. Association for Mexican Cave Studies, Austin, TX.

Moyes, Holley. 2020. "Capturing the Forest: Ancient Maya Ritual Caves as Built Environments." In *Approaches to Monumental Landscapes of the Ancient Maya*, ed. Brett A. Houk, Barbara Arroyo, and Terry G. Powis, 313–34. University Press of Florida, Gainesville.

Moyes, Holley, and Jaime Awe. 1998. "Spatial Analysis of Artifacts in the Main Chamber of Actun Tunichil Muknal, Belize: Preliminary Results." In *The Western Belize Regional Cave Project: A Report of the 1997 Field Season*, ed. Jaime J. Awe, 22–38. Department of Anthropology Occasional Paper 1. University of New Hampshire, Durham.

Moyes, Holley, and Jaime J. Awe. 1999. "Ritual Pathways in the Underworld." Paper presented at the New Directions in Field Research in Maya Cave Studies Symposium, 64th Annual Meeting of the Society for American Archaeology, Chicago, April.

Moyes, Holley, Jaime J. Awe, George Brook, and James Webster. 2009. "The Ancient Maya Drought Cult: Late Classic Cave Use in Belize." *Latin American Antiquity* 20 (1): 175–206.

Moyes, Holley, and James E. Brady. 2005. "The Heart of Creation, the Heart of Darkness: Ritual Cave Use in Mesoamerica." *Expedition* 47 (3): 30–36.

Moyes, Holley, and James E. Brady. 2012. "Caves as Sacred Space in Mesoamerica." In *Sacred Darkness: A Global Perspective on the Ritual Use of Caves*, ed. Holley Moyes, 151–70. University Press of Colorado, Boulder.

Moyes, Holley, and Sheryl A. Gibbs. 2000. "Sacrifice in the Underworld: The Human Remains from Actun Tunichil Muknal, an Ancient Maya Cave Site in Western Belize." Paper presented at the 99th Annual Meeting of the American Anthropological Association, San Francisco, November 15–19, 2000.

Moyes, Holley, and Keith M. Prufer. 2013. "The Geopolitics of Emerging Maya Rulers: A Case Study of Kayuko Naj Tunich, a Foundational Shrine at Uxbenká, Southern Belize." *Journal of Anthropological Research* 69 (2): 225–48.

Nagy, Gregory. 2002. "Can Myth Be Saved?" In *Myth: A New Symposium*, ed. Gregory A. Schrempp and William F. Hansen, 240–48. University of Indiana Press, Bloomington.

Nicholson, Henry B. 1976. "Preclassic Mesoamerican Iconography." In *Origins of Religious Art and Iconography in Preclassic Mesoamerica*, ed. Henry B. Nicholson, 159–81. UCLA Latin American Center Publications, Los Angeles.

Nielsen, Jesper, and James E. Brady. 2006. "The Couple in the Cave: Origin Iconography on a Ceramic Vessel from Los Naranjos, Honduras." *Ancient Mesoamerica* 17 (2): 203–17.

Pendergast, David M. 1971. *Excavations at Eduardo Quiroz Cave, British Honduras*. Art and Archaeology Occasional Papers 21. Royal Ontario Museum, Toronto.

Pendergast, David M. 1974. *Excavations at Actun Polbilche, Belize*. Royal Ontario Museum, Toronto.

Pendergast, David M. 1982. *Excavations at Altun Ha, Belize, 1964–1970*, vol. 2. Royal Ontario Museum, Toronto.

Penner, Hans H. 1968. "Myth and Ritual: A Wasteland or a Forest of Symbols?" *History and Theory* 8, Beiheft 8 (On Method in the History of Religions): 46–57.

Petryshyn, Von Jarslaw Theodore. 2005. Trans. and ed. Pierre Robert Colas. "A Lacandon Religious Ritual in the Cave of the God Tsibanà at the Holy Lake of Mensabok in the Rainforest of Chiapas." In *In the Maw of the Earth Monster: Mesoamerican Ritual Cave Use*, ed. James Brady and Keith Prufer, 328–41. University Press of Colorado, Boulder.

Pohl, Mary. 1981. "Ritual Continuity and Transformation in Mesoamerica: Reconstructing the Ancient Maya Cuch Ritual." *American Antiquity* 46: 513–29.

Pohl, Mary. 1983. "Maya Ritual Faunas: Vertebrate Remains from Burials, Caches, Caves, and Cenotes in the Maya Lowlands." In *Civilization in Ancient America: Essays in Honor of Gordon R. Willey*, ed. Richard Leventhal and Alan L. Kolata, 55–103. University of New Mexico Press and Peabody Museum, Harvard University, Albuquerque, NM, and Cambridge, MA.

Pohl, Mary, and John Pohl. 1983. "Ancient Maya Cave Ritual." *Archaeology* 36 (3): 28–51.

Prechtel, Martin, and Robert Carlsen. 1988. "Weaving and Cosmos amongst the Tzutujil Maya of Guatemala." *RES—Anthropology and Aesthetics* 15: 123–32.

Redfield, R., and Alfonso Villa Rojas. 1962 [1934]. *Chan Kom: A Maya Village*. University of Chicago Press, Chicago.

Reents-Budet, Doris Jane, and Barbara MacLeod. 1997. "The Archaeology of Petroglyph Cave, Cayo District, Belize." Unpublished manuscript, on file at the Department of Archaeology, Belize.

Reimer, Paula J., Edouard Bard, Alex Bayliss, J. Warren Beck, Paul G. Blackwell, Christopher Bronk Ramsey, Caitlin E. Buck, Hai Cheng, R. Lawrence Edwards, Michael Friedrich, Pieter M. Grootes, Thomas P. Guilderson, Haflidi Haflidason, Irka Hajdas, Christine Hatté, Timothy J. Heaton, Dirk L. Hoffmann, Alan G. Hogg, Konrad A. Hughen, K. Felix Kaiser, Bernd Kromer, Sturt W. Manning, Mu Niu, Ron W. Reimer, David A. Richards, E. Marian Scott, John R. Southon, Richard A. Staff, Christian S.M. Turney, and Johannes van der Plicht. 2013. "Intcal13 and Marine13 Radiocarbon Age Calibration Curves 0–50,000 Years Cal BP." *Radiocarbon* 55: 1869–87.

Rissolo, Dominique. 2005. "Beneath the Yalahau: Emerging Patterns of Ancient Maya Ritual Cave Use from Northern Quintana Roo, Mexico." In *In the Maw of the Earth Monster: Mesoamerican Ritual Cave Use*, ed. James E. Brady and Keith M. Prufer, 342–72. University of Texas Press, Austin.

Robicsek, Francis, and Donald Hales. 1981. *The Maya Book of the Dead: The Ceramic Codex*. University of Virginia Art Museum, Charlottesville.

Schávelzon, Daniel. 1980. "Temples, Caves, or Monsters? Notes on Zoomorphic Facades in Pre-Hispanic Architecture." In *Third Palenque Round Table, 1978, Part 2*, ed. Merle G. Robertson, 151–62. University of Texas Press, Austin.

Segal, Robert A. 2006. "Myth and Ritual." In *Theorizing Rituals: Issues, Topics, Approaches, Concepts*, ed. Jens Kreinath, Jan Snoek, and Michael Strasberg, 101–22. Brill, Boston.

Segal, Robert A. 2010. "Myth and Ritual." In *The Routledge Companion to the Study of Religion*, 2nd ed., ed. John Hinnells, 373–96. Routledge, New York.

Smith, A. Ledyard. 1955. *Archaeological Reconnaissance in Central Guatemala*. Publication 608. Carnegie Institution of Washington, Washington, DC.

Smith, William Robertson. 1969 [1889]. *Lectures on the Religion of the Semites: The Fundamental Institutions*. Ktav Publishing House, New York.

Sosa, John R. 1985. "The Maya Sky, the Maya World: A Symbolic Analysis of Yucatec Maya Cosmology." PhD dissertation, State University of New York at Albany.

Stone, Andrea J. 1995. *Images of the Underworld: Naj Tunich and the Tradition of Maya Cave Painting*. University of Texas Press, Austin.

Stone, Andrea J. 2005. "Scribes and Caves in the Maya Lowlands." In *In Stone Houses and Earth Lords: Maya Religion in the Cave Context*, ed. Keith M. Prufer and James E. Brady, 135–66. University Press of Colorado, Boulder.

Tarn, Nathaniel, and Martin Prechtel. 1986. "Constant Inconstancy: The Feminine Principle in Atiteco Mythology." In *Symbol and Meaning beyond the Closed Community: Essays in Mesoamerican Ideas*, ed. Gary Gossen, 173–84. Studies on Culture and Society 1. Institute for Mesoamerican Studies, State University of New York, Albany.

Taube, Karl A. 1985. "The Classic Maya Maize God: A Reappraisal." In *Fifth Palenque Round Table (1983)*, vol. 7, ed. Merle Greene Robertson and Virginia Fields, 171–81. Pre-Columbian Art Research Institute, San Francisco.

Taube, Karl A. 1988. "The Ancient Yucatec New Year Festival: The Liminal Period in Maya Ritual and Cosmology." Vols. 1–2. PhD dissertation, Yale University, New Haven, CT.

Taube, Karl A. 1989. "The Maize Tamale, Wah, in Classic Maya Epigraphy and Art." *American Antiquity* 54 (1): 31–51.

Taube, Karl A. 1992a. "The Iconography of Mirrors at Teotihuacan." In *Art, Ideology, and the City of Teotihuacan*, ed. Janet Berlo, 169–203. Dumbarton Oaks, Washington, DC.

Taube, Karl A. 1992b. *The Major Gods of Ancient Yucatan*. Studies in Pre-Columbian Art and Archaeology 32. Dumbarton Oaks, Washington, DC.

Taube, Karl A. 1993. *Aztec and Maya Myths*. University of Texas Press, Austin.

Taube, Karl A. 1998. "The Jade Hearth: Centrality, Rulership, and the Classic Maya Temple." In *Function and Meaning in Classic Maya Architecture*, ed. Stephen D. Houston, 427–78. Dumbarton Oaks, Washington, DC.

Taube, Karl A. 2004. "Flower Mountain: Concepts of Life, Beauty, and Paradise among the Classic Maya." *RES—Anthropology and Aesthetics* 45: 69–98.

Tedlock, Barbara. 1992. *Time and the Highland Maya*. 2nd revised ed. University of New Mexico Press, Albuquerque.

Tedlock, Dennis. 1996 [1985]. *Popol Vuh: The Definite Edition of the Mayan Book of the Dawn of Life and the Glories of Gods and Kings*. 2nd revised ed. Simon and Schuster, New York.

Tedlock, Dennis. n.d. "The Sowing and Dawning of All the Sky-Earth: Astronomy in the Popol Vuh." Unpublished manuscript in the author's possession.

Thompson, J. Eric S. 1975. "Introduction to the Reprint Edition." In *The Hill-Caves of Yucatan*, by Henry Mercer, vii–xliv. University of Oklahoma Press, Norman.

Tozzer, Alfred M. 1907. *Comparative Study of the Mayas and Lacandones*. Archaeological Institute of America. Macmillan, London.

Tozzer, Alfred M. 1941. *Landa's Relación de las cosas de Yucatán: A Translation*. Papers of the Peabody Museum of American Archaeology and Ethnology 18, Harvard University 18. Peabody Museum, Cambridge, MA.

Turner, Victor. 1982. *From Ritual to Theatre: The Human Seriousness of Play*. Performing Arts Journal Publications, New York.

Vogt, Evon Z. 1998. "Zinacanteco Dedication and Termination Rituals." In *The Sowing and the Dawning: Termination, Dedication, and Transformation in the Archaeological Record of Mesoamerica*, ed. Shirley Mock, 21–30. University of New Mexico Press, Albuquerque.

Vogt, Evon Z., and David Stuart. 2005. "Some Notes on Ritual Caves among the Ancient and Modern Maya." In *In the Maw of the Earth Monster: Mesoamerican Ritual Cave Use*, ed. James E. Brady and Keith M. Prufer, 155–85. University of Texas Press, Austin.

Willey, Gordon R. 1973. "Certain Aspects of the Late Classic to Postclassic Periods in the Belize Valley." In *The Classic Maya Collapse*, ed. T. Patrick Culbert, 93–103. University of New Mexico Press, Albuquerque.

Ximénez, Fr. Francisco. 1929–30 [1722]. *Historia de la provincia de San Vicente de Chiapa y Guatemala*. Biblioteca "Goathemala" de la Sociedad de Georgrafía e Historia de Guatemala Publication 1. 3 Vols. Guatemala Tipografía Nacional, Guatemala City.

PART 3

*Comprehending Classic Maya Art and
Writing through the Myths of the Popol Vuh*

8

The Transmutation of Sustenance

A Narrative of Perennial Reciprocity on Classic Maya Codex-Style Ceramics

BARBARA MACLEOD

Only a tiny fraction of the total Underworld mythic cycle that was extant in Classic times survived the Spanish Conquest, to be recorded in Spanish letters; most of what we have is in the first three sections of the Popol Vuh of the Quiché Maya, and the authors have followed others in finding this a productive (however incomplete) source for their interpretations.

MICHAEL D. COE 1981

PROLOGUE

For decades since the publication of Michael D. Coe's *The Maya Scribe and His World* (1973) and *Lords of the Underworld* (1978), Maya scholars have known that certain narratives in the K'iche' Popol Vuh were rooted in Classic Maya mythology, with antecedents depicted on elite ceramics found in royal tombs. As Coe also observed, amid these myriad scenes, one glimpses other myths—or other chapters and subplots of a great monomyth—that did not survive into modern oral tradition and preservation as did the Popol Vuh. One of these is the story of the Baby Jaguar and its companion narrative, that of the Dragon Lady or Snake Lady (figure 8.1a, b: K5164 and K2208; Robicsek and Hales 1981; figure 8.2: K1815).

Francis Robicsek and Donald Hales (1981) demonstrated that the Baby Jaguar and Snake Lady ceramic constellations were linked by a shared hieroglyphic statement now known to be a nominal phrase. For the time being, I will call it "Seven Vase," while the figure captions will give its suggested reading and translation. It has

DOI: 10.5876/9781646421992.c008

FIGURE 8.1. (a) The Snake Lady conjures the Old God/Serpent. The text reads (13 Muluk 17 Pax) *sihyaj Huk Pul Tzin Yax Kaan U-Mam Ahk* "is born Seven Provider of Sustenance First Snake, Ancestor/Grandfather of the Turtle" (K5164). (b) The Death God throws the Baby Jaguar into the mountain, which Chahk has split with his axe. The text reads (7 Kib 4 K'anasiy/K'ayab) *nut'il? tzahkaj K'awiil Huk Pul Tzin Yax Kaan Chak ??* "at twilight? is conjured K'awiil Seven Provider of Sustenance First Snake, Great ??" (K2208).

FIGURE 8.2. *Nut'il? yahlaj K'awiil Chatan* "at twilight? is thrown (the) K'awiil (of) Chatan" (K1815).

begged for decipherment because the two scenes under consideration display a fascinating and deeply esoteric narrative accompanied by Calendar Round dates. These manifest a tail-chasing complementary opposition, and the occasional conflations

FIGURE 8.3. The jaguar-paw tree with the Rain God, the Death God, the Baby Jaguar, and the Old God/Serpent. The text reads yala(w) Huk Pul Tzin "he throws the Baby Jaguar" (K4013).

(K4013, figure 8.3) show that they are intertwined. The accompanying dates, half of which are nonstandard, are not particularly helpful; and when their authenticity can be verified, they themselves are suggestive of primordial, nonlinear time.

My interest in these vases was kindled by an unpublished 2005 paper by Nicholas Carter (n.d.)—then a student of David Stuart; his epigraphic methodology was exacting, and our subsequent conversations motivated me to investigate the texts from a linguistic perspective. A collaboration between Michel Quenon and myself began in 2011 when he shared a hitherto unknown and remarkable vase—to be discussed shortly—that brought me back to the grammatical and iconographic challenge represented by these texts. In 2012, Penny Steinbach and I undertook a new collaboration that has further aided my understanding of Codex-Style iconography. Following the contributions of Coe and Robicsek and Hales, many investigators (Alexander, Boot, Carrasco, Carter, García Barrios, García Capistrán, Grube, Kerr and Kerr, Lopes, Martin, Reents-Budet, Steinbach, Stone, Stuart, Taube, Valencia Rivera, and Velásquez García) have tackled this fascinating Classic Maya narrative. Much of this myth remains beyond our ken, and any glance sideways from its canon reveals new actors in related stories or familiar actors in new stories. A central goal of my chapter will be—after having animated the chosen tableaux—to read the nominal phrase they share and to consider its implications.

The Maya polity known in ancient times as Kaan, or the Snake Kingdom, was the locus of production of an exquisite black- or brown-on-cream ceramic painting tradition first termed by Coe "Codex Style" due to stylistic similarities with Postclassic screenfold books (Reents-Budet et al. 2010). One must assume that the Baby Jaguar and Snake Lady narratives were of paramount importance to the elite of the Kaan polity, given their prevalence in the Codex-Style corpus.

Attempts to reconcile the Calendar Rounds have been fraught with challenges. While a number of them are Type III or standard CRs, just as many are not, and some are effaced or repainted. The Calendar Rounds merit a study of their own and will not be considered in depth here, but one can immediately observe the frequent pairing of Kib with K'ayab on the Baby Jaguar vases and of Muluk with Pax on the Snake Lady vases. Problematic calendrics and other interpretive problems are complicated by overpainting on the part of subliterate twentieth-century restorers, but it is still often possible, per Penny Steinbach, Justin Kerr, and Dorie Reents-Budet (personal communication, 2013), to distinguish the restoration from the original. I study these texts trusting their expertise.

A PLAY IN TWO ACTS

The two pieces seen in figure 8.1a and 8.1b have much stylistic commonality, and Reents-Budet (personal communication, 2012) thinks they are from the same workshop. They have Calendar Rounds only seven days apart—with the Snake Lady vase's CR date preceding that of the Baby Jaguar vase—but given the range of dates among all these vases, I offer this with caution. The common presence of seven as both the day and month coefficient may allude to the Jaguar God of the Underworld (JGU), as may the "seven" prefixed to the elusive nominal phrase shared by both sets of vases. The head variant of seven is the JGU. Ana García Barrios and Rogelio Valencia Rivera (2011: 73) argue that the frequent occurrence of the month Pa'ax (Pax) in the CRs of Snake Lady vessels (cf. K1813, K6754, K1081, K3702, K4485, K5230, K7838) reflects the role of one of the bundled gods in these scenes: the "Pax God," or Te'. I concur, for reasons to be discussed, but I question their proposition that the "Seven Vase" nominal phrase directly names this bundled god.

In the Baby Jaguar scene (figures 8.1b–8.5 and others to follow), the Death God (God A) throws the infant anthropomorphic jaguar into a cleft in a mountain (*witz* in the Classic language) while the First-Rains Rain God Yax Ha'al Chahk—who has split the *witz* with his lightning axe and his stone knuckle-duster—dances (see Taube and Zender 2009: 180–94 for a discussion of such weapons). Although the suggestion recurs that Chahk bashes the baby with his axe, Justin Kerr (1992) long ago identified the role of Chahk's weapon as the creator of the cleft—a function that, as we will see, underlies the ubiquitous *kaloomte'* title of kings. Extrusions from the mountain have mirrors in the forehead, serpent-skin patterns, fiery vegetal foliation, and belly plates. The infant is once replaced by an adult jaguar (K1152). The transitive verb—whose root is *yal* "throw"—is spelled *yalaw* either logographically

FIGURE 8.4. *Yalaw K'awiil Huk Pul Tzin Yax Kaan Chak ?? Chatan winik* "he throws K'awiil Seven Provider of Sustenance First Snake, Great ??, the Chatan person" (K521).

FIGURE 8.5. *Yalaw K'awiil* "he throws K'awiil" (K1003). Note his tail and the "cruller" of the JGU on the face of the Baby Jaguar.

or syllabically, and it is followed by the nominal phrase and/or other nouns as its object; thus "he (the Death God) throws the Baby Jaguar." The infant may have the "cruller" of the JGU (see figures 8.1b, 8.3) and thus is an aspect of him. The mountain is often surrounded by froth or foam represented as swirling dots or a thin mist-like wash at the bottom register. There are other Codex-Style settings with multiple protagonists who are waist-deep in this liquid; all evidence suggests that it is water (see Robicsek and Hales 1981, vessels 73–107). Forest animals may accompany these scenes; thus the setting has been considered a mountain amid a Primordial Sea, or as suggested by Valencia Rivera and Hugo García Capistrán (2013), Tamoanchan—a misty pan-Mesoamerican place of creation associated with the birth of maize. While theirs is an important frontier of inquiry, I have chosen a narrower focus and will generally restrict ethnohistorical comparisons to portions of the Popol Vuh.

We will find clues that the story of the defeat of Seven Macaw in the Popol Vuh (Christenson 2007: 78–88) is presaged in the tale of the Baby Jaguar. A tree rises

FIGURE 8.6. The Blowgunner Vase: Jun Ajaw shoots the Principal Bird Deity in the jaguar-paw tree (K1226).

from the cleft in the *witz* as the Baby Jaguar falls (see figures 8.2, 8.3). That of K4013 is almost identical to the tree found on the famous Blowgunner Vase; there, as first noted by Karl A. Taube (1993: 64–66), the Hero Twin Jun Ajaw shoots the Principal Bird Deity as he perches in it (figure 8.6; see also K1345 and K4546 for other examples). Evidence for this identity is seen in the TE' trunk icon with its jaguar-paw ear, shared by both trees. The branches and pinnate compound leaves of these trees are much alike as well and suggest the bottle-gourd tree, *Crescentia cujete* (independently suggested by Helmke 2013, figure 5), although David Stuart (2007) regards it as a *ceiba*. Taking into account the San Bartolo murals (Taube et al. 2010), where the penis bloodletting of Jun Ajaw and altars with animal offerings appear before various trees with fruit or pods and the central tree has the same leaves as above, one may posit via this tree that the Baby Jaguar sacrifice is part of a primordial creation event—a tenet of the charter for the origins and relations between gods—in the story, which later relates the defeat of a vainglorious impostor. But at San Bartolo, the bird deity was revered.

Michael Coe first proposed that the Baby Jaguar on the Metropolitan Vase (K521; see figure 8.4) has an antecedent in the infant "were-jaguar" in Olmec iconography. This is due not only to the conflation of human and feline characteristics but to the infant body form and postures seen in both and in the ways these infants are held or touched by adults. While Coe's proposal has been reconsidered by Simon Martin (2002), the "were-jaguar" identity has been disputed in recent years in favor of an ophidian or human embryonic identification (Kent Reilly, personal communication, 2014; Tate 2012: 35–58). Martin notes the presence of a name read Unen Bahlam "baby jaguar" at Early Classic Tikal and Naranjo, which suggests that it was a local patron god and source name for historical individuals. This elevates it above the status of a simple infant sacrifice. Various scholars have noted the range of conflation along a human/feline continuum as well as the *k'awiil* "torch/flame" icon occasionally appended to the infant's tail. The texts inform us that this being is a manifestation of *k'awiil*: lightning, life force, and sustenance.

In the Snake Lady narrative (figures 8.7–8.13, also see figure 8.1a; includes a related conjuring in figure 8.9), set in a temple sanctuary (likely underground per Steinbach [personal communication, 2014]) with a dais and curtains, an aged god appears in the open maw of a being first termed "the Bearded Dragon" (Coe 1975: 19)—a fantastic bearded serpent who is the foot of the god K'awiil. The serpent, whose snout often bears the same mirror motif seen on the animate *witz*, coils around the body of a buxom, lovely, topless young goddess occasionally named as his conjurer, while he is named as her child. The stage is charged with erotic tension as K'awiil and the Old God appear to vie for the lady's favors. The old fellow touches her breasts or offers her a cup or clyster. Her skirt is a leaf whose identity will be explored. In some examples (see figures 8.7b, 8.10, 8.11), two tightly bundled deities, Chahk and the "Pax God" (as a hieroglyph, read TE' "tree"), appear on a dais. The associated texts are often brief and feature the verb *sihyaj* "is born," but investigators disagree about whose birth is referenced. I hope to resolve this question through syntactic analysis of selected texts. I understand the action on these vases to be conjuring (a ritual birth), a spiritual mating, and the ensouling of deity bundles. It is a locus for the source (leaf skirt) and ingestion (cups, clysters) of a psychotropic substance. One notes the presence of human attendants who, seemingly intoxicated, appear transported into an archaic myth. I view their insertion as a storyteller's device that contextualizes the story in contemporary Classic culture. Also pertinent is a manuscript by Helen Alexander (n.d.), who notes the frequent association of God K (K'awiil) with conjuring, drinking, and enemas. Various authors have noted that the Snake Lady scenes suggest visionary states.

Michael Coe (1978: 12) has said that "to attempt to find order in the multiplicity of deities on Maya vases is no mean task." The body of prior scholarship (e.g., Lopes 2005; Carter 2005; García Barrios and Valencia Rivera 2011; Valencia Rivera and García Capistrán 2013; Steinbach 2015b) reflects a range of views regarding the protagonists. I can affirm that these texts have complete grammatical integrity, which facilitates identification of the actors and their roles. Now let's move into the play.

THE BABY JAGUAR, THE DEATH GOD, AND THE RAIN GOD

K1003 (see figure 8.5) sets the stage. Following the CR, the text reads ya-YAL-wa K'AWIL-la *yalaw K'awiil* "he throws K'awiil." The simplest texts help to align names with protagonists. "He" is the Death God (God A) with bony arms extended, gleefully tossing the Baby Jaguar down on an extrusion from the mountain, itself a living being as cued by the T58: 533 SAK BAK "vitality" phrase affixed to its forehead. Yax Ha'al Chahk, having cracked the mountain with his axe, dances back wearing

FIGURE 8.7. (a) The Snake Lady, K'awiil, and the Old God/Serpent (K3202). (b) The partially effaced Snake Lady, K'awiil, the Old God/Serpent, and the awakening effigies (K3716).

FIGURE 8.8. *Sihyaj Huk Pul Tzin* "is born the Old God/Serpent" (K5230).

a vase-with-snake pendant. A naturalistic snake—a portent of the companion act—slides from the heart of the mountain as a sapling sprouts from its summit. The jaguar-tailed baby has the cruller eye of the Jaguar God of the Underworld. The animate extrusion is the mirrored serpent of the Snake Lady scenes, here in nascent

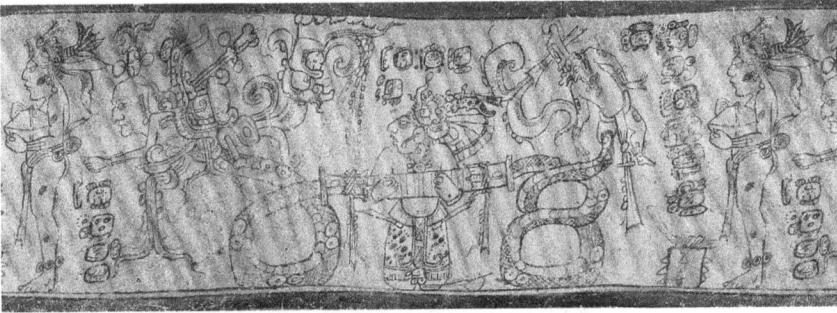

FIGURE 8.9. *U-bah K'awiil Huk Pul Tzin Yax Kaan* "it is his image, K'awiil the Old God/ Serpent First Snake" (K4114).

FIGURE 8.10. *Sihyaj Yuk Ha' Kabal Chahk Huk Pul Tzin* "is born Shakes-Water-and-Earth Chahk (and) the Old God/Serpent" (K6754).

FIGURE 8.11. *Sihyaj Yuk Ha' Kabal [Chahk Huk Pul Tzin]* "is born Shakes-Water-and-Earth [Chahk (and) the Old God/Serpent]" (K4485).

form, with belly plates. The Waterlily Jaguar attends the scene wearing a vomit bib. The Cholan root *yal* "throw" is represented by a logogram YAL; it is never read CH'AM "receive" in this context. I translate *yalaw* as "he throws him," but here—as

FIGURE 8.12. *Sihyaj Yuk Ha' Kabal [Chahk] Huk Pul Tzin [Yax Kaan]* "is born Shakes-Water-and-Earth [Chahk] (and) the Old God/Serpent [First Snake]" (K3702).

FIGURE 8.13. *Leem Uk' Kaan* "Shining Drink Snake"; *Ixik Yal Kopeem Ixik Kamay* "Lady of the Winder's Child, Lady Kamay" (K2067).

with almost all examples—we have ergative extraction, a focusing strategy in transitive sentences in a few Mayan languages (predominantly Yucatec in modern times) wherein the ergative pronoun is deleted. Here it highlights the Death God without his syntactic inclusion. The possibility also exists that this is an antipassive construction. The normal transitive form of the verb would be *u-yalaw-o* "he throws it/him," and occasional examples occur with the ergative pronoun (K4056, not illustrated).

K'awiil is the lightning axe of Chahk—the thunderbolt, the raw, sacred power of nature wielded by gods, mediated by ancestors, received by living diviners and curers. This power is symbolized by a fiery torch or an axe blade bursting from a flashing mirror in the head of a theomorphic, snake-footed being—one we will meet often in these pages. The flames of K'awiil's torch often have a vegetal aspect, containing clusters or lines of maize kernels, as in the lovely K'awiil portraits of K5071. Apart from its embodiment in K'awiil the god (capitalized and not italicized), *k'awiil* is lightning and the primal source of fire. It is a cultural analog of lightning; it is plant fertility and life essence. This lightning is a lineage-based augural current that leaps in the blood of a modern K'iche' daykeeper (Tedlock 1982: 133–47). As Allen J. Christenson (2007: 60–61n65) states:

> These three gods comprise the powers of the sky, symbolized by various aspects of the thunderbolt. Thunderstorms combine the elements of water (rain) and fire (lightning), which the K'iche' see as essential to all life. Lightning is also considered the force that fertilizes the earth and promotes the growth of crops. In modern K'iche' society, lightning is believed to be the inspirational force of the sky. Modern *aj q'ij* priests take note of sensations within their bodies, which they call "lightning in the blood," and interpret them as revelatory messages.

Significantly, in Colonial Yucatec Maya (Roys 1967: 127), *kauil* (*k'awiil*) was an obsolete term for bread or food. J. Eric S. Thompson (1960: 286) believed the name of the Maize God in Yucatan to have been Ah Uaxac Yol Kauil ("He, Eight Heart of K'awiil"); he also states that *kauil* (*k'awiil*) was appended to the name of any deity considered a provider of food. This will find resonance in the decipherment of the "Seven Vase" nominal. Here, K'awiil must refer to the Baby Jaguar, as no one else is being thrown.

On K4013 (see figure 8.3) we have seen, following the date, *yala(w)* "Seven Vase" "he throws 'Seven Vase'" amid a complex scene. The tree grows from the mountain as the infant falls; the serpent arises from a hole in the tree and encircles it as the Old God emerges from its maw. The serpent-like extrusions from the *witz* feature profile heads with mirror infixes. The mirror signals the resplendence accorded to gods and sacred objects. Flame-like volutes with maize-kernel inclusions cue the presence of *k'awiil*. The placement of "Seven Vase" within this scene links it to the Baby Jaguar and not to the tree, as suggested by García Barrios and Valencia Rivera (2011: 73). They do not address the function of the *yal* verb in their study. The mature tree is also seen on K1815 (see figure 8.2).

On the beautiful vase brought to public attention by Michel Quenon (figure 8.14) we see the gleeful Death God; we can almost hear him cackling as he throws the baby down on the snaky extrusion. Quenon astutely noted that the *ahk'ab* vase-and-snake pendant he wears spills forth the same dark frothy liquid that forms the basal layer of the scene. The longer text reads *yalaw k'awiil Chak ??* "he (the Death God) throws K'awiil Great ??." *Yax Ha'al Chahk* "First-Rains Rain God," whose name

FIGURE 8.14. *Yalaw K'awiil Chak ?? Yax Ha'al Chahk* "he (the Death God) throws K'awiil, Great ??." Photographs supplied by Michel Quenon (personal communication, 2011).

is juxtaposed to (but is not a part of) this text and who wears a similar pendant, dances in place. The animal head following *chak* "great" has a dark patch above the eye here and elsewhere, and its visible affixes are syllabic *la*. On the Quenon Vase there is a "percent sign" on the cheek, suggesting it is a *wahy*. Steinbach and I agree that it must close the name phrase (the complex nominal object) in the five texts of its occurrence; all are Baby Jaguar vases. The possibility that it is a nominal subject—that is, a local epithet for the Death God—is foreclosed on K2208 (see figure 8.1b) by the passive verb. We have seen that *k'awiil* alone may designate the Baby Jaguar, who is further qualified in a second phrase containing the elusive "Seven Vase" (properly "VII tzi-INVERTED VASE-la") nominal also found on the Snake Lady vases. Following it here is Yax Kaan "First Snake." It is not just any first snake but one pertaining to the Kaan kingdom, employing a "fish" *ka* syllable in its spelling. Curiously, the only snake visible in this scene is the incipient one emerging from the *witz*. Text and image on these two sets of vases define the relationship as a transition between two personae shared by one being.

Historical texts that cite the imperial presence of the Kaan polity in local royal courts show that the snake head in its name was pronounced as the archaic *kaan* "snake" and not the Cholan equivalent *chan*; this is cued by the prefixed comb-like syllable *ka*. But on these vases, the scribes of Kaan have chosen to conflate the fish head variant of *ka* with the snake head to spell *kaan*. The fish sign often contains the two short black bars that identify a small, tasty freshwater perch (called "two-bar" in Belize) common throughout the region. However, Luís Lopes (2005) observes that a few of these heads more closely resemble the zoomorphic Mams of Classic Fire rituals, and he makes a plausible case for this alternative head—which he considers to be a weasel—as a name for the Old God (in exclusion of the snake) featured in the Snake Lady scenes.

On K2208 (see figure 8.1b) we find, following the date and what is a likely temporal adverb, *tzahkaj k'awiil* "Seven Vase" Yax Kaan Chak ?? at "nu-split AHK'AB is conjured K'awiil 'Seven Vase' First Snake, Great ??." Note the lightning bolt leaping from the mouth of Chahk. Here we have our first example of AHK'AB (a sign that normally means "darkness") with a nu- prefix, a li- suffix, and a split down the middle that likely changes the value of the main sign. The verb is the passive TZAK-ja *tzahkaj* "is conjured." It is much less common than *yalaw* and binds this scene to the conjuring within the Snake Lady narrative. The nominal subject includes an example of the "great/red ??-la" collocation. Here, the passive *tzahkaj* argues firmly against its signaling the Death God. The image of "split darkness" is provocative; while a literal interpretation might suggest an abyss leading to the underworld beneath, a number of these scenes have as witnesses fireflies (*kuhkay*) holding torches, as if the stage requires illumination. Is this a night event or perhaps one bathed in pre-Creation crepuscular light? Nicholas Carter (2005: 19) and Steinbach (personal communication, 2013) cite discussions with Stuart, who observes that this "split AHK'AB" sign substitutes for a well-known sign PAS (literally a verb "to open"), meaning "dawn" at Comalcalco. Stuart regards the prefix as logographic NUK "great" and reads the whole as *nuk ahk'ab* "dawn." Christenson (2005: 52, 78) considers the nature of the dim light that barely lit the world in the time of Seven Macaw, and Karen Bassie-Sweet (2002: 18) observes the role of Junajpu Possum (per Christenson, Xpiyacoc or the Mam) in the Popol Vuh as one who is asked to darken the sky just before dawn. Christenson (personal communication, 2014) also observes that the misty darkness associated with the Baby Jaguar story resonates with the solemn rituals of assembly and disassembly of the Tz'utujil Rilaj Mam (Maximon), wherein absolute darkness is required in the reenactment of the Mam's original mist-enshrouded birth.

A recent article by Albert Davletshin and Péter Bíró (2014) calls into question the apparent semantic equivalence between the "split darkness" collocation and the "dawn" sign at Comalcalco and argues instead that the main sign is a syllable—one that with syllabic nu- spells a *nuC* root that can interchange syntactically with *pas(aj)* "dawn." Their provisional solution, which I find attractive, is to posit that the "split AHK'AB" is a new t'i syllable and that the sequence nu-t'i-li spells a Cholan/Yucatecan word *nut'il* "joining," meaning by extension "twilight" in counterpoint to *pas(aj)* "open(ing)" or "dawn." While *nut'(il)* is unattested as a term for sunset or twilight, I consider the presence of fireflies in many Baby Jaguar scenes to be independent support, as these tropical elaterid beetles are most visible at dusk and in the early nighttime hours.

On K1815 (see figure 8.2) one sees *nut'il*? (nu-"split AHK'AB"-li or nu-t'i-li) *yahlaj* (spelled ya-la-ja) K'awiil Chatan "at twilight? is thrown the K'awiil of Chatan."

Another text names Yax Ha'al Chahk. Chatan is an unidentified toponym within the Kaan sphere, appearing on a number of non-narrative Codex-Style vessels that have the Primary Standard Sequence. It is frequently found in the toponymic title *k'uhul Chatan winik* "holy Chatan person." Does this text inform us that K'awiil—or rather his Baby Jaguar manifestation—is intrinsically bound to Chatan, as Steinbach (personal communication, 2013) believes? If so, it forms a tantalizing bridge to the aforementioned Baby Jaguar patron god of Tikal and Naranjo. Note the "flaming Ajaw" icon attached to the tail of the infant. As a hieroglyph it has the meaning *mijiin* "man's child"; it occurs more often on the tail than does the *k'awiil* "torch" icon. We see the flowering tree mentioned earlier. Like *tzahkaj* above, the verb *yahlaj* is passive. One can just make out the quatrefoil opening in the tree into which the baby will slide; the tree is thus a conduit. On K521 (see figure 8.4) we have *yalaw K'awiil* "Seven Vase" *Yax Kaan Chak ?? Chatan winik* "He throws K'awiil 'Seven Vase' First Snake Great ??, the Chatan person."

We must conclude that K'awiil "Seven Vase" is the Baby Jaguar.

Following are other examples of texts that, due to space constraints, are not illustrated but which may be seen in the Mayavase Database (Kerr n.d.a):

> On K2207 the text is *yalaw* "Seven Vase" "(he) throws the Baby Jaguar." Here the infant is unequivocally represented by the "Seven Vase" compound. The Death God throws a human infant as Chahk dances amid scrolls representing foaming water.

> On K8680 the text is *yalaw K'awiil Chak ??* "(he) throws K'awiil Great ??." The Baby Jaguar has the cruller and the *mijiin* "man's child" motif attached to the tail.

> On K4056 we *find u-yalaw Ba[h] Ha'* "Seven Vase" "he (the Death God) throws him (at) First Water, the Baby Jaguar." Here we see a rare phrase *Bah Ha'*, which Steinbach (2015b: chapter 5) identifies as a primordial toponym, suggesting this to be an event that followed soon after the creation of the world. Note the pronominal prefix on the transitive verb—a unique example.

> The text of K2213 reads *yalaw Ba[h] Tuun* "Seven Vase" "(he) throws the First-Stone Baby Jaguar." As with Bah Ha', Steinbach understands Ba[h] Tuun to be "First Stone," a reference to the locus of sacrifice: the newly formed *witz* in the time of creation. Here the syntax argues that Ba[h] Tuun is a title and not a location, but the term is unequivocally toponymic (as in *u-wahy Ba[h] Tuun* "he is a nagual of Ba[h] Tuun")

THE TRANSMUTATION OF SUSTENANCE 187

on other Codex-Style vessels. Yax Ha'al Chahk is called a *Ba[h] Tuun Ajaw* on the West Tablet of the Inscriptions at Palenque (Steinbach, personal communication, 2014).

On K1152 we find *yal[aw]* "Seven Vase" *Yax Kaan Chatan winik* "(he) throws the Baby Jaguar First Snake, the Chatan person." In separate captions the Rain God is named *Yax Ha'* "First Rains" and the Death God is named *Sak Jal Chamiy u-wahy Bah Tuun* "Turning-White Death, the nagual of First Stone." The lineage connection is significant, hinting at the motive for the sacrifice as a vehicle of access to an ancestral repository of power. The adult jaguar has the scarf and forehead sprout of the Waterlily Jaguar.

We observe that the Baby Jaguar is usually named by K'awiil "Seven Vase" Yax Kaan, in that order. Rarely, the K'awiil component is absent, and occasionally other components are present. The canonical *k'awiil* "torch" icon may attach to the baby's tail, but more often it is the *mijiin* "man's child" sign. The infant never has the torch in the forehead.

THE SNAKE LADY, THE FOOT OF K'AWIIL, THE OLD GOD, AND THE LITTLE GODS

With K3202 and K3716 (see figure 8.7a, b), likely painted by the same scribe, we move into the conjuring chamber of the Snake Lady. In the first scene, the full-breasted young goddess gets a come-hither from crafty K'awiil as the Old God in the serpent's maw protests, jaw agape. In the second, because her head and upper body are eroded, it is hard to be certain whether the old codger has gotten her attention. The light sexual play in these scenes, first noted by Robicsek and Hales, is both humorous and humanizing. The snake of K3202 bears a great "mirror" plume at the back of his head; it marks the beast as shiny, as do the "sparkling spiral" motifs behind the head and at the corner of the mouth. Note that the snake in both scenes originates as the foot of K'awiil, and in both, the Old God's forehead displays the *k'awiil* torch. In these scenes and in others to follow, we see snakeskin-like patterns on the curtains, as first noted by Carter (2005: 7–8). These may be entoptic motifs signaling a drug-induced altered state. Like his snake-footed doppelganger, the Old God is a lightning being. On K3716 (see figure 8.7b) we find the wrapped, diminutive Chahk and the "Pax God" (or Te' "tree") on their dais with bowls of grisly offerings at their feet. In other examples, censers containing blood offerings are positioned at the foot of the dais. As other authors have also observed, the little

Chahk and the mature Yax Ha'al Chahk must be connected. It follows that the tiny Te' must also relate to the mature tree rising from the mountain.

Most of the texts on the Snake Lady vases are short. On K5230 (see figure 8.8) the verb following the date (which includes 15 Pax) is spelled SIH-ya-ja *sihyaj* "he is born." This is an intransitive verb, one ubiquitous in the script corpus. The name that follows it is its subject—the one being born. It is "Seven Vase," known from the mountain sacrifice scene to refer to the Baby Jaguar. But where is he? In place of the Baby Jaguar we now have the Old God wearing the Itzam net headscarf of God N emerging from the snake, which is adorned with the sparkling spirals common to these shiny beings. A fiery maize leaf behind the head of the serpent touches the like-in-kind flame of K'awiil's torch, closing the circle. The odd form of the Inverted Vase sign resembles the eye of the Jaguar God of the Underworld, and the mirror motif appears on the snout of the serpent. Like Lopes (2005), Steinbach (personal communication, 2014) views these as scenes of triple birth, wherein the usual verb *sihyaj* "is born" refers to the conjoined aged god-with-snake and also to the diminutive deities, who resemble swaddled infants. García Barrios and Valencia Rivera (2011: 73–74 and elsewhere) argue that the birth is that of Chahk and Pax (or Te') and never of the Old God/Serpent. But in many of these Snake Lady scenes, only the conjoined Old God and snake appear while the texts state that "Seven Vase" is born. These authors (2011: 74–75) posit that the presence of the "Seven Vase" nominal in the headdress of Te' on K1813 (not illustrated) also suggests that these bundled gods are the only ones being born (a view echoed by Valencia Rivera and García Capistrán [2013: 42–43]). I argue that this unique example—infixed into the forehead of the Piscine Jester God on the headdress—suggests not the primary referent but a derivative one. There is other evidence, to be considered later, linking birth with ancestors in serpents' maws amid their conjuring by women, and K4114 offers proof that "Seven Vase First Snake" names the Old God/Serpent. Michel Quenon (personal communication, 2014) considers the little gods to be deity bundles and not infants and cites a Jaina figurine—to be considered later—representing such a bundle. Its basal platform features the Old God and an inverted vase nominal. In my view, the solution to this syntactic and iconographic riddle demonstrates the "birth" to be that of the Old God/Snake ("Seven Vase") in every case and also that of the bundled gods when they are present and the little Chahk is named. The Old God of the Jaina figurine may likewise be the ontological foundation on which the ritual birth of its bundled god is enacted.

On K4114 (see figure 8.9) we find the text *u-baah K'awiil* "Seven Vase" *Yax Kaan* "(it is) the image of K'awiil 'Seven Vase' First Snake." This non-canonical scene confirms the identity of the conjured Old God-with-snake as K'awiil "Seven Vase" First Snake. Here, a male holds a tube from which the serpent emerges, fused with the

Old God in its maw. A theomorphic K'awiil plume on the snake's head with a K'IN sign in its forehead (likely overpainted on the mirror) terminates in a fiery maize ear whose kernels spill down toward the groundline. As Carter (2005) has noted, when males conjure this being, they must do so while holding flexible woven tubes—clear prototypes for the formal Serpent Bar held by kings in full dress. In contrast, female conjurers are "winders" of the serpent, often allowing it to envelop them.

In the text of K6754 (see figure 8.10), the CR date is the common 7 Muluk 15 Pax and the verb is again *sihyaj* "is born." Now a new phrase appears, followed by Chahk, with "Seven Vase" following in turn. Penny Steinbach and I have identified this phrase as *yuk ha' kabal* "shakes-water-and-earth"; it is a qualifier for Chahk. In the scene, only the Te' deity appears. We see the *k'awiil* torch in the forehead of the Old God.

On K4485 (see figure 8.11) the CR is 7 Muluk 10 Pax. Here, we find the text *sihyaj Yuk Ha' Kabal* "is born, Shakes-Water-and-Earth," but in the text Chahk and "Seven Vase" are effaced. On K1813 (not illustrated) there is a complete form of the phrase, reading sihyaj *Yuk Ha' Kabal Chahk* "Seven Vase" *Yax Kaan* plus an effaced sign resembling a jaguar head. In examining the texts in the full corpus of these vases, I have found that the "Shakes-Water-and-Earth-Chahk" phrase regularly co-occurs with the deity bundles on the dais (in addition to K1813, see also K1081, K4485, K6754, K7838; K1382, with *sihyaj* juxtaposed to the little Chahk, offers proof of another sort). In figure 8.11, the lady's chamber is layered with a bed of leaves, and the old codger makes his move while K'awiil is reduced to a torch at the snake's tail tip. The snake's fiery plume contains a star sign. In the next room, a human attendant leans back in astonishment at the awakening deity bundles, whose collars are formed by the thick string knot seen on the belt of Chahk (see figures 8.1b, 8.2, and 8.4).

On K3702 (see figure 8.12), unusual for being a plate, we find the *Yuk Ha' Kabal* phrase following *sihyaj*; "Seven Vase" appears between two eroded signs, which might by analogy be Chahk and Yax Kaan. Of particular interest are the smoking censer with its plumed heart offering (best exemplified on K7838) at the edge of the scene and the bound, disemboweled young man beneath it. This plate was ritually transformed by the piercing of the eye of the Old God before its placement in a tomb. From the presence of the censer and the sacrifice, we can infer that the bundled deities are just offstage and that Yuk Ha' Kabal [Chahk] is a clue to their proximity. Amid the signs in front of the Old God's face is a pair resembling the undeciphered Chak-?? nominal discussed earlier.

Returning to K5164 (see figure 8.1), the statement is *sihyaj* "Seven Vase" *Yax Kaan U-Mam Ahk* "is born 'Seven Vase' First Snake, Ancestor/Grandfather of the Turtle." This calls to mind the well-known Resurrection Plate (K1892; see also Robicsek and Hales [1981: figure 57]) wherein Te' and a reptile—turtle or toad?—emerge from either end of the turtle shell. The Maize God is born as from a seed, while the Hero

Twins nurture the newborn sprout. The idea that the Old God is a toad is suggested by the epithet *amuch tuun ajaw* "toad stone lord" seen at top left on K5164, preceding the parentage statement *y-al* "he is her child . . ." The theme of birth from the turtle shell has been addressed by various scholars, notably by Taube (1985, 1994) and Quenon and Geneviève Le Fort (1997). I see the story of the Maize God as a tangent to the current study, as the iconography of the Baby Jaguar only rarely conflates with that of maize (see K688 and K1184, discussed by Carrasco 2005: 166–67) and never within the Codex-Style tradition. Although maize foliation and kernels appear regularly with the Old God/Serpent constellation, I view this as a veneer added to a pre-agricultural prescription for arboreal and lineage fertility.

On K5164, via *y-al* "he is her child" the Snake Lady is unequivocally designated as the mother of the Old God/Serpent. In contrast, García Barrios and Valencia Rivera (2011: 76, 79–81) understand the Old God to be the woman's father while tying this suggested relationship to a Rabinal myth. But in further contrast, Valencia Rivera and García Capistrán (2013: 42–43) now accept the syntax of the parentage statement and propose that the Lady—a human female whose proper husband is the attendant sometimes present—gives ritual birth to the Old God, who then mates with her in an act of incestuous hubris, tied to a pan-Mesoamerican myth of the origin of maize. As will become clear, my view of the Lady's nature, role, and relationship to other players differs considerably from the foregoing. The Lady's name was suggested by David Stuart, Stephen Houston, and John Robertson (1999: II-52) to read *Ix Tzak Kotz'oom* (now thought to be *Kopeem*) *Chan (Kaan)* "She Who Conjures the Rolled-up Snake." This is followed by *Ix(ik) Wayib* "She of the Sleeping Place," though one might understand this as a place for dreaming and visions. This "snake" is a nice example of the animal head Lopes (2005) relates to the Mams associated with fire rituals; he believes it names the Old God rather than the snake. I find his argument persuasive and complementary rather than competitive. The Snake Lady appears to have no name independent of her roles as conjurer, mother, and consort. I suggest her to be, among other roles, the deified personification of a psychoactive plant.

I have noted that on K2067 (see figure 8.13) the entangled snake being is now called *Leem Uk' Kaan* "Shining Drink Snake," and it bears one sparkling spiral. A nominal instead featuring Lopes's (2005) animal head is seen on K4113 (figure 8.15), and a related scene appears on K1375 (not illustrated); in both, the Old God presents a jar or basin of liquid to a lord, who on K1375 seems to float off the ground. On K5862 the Old God emerges from a serpent bedecked with sparkling spirals and offers the Lady a clyster. On K2067 the Snake Lady is named as *Ixik Yal Kopeem Ixik Kamay* "Lady of the Winder's Child, Lady Kamay." *Kamay*, which may contain an archaic root *kam* "death," has not been resolved, but its known occurrences

FIGURE 8.15. *Huli Kaan-naah Yajaw Ek' Yax ba-? Winik Hiin Uk' ?-?* "arrives at the Kaan house Star-Lord, First-? person, the Drink-Creature." (The hi- ni *hini* reading was suggested by David Mora-Marín [personal communication, August 2020] to represent the article "the"). *Ubah ti ch'ab yak'abil* "his person (the old man's) is the image of his (the lord's) creation-darkness" (K4113).

FIGURE 8.16. *Ch'ahoomtak yook* "censers of the tripod pedestal" (K1645).

associate it with serpent conjuring. Here, the cup is offered to the Lady; might her leaf skirt represent an admixture plant, if not the primary source of the drink? The attendant is in a visionary state. Time stands still.

K1645 (figure 8.16) is reminiscent of scenes in which a human infant is displayed as an offering (see K8655, K1200, and K5855 for examples wherein a sacrificial priest with attributes of Akan or God A-Prime [Grube 2004: 72] receives the human infant from a lord). Here, the baby lies on a plate above a smoking censer whose spikes mimic the thorns of a young ceiba. This vase is linked to the Snake Lady scenes through the phrase *sihyaj* "Seven Vase" Yax Kaan, although that being is not present. The two attendants, musicians, are named as *ch'ahoomtak yook* "incense offerers of the (tripod) pedestal"; they appear enveloped in a dreamlike vigil, while entoptic jaguar-skin motifs dance on the curtains. One of them wears the vomit bib seen in enema-taking scenes. The little gods Chahk and Te' are wrapped in jaguar pelts, as if to show affinity with the Baby Jaguar. Quenon (personal communication,

2014) believes that whenever the serpent-winding Lady is seen with her aged child and paramour, the *ch'ahoomtak*, the wrapped effigies, their dais with its furnishings, the snake-patterned curtains, and the censer with its plumed heart offering are also present (see Taube 1994: 664–65 for further discussion of the heart-and-knife device in the censer). While this may be so, the accompanying texts (this one excepted) frequently cue the visual presence of the effigies by the phrase "Shakes-Water-and-Earth Chahk." This human infant on the offering plate is unique to the Lady's chamber and recalls the "sacrificial priest" vases mentioned above in what I see as a slightly earlier chapter of the story.

In sum, the nominal phrase employed to describe the Old God/Serpent being is simply "Seven Vase" Yax Kaan. In contrast, the Baby Jaguar is called K'awiil "Seven Vase" Yax Kaan. The ancient storyteller must have felt it necessary to remind his audience that the falling infant was K'awiil in anthropomorphic form.

Simon Martin (2015) has written a thought-provoking essay about the many presentations of the Old God (God N), whom he views as an embodied mountain, an ancient Atlantean sustainer of cosmic order, an aged man (God D) fused with the Principal Bird Deity, and, following Stuart, a sorcerer. He cites Stuart's 1994 observations (in a letter to Linda Schele) suggesting that his name was never "Pauahtun" but rather Itzam "agent of *itz*," with *itz* defined in relevant Mayan languages as both a plant secretion or sap and as the root of "sorcery" and "sorcerer" (Barrera Vásquez 1980: 272). Itzam is also a term for crocodile. Martin makes an excellent case for the Old God as both singular and quadripartite, marvelously free to merge with other beings in both cosmic and chthonic realms.

Significantly, the Old God is termed by Martin a "universal sustainer." While Martin does not specifically address God N's appearances on the Codex-Style vases, he provides an explanatory key not only for the "star" and "toad" epithets (2015) but also for his union with the serpent, or not (as he elects), as seen above on K4113 (see figure 8.15). Here, I note a pair of texts detailing an encounter between a lord of Kaan and the Old God in his role as shamanic purveyor of psychotropic potions. They read:

1. *Huli Kaan-naah Yajaw Ek' Yax ba-? Winik Hini Uk' ?-?* "arrives at the Kaan house Star-Lord, First-? person, the Drink-Creature."
2. *ubaah uch'ahb yahk'abil* "his (the Old God's) person/image is his (the lord's) creation and his darkness."

Now the Old God visits a noble resident of Kaan (spelled as before) without the snake, amid a scene termed *ch'ahb ahk'ab* "creation-darkness" (Barrera Vásquez 1980: 120, 7), the deeply esoteric parentage and ancestor rite associated with conjuring and blood sacrifice cherished by Maya kings from Early Classic times onward.

From the jar with its female profile, might we infer that it contains a drink whose spirit essence is female? On K1650 the Old God/Serpent appears poised to insert his clyster into the anus of the Death God amid yet another gem in the storyteller's repertoire. But K1973 places the clyster in the paw of the Waterlily Jaguar, from which we infer that he, too, is a participant in the Old God's constellation.

As mentioned earlier, Luís Lopes (2005: 4) identifies the animal of the Drink "Snake" here and on K2067 as another animal, perhaps a weasel. The zoological identification may be uncertain, but he astutely links it to one of the fire-drilling gods identified by Nikolai Grube as an opossum Bakab. A quote from Grube (2000: 100) is worth sharing:

> How God N in his different forms is related to the fire rituals in the inscriptions is not known. He is hardly ever, if at all, displayed on incense burners and his association with fire remains opaque, although Taube shows that God N is related to Chahk. Taube cites an early Classic incised ceramic which names God N with the opossum Mam hieroglyph. The same vessel on its opposite side shows Chahk with a burning serpent-footed lightning axe. Perhaps an aspect of God N is associated with lightning and by this way also with fire.

The term spelled ba-ka-ba *baah kab* "head of the earth" is a Classic period title taken commonly by kings and almost never by God N. But we know from Diego de Landa's (1978: 62–65) account of the New Year's rites that the four Year Bearers—who also had individual names—were color/directional *chahks* as well as *pawahtuns* and *bakabs*. If the polymorphic Old God with his *k'awiil* torch is also a *chahk* (for which we will see further argument), then there are three Chahk protagonists in our play: the Old God, the tiny Chahk on the dais, and Yax Ha'al Chahk. In the Popol Vuh, there is a trinity of thunderbolt creator gods who together comprise *Uk'ux Kaj* "Heart of Sky," also known as *Juraqan* (simply, "One Leg" or a reflex of K'awiil, per Christenson 2007: 60n62):

> Then they arranged for the germination and creation of the trees and the bushes, the germination of all life and creation, in the darkness and in the night, by Heart of Sky, who is called Huracan. First is Thunderbolt Huracan, second is Youngest Thunderbolt, and third is Sudden Thunderbolt. These three together are Heart of Sky. Then they came together with Sovereign and Quetzal Serpent. Together they conceived light and life: "How shall it be sown? When shall there be a dawn for anyone? Who shall be a provider? Who shall be a sustainer?" (Christenson 2007: 61)

Let us recall Martin's (2002) discussion of the Baby Jaguar or Scroll Baby motif as a patron deity and historical name at Early Classic Tikal, as well as the role of Yax Ha'al Chahk as the "opener" of the mountain into which the infant falls. Bassie-Sweet

(2002: 48–49), in her consideration of the multiplicity of Chahks among various Mayan communities, recounts folktales in which these rain and lightning deities compete to crack open the mountain in which maize was concealed. An unpublished paper by Elisabeth Wagner (1995) offers an incisive analysis of the Kaloomte' title (superordinate to Ajaw at Tikal from the Early Classic onward) as *kal-oom* "one who opens," with te' referring either to the axe of Chahk or to a tree. While she leans toward its likely relationship to the Chahks who crack the turtle shell for the sprouting Maize God, I view the archaic theonym *kaloomte'* "Chahk-the-splitter (for the tree)" as a mythological counterpoint to the Scroll Baby name. As such, it marks the bearer of the title as *kal-oom* "opener of the portal" for the falling human/feline infant and for the eponymous tree with jaguar-paw ear that rises from the mountain. As evidence, I offer the occasional substitution of the skull of God A at Naranjo (Stelae 6 and 13) for the usual profile head of Chahk in the title.

The quadrangular "Birth Vase" K5113, the subject of a detailed study by Taube (1994), depicts an event clearly related to the Snake Lady scenes. A bearded serpent emerges from the personified mountain on side 1, then rises and disgorges the Old God on side 2. Simultaneously, a young goddess with jaguar features stands in the traditional birth posture, while multiple representations of her aged counterpart Goddess O assist in the birth amid various basins. No newborn is identified in the study, but none is available other than the Old God himself. On side 4 the Old God dialogues with the young goddess while presenting a bowl of sacrificial knives.

READING THE NOMINAL PHRASE AS *HUK PUL TZIN* "SEVEN-PROVIDER-OF-SUSTENANCE"

We have been immersed in a story about a lost portion of a great epic and have reached a change of course. To proceed, we must understand the nominal phrase. Because this chapter is not primarily a work of epigraphy, the bounty of detail that is vital to a convincing decipherment must be deferred to another project (MacLeod n.d.). I hope the evidence I can provide here will suffice.

An analysis by Nikolai Grube (2012) features a reading SIP for the inverted vase sign with crossbands infix. This is the main sign in the phrase I have been calling "Seven Vase" but whose full descriptor is "VII tzi-INVERTED VASE-la." Grube argues that the superfix is not a tzi but rather a stylized deer antler (which it surely is in deer-related contexts; see figure 8.17) that mimics the tzi syllable in this environment. His result: the mystery nominal phrase reads Wuk Sip and refers to the Yucatecan Wuk Yol Sip, "Seven Heart of Sip," the protector god of deer. I contend that Grube's SIP reading applies only to the 819-Day Count protagonist and the Deer God title of Yaxun Bahlam at Yaxchilan, where the superfix is always an antler

FIGURE 8.17. The Old God/Serpent as the Deer God (a: K531, b: K2572).

and never a tzi, and where that compound may be replaced by the full head of the Deer God. Having found additional proof on the Walter Randel Stela for SIP in the 819-Day Count phrase, I accept Grube's reading with conditions. It has cleared the way by setting the deer constellation apart from the "Seven Vase" phrase, where the superfix is a genuine tzi apparently standing pars pro toto for another collocation hidden behind the vase.

Support for this hidden sign appears at Q16 on the Palenque Palace Tablet (see figure 8.18 left side), where we find all the elements—the inverted vase with crossbands, the tzi superfix, the la suffix, and more. It is the first half of the name of a being whose birth is cited in a caption text within the central image and for which House A–D of the palace was dedicated. The "vase with antler" in the 819-Day Count phrase on the same tablet at D2 makes clear that the scribes distinguished that compound, with its unmistakable antler, from the "vase with tzi."

The "Seven Vase" nominal never occurs with the Codex-Style narrative scenes featuring the Old God-with-Serpent as the Deer God (see figure 8.17a, b), where he holds the conch shell trumpet of the hunt and wears the antler and deer ear (Robicsek and Hales 1981: vessels 34–38; see also K556, K998, K1384, K1882). The serpent in these scenes, although likewise the foot of K'awiil, is a distinctive cervid polymorph termed *(sip?)-chih(il) kaan* or *noh chih kaan* "deer(-god) snake," "big deer snake," who never appears in the Snake Lady's chamber. He is also called a *wahy* or *nagual* of sorcerers, while the serpent of the Snake Lady's chamber is not.

The "Inverted Vase with Crossbands" has been one of the more intractable of the unread logographs, and final proof for the PUL (*pul* "provide, cast [down]") value I

FIGURE 8.18. Palenque Palace Tablet, left side. Q16 *Pul Tzin* "Provider of Sustenance." Photograph by Jorge Pérez de Lara.

have long entertained must be detailed elsewhere. The common -la suffix suggests a CVl root. *Pulaab* appears in Tuzantec as *cántaro* "pitcher" (Kaufman and Justeson 2003: 883), and it may be that the Yucatec, Mopan, and Ch'orti' *p'ul* "pitcher" is a later development from *pul, but the "Inverted Vase with Crossbands" is never used with this meaning. Rather, its modern reflexes are found in Yucatecan languages with meanings "throw, cast down, carry, bear, provide," as seen in these entries:

Yucatec:	
pul (t.v., i.v.): *arrojar y desechar y echar de sí.*	Throw, throw out, throw from oneself.
ah pul abich k'iik': hechicero que hace que uno orine sangre.	Sorcerer who makes one urinate blood.
ah pul yah: hechicero.	Sorcerer (lit. "he who throws/casts injury"; noun incorporation).
ah pul: el que lleva o trae algo, conductor, portador.	He who carries or brings something, conductor, bearer.
pula' (pul ha'): proveer la orina o orinar.	Provide urine or urinate.
ah pula' el ofrendador del agua.	The offerer/provider of water (noun incorporation). A rainmaker.
pulba: entregarse, ofrecerse presentándose.	Deliver, offer oneself in presentation.
pul: llevar or traer.	Carry or bring.
ah pul hu'un: cartero, mensajero.	Postman, messenger (lit. "he who carries papers"; noun incorporation).

(Barrera Vásquez 1980: 675–76)

Itzaj:	
pul (t.v., i.v.): *tirar, botar.*	Throw, throw down.
Pul-che': tumbar palos.	Fell trees (noun incorporation).
pulik k'ax: tumbar bosque.	Fell forest.
pulik k'ik': botar sangre.	Bleed (lit. "throw blood").

(*Hofling and Fernando Tesucún 1997: 525*)

The following entries from the Qanjob'alan subfamily are included in the same cognate set with Yucatec, Mopan, and Itzaj *pul* "throw, throw away":

Tuzantec:	
pul (t.v.): *sacar comida/agua con cuchara/balde.*	Take out food/water with spoon/pail.
pulaab' (n.): *cántaro.*	Pitcher.
Mocho:	
pul (t.v.): *sacar agua.*	Draw water.
puul-i' (t.v.): *bombear (agua).*	Pump (water).

(*Kaufman and Justeson 2003: 883*)

Relevant but not cognate is proto-Cholan **pul* "burn" (Kaufman and Norman 1984: 129).

An unpublished manuscript by Kerry M. Hull and Alejandro Sheseña (n.d.) that circulated in April 2009 generated lively email discussion. While their TZIK proposal has been set aside by the authors, it was this compendium of examples and ensuing dialogue that affirmed the constraints on my PUL proposal. Here is my reasoning:

1. The sign often has a -la suffix, but it is not obligatory; this suggests a CVl or CVVl root. There is no parsimonious alternative explanation.

2. A common title of royal women in which a K'IN "sun" sign is infixed into the vase suggests *pul-k'iin ixik k'uh/k'uh ixik* "sun/augury-casting holy woman/goddess" and on Yaxchilan L. 32, *pulab (PUL-la-ba) k'iin ixik k'uh* "sun/augury-bowl (the archaic *pulab*, perhaps here meaning 'instrument for burning'?) holy woman/goddess." This title may reference the serpent/ancestor-conjuring rites of women at Yaxchilan. A related title on K2324 (Hull and Sheseña n.d.: figure 30) depicts drops spilling from the vase.

3. The name of the Palenque Temple of the Sun is *Bolon Pul-K'ahk' Witz K'inich Paskab* "Nine Cast-Down-Fire Mountain Sunny Dawn." David Stuart (2006: 157–58) recognized that the fully visual form of the sign appeared in Almendáriz's eighteenth-century drawings of the *alfardas*: from the unseen

vase fall inverted the number nine, fire, *witz*, and maize, as well as the rest of
the name meaning "sunny dawn." This recalls the fiery leaf and falling maize
kernels on K4114 (see figure 8.9) where the Serpent/Old God entity is named
K'awiil "Seven Vase" *Yax Kaan*. I propose that in both names the Inverted
Vase represents *pul* "provide" and in these examples literally "cast down." In
both, one may envision a divine gift of fertility and abundance symbolized as a
spilling earthward of sun-heated ears or kernels of maize.

4. In the April 2009 email thread cited above, Carlos Pallán shared a photo of the
east side of Moral Reforma Stela 4, noting a rare verbal function for the "Inverted Vase with Crossbands" with a possible *yi* suffix, followed by *utok' (u)pakal*
"his flint knife, his shield." The couplet is a metaphor for both a military campaign and an ancestral directive to conduct war. The "defeat-in-battle" verbs that
otherwise accompany *utok' upakal* are *jubuy* "gets downed" and *hayi* "collapses."
Given the gloss "throw down" for the transitive *pul*, this looks like a mediopas-
sive verb *pu[h]luy* "gets thrown down."

In the collocation at Q16 on the Palace Tablet, with the Inverted Vase-la now
resolved, the tzi suggests an initial consonant plus vowel, and the unequivocal ni to
the right of the vase must provide the final consonant. The sign to the left—a shark,
a fish, or a piscine polymorph—is assumed to be the sign normally hidden in our
mystery nominal phrase. The "shark" and ni appear as the head and tail of the same
creature, cued by the widening of the tzi to rest on both of them; thus the creature is
named by tzi-"shark"-ni and cannot be read XOOK "shark." Its vegetal tendril suggests its identity with the Piscine Jester God affixed to the "drum-major" headdress
in the tablet's central image. That motif fuses fish with waterlily imagery (Steinbach
2015a). A reading TZIN *tzin* "sustenance" for the sign at Q16 is attractive. *tzin* is
here proposed for Classic Cholan as cognate with Yucatec *tzéen* (< *tzehn* "food, sustenance"), although the phonological relationship is not the expected *CeeC* > *CiiC*.

tzen, tzéen (n.): *alimento, sustento, manutención.*	Food, sustenance, maintenance.
Aj Tzenulo'ob: los que mantienen o proveen alimentos a otros; uno de los nombres con quien también son conocidos los Chakes.	Those who maintain or provide food to others; one of the names by whom the Chahks are also known.
(*Barrera Vásquez 1980: 858*)	

Signs identical to the "shark" prefix at Q16 flank the front-facing head of the
Old God on the Jaina molded figurine brought to my attention by Michel Quenon
(figure 8.19). The associated text features the Piscine Jester God and an inverted
vase with a-la suffix and a possible T507 tzi infix. Together, these appear to be a

FIGURE 8.19. Jaina figurine of a bundled Monkey Scribe on a four-sided God N throne: (a) full image of bundled Monkey Scribe on throne, (b) detail of throne: Old God with flanking "shark" motifs and text with Piscine Jester God above Inverted Vase. Photographs by Michel Quenon.

FIGURE 8.20. (a) The Jaguar God of the Underworld on Era Day; Vases of the Eleven (K7750) and Seven (K2796) Gods (K7750). (b) Close-up of glyph. The Jaguar God of the Underworld on Era Day; Vases of the Eleven (K7750) and Seven (K2796) Gods. (c) The Jaguar God of the Underworld on Era Day; Vases of the Eleven (K7750) and Seven (K2796) Gods.

variant of our Codex-Style nominal phrase, qualifying the Old God on the four-sided throne as the "Provider of Sustenance" that awakens the bundled Monkey Scribe deity seated above.

Additional evidence that this head is TZIN is found on the famous Vase of the Eleven Gods (K7750, figure 8.20a), where a sign resembling the Piscine Jester God names a Roman-nosed god with a jaguar-pelt skirt. Its main sign, referencing the seated Jaguar God of the Underworld (JGU), is superfixed by a tzi syllable. Dorie Reents-Budet (personal communication, 2012) notes some overpainting on his face, but we agree that a tau tooth was present. On the identically themed Vase of the Seven Gods (K2796, figure 8.20b), the best candidate for the JGU wears the Piscine Jester God on his forehead (Steinbach 2015a: figure 2.3e). It seems that the JGU—whom we know to be a god of war and an avatar of the Baby Jaguar—can be named as *tzin* "sustenance." Further support appears in the text of Lamanai Stela 9 at B8 (Closs 1988: 10; not illustrated here), where a toothsome Piscine Jester God with K'IN in the forehead has a tzi superfix, suggesting *K'inich Tzin* "Sunny Sustenance."

THE PALENQUE PALACE TABLET: SUSTENANCE IN CONTEXT

The Palace Tablet seems a fitting place to explore the productivity of *Pul Tzin* "provider of sustenance." Karen Bassie-Sweet, Nicholas A. Hopkins, and J. Kathryn Josserand (2012) propose that the narrative structure and positioning of the protagonists (a living king flanked by deceased parents) in its tri-figural panel highlight the birth and, decades later, the transfer of a mosaic "drum-major" headdress called

Ux Yop Huun "Three-Leaf Paper." The placement of the birth statement next to the headdress held by the father is suggestive. They also argue that the house dedication in the closing passage (which includes Q16, discussed above) demonstrates that House A–D was intended for storage of this headdress. This is countered by Stuart (2012: 126–27) amid evidence that the Ux Yop Huun is not the mosaic headdress (elsewhere termed *ko'haw* "helmet") but rather "the animate essence of paper." As such, it not only embraces the headband or royal crown of kingship, the bark paper of which it is made, and the *Ficus* or strangler-fig tree that is its source but as a living being and "historicized proto-ruler" (2012: 128) also embraces its animate, archaic power. As both a hieroglyph and a form of the Avian Jester God, it has an ancient pedigree as part Principal Bird Deity, part *Ficus*; and early examples show it as a three-leaf plant or tree with an avian base (see also Fields 1991; Steinbach 2015a). To clarify:

> This statement resonates once we realize that Ux Yop Huun is at once a symbol and a mythical actor, the active personification of the substance of royal headbands used in accession rituals to embody one's newly acquired royal name, or what the Classic Maya literally called "the white-paper-name" (sakhuunil k'aba'). This convergence of Ux Yop Huun and royal names is precisely what we have just seen visually communicated by the iconography of Lamanai Stela 9 and Copan Stela 2. There can be little doubt that paper headbands, the royal crowns of Mesoamerica, were the physical material by which kingly names were bestowed upon new rulers. This is, I believe, the crux of the message behind the Palace Tablet's caption, if not the monument as a whole. By referencing the birth on 1 Ajaw 3 Wayeb and the subsequent "fastening" in association with royal names, Ux Yop Huun is rhetorically treated much like a royal persona, a figure who himself is born and assumes a sort of office well into adulthood—a poetic device, I would argue, that has led to long-standing problems in understanding his true identity. The final passage of the caption resolves much of the confusion by telling us that the fastening of the name of Ux Yop Huun was the foundational event that established the pattern of dynastic naming, wherein kings would "take turns" donning the headband and its persona in the name of Ux Yop Huun. Rather than see Ux Yop Huun as some obscure royal figure from Palenque's dynasty or as the name of the large helmet depicted in the scene, Ux Yop Huun is best interpreted as the animate basis for bark paper and all its charged meanings in the all-important rituals associated with royal crowning. (Stuart 2012: 138)

Stuart (2012: 124n3) briefly considers the sign at Q16—which I now read as *Pul Tzin*—to be either "an extension of a name phrase or a separate personal name." It is followed at R16 by none other than Ux Yop Huun (see figure 8.18 right side) amid

the house dedication statement (2012: 124), which—with my amendments—reads:
Och-iiy k'ahk' K'alhuun-Naah u k'aba'. Ux k'iin ja(b)' ta y-otoot Pul-Tzin Ux Yop Huun. Y-e'tej K'inich K'an Joy Chitam K'uhul Baakal Ajaw.

"The fire entered (into) the Headband-Binding House (which) is its name. Three days (the rite) occupied in the dwelling of Provider of Sustenance Three-Leaf Paper. It is the sacred service of K'an Joy Chitam, the Holy Baakal Lord."

The pallet on which the king sits is designated as a "'shark' bone throne" by its flanking zoomorphs and so is linked to the sign at Q16 and to the piscine plant diadem on the headdress he receives. Quenon and Le Fort (1997: 888–89) cite independent suggestions by Taube and Reilly that the "Xook" head is the alligator gar *Lepisosteus tristoechus*—a denizen of brackish waters—and not a shark. Given the above discussion and the argument that the parents of K'an Joy Chitam are deceased, I understand the drum-major headdress presented by the father to be incorporeal and symbolic of a transferable obligation resident in this "animate essence of paper" and the status it confers (see Stuart 2012: 126 regarding the war-related Teotihuacan origin of this headdress). The *tok' pakal* "flint knife and shield" presented by the mother is likewise incorporeal and symbolic. While the headband-binding rites of House A–D were undoubtedly historical, the tri-figural scene on the tablet is supernatural. Waterlily iconography, signaling the waters of creation, is omnipresent, and the Piscine Jester God is in part a waterlily blossom (Steinbach 2015a). If its hieroglyph means "sustenance," we may better understand it as "the animate essence of sustenance." The earlier "birth" of this iteration of the Ux Yop Huun was likely a conjuring—a birthing of the sort we have seen on Codex-Style vases. What is being successively transferred—through the mosaic headdress and the flint knife and shield—is the formal obligation to conduct war and to perform both captive sacrifice and auto-sacrifice. I concur with Bassie and her colleagues that the headdress (with its piscine diadem, notably) is featured in a visual narrative moving through the caption text and across the stations of the protagonists. But I am persuaded by Stuart's argument that House A-D was a locus for the rites of office taking and not a storage chamber for a physical heirloom. The "Provider of Sustenance" half of the name at Q16-R16 represents an office ordained by the perennial reciprocity between Maya elites and their ancestors in the maintenance of agricultural and lineage fecundity. Blood offerings are required. We will consider the archaic substratum for the concept "provider of sustenance" as we return to our tale on the Codex-Style vases.

THE TRANSMUTATION OF SUSTENANCE

We can now name the Baby Jaguar and the Old God/Serpent as *Huk Pul Tzin* "Seven-Provider-of-Sustenance." Within the supernatural realm, *tzin* is incorporeal energy that has parity with *k'awiil*; it is a life-giving force, the source of the blood of a plant, tree, or human fetus; it is precious invisible nourishment that allows these entities to thrive and protects them from danger. In the material realm, sustenance in its fiery form (*k'awiil*) and its watery form (*tzin*) nourishes the physical bodies of man, animals, and plants as heat and light from the sun, nurturing rains, favorable winds, good soil, and water. They encourage robust growth and abundance and spawn the diverse utilitarian and beautiful produce of forests, savannahs, *milpa*, rivers, lakes, and the ocean. Sustenance is returned to the supernatural realm as offerings of incense, sacrificial blood, prepared foodstuffs, fragrant flowers, music, song, and prayer in rites honoring lineage ancestors; celestial, arboreal, and earth deities; the deities of calendric cycles, of war, the hunt, and the cornfield. As Taube (2004: 73) observes, the gods' food consists of fragrances and aromas arising from offerings. I noted above that the role of "Provider of Sustenance Three-Leaf Paper" is transferred to successive royal heirs in service to deities and deified lineage ancestors. The concept thus encodes a reciprocal contract between men and gods. The number seven occurs with various gods; familiar examples are Seven Junajpu, Seven Macaw, Seven Heart of Sip. As stated earlier, seven is a numeral closely associated with the Jaguar God of the Underworld; its head variant is this god.

Following are complete texts from both scenes:

K2208: *Nut'il? tzahkaj K'awiil Huk Pul Tzin Yax Kaan Chak ??*: "At twilight? is conjured K'awiil Seven-Provider-of-Sustenance First Snake, Great ??."

K521: *Yalaw K'awiil Huk Pul Tzin Yax Kaan Chak ?? Chatan winik*: "He throws K'awiil Seven-Provider-of-Sustenance First Snake Great ?? the Chatan Person."

K5164: *Sihyaj Huk Pul Tzin Yax Kaan U-Mam Ahk*: "Is born Seven-Provider-of-Sustenance First Snake, Ancestor/Grandfather of the Turtle."

K6754: *Sihyaj 'Yuk Ha' Kab Chahk Huk Pul Tzin*: "Are born Shakes-Water-and-Earth Chahk (and) Seven-Provider-of-Sustenance."

The Palace Tablet has helped us contextualize the function of "Provider of Sustenance" by tying it to a responsibility to conduct war and blood sacrifice. As we consider the Codex-Style narrative as a cycle of sacrifice and rebirth, we might ask how this story operated as a template for elite Maya practice. We recall K3702 (see figure 8.12), where a disemboweled youth lies below the Snake Lady's conjuring chamber; K3716 (see figure 8.7b), where bowls with bones and a decapitated head sit at the foot of the dais before the bundled deities; and K1645 (see figure 8.16), where a baby on an offering plate is censed and displayed before these deities. We observe a transformation: the Baby Jaguar falls into the mountain and the Old God with serpent—his namesake—is conjured into the Snake Lady's chamber; in one case (see figure 8.3) he emerges directly from the tree. These are actions in a supernatural world, wherein the transformation of beings into alter-egos is—dare I say—natural. Equally natural in that world is the merger of identities, the assumption of many guises by a fundamental constant, and divine immortality. One observes these phenomena in the Popol Vuh amid the marvels of Junajpu and Xbalanke as they are consumed by fire and their bones ground to dust and cast into the river so they can be reborn first as fish, then as trickster-orphans who sacrifice themselves and come back to life to trick the Lords of Death.

In the realm of men, the rules apply accordingly. Dreaming attendants called *ch'ahoomtak yook* "incense offerers of the (tripod) pedestal" appear in the Snake Lady scenes, usually facing the bundled deities on the dais. Accompanying them are censers, musical instruments, entoptic-spattered curtains, bowls with body parts, a living baby on a tripod (once), the chamber itself, and, below it, a disemboweled captive. These all belong to what I call "scribal present time." Also contemporaneous are the wrapped deities themselves; they are effigies being awakened (and, at the same time, supernatural infants being fed) during the conjuring of Seven-Provider-of-Sustenance—a rite requiring censing, music, and blood offerings. Their bundled appearance, per Michel Quenon (personal communication, 2014), indicates their quiescent state prior to ritual activation. This tableau is a recipe for lineage and vegetal fecundity and life-giving rains in the following manner: a rite of *ch'ahb ahk'ab* "creation-darkness" is undertaken; a potent hallucinogenic beverage is drunk or taken as an enema; amid music and song, a sacrificial offering is burned with copal in a censer before the wrapped deities Chahk and Te' (with the *ch'ahoomtak* standing in for the supplicants); a conjuring occurs within the visionary state that brings forth the Old God/Serpent who is Itzam, "sorcerer"; and a dialogue and reenactment of a primordial conception ensues. Itzam is the Earth Lord; his powers are profound and treacherous, and his favors are greatly desired. The Snake Lady is the personified essence of a psychotropic plant and a youthful aspect of the creator-mother goddess—Xmucane being the crone—and a vessel for fertility magic. She has neither lunar nor jaguar features, but we can guess that, like Goddess O, she has both young and old aspects. Itzam is her child, named as such because she winds the serpent and opens the portal for him; he is her lover because his sorcery is required for conception (human conception, that is, without our knowing whose) and induction of the soul of the lineage into a fetus or baby. That sorcery directed toward the effigies gives them birth—amid shock and awe—into the sphere of men so they may provide, as Chahk, thunderstorms and vital rains and, as Te', the bounty of forest and field. In the material sense, these deities are also "providers of sustenance"; this may explain the presence in their headdresses of the Piscine Jester God (K1813, K7838, K3716) and a diminutive Huk Pul Tzin (K1813).

Further support for the bundled deities as *tzin* was shared by Guido Krempel (personal communication) in February 2015. On K8719 a white coati, an attendant at a grisly beheading, wears the signature "Xibalba red neck scarf" and a headdress with a prominent Piscine Jester God. The short text naming him concludes with SAK-tzi-ni *sak tzin* "white/pure sustenance."

In the realm of gods, Yax Ha'al Chahk splits the *witz* that receives the K'awiil, the half-feline baby—the quintessential *wahy* being who is also the Old God, a bearer of the essence of the sacrificed human infant tagged as *mijiin* "man's child," and a promise of continuity for the lineage. The waters surrounding the *witz* erupt in waves and froth at the blows from the now mature "Chahk Who Shakes Water and Earth." The verdant tree rises from the mountain laden with the gifts of the forest, granting men arboreal and agricultural abundance. It is an act of parturition that brings K'awiil as the Old God/Serpent forth from the living *witz* as a nascent extrusion; it is an entanglement both convoluted and complete. Pertinent is Taube's (1994: 664) mention of Tz'utujil and K'iche' birth and *tzolk'in* anniversary rites in which the Mam (the Old God) must be summoned.

Taube (1994: 669–74) cites the Baby Jaguar as a specific example of a *k'ex* sacrifice. *K'ex*—a word meaning "substitute"—appears in modern Yucatec and Tzotzil ethnographic sources, among others. Typically, this rite takes the form of libations poured or animals and birds offered to the Earth Lord amid a petition—which, in turn, takes any number of forms including protection, revenge, healing, or the recovery of something lost, including a lost soul. House dedications will feature such an offering to secure the dwelling against dangerous entities or winds. The item offered—be it alcohol, copal, tobacco, a maize drink, or a live chicken or turkey—is intended as a gift to the earth and a substitute for something in its clutches. The Earth Lord is seen as a trickster, dangerous and fickle, with whom one must delicately negotiate. While the delicacy of this engagement may not seep ostensibly from the scenes on Classic stelae, we know it by its nature to be dangerous, as it concerns matters of harvests and weather, royal succession, birth of an heir, or success in warfare.

CREATION AND DARKNESS

We have had more than a hint that for the Maya of Kaan, death engenders the nourishment of gods and ancestors. This is clear in the text of Tortuguero Monument

6 (Gronemeyer and MacLeod 2010: 48-49n49), where the sacrifice of war captives ("piling of skulls, pooling of blood") "strengthens nine times over the vitality and breath" of the lineage. On the Tonina "labyrinth of the underworld" frieze, the Turtle-Footed Death God with his *ahk'ab* vase/snake pendant dances while carrying a decapitated head (Yadeún Angulo 1992).

The Baby Jaguar narrative texts say nothing directly about the Death God, as if depicting him was sufficient and invoking him was dangerous (though—as on K1152—he can be named with his own caption). But without him, no part of the transmutation is possible. On the Quenon Vase (see figure 8.14), I noted that the *ahk'ab* vase pendant the Death God wears is unique: unlike all the other inverted vase pendants he and Chahk display on these vases, this one emits a stream of dark froth along with a tzi sign. It joins an undulating, speckled layer of mist that surrounds the *witz*. If we understand the metaphorical contents of the vase here and in the nominal phrase as *tzin*, "sustenance" (which water is in all forms), then that misty, swirling register here and in similar scenes must be *tzin* (as the little snake in the orifice must be), though we cannot completely discount that it could be *ahk'ab* "darkness." Creeping forward on a speculative limb, I suggest that the red misty swirls emanating from sacrificial offerings on the San Bartolo murals are an early representation of *tzin*.

While the many varieties of *ahk'ab* "darkness" jars warrant a study of their own, a brief review of them is in order. I have noted the *ahk'ab* vase pendants worn by Chahk and God A; they are also regularly worn by God A-Prime and other underworld beings. On the Resurrection Plate (K1892), Yax Bahlam (Xb'alanke) pours the contents of an *ahk'ab* jar on the turtle shell as Jun Ajaw (Junajpu) greets the nascent Maize God in yet another lost tale of the Hero Twins. From this we infer that an *ahk'ab* jar contains vital nourishment—in the material sense, rain. It is noteworthy that the inverted vase hieroglyph in our nominal phrase is never an *ahk'ab* jar; while both *ahk'ab* and *tzin* are nourishing substances, they are not the same. The *ahk'ab* jar is frequently associated with Akan or God A-Prime, a liminal, often anthropomorphic *wahy* figure, the god of pulque and of bees (Grube and Nahm 1994; Grube 2004: 67–68; Kerr n.d.a). He is once called *took jatz'oom mok chih* "sparking-striking pulque sickness"—presumably a term for hellish drunkenness (note K2284 and Zender 2004 for the *jatz'* reading). One thus assumes that these jars contain pulque or, more likely, a potent admixture. A god named *Chihil Akan* "pulque Akan" is named as a patron deity of the king of Tortuguero (Gronemeyer and MacLeod 2010: 45). As noted above, it is a priest with Akan attributes who receives human infants destined to be the *k'ex* for the Baby Jaguar (K8655, K1200, K5855), though I have not had time to explore that story. *Ahk'ab* jars, both at rest and carried using handles amid a dance—appear in a variety of underworld group-intoxication scenes, but I am not aware of any associated with *ch'ahbahk'ab* "creation-darkness." *Ahk'ab* operates metaphorically as a two-sided scrying mirror, with Akan's side a conduit to chaos, madness, and malevolent entities; but if the sacrificer who receives infants is indeed a priest of Akan, then that god also has a vital role in the transmutation of sustenance. Taube (2004: 77, figure 8.6a) considers an Early Classic stucco vase from Tikal featuring a large serpent framing an *ahk'ab* sign being lifted from the water by the Sun God while the Wind God tickles the ophidian's chin. He ties this imagery to rain—specifically, the rising of morning mist from bodies of water as it is heated by the sun and nudged by the wind. He views the *ahk'ab* "snake jar" sometimes carried by Chahk as symbolic of rain-laden nimbus clouds. It follows that an inverted *ahk'ab* jar suggests rainmaking, and the frequent association of Yax Ha'al Chahk with the inverted jar pendant is supportive. We can infer that the Death God's identical pendant signals his role in the sacrificial component of rain production. But there is an aspect of *ahk'ab* having to do with the absolute darkness of original creation and the coming into being of the K'iche' Rilaj Mam, who is the reflex of the archaic Old God himself.

A unique example of the *ahk'ab* jar—carried upright in the right hand with its companion snake—is found on the Dumbarton Oaks Panel, unquestionably from Palenque but without provenance (Schele and Miller 1986: 274–76). It is to my knowledge the only *ahk'ab* jar carried by a historical individual, one we have met on the Palace Tablet: K'inich K'an Joy Chitam, the last son of K'inich Janab Pakal. In the scene he is flanked by his parents: his mother on his right holds a diminutive full-figure K'awiil, as if displaying a living infant; his father on his left holds in the same manner a diminutive composite (anthropomorphic, avian, and piscine) Jester God (Steinbach 2015a: figures 2–6). K'an Joy Chitam impersonates Yax Ha'al Chahk and in his left hand holds a bearded serpent wrapped around an eccentric axe blade as he dances. The text features two dates. The first is the ninety-two-sidereal-year canonical nadir anniversary of the death of his predecessor K'an Joy Chitam I, on which the young heir (age twelve, named by both his pre-accession and regnal names) is taken by his father, K'inich Janab Pakal, into the sanctuary (*waybil*) of the "Three and the Nine Chahks" and wherein "his foot treads on the mountain of his gods." The second date is controversial: it falls either thirteen years after the first date (when the heir, not yet king, is twenty-five) or fifty-two years after that, as suggested by Schele and Miller. This would be two years after the dedication of House A–D of the palace (the heir, who would now be seventy-eight, has been king for twenty years) on which the event is *och k'awiil ta tzihl? ti Ux Chahk Balun Chahk*: "*k'awiil* enters into the cleft? of the Three Chahks and the Nine Chahks." From the text we infer that the dance scene portrays the first event, but the two dates are entangled with text and image, with no mention of the king's accession or other events of his life. There are reasons to speculate that the T124 tzi sign when suffixed in this orientation is a rare logogram TZIL, here representing the Cholan noun *tzihl* "break, crack, cleft" (Wisdom 1950), but the details must be deferred to an epigraphic analysis (MacLeod n.d.). If this is correct, it suggests that the elusive "entering of *k'awiil*" is an offering like that of the Baby Jaguar, adding to a lineage repository of power that could be tapped at requisite intervals by future heirs. This impersonation of Yax Ha'al Chahk in a rite of heir apparency resonates with the K'iche' concept of heritable "lightning in the blood" and likely signifies an activation of the effigies K'awiil and the Jester God (a composite of *huun*, *tzin*, and maize) in the laps of the parents. I have considered this panel in detail because it exemplifies the percolation of now familiar mythic elements—*ahk'ab*, *k'awiil*, *tzin*, lineage ancestors, Yax Ha'al Chahk, the cleft in the primordial mountain, the Bearded Serpent, the plant-like Jester God, the activation of "infant" effigies—up from an archaic substratum into state-level practice regarding the ancestors, royal succession, and the afterlife.

We have seen a personified (but plain) jar amid a conjuring of the Old God termed "creation-darkness" (figure 8.15). The phrase *u-bah tu ch'ahb ti y-ahk'ab* "(it is) his image amid his creation and/within his darkness" appears regularly in association with rites of penitence and humiliation of war captives on Classic monuments, as on Yaxchilan Stela 18. The blood offered to gods and ancestors in these rites is shed amid a deliberate erasure of the boundary between captor and captive. This may explain why some captives are said to have no creation-darkness, as if it is a vital force that can be appropriated. References to *ch'ahb ahk'ab* and serpent winding in the parentage statements of Classic Maya kings point to procreative and ensouling rituals, as depicted on Yaxchilan Lintel 13 (note the bloodletters, the serpent with the *k'awiil* of the newborn son in its maw, and *ch'ahb* in the offering plate) and seen in the following examples:

u-bah u-chiit-ch'ahb	"he (the son) is the person of her co-creation" (mother)
u-nich u-kopeem	"he (the son) is the flower of his winder-serpent" (father) (Tortuguero Monument 6)
u-bah u-ch'ahb ahk'ab	"he (the son) is the person of her creation-darkness" (mother)
u-sih u-ch'ahb ahk'ab (*Yaxchilan Stela 7*)	"he (the son) is the gift of his creation-darkness" (father)

Postclassic evidence for the identity of creation-darkness with parentage is found in the Yucatec Maya *Ritual of the Bacabs* (Roys 1965), a collection of esoteric incantations for curing. Amid these, the curer invokes the progenitors—the *ch'ahb* and *ahk'ab*—of the affliction, as seen in the words for jaguar-macaw-seizure:

Mac cech tah ch'ab mac cech tah akab . . . ca   "Who was your creator? Who was your
sihech? Max a na max a coob cit ca ch'abtab   darkness . . . when you were born? Who was your
ech   mother? Who was your begetter, father . . . ?"

(Roys 1965: 3, 72)

In these incantations, the power of malevolent beings (akin to the *wahyob* depicted on Classic ceramics) is named and mitigated by the curer as he stands at the permeable boundary between the destructive and restorative aspects of sorcery. At this interface between chaos and order, *ahk'ab* partakes of both. Its ordered side manifests as (1) a distillation of heritable ancestral power; (2) a reservoir of that power in primordial time; (3) when present on a jar in some contexts (benevolent elemental processes, deity birth, Chahk impersonation), a signifier of divine nourishment; and (4) as *ch'ahb ahk'ab*, a reenactment by lineage heirs of an ancestral genesis within a primal darkness:

Nothing stirs. All is languid, at rest in the sky. There is not yet anything standing erect. Only the expanse of the water, only the tranquil sea lies alone. There is not yet anything that might exist. All lies placid and silent in the darkness, in the night. (Popol Vuh, Christenson 2007: 58)

The syntax and contexts of *ch'ahb ahk'ab* statements suggest that both of these are true: (1) creation takes place within darkness, and (2) creation and darkness are parallel generative entities. I must point out that *ch'ahb*, in addition to meaning "create (from nothing)" in Yucatec, also means "fasting, abstention, penitence" in many lowland Mayan languages (Kaufman and Justeson 2003: 714). But the Classic monuments demonstrate these to be Christianized dilutions of an original meaning: "blood sacrifice."

As for the Classic Mayas' offering of human lives to the underworld, there is bounteous archaeological evidence in caves. An unpublished monograph (Reents-Budet and MacLeod 1997) on a spectacular river cave in Belize with remote, formation-filled chambers documents the crystal-encrusted skeletons of tiny infants once cast into pools, as well as remains of young adults associated with hearths, unslipped pottery jars, metates, bone awls, obsidian blades, shell jewelry, and enema tubes (for additional examples, see chapter 7, this volume). Given the location of bloodletters and jars in remote niches far from daylight and the suitability of these retreats for extended vigils, I have suggested that visionary rites also took place in total darkness (MacLeod and Puleston 1978). Perhaps the Baby Jaguar story was a prescription for these hidden rituals in caves.

GIFTS OF THE FOREST PRIMEVAL

Maya iconographers have sometimes invoked the First Tree as the *axis mundi*, or vertical core, of a layered color/directional cosmogram, a concept dear to students of comparative religion. Steinbach (2015a) has recently considered the *axis mundi* in her study of the vertical assignments to Maya costume of celestial (avian), earthly (anthropomorphic), and underworld (piscine) forms of the Jester God. Erich Neumann (1974: 48–54) synopsizes what several generations of Jungian scholars have said:

> The Great Earth Mother who brings forth all life from herself is eminently the
> mother of all vegetation. The fertility myths and rituals of the whole world are
> based upon this archetypal context. The center of this vegetative symbolism is the
> tree. As fruit-bearing tree of life it is female: it bears, transforms, nourishes; its leaves,
> branches, twigs are "contained" in it and dependent on it. The protective character
> is evident in the treetop that shelters nests and birds. But in addition the trunk is a
> container, "in" which dwells its spirit, as the soul dwells in the body. (1974: 48–49)

This is qualitatively and poetically applicable to the tree at the center of our attention. Whether it is feminine remains to be known, but then, why not? Nicholas Carter (n.d.: 27) was among the first to have given the emerging tree its due recognition:

> One of the most important optional elements in scenes dealing with the Baby Jaguar
> sacrifice is the tree which sprouts from the infant's grave in certain depictions of
> the sacrificial event. In fact, this tree—the World Tree, so central to Maya religious
> thought—implies a whole set of images and ideas which are, in my view, the key to
> understanding the Baby Jaguar series, the Snake Lady series, and the connection
> between them.

Carter (n.d.: 28) states that he had "to conclude that the Baby Jaguar, the Pax God/World Tree, and the Uk' Kaan/God N entity are in some sense all the same being." This conclusion rests upon an identity between the Baby Jaguar and the jaguar-paw ear of the tree, a view shared by García Barrios and Valencia Rivera (2011: 80 and elsewhere), who also regard the tree as fundamental. It is both tempting and problematic to see the tree as a transformation of the Baby Jaguar, but we can certainly understand the Old God (God N), the serpent, and the Baby Jaguar to be the same being. To this unity, let us add another occasional player: the Jaguar God of the Underworld.

In the Popol Vuh (Christenson 2007: 85), the tree in which Seven Macaw perches is identified as a nance, *Byrosinima crassifolia*, a ubiquitous native cherry-like fruit that the bird feasted upon. Stuart identifies the tree with the jaguar-paw ear on the

FIGURE 8.21. Waterlily plant with a TE' base, a jaguar-paw ear, and a white heron perching in it.

Blowgunner Vase (see figure 8.6) as a ceiba due to a largely effaced YAX sign to the left of the basal TE', yielding *yaxte'* "ceiba" (*Ceiba pentandra*) in Cholan. I have suggested that the leaves and fruit of that tree and similar ones on these vases signal the bottle-gourd tree *Crescentia cujete*. Stuart (2012: 133) has also proposed that the central tree associated with the Principal Bird Deity at San Bartolo is the strangler fig *Ficus cotinifolia*, although to me its double-helix trunk is vine-like and its leaves and fruit are more like the immature bottle gourd. Elsewhere on the mural a bursting, constricted bottle gourd ejects newborn anthropomorphic "seeds" with umbilici. In testimony to ever-flowering divine reciprocity, the same pinnate compound leaves appear on the living perforators used by the Jun Ajaw supplicants offering genital blood to the trees from which the wood was taken. Might these explain the elusive Chahk title *yop-aat* "leafed stinger?"

While the three forms of the Jester God—avian, anthropomorphic, and piscine—are assignable to fig, maize, and waterlily, respectively, and may appear as trees (Steinbach 2015a; Stuart 2012: figures 11, 18, and elsewhere), perhaps we cannot identify the tree of creation. *Yax-te'* might simply mean "first tree." The ambiguity seems purposeful, as if the First Tree stood for all the woody sustenance of the tropical forest—ceiba, fig, gourd, nance, *t'iney*, cacao, mamey, avocado, breadnut, *tz'ite'*, *sihom*, *balche'*, copal, zapote, and many more—which nourished and sheltered birds, insects, animals, and man and provided beautiful hardwoods and utensils and implements, essential oils, fruit, soap, bedding, paper, incense, and, not least, medicines. In a bow to ambiguity, consider the Te' on K555 (figure 8.21); it is a waterlily plant with a TE' base, a jaguar-paw ear, and a white heron perching in it. Fish, snails, and humans may eat parts of the waterlily plant, and its green blanket on still waters shelters myriad forms of aquatic life. Its fronds symbolize the watery underworld and adorn the skull (*baak* "regenerative bone") from which the Maize

God is reborn. A fascinating variant of the waterlily tree appears on K1609, where Chahk, up to his waist in water, sprouts supple branches from his head that become the Bearded Serpent and the Piscine Jester God with its waterlily blossom. Here we see in a new permutation the emergence of *k'awiil* and *tzin* from the waters of creation and recognize familiar actors—the snake, the "shark"—in a fully vegetal expression. A fusion of Yax Ha'al Chahk with the Bearded Serpent is seen on K2772, where Chahk's foot (in the tradition of K'awiil) becomes the Serpent/Old God who encircles the pillar of an underground chamber; on its dais, the Snake Lady sits with two other young goddesses.

One wonders why the shark-like Piscine Jester God and its waterlily blossom should represent or be read as "sustenance" on the Palace Tablet (see figure 8.18), on the Jaina figurine (see figure 8.19), and in this Codex-Style narrative. As Steinbach (2015a) and Stuart (2012: 128–29) have observed, the Avian and Piscine Jester Gods were clearly differentiated in the Olmec Preclassic milieu of their origin and in the Maya Early Classic, but they later often merged into composite forms or traded roles as generic emblems of sovereignty (Steinbach, personal communication, 2014). Thus one finds on K760 the Piscine Jester God gracing the page of a codex as the animate *huun*. But a pure semantic pedigree for the Piscine Jester God must have endured as well, preserving an association among the waters of creation, fish, and incorporeal nourishment. This may explain the connections among fishing, rainmaking, and conjuring as well as the presence of fish embedded in Late Preclassic representations of the vegetal *witz* (Taube 2004: 74–77, 83 [figure 11a]). It is perhaps also reflected in the transformation of Junajpu and Xb'alanke into fish prior to their rebirth, as if the ancient Maya and their forebears viewed the denizens of the waters as the foundation of the chain of life. Fish would have been the staple protein in the diets of Formative peoples living in the swampy, riverine lowlands of the Gulf Coast. Given what we now know, the presence of the Piscine Jester God as the tooth of the Bearded Serpent (K3716, K3202) suggests that being is *tzin*: sustenance from the waters of creation.

Mayan communities into the first half of the twentieth century had a rich pharmacopoeia of herbs used as teas, poultices, and chewable leaves and roots, with detailed prescriptions for their use in curing (Roys 1931). They named all the plants of the forest and knew their habits and applications. Among the Maya and across the Americas, tobacco (*Nicotiana tabacum*) was smoked, chewed, and taken as snuff, often within ritual. Its indigenous use as snuff survives in Tzotzil and Tzeltal communities (Groark 2010) and among the Lacandon (Robicsek 1978; Roberto Bruce, personal communication, 1978). I have smoked traditional cigars and drunk *balché* with the Lacandon of Naha' and know their potency firsthand. Tobacco has abundant medicinal uses, and for some years, by analogy from Amazonia where it is a potent psychoactive decoction, it had been considered a likely ingredient in the jars, cups, and clysters seen on Classic Maya vases (Robicsek 1978: 21–23, citing Furst 1976). If God L, the theomorphic form of the plant, is an aspect of the Old God as Martin suggests, then one might propose tobacco as an ingredient in scenes involving that old sorcerer with his paraphernalia. We know from John B. Carlson's (2007) analysis of a private collection of snuff bottles that the Maya had a distinctive icon for the tobacco leaf that substitutes for a glyphic spelling *may* "tobacco." The leaf appears on these tiny bottles as well as on examples of God L; it has three circles at the leaf's tip representing the small yellow flowers or seed pods. Because these never occur on the many examples of the Snake Lady's leaf skirt, her plant is likely not tobacco. In conformity with indigenous medicinal practice in the Americas, either several plants (perhaps including tobacco) or hers alone (not tobacco) might be in the brew that propels our narrative and the *ch'ahb ahk'ab* rite of K4113.

Barbara Kerr (2007) has made a compelling argument for Datura as the plant source in a woman's snake conjuring on Yaxchilan Lintel 25. These rites of women—tied to the *pul k'iin* "cast augury" title proposed above—involve tongue piercing and scrying through the smoke of burning cord and blood-spattered paper. Kerr proposes that the conjured serpent with an ancestor in its maw has Datura flowers on its head. It confirms what Brian Stross and Justin Kerr (1990) and Adrian Andreacchio (2013: 37–45) have proposed in essays featuring ethnohistorical and ethnographic data on *Datura inoxia* ingestion. *Datura* and *Brugmansia* species, which contain scopolamine and other tropane alkaloids, have long been used by indigenous tribes on both American continents as potent facilitators of initiations, dream states, and communion with the dead. Stross and Kerr (1990: 354) argue that the clyster—for which they have ethnographic evidence—was the safest method of delivery because it circumvented the more dangerous side effects of the drug. In addition (354), Datura visions reported by ethnographers often feature serpents. A case is made for a Classic Maya blend of Datura and pulque taken either orally or rectally. Ralph L. Roys (1931: 285) gives the Yucatec Maya names for Datura inoxia as *toh ku* "true god" and *cheles ku* "rainbow god," citing the plant's primary use as a cure for hemorrhoids. One recognizes in these names a deeper history.

A matter still to be clarified is the depiction of purging in the Maya enema scenes accompanied by the donning of "vomit bibs" (Nicholas Hellmuth, personal communication, 1976). Examples are noted on K1645 (figure 8.16, an off-stage Snake Lady scene) and on K1973, K8763, and K9294. Stross and Kerr (1990) cite Amazonian ayahuasca brews (which may contain *Brugmansia*) as famous for producing visions of snakes but lament the unlikely availability of the ingredients to the Maya. Ayahuasca is a powerful psychoactive and purgative brew that contains dimethyltryptamine (DMT) and harmine, a monoamine oxidase inhibitor that potentiates DMT orally. What is little known is that a close relative of the woody vine *Banisteriopsis caapi* (the harmine source) is native to Chiapas (Dennis Breedlove, personal communication 1979; Rätsch 2005: 719). If the Chiapas vine *Banisteriopsis muricata* and the native DMT-containing Mimosa species were known to the Classic Maya, then the purging, the birthing of the Old God, and the visionary immersion in the primordial realm could all be explained in this way. Visually, a leaf of either *D. inoxia* or *B. muricata* could account for the pattern on the Snake Lady's skirt. Finally, to my foregoing conjectures about *ch'ahb ahk'ab*, I can add that *ahk'ab* jars are likely to have contained psychoactive plant decoctions (Braakhuis 2005: 186–88), which are conduits to the ancestors and to the teeming netherworld, and that *ch'ahb* "creation"—as noted on K4113—refers to the rites of ingestion, conjuring, and blood sacrifice.

EPILOGUE

I have used the words *story*, *tale*, *narrative*, and *myth* interchangeably, and in most respects this seems right. The Popol Vuh is all of these, as is the account of the Baby Jaguar and the Snake Lady. Both partake of a shared Mayan heritage—one that belongs to a vast, ancient Mesoamerican matrix. What is noteworthy with respect to myth is that it encodes fundamental beliefs and ideologies at the heart of the social order. It exemplifies and reinforces them in accounts of gods and heroes with extraordinary qualities, in settings that lie in primordial time reaching back to a genesis. Under it all rumbles a voice of authority like a river in a deep chasm. What we distill from Classic Maya art and literature suggests not a single underlying ontology but rather a benthic repertoire from which the elite chose symbols and themes to orchestrate their own ideologies. As we endeavor to do (clumsily, with far fewer pieces), they were navigating and interpreting archaic, perhaps opaque layers of a history whose true origins were unknown, shaping its relevance to a current agenda, adding new layers as ears of maize affixed to pre-agricultural protagonists. We glimpse manifestations of the narrative of the Baby Jaguar and the Snake Lady as they have surfaced on public monuments, interwoven with the politics of the ruling dynasty. Among these we have noted the Scroll Baby as an Early Classic patron god and companion to the *kaloomte'* title at Tikal; at Yaxchilan, we have seen serpent/ancestor conjuring by royal women amid tongue perforation and transformation of blood into smoke; in the trifigural panels of Palenque, we have observed reifications of ancestral rites of succession and obligations to nourish the gods. These are mirrors of the arcane discourse on elite ceramics used in private rituals, gifted in the forging of alliances, and finally consigned to tombs of dead kings embarking on their journey through Xibalba.

Because the mythology on Classic Maya polychrome ceramics is almost entirely visual, we can witness the strategies the artists employed to mark the boundary between "scribal present" and the timeless realm of the primordial and the unconscious—that being dreams, visions, ancestors, progenitor gods, and first creations. It is the subtle back-and-forth shift across this boundary that weaves the whole into one tapestry and transmits the core ideology of our myth: that of perennial sacred reciprocity.

We read in the Popol Vuh of the attempts by the Framer and the Shaper to create a being who will be "a provider and a sustainer" (see Christenson 2003), whose progeny will recognize and be thankful for their birth and their hearts, who will have language with which to hold the memory of their creation and to forever express their gratitude. After two failures—the mud people and the wooden effigies; after the defeat of Seven Macaw; after the adventures of the Hero Twins and their fathers on the earth and in Xibalba; after the discovery of the cleft mountain Paxil (a rich reflex of our *witz*) full of maize and honey and trees with many kinds of sumptuous fruit, the Framer and the Shaper now make man from ground corn and water as flesh and blood. However:

> Perfect was their sight, and perfect was their knowledge of everything beneath the sky. If they gazed about them, looking intently, they beheld that which was in the sky and that which was upon the earth. Instantly they were able to behold everything. They did not have to walk to see all that existed beneath the sky. They merely saw it from wherever they were. Thus their knowledge became full. Their vision passed beyond the trees and the rocks, beyond the lakes and the seas, beyond the mountains and the valleys . . . thus their vision of everything beneath the sky was completed, and they gave thanks to the Framer and the Shaper: . . . "We thank you, therefore, that we were created, that we were given frame and shape. We became because of you, our Grandmother, and you, our Grandfather," they said when they gave thanks for their frame and shape. Their knowledge of everything that they saw was complete—the four corners and the four sides, that which is within the sky and that which is within the earth. (Popol Vuh, Christenson 2007: 185–86)

The Framer and the Shaper are troubled and decide to retrieve some of the knowledge given to the first men so that these would not be equal to gods. Christenson (2007: 197n494) explains:

> Although the creator gods eventually clouded the vision of the first men, the progenitors of the Maya and their descendants nevertheless believe themselves to bear within their blood the potential for divine sight. Present-day aj q'ij priests believe that their divine ancestors, who set the pattern for contemporary rituals, continue to operate

through them as conduits. It is this ancestral vision that allows the aj q'ij to "see" beyond the limits of time and distance.

Of relevance to the closing of our tale about this myth is the term *k'ajb'* "blood sacrifice" in K'iche', cited in the Popol Vuh as a token of the peoples' gratitude after the foundation of the K'iche' lineage. *K'ajb'*, as Christenson (2007: 190n502) learned from Mayanists Stephen Houston and Karl Taube, is cognate with the Classic Cholan *ch'ahb*, which we know well in *ch'ahb ahk'ab*, "creation/sacrifice-darkness." With this we return to the procreative visionary rite, to the transmutation of the lightning-being Seven Provider of Sustenance. We do so with new knowledge: although the gods did not want men to have omniscience, amid the conjuring of the sustenance of the lineage and obedience to divine prescriptions for reciprocity, brief glimpses were permitted.

ACKNOWLEDGMENTS

The original version of this chapter was presented at the Popol Vuh Conference at the University of California, Merced in March 2012. I am grateful to the organizers Holley Moyes, her students, and all those who helped make the conference such a success. I give abundant gratitude as well to the friends and colleagues who have helped me along the way by sharing images, data, inspiration, and encouragement: Nicholas Carter, Michael Grofe, Kerry Hull, Justin Kerr, Michel Quenon, Dorie Reents-Budet, and Penny Steinbach. Without them, this project would never have reached fruition. Bounteous thanks as well to Allen Christenson, Michael Grofe, Justin Kerr, Guido Krempel, Michel Quenon, and Penny Steinbach for comments on an earlier draft. I am grateful as well to Holley Moyes, Allen Christenson, and Frauke Sasche for their hard work in preparing this volume for publication. Most of all, I thank Justin and Barbara Kerr for the Mayavase Database, a conduit to the gods and ancestors. *Un fuerte abrazo*; prayers for safe passage.

REFERENCES CITED

Alexander, Helen. n.d. "God K on Maya Ceramic Vessels: Notes and Commentary." Mayavase Archive, www.famsi.org/kerrmaya.html.

Andreacchio, Adrian. 2013. "The Role of Psychoactive Substances as Entheogens and Medicines in Pre-Columbian Mexico." MA thesis, University College, London. http://erowid.org/history/history_article3_psychoactives_in_precolumbian_mexico.pdf.

Barrera Vásquez, Alfredo. 1980. *Diccionario Maya Cordemex: Maya-Español, Español-Maya*. Ediciones Cordemex, Editorial Porrúa, Mérida, Mexico City.

Bassie-Sweet, Karen. 2002. "Maya Creator Gods." http://www.mesoweb.com/features/bassie/CreatorGods/CreatorGods.pdf.

Bassie-Sweet, Karen, Nicholas A. Hopkins, and J. Kathryn Josserand. 2012. "Narrative Structure and the Drum Major Headdress." In *Parallel Worlds: Genre, Discourse, and Poetics in Contemporary, Colonial, and Classic Maya Literature*, ed. Kerry M. Hull and Michael D. Carrasco, 195–219. University Press of Colorado, Boulder.

Braakhuis, H.E.M. 2005. "Xbalanque's Canoe." *Anthropos* 100 (2005): 173–91.

Carlson, John B. 2007. "Entries 16–19, 118." In *The Jay I. Kislak Collection at the Library of Congress: A Catalog of the Gift of the Jay I. Kislak Foundation to the Library of Congress*, ed. Arthur Dunkelman, 11–13, 42. Library of Congress, Washington, DC.

Carrasco, Michael D. 2005. "The Mask Flange Iconographic Complex: The Art, Ritual, and History of a Maya Sacred Image." PhD dissertation, Department of Art and Art History, University of Texas, Austin.

Carter, Nicholas. n.d. "Drink-Snakes, Snake Ladies, and Baby Jaguars: An Examination of Certain Codex Style Vessels Connected by Textual and Iconographic Content." Unpublished manuscript. Paper submitted to David Stuart's 2005 class Maya Hieroglyphic Writing, Department of Art and Art History, University of Texas, Austin.

Christenson, Allen J. 2007. *Popol Vuh: Sacred Book of the Quiché Maya People*. Electronic version of original 2003 publication. Mesoweb, http://www.mesoweb.com/publications/Christenson/PopolVuh.pdf.

Closs, Michael P. 1988. "The Hieroglyphic Text of Stela 9, Lamanai, Belize." Research Reports on Ancient Maya Writing 20–22. Center for Maya Research, Washington, DC.

Coe, Michael D. 1973. *The Maya Scribe and His World*. Grolier Club, New York.

Coe, Michael D. 1975. *Classic Maya Pottery at Dumbarton Oaks*. Dumbarton Oaks, Washington, DC.

Coe, Michael D. 1978. *Lords of the Underworld: Masterpieces of Classic Maya Ceramics*. Art Museum, Princeton University Press, Princeton, NJ.

Coe, Michael D. 1981. "Foreword." In *The Maya Book of the Dead: The Ceramic Codex*, by Francis Robicsek and Donald M. Hales. University of Virginia Art Museum, Charlottesville.

Davletshin, Albert, and Péter Bíró. 2014. "A Possible Syllable for t'i in Maya Writing." *PARI Journal* 15 (1): 1–10.

Fields, Virginia M. 1991. "The Iconographic Heritage of the Maya Jester God." In *Sixth Palenque Round Table, 1986*, ed. Virginia M. Fields, 167–74. University of Oklahoma Press, Norman. Mesoweb, http://www.mesoweb.com/pari/publications/RT08/JesterGod.pdf.

Furst, Peter. 1976. *Hallucinogens and Culture*. Chandler and Sharp, San Francisco.

García Barrios, Ana, and Rogelio Valencia Rivera. 2011. "Relaciones de Parentesco el el Mito del Dios Viejo y la Señora Dragón en las Cerámicas del Estilo Códice." Texto, *Imagen E Identidad en la Pintura Maya Prehispánica.* Centro de Estudios Mayas Cuaderno 36, ed. Merideth Paxton and Manuel A. Hermann Lejarazu. Universidad Nacional Autónoma de Mexico, Mexico City.

Groark, Kevin P. 2010. "The Angel in the Gourd: Ritual, Therapeutic, and Protective Uses of Tobacco (Nicotiana tabacum) among the Tzeltal and Tzotzil Maya of Chiapas, Mexico." *Journal of Ethnobiology* 30 (1): 5–30.

Gronemeyer, Sven, and Barbara MacLeod. 2010. "What Could Happen in 2012: A Re-Analysis of the 13-Bak'tun Prophecy on Tortuguero Monument 6." *Wayeb Notes* 34, http://www.wayeb.org/notes/wayeb_notes0034.pdf.

Grube, Nikolai. 2000. "Fire Rituals in the Context of Classic Maya Initial Series." In *The Sacred and the Profane: Architecture and Identity in the Maya Lowlands*, ed. Pierre Robert Colas, Kai Delvendahl, Marcus Kuhnert, and Annette Schubart, 93–109. Third European Maya Conference, University of Hamburg, November 1998, Verlag Anton Saurwein, Markt Schwaben.

Grube, Nikolai. 2004. "Akan, the God of Drinking, Disease, and Death." In *Continuity and Change: Maya Religious Practices in Temporal Perspective*, ed. Daniel Graña Behrens, Nikolai Grube, Christian M. Prager, Frauke Sachse, Stefanie Teufel, and Elisabeth Wagner, 59–76. Acta Mesoamericana 14. Verlag Anton Sauerwein, Markt Schwaben.

Grube, Nikolai. 2012. "A Logogram for SIP, 'Lord of the Deer.'" *Mexicon* 34 (4): 138–41.

Grube, Nikolai, and Werner Nahm. 1994. "A Census of Xibalba: A Complete Inventory of Way Characters on Maya Ceramics." In *The Maya Vase Book*, vol. 4, ed. Justin Kerr and Barbara Kerr, 686–715. Kerr Associates, New York.

Helmke, Christophe. 2013. "Mesoamerican Lexical Calques in Ancient Maya Writing and Imagery." *PARI Journal* 14 (2): 1–15.

Hofling, Charles Andrew, and Félix Fernando Tesucún. 1997. *Itzaj Maya-Spanish-English Dictionary Diccionario Maya Itzaj-Español-Inglés.* University of Utah Press, Salt Lake City.

Hull, Kerry M., and Alejandro Sheseña. n.d. "Drenched in Tradition: A Reading for the Inverted Vase Glyph." Manuscript in author's possession.

Kaufman, Terrence, with John Justeson. 2003. "A Preliminary Mayan Etymological Dictionary." *FAMSI*, http://www.famsi.org/reports/01051/index.html.

Kaufman, Terrence, and William M. Norman. 1984. "An Outline of Proto-Cholan Phonology, Morphology, and Vocabulary." In *Phoneticism in Mayan Hieroglyphic Writing*, ed. John S. Justeson and Lyle Campbell, 77–166. Institute for Mesoamerican Studies 9. State University of New York, Albany.

Kerr, Barbara. 2007. "Datura and the Vision." Mayavase, http://www.mayavase.com/datura.pdf.

Kerr, Justin. 1992. "Please, Let's Stop Bashing the Baby." March 28, 1992, letter written to Linda Schele with a few recent revisions. Mayavase, http://www.mayavase.com/bashing baby.pdf.

Kerr, Justin. n.d.a. *Justin Kerr's Mayavase Archive*. Mayavase, http://www.famsi.org/kerr maya.html.

Kerr, Justin. n.d.b. "The Transformation of Xbalanqué, or the Many Faces of God A-Prime." Mayavase, http://www.mayavase.com/tran/trans.html.

Landa, Diego de. 1978. *Relación de las cosas de Yucatán, 1566*. Translated by William Gates as *Friar Diego de Landa—Yucatan Before and After the Conquest*. Publication 20. Maya Society, Baltimore, 1937. Dover reprint.

Lopes, Luís. 2005. "A New Look at the Name Phrase of the 'Snake Lady.'" *Wayeb Notes* 19. http://www.wayeb.org/notes/wayeb_notes0019.pdf.

MacLeod, Barbara. n.d. "Provider of Sustenance: The Decipherment of a Mystery Phrase on Narrative Codex Style Vases." Manuscript in author's possession.

MacLeod, Barbara, and Dennis E. Puleston. 1978. "Pathways into Darkness: The Search for the Road to Xibalba." In *Tercera Mesa Redonda de Palenque*, vol. 4, ed. Merle Greene Robertson and Donnan Call Jeffers, 71–77. Hearld Peters, Monterey. Mesoweb, http://www.mesoweb.com/pari/publications/RT04/Pathways.html.

Martin, Simon. 2002. "The Baby Jaguar: An Exploration of Its Identity and Origins in Maya Art and Writing." In *La organización social entre los mayas prehispánicos, coloniales y modernos: Memoria de la Tercera Mesa Redonda de Palenque*, vol. 1, ed. Vera Tiesler Blos, Rafael Cobos, and Merle Greene Robertson, 49–78. Consejo Nacional para la Cultura y las Artes, Mexico City.

Martin, Simon. 2015. "The Old Man of the Maya Universe: Unified Aspects to Ancient Maya Religion." In *Maya Archaeology*, vol. 3, ed. Charles Golden, Stephen Houston, and Joel Skidmore, 186–227. Precolumbia Mesoweb Press, San Francisco.

Neumann, Erich. 1974. *The Great Mother*. Bollingen Series XLVII. Princeton University Press, Princeton, NJ.

Quenon, Michel, and Geneviève Le Fort. 1997. "Rebirth and Resurrection in Maize God Iconography." In *The Maya Vase Book*, vol. 5, ed. Justin Kerr and Barbara Kerr, 884–902. Kerr Associates, New York.

Rätsch, Christian. 2005. *The Encyclopedia of Psychoactive Plants*. Park Street Press, Rochester, VT.

Reents-Budet, Dorie, Sylviane Boucher Le Landais, Yoly Palomo Carrillo, Ronald L. Bishop, and M. James Blackman. 2010. "Codex Style Ceramics: New Data Concerning Patterns of Production and Distribution." Paper presented at the 24th Symposium of Archaeological Investigations in Guatemala, July 19–24, Museo Nacional de Arqueología E Etnología, Guatemala City.

Reents-Budet, Dorie, and Barbara MacLeod. 1997. "The Archaeology of Petroglyph Cave, Cayo District, Belize." Unpublished manuscript, on file at the Department of Archaeology, Belize. Report on the 1978 season.

Robicsek, Francis. 1978. *The Smoking Gods: Tobacco in Maya Art, History, and Religion.* University of Oklahoma Press, Norman.

Robicsek, Francis, and Donald Hales. 1981. *The Maya Book of the Dead: The Ceramic Codex.* University of Virginia Art Museum, Charlottesville.

Roys, Ralph L. 1931. *The Ethno-Botany of the Maya.* Tulane University of Louisiana Middle American Research Series 2. Tulane University, New Orleans.

Roys, Ralph L. 1965. *Ritual of the Bacabs.* University of Oklahoma Press, Norman.

Roys, Ralph L. 1967. *The Book of Chilam Balam of Chumayel.* University of Oklahoma Press, Norman.

Schele, Linda, and Mary Ellen Miller. 1986. *The Blood of Kings: Dynasty and Ritual in Maya Art.* Kimbell Art Museum, Fort Worth, TX.

Steinbach, Penny. 2015a. "Aligning the Jester God: The Implications of Horizontality and Verticality in the Iconography of a Classic Maya Emblem." In *Maya Imagery, Architecture, and Activity: Space and Spatial Analysis in Art History*, ed. Maline Werness-Rude and Kaylee Spencer, 106–39. University of New Mexico Press, Albuquerque.

Steinbach, Penny. 2015b. "Sacrificing the Jaguar Baby: Understanding a Classic Maya Myth Depicted on Codex Style Ceramics." PhD dissertation, University of Texas, Austin.

Stross, Brian, and Justin Kerr. 1990. "Notes on the Maya Vision Quest through Enema." In *The Maya Vase Book*, vol. 2, ed. Justin Kerr and Barbara Kerr, 348–62. Kerr Associates, New York.

Stuart, David. 2006. "The Palenque Mythology." In *Sourcebook for the 30th Maya Meetings, March 14–19, 2006*, ed. David Stuart, new index by Linda Quist, 85–194. Mesoamerican Center, Department of Art and Art History, University of Texas, Austin.

Stuart, David. 2007. "The Ceiba Tree on K1226." Maya Decipherment, https://decipherment.wordpress.com/2007/04/14/the-ceiba-tree-on-k1226/.

Stuart, David. 2012. "The Name of Paper: The Mythology of Crowning and Royal Nomenclature on Palenque's Palace Tablet." In *Maya Archaeology 2*, ed. Charles Golden, Stephen Houston, and Joel Skidmore, 116–42. Precolumbia Mesoweb Press, San Francisco.

Stuart, David, Stephen Houston, and John Robertson. 1999. "Recovering the Past: Classic Maya Language and Classic Maya Gods." In *Notebook for the XXIIIrd Maya Hieroglyphic Forum*, ed. David Stuart, Stephen Houston, and John Robertson, II-1–II-80. University of Texas, Austin.

Tate, Carolyn E. 2012. *Reconsidering Olmec Visual Culture: The Unborn, Women, and Creation.* University of Texas Press, Austin.

Taube, Karl A. 1985. "The Classic Maya Maize God: A Reappraisal." In *Fifth Palenque Round Table (1983)*, vol. 7, ed. Merle Greene Robertson and Virginia Fields, 171–81. Pre-Columbian Art Research Institute, San Francisco.

Taube, Karl A. 1993. *Aztec and Maya Myths*. University of Texas Press, Austin.

Taube, Karl A. 1994. "The Birth Vase: Natal Imagery in Ancient Maya Myth and Ritual." In *The Maya Vase Book*, vol. 4, ed. Justin Kerr and Barbara Kerr, 652–85. Kerr Associates, New York.

Taube, Karl A. 2004. "Flower Mountain: Concepts of Life, Beauty, and Paradise among the Classic Maya." *RES—Anthropology and Aesthetics* 45: 69–98.

Taube, Karl A., William A. Saturno, David Stuart, and Heather Hurst. 2010. *The Murals of San Bartolo, El Petén, Guatemala, Part 2: The West Wall*. Ancient America 10. Boundary End Archaeology Research Center, Barnardsville, NC.

Taube, Karl, and Marc Zender. 2009. "American Gladiators: Ritual Boxing in Ancient Mesoamerica." In *Blood and Beauty*, ed. Heather Orr and Rex Koontz, 161–220. Cotsen Institute of Archaeology Press, Los Angeles.

Tedlock, Barbara. 1982. *Time and the Highland Maya*. University of New Mexico Press, Albuquerque.

Thompson, J. Eric S. 1960. *Maya Hieroglyphic Writing: An Introduction*. University of Oklahoma Press, Norman.

Valencia Rivera, Rogelio, and Hugo García Capistrán. 2013. "In the Place of the Mist: Analysis of a Maya Myth from a Mesoamerican Perspective." In *The Maya in a Mesoamerican Context: Comparative Approaches to Maya Studies*, ed. Jesper Nielsen and Christophe Helmke, 35–50. Acta Mesoamericana 26. Verlag Anton Sauerwein, München.

Wagner, Elisabeth. 1995. "Thoughts on the Chak-te'/Kalom-te' Title." Unpublished manuscript.

Wisdom, Charles. 1950. *Ch'orti' Dictionary*, transcribed and transliterated by Brian Stross. www.scribd.com/doc/921634/CHARLES-WISDOM-CHORTI-DICTIONARY.

Yadeun Angulo, Juan. 1992. *Toniná, El Laberinto del Inframundo*. Gobierno del Estado de Chiapas, Mexico City.

Zender, Marc. 2004. "Glyphs for 'Handspan' and 'Strike' in Classic Maya Ballgame Texts." *PARI Journal* 4 (4): 1–9.

9

Predatory Birds of the Popol Vuh

KAREN BASSIE-SWEET AND NICHOLAS A. HOPKINS

Beginning in the Epiclassic period, there was a cultural horizon extending from Morelos and Puebla to the Gulf Coast and the Yucatan Peninsula, including such sites as Tula, Cholula, Cacaxtla, El Tajín, Xochicalco, and Chichen Itza (Ringle et al. 1998; Ringle and Bey 2012). There is ample evidence that the K'iche' participated in this cultural horizon. Allen J. Christenson (2007: 26–31) has summarized the well-known affiliations of the highland K'iche' with Epiclassic Chichen Itza and Tula and the Postclassic Nahua cultures of Central Mexico and the Gulf Coast. The Popol Vuh recounts a foundation story that has elements from both the Classic period Maya and Epiclassic-Postclassic Nahua mythologies. This ancient tale explains how a family of primordial deities created the world, established its structure and order, and created humans to inhabit it and worship them. The meager visual arts record left behind by the K'iche' does not even hint at this rich mythology; however, episodes from the Popol Vuh story have long been used to explain some of the mythology illustrated in lowland Classic period art.

The Popol Vuh relates the deeds of three generations of deities: the creator grandparents called Xpiyacoc and Xmucane; their sons, One Junajpu and Seven Junajpu; and One Junajpu's sons, named One Chowen, One B'atz, Junajpu, and Xb'alanke. Classic period lowland parallels for all of these gods, their spouses, and their in-laws have been identified (Coe 1973, 1977, 1989; Taube 1985, 1992; Bassie-Sweet 1996, 2002, 2008; Zender 2004a). The Maya as well as other Mesoamerican cultures often categorize, organize, and structure their world using

DOI: 10.5876/9781646421992.c009

complementary opposition such as male/female, right/left, and senior/junior (Bassie-Sweet 2008: 3–4). This concept was a fundamental principle in ancient Maya worldview, and it was reflected in all aspects of life. The creator deities were the embodiment of complementary opposition and represented the ideal state for humans to achieve. The creator deities were role models for humans, in particular, for the ruling elite.

Birds are ubiquitous in Maya art. Avian creatures played key roles in Maya mythology as avatars and messengers of various gods, rulers, and secondary lords. The Popol Vuh relates important information about a number of predatory birds: the eagle, laughing falcon, owl, and vulture. This study focuses on the nature of the eagle and the laughing falcon, their relationship to specific deities, and their parallels with the birds of the Classic period lowland Maya, Epiclassic Chichen Itza, and the Epiclassic-Postclassic Nahua cultures of Central Mexico. Teotihuacan was the major influence on the Epiclassic-Postclassic Nahua cultures of Central Mexico. A discussion of Teotihuacan imagery is beyond the scope of this study, but it must be noted that eagles and owls are well represented in the art of this great city.

THE EAGLE

As discussed at length by Christenson (2007: 42–52), the Popol Vuh is a composition of rich and elegant poetry. He identified sixteen different types of parallelisms in the manuscript, including metonyms (merismus). In the Popol Vuh, the eagle and the vulture form a couplet in a passage that describes the reaction of the animals to the first rising of the Hero Twin Junajpu in his role as the sun of the new era:

True that they rejoiced all animals	*Qitzij chi xkikot ronojel chikop*
They spread their wings	*Xkirip ki xik'*
Eagle	*Kot*
White vulture	*Saq k'uch*
Small birds	*Ch'uti tz'ikin*
Great birds	*Nima tz'ikin*
(Christenson 2003: 188).	

A metonym is a term in which two typical members of a class are juxtaposed to stand for the whole domain (Hopkins 1996). The two members of a metonym are usually the best examples of the domain and are often complementary or contrasting opposites. For example, the Maya term for ancestors is mother-father. In the Popol Vuh, mountain and valley are paired to describe the earth, sky and earth are paired to describe the world, and Heart of Sky (the three thunderbolt gods) and Heart of Earth (the creator grandparents) are paired to describe all of the creator deities (Christenson 2003: 16, 19, 20). In this same manner, *cho* "lake" and *palow* "sea" are paired as a reference to all water (Tedlock 1987: 148; Christenson 2003: 16, 157). These two terms are a contrast between the largest body of freshwater and the largest body of saltwater. The pairing of an eagle with a vulture contrasts raptors that eat freshly killed prey with those that consume carrion (Atran 1999: 173). It is a poetic reference to all birds of prey.

In Aztec worldview, the eagle (Nahuatl *cuauhtli*) was a supreme symbol of authority and spiritual power, and it was considered an avatar of the sun (Caso 1958). The association of eagles with the sun is reflected in the Nahuatl terms for the rising sun (*cuauhtlehuanitl* "ascending eagle") and the setting sun (*cuauhtemoc* "descending eagle"). In his list of Aztec birds, Fray Bernardino de Sahagún (1959–63: vol. 11: 40–41) describes a number of eagle and eagle-like birds, most notably the golden eagle (*Aquila chrysaetos*):

> The eagle is yellow-billed—very yellow; the bill is yellow, very yellow. The bill is thick, curved, humped, hard. The legs are yellow, an intense yellow, very yellow, exceedingly yellow. They are thick. The claws are curved, hooked. The eyes are like coals of fire. It is large, big . . . The eagle is fearless, a brave one, daring, a screamer, a wing-beater. It is ashen, brown. It beats its wings, constantly beats its wings, it grooms itself, it constantly grooms itself . . . It is called itzquauhtli because the feathers of its breast, of its back are very beautiful; they glisten as if blotched with gold, and they are called quauhxilotl. Its wings, its tail are blotched with white; they are somewhat golden like the feathers of the falcon. And it is called itzquauhtli because it is a great bird of prey. It preys on, it slays the deer, the wild beasts. To kill them, it beats them in the face with its wings and then pecks out their eyes. It can slay very thick snakes, and can kill whatever kind of bird flies in the air. It carries them off wherever it wishes to go to eat them.

The fifteenth day in the Aztec calendar was *Cuauhtli* "eagle," and it is represented by a raptor with a crest of feathers and a yellow beak. There has been some debate as to whether this eagle was based on a golden eagle or a harpy eagle (*Harpia harpyja*) (Seler 1902–23: vol. 4; Kendall 1992: 118–19; Miller and Taube 1993: 82). The harpy eagle and golden eagle have dramatically different features, habits, and habitats. In Mesoamerica, the range of the harpy eagle is restricted to the jungles of southern Veracruz and the southern Maya lowlands. Although it is the largest bird in the world, the harpy eagle is extremely rare and is seldom seen even in areas of undisturbed forest (Howell and Webb 1995: 208). It hunts within the lowland forest and preys primarily on medium-sized arboreal mammals such as monkeys and sloths. It does not soar. The harpy eagle has a ruff of feathers around its face and an elongated crest that is divided into two. Its beak is gray. The golden eagle, a resident of Central and Northern Mexico, prefers open country where it is frequently seen soaring high in the sky. In contrast to the dark gray and white plumage of the harpy eagle, the brown feathers of the golden eagle appear golden, hence its name.

Sahagún's description of the golden eagle stresses its very yellow beak and feet. The beak of the bird used in the *Cuauhtli* day sign is yellow. The reason the harpy eagle was considered a possible model for the *Cuauhtli* bird was because this day sign bird has a crest of feathers the golden eagle appears to lack. The head feathers of the golden eagle can, however, take a crested form when they are ruffled. In some examples of the *Cuauhtli* bird, the crest feathers are tipped with blades. This is a common convention in Mesoamerica where the feathers of raptorial birds such as owls and laughing falcons are marked with obsidian or flint blades. As noted above, an alternative name for the golden eagle is Itzquauhtli "obsidian eagle," which again suggests that the *Cuauhtli* day sign bird was based on a golden eagle. The likelihood that the golden eagle rather than the harpy eagle was the role model for the day name *Cuauhtli* is suggested by the golden eagle remains that have been found in elite caches at Tenochtitlan and for that matter at Teotihuacan as well. Furthermore, the traits of the golden eagle reflect the cultural associations the Aztecs had between eagles and the sun while those of the harpy eagle do not.

In a Nahuatl myth, the deities Nanahuatzin and Tecuciztecatl jumped into a primordial fire and transformed into the sun and moon, respectively (Sahagún 1959–63: vol. 7: 3–6). An eagle (*cuauhtli*) and a jaguar (*ocelotl*) then followed them into the fire. These creatures were role models for the eagle-jaguar warriors (*cuauhtli ocelotl*) who were the most accomplished and highest-ranked Aztec soldiers. The Nahuatl term *eagle-jaguar* is a metonym that contrasts a powerful predator of the sky with a powerful predator of the land. The Aztec eagle-jaguar soldiers were the best examples of the warrior class. The throne of Moctezuma was composed of an eagle seat and a jaguar back rest, suggesting that the ruler was the quintessential eagle-jaguar warrior (Sahagún 1959–63: vol. 2: 123).

Epiclassic buildings at both the Toltec site of Tula and the Maya site of Chichen Itza prominently display similar Central Mexican–style eagles and jaguars devouring bloody hearts (Davies 1977: 241–43, 250–51; Tozzer 1957: figures 431, 432, 435, 444). Eagles and jaguars are found in several Popol Vuh episodes. The first four K'iche' lineage heads made a pilgrimage to a city called Tulan Suywa, Seven Caves, Seven Canyons, where they obtained patron deities (Christenson 2007: 208–13). There has been long debate about the specific location of this city, with various researchers favoring Tula, Chichen Itza, or Cholula, among others. Each K'iche' lineage head provided his patron deity with sacrificial offerings and cared for the idol and deerskin bundle that represented his god. In other words, the lord functioned as a priest. The Popol Vuh and the *Título de Totonicapán* indicate that Tojil and Awilix, who were the patron gods for the two leading K'iche' lineages, were represented by a jaguar (*b'alam*) and an eagle (*kot*), respectively (Christenson 2007: 243–45; Edmonson 1971: 201). The *Título de Totonicapán* describes the mountain associated with Tojil as inhabited by jaguars and eagles and rattlesnakes and pit vipers (Carmack and Mondloch 1983: 109, 184). This description indicates that the K'iche' god was identified with the most dangerous and powerful animals.

The second generation of lords returned to Tulan and received symbols for their offices and duties (Christenson 2007: 256–58). The Popol Vuh lists these symbols in couplet form: canopy and throne (*muj, q'alib'aj*), flute bone and drum (*su' b'aq, cham cham*), bright black powder and yellow stone (*tatil, q'an ab'aj*), puma paws and jaguar paws (*tz'ikwil koj, tz'ikwil b'alam*), head and hooves of deer (*jolom, pich kej*), arm band and snail shell rattle (*makutax, t'ot' tatam*), tobacco gourd and food bowl (*k'us b'us, kaxkon*), and macaw feathers and heron feathers (*chiyom and astapulul*). The *Título de Totonicapán* states that these lords were also given eagle feet and jaguar paws (*tzikil wil kot tzikil b'alam*), indicating that their regalia reflected the same symbols of power as the Aztec eagle-jaguar warriors (Carmack and Mondloch 1983: 99, 183). Another reference to the eagle and jaguar is found in the description of the K'iche' lord Q'ukumatz, who was thought to be able to transform into these animals:

> One transformation again as well he would be as eagle, One transformation again as jaguar, Truly then eagle, Then jaguar his appearance he would come to be (*Ju wuq' chi nay puch chub'ano chi kotal, Ju wuq' chik chi b'aalamil, Qitzij wi chi kot, Chi b'alam u wachib'al chuxik*).
>
> (Christenson 2003: 238)

The pairing of eagle-jaguar is also seen in the modern dance drama known as the *Rabinal Achi*, where the warriors are referred to as eagle-jaguar (Breton 1994: 34).

The only resident eagle of highland Guatemala is the very rare solitary eagle (*Harpyhaliaetus solitaries*). There are other eagles and eagle-like birds on the Pacific Coast of Guatemala and in the Maya lowlands, such as the harpy eagle (*Harpia harpyja*), crested eagle (*Morphnus guianensis*), ornate hawk-eagle (*Spizaetus ornatus vicarious*), black and white hawk-eagle (*Spizaetus melanoleucus*), and black hawk-eagle (*Spizaetus tyrannus serus*) (Howell and Webb 1995: 206–11). In various Mayan languages, these eagles are named using cognates of *t'iiw* and *xik*, which Terrence Kaufman (Kaufman and Justeson 2003: 606–8) has reconstructed as proto-Mayan terms for hawk. Kaufman and William M. Norman (1984: 133) list *t'iw* as the proto-Cholan term for eagle.

A Ch'ol word list from 1789 has the entry *t'iw* "eagle" (Hopkins et al. 2008: 109). *T'iw* has disappeared in modern Ch'ol, but *xiye'* (a cognate of *xik*) refers to both eagles and hawks (Aulie and Aulie 1978: 136; Whittaker and Warkentin 1965: 170). The sixteenth-century Ch'olti' dictionary gives *tzununtibu* (*tz'unun t'iw*), literally, hummingbird eagle, for eagle and eaglet (Stross n.d.). Robert M. Laughlin (1988: 323) lists cognates for eagle as *t'iv* (colonial Tzotzil) and *thiuh* (colonial Tzeltal). In Chuj and Mam, *t'iw* is eagle (Pérez Hernández 2003; Hopkins 2012). Q'eqchi' also has *t'iw* "eagle" as a term for the harpy eagle or solitary eagle (Wilson 1972: 412). Laughlin (1988: 323) lists *t'iiw* "eagle" for modern Mopán Maya, while Kerry M. Hull and Rob Fergus (2009: 89) note that this term is used to name the harpy eagle. In Huastec, *t'iiw* is recorded as a term for eagles that migrate from the north through the Huasteca area in mid-October (Alcorn 1984: 45, 80). The Huastecans inhabit an area in northeastern Mexico that is outside the range of the eagles listed above, so it is likely that this term refers to migratory golden eagles whose southern range extends to Morelos and northern Puebla or possibly to bald eagles that migrate south along the coastal area to the north of the Huastecans.

In some Mayan languages, the double-headed Hapsburg eagle associated with Spanish rule is named using cognates of *t'iiw* and *xik*, but it is also referenced using the Nahua loan word *kot* (Nahuatl *cuauhtli*) (Campbell 1977; Justeson et al. 1985: 24–26; Kaufman and Justeson 2003: 606–8, 694). It is noteworthy that the word used for jaguar in the Popol Vuh and other colonial K'iche'an documents is the term *b'alam* (proto-Mayan *b'ahlam*), but for eagle it is the loan word *kot*. In addition to K'iche', the Nahua loan word *kot* "eagle" also appears in Yucatec Maya and the highland languages of Kaqchikel, Uspanteko, Poqomam, and Q'anjob'al (Kaufman and Justeson 2003: 606–8). Given the intimate cultural ties highland Guatemala and Epiclassic Chichen Itza had with Central Mexican culture, it is not surprising that such a term would be adopted. It seems highly likely that the eagle form of Awilix and Q'ukumatz and the eagle feet given to the K'iche' lords were those of the golden eagle as a symbol of foreign-anointed status. Furthermore, the Chichen Itza images of eagles devouring hearts are likely also based on the golden eagle of Central Mexico.

The sixteenth-century Vienna dictionary of Yukatec Maya records the terms *coot* and *coot max* to describe an Águila bermeja "brownish eagle" (Bolles 2003). *Maax* is the proto-Mayan word for spider monkey (Kaufman and Justeson 2003: 561). The term *coot max* "eagle monkey" is surely a reference to the harpy eagle that preys on monkeys, although harpy eagles are gray, not brown. The presence of the Nahua loan word *kot* "eagle" in the contact period Yucatec Maya language explains its use by the modern Lacandon Maya of Chiapas. During the Postclassic period, Yucatec Maya speakers from northern Yucatan migrated into the lowland forests of the Peten. During the subsequent Conquest period, Yucatec Maya refugees fleeing Spanish oppression also moved into this zone. The Lacandon Maya who now reside in the lowland forests of Chiapas are descendants of these Yucatec Maya speakers

(Palka 2005). One of the terms used by the Lacandon Maya to refer to the harpy eagle (*Harpia harpyja*) is *kot maax* "eagle monkey" (Bruce 1976: 25, 69). There is a modern Lacandon Maya belief that the creator deity painted a *kot maax* on the clothing of the Sun God (K'ayum Ma'ax and Rätsch 1984: 42–43). The connection of an eagle with the sun may stem from the Epiclassic Nahua eagle-sun complex.

Federico G. Neiburg (1988) has suggested that the origin of the Mazatec stories of giant eagles carrying farmers away and devouring them may be based on the distant memory of Aztec eagle warriors who raided the Mazatec for sacrificial victims and slaves. There are many similar stories in the Maya region of eagles, great hawks, or vultures that carry away children or people (Arcos 1988; Guiteras Holmes 1961: 187; Hull and Fergus 2009: 108–18; Sánchez Díaz 1986: 62–63). Such birds are thought to be the animal co-essences of people or supernatural beings. Known variously as *way* (*uay*), *nagual*, or *lab*, a co-essence is the part of the spiritual essence of a person that can take the form of an animal or a phenomenon like lightning, wind, or meteors. Leaders use their co-essences to defend their communities, but they can also be used irresponsibly to inflict punishment or cause illness in others. In Yucatec Maya Chan Kom, one of the animal co-essences is the *uay kot*, which is specifically identified with greedy shop owners who exploit the people (Re Cruz 1993: 69–70, 77). At Tzotzil Chalchihuitán, *t'iv* "eagle" is a very large supernatural bird that is the co-essence of the *j'ik'al* (black cave-dwelling beings who kidnap and eat people) (Laughlin 1988: 323). In the Tzotzil community of Chenalho, *chohchohotro* is thought to be an eagle or great hawk that is related to destructive powers and to the eclipse, which the Maya associate with harmful forces (Guiteras Holmes 1961: 334).

In their *Diccionario del Tzeltal de Tenejapa*, Brent Berlin and Terrence Kaufman (1962: 138) have the entry "*kokmut, xkokmut.* n [nominal] uno que tenía nagual de cuervo o zanate; nagual de persona que había anteriormente." Brian Stross (personal communication, 2013) noted that his Tzeltal informants identified the *kok mut* as an *águila* "eagle." Although it is only known from stories, it is described as a hawk-like lowland bird that is larger than a hawk. An alternative name is *me'tak'in*, literally "mother of gold." In the course of his study of Tzeltal animal names, Eugene Hunn (1977: 142–43) took his Tenejapan informants to the Tuxtla Gutiérrez, Chiapas, zoo to see various animals that included a harpy eagle. The extremely rare harpy eagle does not reside in Tzeltal territory, and his Tenejapan informants had never seen one before. While some informants gave the term *ákila* (a loan of Spanish *águila* "eagle" used to describe the golden eagle on the Mexican national flag), others provided the term *kok mut* to name this bird. Hunn also noted that another name given for *kok mut* is *me' tak'in* "mother of gold" and that this name is in reference to a belief that by praying to the *me' tak'in* on certain mountains, the bird will bring you money. In Tzeltal Cancuc (16 km northeast of Tenejapa), Pedro Pitarch

(2010: 40) noted that the co-essence called *kok mut* was an eagle that was "capable of stealing the silver coins that are kept in San Juan's coffer—otherwise known as the *me'tak'in* (mother-money), perhaps because it appears as the national emblem on Mexican coins." The Mexican national bird is the golden eagle. Given the identification of the *kot mut* with the harpy eagle and the golden eagle found on Mexican flags and money, it seems likely that any eagle or hawk-eagle might be viewed as the mythical *kok mut* by the Tzeltal. Furthermore, in the adjacent Tzotzil area, the *me'tak'in* is identified with the rare king vulture (*Sarcoramphus papa*), which suggests that the *kok mut* might be any large bird of prey (Hunn 1977: 143).

San Pedro Cancuc was the center of the 1712 rebellion against the San Cristóbal de Las Casas secular and religious authorities, and indigenous stories about the war are still told in the region (Calnek 1988). During their revolt, the Cancuc rebels demanded that the wealth of the surrounding communities be consolidated at Cancuc, and most communities forfeited their church silver to the rebel cause. Noteworthy in the tales of the rebellion is the inability of the wind and thunderbolt co-essences of the indigenous rebels to defeat the colonial forces. The inference is that the co-essences of the ladino authorities were stronger. The prominent role of the eagle in colonial emblems suggests the possibility that the *me'tak'in* eagle was identified with that group and that the ability of the *me'tak'in* to steal the silver coins of the patron saint San Pedro of Cancuc was related to the colonial authorities' defeat of the rebels and confiscation of the rebels' silver.

A number of predatory birds appear in the art and hieroglyphic writing of the Classic period and in the Postclassic codices. Vultures, owls, and a certain kind of hawk (*muwan*) have been securely identified by caption texts that accompany their portraits (Grube and Schele 1994; Grube and Nahm 1994; Stuart 2006). In contrast to most other birds, owls are frequently shown in Mesoamerican art in a full frontal pose. The reason for this kind of depiction is based on the physical characteristics of owls. Typically, an owl will sit motionless in a tree, watching and listening for prey. Its keen hearing is enhanced by the facial ruff, a concave surface of stiff dark-tipped feathers. The ruff functions as a reflector, channeling sounds into the ears. The owl's large forward-facing eyes provide it with stereoscopic vision. Without moving its body, an owl can turn its head 270 degrees to follow the movement it sees or the direction of a sound. Consequently, when a person approaches an owl, the owl will most likely be looking directly at the person. Nikolai Grube and Werner Nahm (1994) noted that several of the supernatural *way* birds illustrated on Maya pottery are phonetically named in their caption texts as *kuy*, which is a term for an owl in Yucatec Maya, Chol, and Tzeltal. These *kuy* owls are portrayed with round eyes, ear tufts, and black-tipped feathers. The avian manifestation of God L is an owl, and his name phrase has been deciphered as Oxlahun Kan Kuy "13 sky owl" (Grube and Schele 1994). Its standard depiction is in profile view, and its ear tufts are often represented by a single black-tipped feather. As noted by David Stuart (2005: 105), a portrait of an owl or just the black-tipped feather of an owl is used in hieroglyphic writing for the phonetic sound '*o*, which is likely an onomatopoeic word for the call of an owl. The use of a diagnostic element to represent the full form of glyph is common in Mayan hieroglyphic writing.

A number of raptorial birds have been identified as eagles, such as the head variants used in the Bak'tun, k'atun, and tun periods of the Long Count; the head variant for the sky glyph; the so-called Principal Bird Deity; the bird employed to represent the day name Men in the Classic period calendar; and the avian manifestation of the creator deity Itzamnaaj (Xpiyacoc's lowland parallel) (Hull and Fergus 2009; Miller and Taube 1993: 82; Taube et al. 2010). Many of these eagle identifications have been simply asserted without evidence to support the claim. In the case of the Long Count birds and the sky glyph bird, their common diagnostic trait is ear tufts represented by a single black-tipped feather. We therefore question the assertion that these are eagles and not owls. The following is a review of the Men bird and the so-called Principal Bird Deity.

THE MEN BIRD

The fifteenth day in the calendars of the eastern Mayan languages and in the Tzeltal-Tzotzil calendars is Tz'ikin (Thompson 1950: 82). Kaufman (Kaufman and Justeson 2003: 618) lists *tz'ikin* as a proto-Mayan word for bird. In the Yucatec Maya calendar, the fifteenth day is Men. There are no recorded Cholan day name lists, but day names do occur as personal names in Colonial documents from the Lacandon Ch'ol and Tila-Tumbala Ch'ol regions. Men is one of these names, which suggests that the fifteenth day in the Classic period inscriptions was called Men (Thompson 1977: 225; Campbell 1984: 179, 1988: 373–86). J. Eric S. Thompson (1950: 82) related the name Men to the modern Yucatec Maya ritual specialist called *men*. The *menob* are priests and shamans who perform divinations and healing rituals and direct agricultural rituals to ensure abundant harvest (Tozzer 1907: 104, 163–64; Redfield and Villa Rojas 1934: 74–77, 170–71, 349). When the *men* is inducted into his profession, he is given a headdress of vines and red *nicte* flowers. Although the Lacandon Maya no longer have community ritual specialists, the head of each household performs these duties. During various ceremonies, these men wear bark cloth headbands that are dyed red (Tozzer 1907: 72, plate XXVI).

In the Classic and Postclassic inscriptions, Men is represented by a bird wearing a wide headband that is tied at the back of the head (Thompson 1950: figure 9). Although the specific meaning of the headband is unknown, such headbands made from bark cloth are commonly seen in Maya art. Marc Zender (2004b) has detailed the many types of headbands that are worn by Maya deities and Classic period lords, and he noted that these individuals had priestly duties. Some day signs like Ak'bal, Ik', and Ajaw retain the same value outside of their day name context while others do not. Although the Men bird has been tentatively translated as *tz'ikin* in non-calendrical contexts (Boot 2005, 2008; Martin 2005: 6; Taube et al. 2010: 54), there are no known phonetic substitutions to verify such a reading. We will thus continue to refer to the sign as the Men bird.

The Men bird appears in the name phrase of the Classic period sun god. There are a number of different Classic period gods who have anthropomorphic form with Roman noses and large circular eyes. One of these gods (God G) has *k'in* "sun, day" signs on his face or body, and he has long been identified as the Sun God (Schellhas 1904: 27). He appears in contexts where his portrait is used to represent the word *k'in* and where he clearly represents the sun itself. The T544 *k'in* sign is a stylized red flower with four petals (Thompson 1950: 88, 142; Stone and Zender 2011: 153). The full form of this sign is composed of an eccentric flint or shell cartouche with the *k'in* sign at its center (Taube 2003: 412–13). A skeletal centipede head projects out from each corner. In Maya worldview, the surface of the earth was thought to contain a quadrilateral space. The solstice sun rose and set at the corners of this space, and the sun hovered above its center at noon on the two annual zenith passages (Bassie-Sweet 1996: 21–29, 195–99, 2008: 58–78). Stone and Zender (2011: 153) noted that the four petals of the *k'in* sign invoke the four world directions, and they stated that "the four-petaled flower stood for the bright heavens of the diurnal sun, conceived as a flower- and bird-filled paradise." Their observation can be extended to the full form of the *k'in* cartouche with its centipede corners. The Maya believed the sun rose from the underworld through a cave and that the mouth of that cave took the form of a skeletal centipede mouth (Bassie-Sweet 1996: 90–91; Taube 2003: 411–13). In terms of the *k'in* cartouche, each centipede corner represents the cave from which the sun was thought to rise and set on the solstices. The *k'in* cartouche is a solar-celestial cosmogram, with the center of the flower representing the position of the sun on zenith passage.

The Sun God is depicted on an unprovenanced vessel that illustrates the celestial court of the creator grandfather Itzamnaaj (Boot 2008). It is likely that his court was thought to be located at the zenith position of the sun in the sky, that is, directly overhead (Bassie-Sweet 2008: 58). Itzamnaaj is pictured sitting in his palace with his avian form perched behind him. The Sun God and two other deities are seated on a sky band facing Itzamnaaj. The caption text adjacent to the Sun God gives the Sun God's full nominal phrase that is composed of three names: Uhuk Chapat Men bird (seventh centipede Men bird), K'inich Ajaw, and Bolon

Yokte' K'uh (Boot 2008). On K1398, the Sun God wears a headdress composed of a paper headband and a centipede head (Stuart and Stuart 1993: 171). On Yaxchilan Hieroglyphic Stair III, Step III, the Sun God also wears the centipede head as a headdress (Graham 1982: 169). In another example of the Sun God, the centipede head has a feather crest (Franco 1968: 19). It would appear that this centipede is the Uhuk Chapat Men bird referred to in the Sun God's name phrase. How this name relates to the centipede corners of the *k'in* sign is unclear. Bird names that contain numbers are common. As an example, the owl avatar of God L is called 13 Chan Kuy (Grube and Schele 1994). The Yucatec Maya and Tzotzil name for the ornate hawk-eagle is *ajjun k'uuk'* "one feather" or *jun xulub* "one horn" (Hofling and Tesucún 1997: 76; Laughlin 1988: 216; Köhler 1995: 129). While the name of the ornate hawk-eagle likely refers to the fact that its feather crest often looks like one feather or a horn standing straight up, the meaning of these numbered supernatural bird names remains opaque.

Examples of directional birds are well-known in Maya colonial sources (Roys 1933: 100). The Men bird appears in the names of four deities found on the walls of Río Azul Tomb 12 (Stuart 1985). Moving in a counterclockwise fashion, these names have been glossed as *k'in tz'ikin ajaw* east "day bird lord of the east," *uh tz'ikin ajaw* north "moon bird lord of the north," *ak'ab tz'ikin ajaw* west "night bird lord of the west," and *ek' tz'ikin ajaw* south "star bird lord of the south" (Taube et al. 2010: 54). A slight digression is in order to discuss the contexts in which these names appear.

The Popol Vuh begins by describing the creator grandparents (the embodiment of complementary opposition) and the pooled body of water in which they lived. It was from this place of duality that the earth was formed. The creator deities ordered and structured the world into its quadrilateral form, and they established a household for themselves at its center (the court of Itzamnaaj discussed above was the celestial counterpart to this terrestrial place of duality). Whenever the Maya created a house or a quadrilateral ritual space, they were replicating the household of the creator deities. The ideal state for humans to achieve was the duality of the creator deities. To create a proper ritual state, this duality must be present.

One of the contexts in which complementary opposition is most readily seen in hieroglyphic writing is in the *tz'ak* "whole, complete" glyph (Hopkins 1996; Hull 1993, 2003, 2012; Knowlton 2002; Stuart 2003). The standard form of this sign is often replaced with a pair of signs such as day-night, sun-moon, star-moon, cloud-water, wind-water, unripe-ripe. Formal language, that is, sacred language, is thought to be hot (Gossen 1974). The principal element that gives a discourse its formality, its "heat" or holiness, is the use of the couplet, a pair of lines that differs minimally. These can occur in everyday conversation, but the density of couplets increases through heated speech—including court language—and reaches its maximum in sacred speech and prayer, where virtually the entire discourse is in couplet form. To sanctify ritual space, prayers are said in couplet form. The same kind of duality was created in Río Azul Tomb 12, where the glyphs painted on opposite walls are complementary opposites of each other: k'in/east (A), ak'bal/west (A), moon/north (B), and star/south (B). Counterclockwise ritual circuits are common in Maya culture. Beginning with the east wall and moving in a counterclockwise motion, the Río Azul glyphs form alternating couplets (A-B-A-B) of k'in-east (A), moon-north (B), ak'bal-west (A), and star-south (B). The edge of the Copan Structure 66C bench has similar pairs of couplets carved on its edge (Webster et al. 1998). From left to right are portraits of One Ixim as a lunar patron (A), as an ak'bal deity representing night (ak'bal) (B), the Sun God representing day (k'in) (B), and a scorpion deity representing Venus (A). This is the well-known chiasmus, or "nested couplet," form of A-B-B-A (Hopkins and Josserand 2012: 29). These couplets transform the Copan bench and the Río Azul tomb into proper quadrilateral ceremonial spaces for a lord to sit on and to be buried in, respectively.

Another example of these k'in-ak'bal and sun-moon couplets is found on a large earring in the Kislak Collection (Taube et al. 2010: figure 36a). The rim of this earring has four glyphs carved on it. Each glyph is composed of a bird head and one of the four elements (k'in, ak'bal, moon, and star). Moving counterclockwise from the top, the glyphs are k'in bird, ak'bal bird, moon bird, and star bird. Karl A. Taube, William A. Saturno, David Stuart, and Heather Hurst (2010: 56) were puzzled that these glyphs did not follow the directional order of the Río Azul glyphs, but when viewed as a poetic construction, they form the well-known couplet of AA-BB.

In summary, the Men bird appears in the Seven Chapat Men bird name phrase of the Sun God and in the name phrases of four avian deities. Whether the Men bird represents the word Men or the word tz'ikin "bird" in these contexts is unclear. The question that is pertinent to this discussion is, what bird species does the Men bird represent? Although they do not state the specific species, a number of researchers have identified the Men bird as an eagle and have even translated tz'ikin as eagle rather than bird based solely on the fact that the fifteenth day name in the Aztec and Mixtec 260-day calendar is Cuauhtli "eagle" (Boot 2004, 2005: 255, 2010: 156; Houston and Martin 2012; Martin 2005; Taube et al. 2010; Zender 2004b: 232). Given that only 50 percent of the Aztec-Mixtec day names match those of the Maya, there is reason to doubt this equivalency. An obvious question to ask is, if the Maya conceived of the fifteenth day name as an eagle, why was the highland day name tz'ikin "bird" rather than t'iw "eagle?" At present, there is no internal Maya evidence to indicate what species the Men bird was, and we believe it is more prudent to leave this question unanswered than to assume a parallel with Central Mexican mythology. Taube, Saturno, Stuart, and Hurst (2010: 56) refer to the Men birds and the Kislak birds as Principal Bird Deities, which is the next topic of discussion.

THE ALLEGED PRINCIPAL BIRD DEITY

Lawrence W. Bardawil (1976) proposed that all supernatural birds with serpent wings and hooked beaks were variations of the same creature, and he nicknamed these birds the Principal Bird Deity complex. A serpent wing is a conflation of a serpent head and a bird wing. The serpent head replaces the bones of the wing. Such serpent wings appear frequently in the headdresses of Maya rulers. Although Bardawil noted that his Principal Bird Deity could have the head of Itzamnaaj, the deity GIII, or an owl, he concluded that these were celestial and underworld manifestations of the same deity. Most researchers have unquestioningly accepted Bardawil's premise that any bird with a serpent wing is the same despite the fact that more examples of deities with serpent wings have emerged over the years, such as the avian form of One Ixim (K1387, K1388), the vulture deity (K5356), hummingbirds, and numerous water birds (Berjonneau et al. 1985: figures 329, 335, 340). Lumping together all avian supernaturals into one category is simply wrong, and in our opinion the term *Principal Bird Deity* should be permanently retired.

The word *mo'* "macaw" is represented in hieroglyphic writing by a realistic portrait of a scarlet macaw (Stuart 2005: 150; Stone and Zender 2011: 211). The beak of the macaw is distinguished from other birds by its hooked shape and black markings. The feathers of the scarlet macaw were highly prized across Mesoamerica, and some Classic period rulers incorporate the macaw in their name phrases (Martin and Grube 2008: 156, 192). Avian deities at the Preclassic site of Izapa, a macaw deity at the site of Copan, and an avian deity labeled as a macaw at the site of Tonina have attributes that suggest they may be parallel to Seven Macaw of the Popol Vuh (Lowe et al. 1982; Cortez 1986; Fash 1998; Zender 2005; Guernsey 2006). The raptor manifestations of Itzamnaaj, GIII, and One Ixim do not appear with macaw attributes. The diagnostic trait that distinguishes the Itzamnaaj bird from other avian supernaturals is his *ak'bal* floral headband that he shares with the deity Itzamnaaj (God D) (Bassie-Sweet 2008: 130–45). The Itzamnaaj bird is frequently seen carrying a double-headed serpent in his beak, and he is also often pictured with *k'in* and *ak'bal* signs on his wings. These wings have been characterized as an indication of his solar association, and it has been suggested that he was a particular aspect of the sun (Taube et al. 2010: 33). Given the examples of avian complementary opposition discussed above, it seems far more likely that these signs mark the Itzamnaaj bird as an embodiment of complementary opposition, which is precisely what the creator grandfather was.

In the Popol Vuh, Seven Macaw and his two sons were false deities who the Hero Twins defeated with the help of the creator grandparents. There are several Classic period pottery scenes in which the Hero Twins are pictured shooting avian deities with their blowguns (Blom 1950; Coe 1978). On K4546 and K1226, the Itzamnaaj bird is such a victim. Before researchers had identified this bird as a manifestation of the creator grandfather, it was proposed that these blowgun scenes were parallel to the Popol Vuh episode where the Hero Twins hide in the leaves of a nance tree and shoot the deity Seven Macaw in the jaw when he comes to eat the fruit (Cortez 1986; Robicsek and Hales 1981: 147–48, 1982: 56–57). Many researchers have continued to associate the blowgun scenes with the Seven Macaw episode (Coe 1989; Freidel et al. 1993: 69–71; Houston et al. 2006: 234–36; Stuart 2005: 118; Taube 1987; Taube et al. 2010: 19, 30, 39). While the setting of a tree is shared by both stories, the fatal flaw in this interpretation is that there is no equivalency between the creator grandfather Itzamnaaj and the false deity Seven Macaw. As Nicholas Hellmuth (1987) first proposed, a better parallel is found in the Popol Vuh episode where the Hero Twins shoot the messenger bird Wak (Bassie-Sweet 2002, 2008; Zender 2005).

THE MESSENGER BIRD WAK (*HERPETOTHERES CACHINNANS* LAUGHING FALCON)

The Popol Vuh describes two species of messenger birds: the laughing falcon and owls. The concept of birds as messengers is well documented in Classic Maya art and hieroglyphic writing. As Stephen Houston (2000: 174–75) has stated in regard to secondary lords who appear in tribute scenes:

> The description of these lords seems to have been *y-ebe:t* (**ye-b'e-ta** [early] or **ye-b'e-te** [late]) or "his messenger" (David Stuart, personal communication, 1997), implying that they were sent by another, unseen and higher-ranking tributary who wished for some reason (perhaps self-preservation!) not to be present at the rendering of objects. The term for "messenger" may also have applied to deities with avian characteristics, rather like a Mercury concept of a winged emissary. Some supernaturals of this sort were likely to have been *way* or "companion spirits" (coessences or shared souls) of gods who did not ordinarily sprout wings. The connection between these spirits and "sleep" (*way*) and dream visions reveals something of how the Maya understood the mechanism of communication between gods and humans. It is possible that another glyphic term used by messengers, *mu:t* or "bird" (a term in Yukatek Maya for "fame" or "news"), expresses an overlap between the notion of winged news, the motion of birds as metaphors for long-distance speech, and tribute embassies.

Like *tz'ikin*, *muut* is a general term for bird that is found in Yucatekan and Greater Tzeltalan languages (Kaufman and Justeson 2003: 619). In the codices, a number of birds are identified in the adjacent caption texts as *muut* birds, and the word *muut* appears in Classic period bird contexts where it forms the names of certain birds (Kelley 1976: 131, 181; Houston, Stuart, and Taube 2006). The difference between *tz'ikin* and *muut* may rest in the fact that particular birds were thought to be bearers of omens or messages. Two common examples are that the call of an owl is thought to be an omen of death while the call of the laughing falcon is an omen of rain. In the Ritual of the Bacabs, a series of couplets pair *ch'ich'* "bird" (the Yucatec Maya cognate of *tz'ikin*) with *mut*:

The cry of this bird	*yauat u ch'ich'il*
his bird of tidings	*u mutil*
The red oo, the white oo	*ix chac oo bacan u che sac tan oo*
are his bird	*bacan u ch'ich'il*
his bird of tidings	*u mutil*
His bird	*u ch'ich'il*
his bird of tidings	*u mutil*
What is his bird?	*bax u ch'ich'il*
Who is his bird of tiding?	*max u mutil*
These are the birds	*la u ch'ich'il*
these are the birds of tiding	*la u mutil*
These are his birds	*la baca u ch'ich'il*
these are his birds of tiding	*la ba ca u mutil*
Who is his bird?	*max u ch'ich'il*
Who is his bird of tiding?	*u mutil*
The red tacay-bird would be his bird	*chacal tacay bin u ch'ich'il*
his bird of tidings	*u mutil*
What, how is his bird?	*balx bacin u ch'ich'il*
What, how is his bird of tidings?	*balx bacin u mutil*

(Roys 1965: xxi, 5(10), 8(22), 9(24), 25(69), 36(104), 41(119), 47(138), 60 (179), 70(210))

Although Ralph Roys translated *muut* as bird of tidings, a more succinct translation for these couplets would be his bird (*u ch'ich'il*), his omen (*u mutil*).

The Popol Vuh describes a series of animals that act as messengers for the creator grandmother Xmucane (Christenson 2007: 154–59). In this episode, Junajpu and Xb'alanke (the grandsons of Xmucane) recover the gaming equipment of their father and uncle that was hidden in their house. They joyfully proceed to their father's ballcourt located on the road to Xibalba (the underworld) and play ball. Just as when their father and uncle played ball at this location, their actions are viewed as territorial trespassing by One Death and Seven Death (the rulers of Xibalba). The Lords of Death send their four owl messengers (Arrow Owl, One Leg Owl, Macaw Owl, and Skull Owl) to their household to demand that the Twins come to the underworld. In addition to being messengers, these four owl messengers were also war councilors and the underworld lords who performed heart sacrifices. Arriving at the house, the owls discover that only Xmucane (the Hero Twins' grandmother) is at home, so they deliver the message to her. Xmucane is distraught because these are the same owls who gave the earlier message to One Junajpu and Seven Junajpu to come to the underworld, which resulted in their death. All across Mesoamerica, an owl entering a house is a sure sign that a member of the household will die. Xmucane bitterly weeps, knowing that these owls are omens of death for her grandsons.

Xmucane sends a louse from her head to the ballcourt to convey the message to the Hero Twins. The slow-moving louse proceeds down the road, where he encounters a toad called Tamazul sitting on the path. Tamazul suggests to the louse that he can get to the ballcourt faster if he allows Tamazul to swallow him and continue the journey. The toad licks up the louse and sets out down the road, but soon he meets a great snake (*nima cumatz*) named Saqi K'as who volunteers to take him at an even faster rate of speed. Saqi K'as swallows the toad, and again the journey continues. Then the snake encounters a Great Bird (*nima tz'ikin*) called Wak, who swallows him. When Wak arrives at the ballcourt, he alights at the head of the court and calls out *wak-ko! wak-ko!* The Twins grab their blowguns and shoot the bird in the eye because they want to know what his message is. Wak falls to the ground, where the Twins seize him and demand to know why he has come. Wak informs them that he has a message for them in his belly, but he will not give it to them unless they can cure his eye. They take a slice of rubber resin from their ball and place it on the eye, which miraculously restores his sight. Wak vomits up the snake Saqi K'as, who, in turn, vomits up the toad Tamazul. In the teeth of Tamazul, the Twins find the louse, who finally delivers the message.

Wak is a laughing falcon (Tedlock 1996: 114). It is curious that the Popol Vuh refers to Wak as a *nima tz'ikin* "Great Bird," given that the laughing falcon is a physically smaller bird of prey (18–22 inches) compared to the golden eagle (31–36 inches) or harpy eagle (34–42 inches). However, the principal diet of the laughing falcon is snakes, often highly venomous snakes, and it is viewed as a powerful bird because of its ability to overcome such deadly prey. Throughout Mesoamerica, these birds are also thought to be great healers (Bassie-Sweet 2008: 142). As an example, a laughing falcon cures the Virgin Mary when she is bitten by a snake while spinning her cotton (Joljá Cave Project field notes). To cure a snake bite, Tzeltal shamans imitate the *wako koh koh koh* call of the laughing falcon in their healing chants (Köhler 1975).

The Popol Vuh emphasizes that the Hero Twins are the proper replacements for their father and, by extension, their grandfather Xpiyacoc. The Wak messenger episode demonstrates that they had the healing skills of their grandfather. In fact, Wak is testing the Hero Twins' healing skills when he demands that they repair his eye. There is also an agricultural element to this episode because just before the Hero Twins leave for the ballcourt, they prepare a cornfield for cultivation. Across Mesoamerica, the song of the laughing falcon is said to be an indication of the coming of the rains. The laughing falcon has two vocal patterns: *wako* and ha, ha, ha. The Mayan words for water and rain have glottal stops, *ha'* and *ha'al*, although in many sources glottal stops are not recorded. When the laughing falcon sings, he is literally calling for the rain (Alonso Méndez, personal communication, 2001).

On K1226, the scene shows the moment One Ajaw shoots the Itzamanaaj bird with the blowgun pellet exiting the tube of his blowgun. The mouth of the Itzamnaaj bird is wide open, as though it were calling out just before he is shot. This action parallels that of Wak, who calls out just before he is shot. In the Preclassic San Bartolo murals, the Itzamnaaj bird is illustrated five times. In one example, he descends from a rain-filled cloud, which indicates the Itzamnaaj bird's association with rain (Taube et al. 2010: figure 30). His wings are marked with stone projectile points. This is a common convention found on Mesoamerican raptors that marks these birds of prey as warriors. In the other four examples, the bird is pictured at the top of a tree, clutching a double-headed serpent in his mouth. His wings are spread out as though he had just landed. The double-headed serpent held by the Itzamnaaj bird frequently has water and cloud symbols on its body, indicating its association with water (Bassie-Sweet 2008: 144). A male drawing blood from his penis stands before each San Bartolo tree. At the base of three trees are offerings of fish, deer, and turkey, respectively. In the case of the tree with the deer offering, the snake held by the Itzamnaaj bird has its front head ripped off, and it bleeds on the offering. The meaning of the action is unclear, but when a laughing falcon kills a snake, it first rips the head off of the snake in a manner similar to this scene.

The creator grandfather Itzamnaaj was the quintessential priest and healer, as was his counterpart Xpiyacoc. One of the primary functions of these ritual specialists was rain petitions. The attributes of Itzamnaaj and his snake-eating avian manifestation match those of the laughing falcon.

YAXCOCAHMUT

The etymologies of nominal phrases are complex; however, the term *piyakok* is the name for a slider turtle (*Trachemys scripta elegans*) and for a turtle design in the weavings of Rabinal, which suggests that the creator grandfather Xpiyacoc had a turtle form (Akkeren 2000: 207, 261–64; Christenson 2007: 63). *Kok* is a word for a small turtle in Yucatec Maya and the Central Mayan languages (Barrera Vásquez 1980: 329; Kaufman and Justeson 2003: 635). The creator grandfather Itzamnaaj in his God N manifestation also had a turtle form, although his Classic period turtle name was the proto-Cholan *ahk* "turtle" (Bassie-Sweet 2008: 135–37; Kaufman and Norman 1984: 115; Stuart 2005: 93, 2007). The name of Itzamnaaj (God D) is a compound composed of a portrait glyph of God N and a portrait glyph of the Itzamnaaj bird wearing the *ak'bal* headdress. There are no known phonetic substitutions for either of these logographs, so their pronunciation is still to be determined, although epigraphers favor the reading of Itzam or Itzamnaaj for the God N portrait. Stuart (2007; Houston et al. 2006: 236) has noted that several Classic period examples of the name of Itzamnaaj and his bird are preceded by the word *mut* "bird-omen."

In the sixteenth-century Vienna dictionary, there is an entry for Itzamnaaj that includes the name *yaxcocahmut*. Bishop Diego de Landa mentioned this avian manifestation of Itzamnaaj in reference to the deities honored during the New Year ceremonies for Muluk years, as did Diego López de Cogolludo (Cogolludo 1957: 249; Tozzer 1941: 145). The Franciscan priest Andrés de Avendaño y Loyola (1987: 32) stated that the deity *ahcocahmut* was depicted on a building facade at Tayasal and illustrated in Yucatec Maya codices he had seen. Much later references in the Chilam Balam of Chumayel and Tizimin refer to an *ek co coh mut* amd *ek co cay mut*, respectively (Barrera Vásquez and Rendón 1965: 21v; Gordon 1913: 92). While these two names are likely corruptions of the name *cocahmut*, the black prefix suggests the possibility that the avian *cocahmut* had five manifestations: one for each direction (red, white, black, and yellow) and one for the center (blue-green). The incantations in the Ritual of the Bacabs refer to a red, white, black, and yellow Itzamnaaj, suggesting this is the case (Roys 1965: 23, 27, 28).

Regarding the name *yaxcocahmut*, the meanings of the words *yax* (blue-green, first) and *mut* (omen-bird) are transparent, but it is not clear whether *cocah* represents one word or two. If two words, the name could be translated as *yax coc* "blue-green turtle" or possibly "first turtle," *ah mut* "the omen-bird." The name *ahcocahmut* would simply be translated as "the turtle, the omen-bird." This seems an apt description of the creator grandfather, who had both a turtle and a messenger bird form.

On the Palenque Temple 19 platform, Itzamnaaj's name phrase is preceded by *yax naah* "first house." Stuart (2005: 196) relates this name to a house dedication event recorded on the Copan hieroglyphic staircase that refers to a mythological dedication for the house of Itzamnaaj. In the Popol Vuh, the creator grandparents had the first house on the surface of the earth. Erik Boot (2004, 2008) has suggested that *cocahmut* was the Classic period reading for the portrait glyph of the Itzamnaaj bird. He reordered the Palenque name phrase to read Itzam Nah Yax Kokaj Mut. There is, however, no precedent for such an arbitrary reordering. Boot further argued that *cocahmut* was cognate with the Tzeltal term *kokmut*, discussed above. Given that one of the birds identified by the Tzeltal as a *kokmut* was the harpy eagle, he also proposed that the Itzamnaaj bird was based on a harpy eagle. Other than this tenuous connection, there is nothing in the imagery or hieroglyphic text to suggest that the snake-eating Itzamnaaj bird was identified with the monkey-eating harpy eagle. The pervasive Mesoamerican beliefs concerning the laughing falcon's abilities as a healer and rainmaker make it an obvious role model for the avian manifestation of the creator grandfather Itzamnaaj.

In this chapter, we have used data from multiple domains such as epigraphy, iconography, mythology, ethnography, linguistics, archaeology, and natural history to tease out the nature and role of the eagle and laughing falcon of the Popol Vuh. While golden eagles played important roles in the sun mythology of Central Mexico and certainly appear in the Epiclassic and Postclassic art of the Maya region where Central Mexican influences were common, there is little direct evidence that golden eagles or any other species of eagle played a significant role in Maya Classic period mythology. While it is possible that the Men bird was based on an eagle, the question has to remain open until further evidence is forthcoming.

REFERENCES CITED

Akkeren, Ruud van. 2000. *Place of the Lord's Daughter: Rab'inal, Its History, Its Dance-Drama*. Publication 91. Center for Non-Western Studies, Leiden.

Alcorn, Janis B. 1984. *Huastec Mayan Ethnobotany*. University of Texas Press, Austin.

Arcos, Francisco. 1988. "Kolem bä xiye." In *Wajalix bä t'an; narrativa tradicional ch'ol de Tumbalá, Chiapas*, ed. José Alejos García, 25–30. Centro de Estudios Mayas 20. Universidad Nacional Autónoma de México, Mexico City.

Atran, Scott. 1999. "Itzaj Maya Folk-Biological Taxonomy." In *Folk-Biology*, ed. Douglas L. Medin and Scott Atran, 119–204. MIT Press, Cambridge, MA

Aulie, H. Wilbur, and Evelyn W. de Aulie. 1978. *Diccionario ch'ol-español, español-ch'ol*. Instituto Lingüístico de Verano, Mexico City.

Avendaño y Loyola, Andrés de. 1987. *Relation of Two Trips to Peten: Made for the Conversion of the Heathen Ytzaex and Cehaches*, ed. Frank Comparato. Labyrinthos, Culver City, CA.

Bardawil, Lawrence W. 1976. "The Principal Bird Deity in Maya Art: An Iconographic Study of Form and Meaning." In *The Art, Iconography, and Dynastic History of Palenque, Part III*, ed. Merle Greene Robertson, 195–209. Proceedings of the Segunda Mesa Redonda de Palenque, 1974. Pre-Columbian Art Research, Pebble Beach, CA.

Barrera Vásquez, Alfredo. 1980. *Diccionario Maya Cordemex: Maya-Español, Español-Maya*. Ediciones Cordemex, Editorial Porrúa, Mérida, Mexico.

Barrera Vásquez, Alfredo, and Silvia Rendón. 1965. *El libro de los libros de Chilam Balam*. Fondo de Cultura Económica, Mexico City.

Bassie-Sweet, Karen. 1996. *At the Edge of the World*. University of Oklahoma Press, Norman.

Bassie-Sweet, Karen. 2002. "Corn Deities and the Complementary Male/Female Principle." In *La Organización Social entre los Mayas Prehispánicos, Coloniales y Modernos: Memoria de la Tercera Mesa Redonda de Palenque*, vol. 2, ed. Vera Tiesler Blos, Rafael Cobos, and Merle Greene Robertson, 105–25. Instituto Nacional de Antropología e Historia and Universidad Autónoma de Yucatán, Mexico City.

Bassie-Sweet, Karen. 2008. *Maya Sacred Geography and the Creator Deities*. University of Oklahoma Press, Norman.

Berjonneau, Gérald, Emile Deletaille, and Jean-Louis Sonnery. 1985. *Rediscovered Masterpieces of Mesoamerica: Mexico-Guatemala-Honduras*. Editions Arts, Boulogne.

Berlin, Brent, and Terrence Kaufman. 1962. "Diccionario del Tzeltal de Tenejapa, Chiapas." Mimeograph. Material prepared for use by Stanford University and University of Chicago Chiapas projects.

Blom, Frans. 1950. "A Polychrome Maya Plate from Quintana Roo." *Notes on Middle American Archaeology and Ethnology* 4 (98): 81–84. Carnegie Institution, Washington, DC.

Bolles, David. 2003. *Combined Dictionary-Concordance of the Yucatecan Mayan Language*. Foundation for the Advancement of Mesoamerican Studies, Inc. http://www.famsi.org/reports/96072/c/coo_cor.htm.

Boot, Erik. 2004. "Kerr No. 4546 and a Reference to an Avian Manifestation of the Creator God Itzamnaj." http://www.mayavase.com/Kerr4546.pdf.

Boot, Erik. 2005. *Continuity and Change in the Text and Image at Chichén Itzá, Mexico: A Study of the Inscriptions, Iconography, and Architecture at a Late Classic to Early Postclassic Maya Site*. Leiden: CNWS Publications.

Boot, Erik. 2008. "At the Court of Itzam Nah Yax Kokaj Mut: Preliminary Iconographic and Epigraphic Analysis of a Late Classic Vessel." http://www.mayavase.com/God-D-Court-Vessel.pdf.

Boot, Erik. 2010. "Loan Words, 'Foreign Words,' and Foreign Signs." In *Idea of Writing: Play and Complexity*, ed. Alexander J. De Voogt and Irving L. Finkel, 129–76. Brill Academic Publishers, Boston.

Breton, Alain. 1994. *Rabinal Achi: A Fiftteenth-Century Maya Dynastic Drama*. University Press of Colorado, Boulder.

Bruce, Robert. 1976. *Textos y dibujos lacandones de Najá*. Departamento de Lingüística 45. Colección Científica Lingüística, Mexico City.

Calnek, Edward. 1988. *Highland Chiapas before the Conquest*. Papers of the New World Archaeological Foundation 55. Brigham Young University, Provo, UT.

Campbell, Lyle. 1977. *Quichean Linguistic Prehistory*. University of California Publications in Linguistics 81. University of California, Berkeley.

Campbell, Lyle. 1984. "El pasado lingüístico del sureste de Chiapas." In *Investigaciones recientes en el área maya; XVII Mesa Redonda*, 165–84. Sociedad Mexicana de Antropología, San Cristóbal de las Casas, Chiapas.

Campbell, Lyle. 1988. *Linguistics of Southeast Chiapas, Mexico*. Papers of the New World Archaeological Foundation 50. Brigham Young University, Provo, UT.

Carmack, Robert M., and James Mondloch. 1983. *El Título de Totonicapán: Texto, traducción y comentario*. Instituto de Investigaciones Filológicas, Centro de Estudios Mayas. Fuentes para el Estudio de la Cultura Maya 3. Universidad Nacional Autónoma de México, Mexico City [1554].

Caso, Alfonso. 1958. *The Aztec: People of the Sun*. University of Oklahoma Press, Norman.

Christenson, Allen J. 2003. *Popol Vuh*, vol. 2: *Literal Poetic Version: Translation and Transcription*. O Books, Winchester.

Christenson, Allen J. 2007. *Popol Vuh—the Sacred Book of the Maya*, 2nd revised ed. University of Oklahoma Press, Norman.

Coe, Michael D. 1973. *The Maya Scribe and His World*. Grolier Club, New York.

Coe, Michael D. 1977. "Supernatural Patrons of Maya Scribes and Artists." In *Social Process in Maya Prehistory*, ed. Norman Hammond, 327–47. Academic Press, London.

Coe, Michael D. 1978. *Lords of the Underworld: Masterpieces of Classic Maya Ceramics*. Art Museum, Princeton University Press, Princeton, NJ.

Coe, Michael D. 1989. "The Hero Twins: Myth and Images." In *The Maya Vase Book*, vol. 1, ed. Justin Kerr, 161–84. Kerr Associates, New York.

Cogolludo, Diego López de. 1957. *Historia de Yucatán*. Comisión de Historia, Gobierno del Estado de Campeche, Campeche.

Cortez, Constance. 1986. "The Principal Bird Deity in Late Preclassic and Early Classic Maya Art." MA thesis, Department of Art and Art History, University of Texas, Austin.

Davies, Nigel. 1977. *The Toltecs*. University of Oklahoma Press, Norman.

Edmonson, Munro. 1971. *The Book of Counsel: The Popol Vuh of the Quiche Maya of Guatemala*. Middle American Research Institute, New Orleans.

Fash, William L. 1998. "Dynastic Architectural Programs: Intention and Design in Classic Maya Buildings at Copan and Other Sites." In *Function and Meaning in Classic Maya Architecture*, ed. Stephen Houston, 223–70. Dumbarton Oaks, Washington, DC.

Franco, José Luis. 1968. *Objetos de hueso de la época Precolombina*. Museo Nacional de Antropología, Instituto Nacional de Antropología e Historia, Mexico City.

Freidel, David, Linda Schele, and Joy Parker. 1993. *Maya Cosmos: Three Thousand Years on the Shaman's Path*. William Morrow, New York.

Gordon, George B. 1913. *The Book of Chilam Balam of Chumayel*. University of Pennsylvania Museum Anthropological Publications 5. University of Pennsylvania, Philadelphia.

Gossen, Gary. 1974. *Chamulas in the World of the Sun*. Harvard University Press, Cambridge, MA.

Graham, Ian. 1982. *Corpus of Maya Hieroglyphic Inscriptions*, vol. 3, part 3. Harvard University Press, Cambridge, MA.

Grube, Nikolai, and Werner Nahm. 1994. "A Census of Xibalba: A Complete Inventory of Way Characters on Maya Ceramics." In *The Maya Vase Book*, vol. 4, ed. Justin Kerr, 686–715. Kerr Associates, New York.

Grube, Nikolai, and Linda Schele. 1994. "Kuy, the Owl of Omen and War." *Mexicon* 16 (1): 10–17.

Guernsey, Julia. 2006. *Ritual and Power in Stone: The Performance of Rulership in Mesoamerican Izapan Style Art*. University of Texas Press, Austin.

Guiteras Holmes, Calixta. 1961. *Perils of the Soul*. Free Press, Glencoe, NY.

Hellmuth, Nicholas. 1987. *The Surface of the Underwaterworld: Iconography of the Gods of Early Classic Maya Art in Peten, Guatemala*. PhD dissertation, Karl-Franzens-Universität Graz, Austria. Published by Foundation for Latin American Anthropological Research, Culver City, CA.

Hofling, Charles Andrew, and Félix Fernando Tesucún. 1997. *Itzaj Maya-Spanish-English Dictionary Diccionario Maya Itzaj-Español-Inglés*. University of Utah Press, Salt Lake City.

Hopkins, Nicholas A. 1996. "Metonym and Metaphor in Chol (Mayan) Ritual Language." Paper presented at the annual meeting of the American Anthropological Association, November 20–24, San Francisco.

Hopkins, Nicholas A. 2012. *A Dictionary of the Chuj (Mayan) Language: As Spoken in San Mateo Ixtatán, Huehuetenango, Guatemala*. Foundation for the Advancement of Mesoamerican Studies, Inc. http://www.famsi.org/mayawriting/dictionary/hopkins/dictionaryChuj.html.

Hopkins, Nicholas A., Ausencio Cruz Guzmán, and J. Kathryn Josserand. 2008. "A Ch'ol (Mayan) Vocabulary from 1789." *International Journal of American Linguistics* 74 (1): 83–114.

Hopkins, Nicholas A., and J. Kathryn Josserand. 2012. "The Narrative Structure of Chol Folktales: One Thousand Years of Literary Tradition." In *Parallel Worlds: Genre,*

Discourse, and Poetics in Contemporary, Colonial, and Classic Period Maya Literature, ed. Kerry M. Hull and Michael D. Carrasco, 21–42. University Press of Colorado, Boulder.

Houston, Stephen. 2000. "Into the Minds of Ancients: Advances in Maya Glyph Studies." *Journal of World Prehistory* 14 (2): 121–201.

Houston, Stephen, and Simon Martin. 2012. *Mythic Prototypes and Maya Writing*. http://decipherment.wordpress.com/2012/01/04/mythic-prototypes-and-maya-writing/.

Houston, Stephen, David Stuart, and Karl A. Taube. 2006. *The Memory of Bones: Body, Being, and Experience among the Classic Maya*. University of Texas Press, Austin.

Howell, Steve N.G., and Sophie Webb. 1995. *A Guide to the Birds of Mexico and Northern Central America*. Oxford University Press, New York.

Hull, Kerry M. 1993. "Poetic Discourse in Maya Oral Tradition and in the Hieroglyphic Script." Master's thesis, Georgetown University, Washington, DC.

Hull, Kerry M. 2003. "Verbal Art and Performance in Ch'orti' and Maya Hieroglyphic Writing." PhD dissertation, University of Texas, Austin.

Hull, Kerry M. 2012. "Poetic Tenacity." In *Parallel Words: Genre, Discourse, and Poetics in Contemporary, Colonial, and Classic Period Maya Literature*, ed. Kerry M. Hull and Michael D. Carrasco, 73–122. University Press of Colorado, Boulder.

Hull, Kerry M., and Rob Fergus. 2009. "Eagles in Mesoamerican Thought and Ideology." *Reitaku Review* 15: 83–134.

Hunn, Eugene. 1977. *Tzeltal Folk Zoology*. Academic Press, New York.

Justeson, John S., William M. Norman, Lyle Campbell, and Terrence Kaufman. 1985. *The Foreign Impact on Lowland Mayan Language and Script*. Middle American Research Institute Publication 53. Tulane University, New Orleans.

Kaufman, Terrence, with John Justeson. 2003. *A Preliminary Mayan Etymological Dictionary*. Foundation for the Advancement of Mesoamerican Studies, Inc. http://www.famsi.org/reports/01051/index.html.

Kaufman, Terrence, and William M. Norman. 1984. "An Outline of Proto-Cholan Phonology, Morphology, and Vocabulary." In *Phoneticism in Mayan Hieroglyphic Writing*, ed. John S. Justeson and Lyle Campbell, 77–166. Institute for Mesoamerican Studies 9. State University of New York, Albany.

K'ayum Ma'ax, and Christian Rätsch. 1984. *Ein Kosmos im Regenwald*. Eugen Diederichs Verlag, Cologne.

Kelley, David. 1976. *Deciphering the Maya Script*. University of Texas Press, Austin.

Kendall, Jonathan. 1992. "The Thirteen Volatiles: Representation and Symbolism." *Estudios de Cultura Nahuatl* 2: 99–131.

Knowlton, Timothy W. 2002. "Diphrastic Kennings in Mayan Hieroglyphic Literature." *Mexicon* 24 (1): 9–14.

Köhler, Ulrich. 1975. "Ein Zauberspruch auf Maya-Tzotzil zur Heilung von Schlangenbissen." *Zeitschrift für Ethnologie* 100: 238–47.

Köhler, Ulrich. 1995. *Chonbilal ch'ulelal-alma vendida: elementos fundamentales de la cosmología y religion mesoamericanas en una oración en maya-tzotzil.* Universidad Nacional Autónoma de México, Instituto de Investigaciones Antropológicas, Mexico City.

Laughlin, Robert M. 1988. *The Great Tzotzil Dictionary of Santo Domingo Zinacantán.* Smithsonian Contributions to Anthropology 31. Smithsonian Institution Press, Washington, DC.

Lowe, Gareth W., Thomas A. Lee Jr., and Eduardo Martínez Espinosa. 1982. *Izapa: An Introduction to the Ruins and Monuments.* Papers of the New World Archaeological Foundation 31. Brigham Young University, Provo, UT.

Martin, Simon. 2005. "Caracol Altar 21 Revisited: More Data on Double Bird and Tikal's Wars of the Mid-Sixth Century." *PARI Journal* 6 (1): 1–9.

Martin, Simon, and Nikolai Grube. 2008. *Chronicle of the Maya Kings and Queens.* 2nd ed. Thames and Hudson, London.

Miller, Mary Ellen, and Karl A. Taube. 1993. *The Gods and Symbols of Ancient Mexico and the Maya: An Illustrated Dictionary of Mesoamerican Religion.* Thames and Hudson, London.

Neiburg, Federico G. 1988. *Identidad y conflicto en la Sierra Mazateca: el caso del Consejo de Ancianos de San Jose Tenango.* Colección Divulgación. Instituto Nacional de Antropología e Historia, Escuela Nacional de Antropología e Historia, Mexico City.

Palka, Joel. 2005. *Unconquered Lacandon Maya: Ethnohistory and Archaeology of Indigenous Culture Change.* University of Florida Press, Gainesville.

Pérez Hernández, Jeremias Misael. 2003. *Pujb'il Yol Mam—Vocabulario Mam: K'ulblil Yol Twitz Paxil.* Academia de las Lenguas Mayas de Guatemala, Guatemala City.

Re Cruz, Alicia. 1993. *The Two Milpas of Chan Kom: Scenarios of a Maya Village Life.* State University of New York Press, Albany.

Pitarch, Pedro. 2010. *The Jaguar and the Priest.* University Press of Texas, Austin.

Redfield, Robert, and Alfonso Villa Rojas. 1934. *Chan Kom: A Maya Village.* Carnegie Institution, Washington, DC.

Ringle, William, and George J. Bey III. 2012. "The Late Classic to Postclassic Transition among the Maya of Northern Yucatán." In *The Oxford Handbook of Mesoamerican Archaeology,* ed. Deborah L. Nichols and Christopher A. Pool, 385–99. Oxford University Press, New York.

Ringle, William, Tomás Gallareta Negrón, and George J. Bey III. 1998. "The Return of Quetzalcoatl: Evidence for the Spread of a World Religion during the Epiclassic Period." *Ancient Mesoamerica* 9: 183–232.

Robicsek, Francis, and Donald Hales. 1981. *The Maya Book of the Dead: The Ceramic Codex*. University of Virginia Art Museum, Charlottesville.

Robicsek, Francis, and Donald Hales. 1982. *Maya Ceramic Vases from the Classic Period: The November Collection of Maya Ceramics*. University of Virginia Art Museum, Charlottesville.

Roys, Ralph. 1933. *The Book of Chilam Balam of Chumayel*. Carnegie Institution of Washington 523, contribution 31. Carnegie Institution, Washington, DC.

Roys, Ralph. 1965. *Ritual of the Bacabs*. University of Oklahoma Press, Norman.

Sahagún, Fray Bernardino de. 1959–63. *Florentine Codex: General History of the Things of New Spain*, trans. Charles E. Dibble and Arthur J.O. Anderson. Monographs of the School of American Research and the Museum of New Mexico. 13 vols. University of Utah and School of American Research, Salt Lake City.

Sánchez Díaz, Juan. 1986. "Ili xiye' tzabu ik'uxu wiñikob." In *K'uk' Witz, Cerro de los Quetzales: tradición oral chol del Municipio de Tumbalá*, by Miguel Meneses López, 62–63. Dirección de Fortalecimiento y Fomento a las Culturas, Sub-Secretaría de Asuntos Indígenas, Secretaría de Desarrollo Rural, Chiapas.

Schellhas, Paul. 1904. *Representations of Deities in the Maya Manuscripts*. Papers of the Peabody Museum of Archaeology and Ethnology 4, no. 1. Harvard University, Cambridge, MA.

Seler, Eduard. 1902–23. *Gesammelte Abhandlungen zur 1923 Amerikanischen Sprach- und Alterthumskunde*. 5 vols. Ascher, Berlin.

Stone, Andrea, and Marc Zender. 2011. *Reading Maya Art: A Hieroglyphic Guide to Ancient Maya Painting and Sculpture*. Thames and Hudson, London.

Stross, Brian. n.d. "Moran's Cholti Dictionary." Manuscript in possession of the authors.

Stuart, David. 1985. "The Painting of Tomb 12, Rio Azul." In *Rio Azul Reports Number Three, the 1985 Season*, ed. Richard E.W. Adams, 161–67. University of Texas, San Antonio.

Stuart, David. 2003. "On the Paired Variants of Tz'ak." Mesoweb, http://www.mesoweb.com/stuart/notes/tzak.pdf.

Stuart, David. 2005. *The Inscriptions from Temple 19 at Palenque*. Pre-Columbian Art Research Institute, San Francisco.

Stuart, David. 2006. *Vulture Hill: The Placename of Bonampak*. Maya Decipherment, http://decipherment.files.wordpress.com/2008/03/bonampak-place-glyph.pdf.

Stuart, David. 2007. *Old Notes on the Possible ITZAM Sign*. Maya Decipherment, http://decipherment.wordpress.com/2007/09/29/old-notes-on-the-possible-itzam-sign/.

Stuart, George, and Gene Stuart. 1993. *Lost Kingdoms of the Maya*. National Geographic Society, Washington, DC.

Taube, Karl A. 1985. "The Classic Maya Maize God: A Reappraisal." In *Fifth Palenque Round Table (1983)*, vol. 7, ed. Merle Greene Robertson and Virginia Fields, 171–81. Pre-Columbian Art Research Institute, San Francisco.

Taube, Karl A. 1987. *A Representation of the Principal Bird Deity in the Paris Codex.* Research Reports on Ancient Maya Writing 6. Center for Maya Research, Washington, DC.

Taube, Karl A. 1992. *The Major Gods of Ancient Yucatan.* Studies in Pre-Columbian Art and Archaeology 32. Dumbarton Oaks, Washington, DC.

Taube, Karl A. 2003. "Maws of Heaven and Hell: The Symbolism of the Centipede and Serpent in Classic Maya Religion." In *Antropología de la eternidad: La muerte en la cultura maya*, ed. Andrés Ciudad Ruiz, Mario Humberto Ruz Sosa, and María Josefa Iglesias Ponce de León, 405–42. Sociedad Española de Estudios Mayas, Madrid.

Taube, Karl A., William A. Saturno, David Stuart, and Heather Hurst. 2010. *The Murals of San Bartolo, El Petén, Guatemala*, Part 2: *The West Wall.* Ancient America 10. Boundary End Archaeology Research Center, Barnardsville, NC.

Tedlock, Dennis. 1987. "Hearing a Voice in an Ancient Text: Quiché Maya Poetics in Performance." In *Native American Discourse*, ed. Joel Sherzer and Anthony C. Woodbury, 140–75. Cambridge University Press, Cambridge.

Tedlock, Dennis. 1996. *Popol Vuh: The Definitive Edition of the Mayan Book of the Dawn of Life and the Glories of Gods and Kings.* 2nd revised ed. Simon and Schuster, New York.

Thompson, J. Eric S. 1950. *Maya Hieroglyphic Writing: An Introduction.* Carnegie Institution of Washington, Washington, DC.

Thompson, J. Eric S. 1977. "Nombres de días entre los Mayas Putunes." *Estudios de Cultura Maya* 10: 223–29.

Tozzer, Alfred M. 1907. *Comparative Study of the Mayas and Lacandones.* Archaeological Institute of America. Macmillan, London.

Tozzer, Alfred M. 1941. *Landa's Relación de las cosas de Yucatán: A Translation.* Papers of the Peabody Museum of American Archaeology and Ethnology 18, Harvard University 18. Peabody Museum, Cambridge, MA.

Tozzer, Alfred M. 1957. *Chichen Itza and Its Cenote of Sacrifice: Comparative Study of Contemporaneous Maya and Toltec.* Memoirs of the Peabody Museum of Archaeology and Ethnology, vols. 11 and 12. Peabody Museum, Cambridge, MA.

Webster, David, Barbara Fash, Randolph Widmer, and Scott Zeleznik. 1998. "Skyband Group: Investigation of a Classic Maya Elite Residential Complex at Copan, Honduras." *Journal of Field Archaeology* 25 (3): 319–43.

Whittaker, Arabelle, and Viola Warkentin. 1965. *Chol Texts on the Supernatural.* Publication in Linguistics and Related Fields 13. Summer Institute of Linguistics of the University of Oklahoma, Norman.

Wilson, Michael. 1972. "A Highland Maya People and Their Habitat: The Natural History, Demography, and Economy of the Kekchi." PhD dissertation, University of Oregon, Eugene.

Zender, Marc. 2004a. "Glyphs for 'Handspan' and 'Strike' in Classic Maya Ballgame Texts." *PARI Journal* 4 (4): 1–9.

Zender, Marc. 2004b. "A Study of Classic Maya Priesthood." PhD dissertation, University of Calgary, Alberta, Canada.

Zender, Marc. 2005. "The Raccoon Glyph in Classic Maya Writing." *PARI Journal* 5 (4): 6–16.

PART 4

Mythological Continuities and Change

10

The Solar and Lunar Heroes in Classic Maya Art

OSWALDO CHINCHILLA MAZARIEGOS

In his pioneering book *The Maya Scribe and His World* (1973), Michael D. Coe presented convincing arguments about the correspondence between characters depicted on Classic Maya ceramic vases and the heroes of the Popol Vuh. Since then, the sixteenth-century K'iche' text has been widely employed as a source for the interpretation of ancient Maya art, stimulating important debates for the study of Maya religion and mythology.

Coe paid special attention to Junajpu and Xb'alanke, the heroes who, according to the Popol Vuh, defeated the forces of darkness and death and finally rose to the sky, apotheosed as the sun and the moon, respectively. Initially, Coe identified them with the characters he called "Young Lords," who often showed up as a pair in Classic Maya ceramics, but he also noted that there was another pair, the "Headband Gods," that also showed correspondences. Their relationship with each other and with the characters of the Popol Vuh was initially unclear to him, as noted in his *Lords of the Underworld*:

> On some vases . . . they appear as twins, both with black spots. On others, one has
> black spots while the other has jaguar-skin patches covering his lower face . . . My own
> feeling is that the Headband Gods are the same as the Young Lords (i.e., the Hero
> Twins), but in another role and thus with different characteristics. (Coe 1978: 58)

Despite his initially cautious approach, subsequent work by Coe and other scholars resulted in the unambiguous identification of the Headband Gods with

DOI: 10.5876/9781646421992.c010

Junajpu and Xb'alanke, the Hero Twins of the Popol Vuh, while his Young Lords came to be identified with their father, Jun Junajpu. The latter idea originated from Francis Robicsek and Donald Hales (1981: 150), who misread a hieroglyphic tag on Codex-Style plate K1892 as *Hun Ahau* or *Hun Hunahpu*, suggesting that the Young Lord corresponded to the father of the Hero Twins in the Popol Vuh (Kerr database, http://www.mayavase.com). In an influential paper, Karl A. Taube (1985) criticized Robicsek and Hales's reading of the name but followed their suggestion about the god's correspondence to Jun Junajpu. Moreover, he recognized Coe's Young Lords as representations of the Maya Maize God, initially identified in the Postclassic codices by Paul Schellhas (1904). In subsequent work, both Coe (1989) and Taube (1992: 48) reiterated the correspondence of the Classic Maya Headband Gods with Junajpu and Xb'alanke and of the Maize God with their father, Jun Junajpu.

This interpretation has become paradigmatic, and many authors have restated it in their own work (for example, Bassie-Sweet 2008; Florescano 2004; Freidel et al. 1993; McAnany 2010: 127; Miller and Martin 2004: 56; Stone and Zender 2011: 45). Yet the prevailing identification of these characters is far from conclusive, and many questions remain about the ways the Popol Vuh has been used as a source for the study of ancient Maya religion, as recently remarked by David and George Stuart (2008: 256): "Interpretations of Classic Maya religious iconography based on the Popol Vuh have been overemphasized over the last few decades (Coe 1973 and Tedlock 1985). While strands of individual stories that we read in the Popol Vuh have deep and obvious reflections in ancient art, they are few."

Are these reflections so distant that they cannot lead to credible explanations of ancient Maya religion and art? Is it worth following those strands in search of new explanations?

In this chapter, I return to Coe's initial assessment in which the identity of these characters was not clear-cut. I question the possibility of finding precise one-to-one correspondences between the characters depicted in ancient Maya art and the heroes of the Popol Vuh while acknowledging that the parallels are indeed significant for the study of ancient Maya religion. I propose an alternative approach, grounded in a comparative study of Mesoamerican mythology, which results in a reassessment of the mythological identities of the Headband Gods and the Maya Maize God.

This chapter does not contain a full review of these complex deities; nor does it purport to analyze all known representations. My purpose is to reopen the debate from a broader perspective, as proposed more extensively in recent books (Chinchilla Mazariegos 2011, 2017). These problems require extensive discussion, and I will only outline some of them within the bounds of this chapter.

METHODOLOGY

In the final section of *Maya History and Religion* (1970), J. Eric S. Thompson compared the myths of the Popol Vuh with narratives collected throughout Mesoamerica, from Colonial times to the present. While he made no explicit statement in this regard, he clearly understood that the mythical narratives written by the sixteenth-century K'iche' authors of the Popol Vuh did not represent fixed, definitive accounts of Maya mythology. Instead, they represented particular versions of broadly distributed myths that had circulated since very ancient times in the Guatemala highlands, the Peten, and elsewhere in Mesoamerica. This premise is based on the recognition that the cultural and religious ties between the Classic period lowland Maya and the Early Colonial K'iche' do not conform to an unbroken line of direct transmission. These ties are better explained in terms of peoples' participation in complex networks of interaction that originated long before the Preclassic period and extended well beyond the Maya area. There are good reasons to think that Classic and Preclassic variants of lowland and highland Maya mythical narratives shared essential themes with each other and with the version we know from the Popol Vuh, but there is no justification to think they were identical or even especially close.

Modern versions recorded throughout Mesoamerica attest to the spread and resilience of these myths while revealing their multiple variations. Decades ago, George M. Foster (1945) noticed intriguing parallels with the Popol Vuh in the stories he recorded among the Popoluca of southern Veracruz. Since then, many authors have noted similar correspondences in narratives collected throughout Mesoamerica, from the sixteenth century to the present. These parallels are not casual, and they do not derive from late contacts in Postclassic or Colonial times. As noted by Alfredo López Austin (1993: 18–20), the shared subjects in Mesoamerican mythology are best explained as resulting from their common origins—going back to very ancient times—and from the intense historical interaction among diverse Mesoamerican peoples through millennia.

In his book *The Myths of the Opossum* (1993) and other works, López Austin structured a theoretical and methodological approach for the comparative study of Mesoamerican mythology. Especially relevant for this chapter is his distinction between the "heroic subjects" and the "nodal subjects" of myths. The first refer to "vivid, colorful specific stories, almost impossible to repeat in the same way in every version of the myth." They may include the protagonists' exploits and their very names, which are prone to change easily across time and space. The nodal subjects form the basic structures that underlie the core of mythical beliefs, "an order present in different versions of the same myth" (López Austin 1993: 249).

As suggested by López Austin, the nodal subjects of myths can be traced by comparing multiple versions in search of analogous passages, found repeatedly in multiple versions. Despite their diversity, Mesoamerican myths share nodal subjects that are surprisingly resilient and therefore more likely to be represented in ancient artworks. With these concepts in mind, I turn to the gods Coe initially characterized as the "Young Gods" and the "Headband Gods." Instead of comparing them directly with the heroes of the Popol Vuh, I compare them with the solar and lunar heroes and the maize heroes of Mesoamerican mythology, including among them the Hero Twins of the Popol Vuh.

THE HEADBAND GODS

In his survey of the gods of Yucatan, Taube (1992) used the letters CH and S to designate Coe's Headband Gods (figure 10.1). These labels are employed throughout this chapter instead of the readings that have been proposed for their hieroglyphic names. Currently, the prevailing readings for their names are *Juun Ajaw* and *Yax Baluun*, or variants thereof (Miller and Martin 2004: 56; Stone and Zender 2011: 45). However, those readings are not based on robust patterns of phonetic substitution or complementation—the basic keys employed to unravel the phonetic values of logograms in Maya writing (Chinchilla Mazariegos 2017: 173–74, 178–79, 2020). Considering their tentative status, they provide weak indications about the links of Gods CH and S with the Popol Vuh heroes. Moreover, López Austin (1997) warns that names are among the most superficial elements of mythical narratives and may change easily when the myths are transmitted across time and space. Therefore, the purported readings of their names offer meager information about the identity of the ancient Maya heroes.

God CH is the god of the number nine, a young man distinguished by the jaguar-skin patches on his face and body. While often paired with God S, he can also appear by himself and, very rarely, as a pair of identical twins. Taube (1992: 60–63, 2003) has shown that he is a lord of the wilderness and of wild animals. In his 2003 essay about Maya conceptions of the field and forest, he analyzed Vase K3413, which shows two Gods CH—both with jaguar-skin patches—receiving food and drink from a host of wild animals, like human lords receiving presents or tribute in a royal court. Both Gods CH are holding blowguns, but they are not using them to hunt the animals. In fact, this is a lone example that shows God CH holding that instrument. While the Headband Gods are often characterized as blowgun hunters, a careful comparison shows that this role corresponds largely to God S.

The black spots that mark the face and body of God S are the same ones that mark the skeletal body of death gods (Taube 1992: 11). In his survey of Yucatec gods, Taube emphasized the close association of God S with death and sacrifice. He is a denizen of the wilderness, but unlike God CH, he does not appear to receive

FIGURE 10.1. Gods CH and S. Detail from Vase K0732. Drawing by the author.

presents or food from the animals. He is commonly shown as a hunter, bringing down prey—most often birds—with his blowgun. While sometimes joined
by other hunters with blowguns, none of them has the characteristic jaguar-skin
patches that distinguish God CH. Robicsek and Hales (1981: 147) first noted that
God S often wears a simple straw hat, as befits a hunter in the wilderness. The wild
setting of his exploits is indicated by the Pax God tree—whose trunk is the god
himself—with serpents coiled around its branches (Taube 2003).

Elsewhere in Mesoamerica, the young solar and lunar heroes are sometimes characterized as hunters. Examples include the Mazatec heroes from Oaxaca, who lived with
an evil old woman and hunted birds and other animals for her (Incháustegui 1977:
27–29; Portal 1986: 54). They are visibly close to the heroes of the Popol Vuh, who
were born in the mountains and grew up there. They hunted birds and brought them
to the house, but they were denied food by their grandmother and their older brothers, who rejected them (Christenson 2003: 141–42). In the Maya area, similar passages are found in modern Q'eqchi' narratives (Thompson 1930: 120, 1970: 355–56).

Their role as blowgun hunters was one of the features that led Coe to associate
the Headband Gods with Junajpu and Xb'alanke. He and many others interpreted
the scenes in which God S shoots at a great mythical bird in terms of an important
passage of the Popol Vuh: the defeat of Seven Macaw, a primeval being that pretended to shine like the sun and the moon in a previous creation. But the relevant
scenes show only the spotted God S or a pair of identical spotted gods shooting the

bird. Other blowgun hunters appear occasionally, but no known example shows God CH in that role.

THE SUN AND THE MOON

A number of ancient Maya representations have been linked to the Popol Vuh story of Seven Macaw (figure 10.2). Yet they are better understood as derived from myths that have coexisted in multiple variants throughout Mesoamerica, from ancient times to the present. Many authors have identified artistic representations of episodes from this myth, attested since the Late Preclassic period at Izapa; during the Early Classic period at Teotihuacan, Copan, and the Pacific Coast of Guatemala; and during the Late Classic period in Veracruz, Oaxaca, and the Maya lowlands (Chinchilla Mazariegos 2017: 131–48; Fash and Fash 1996; Lowe 1982: 297; Nielsen and Helmke 2015; Taube 2005a; Urcid 2008). This section of the Popol Vuh finds parallel in multiple stories that tell how the heroes that were destined to become the sun and the moon defeated a monster—an eagle or a hawk, but sometimes a serpent or an unspecified monster—who pretended to be the sun or concealed the sunrays with its open wings. Modern versions are found in Oaxaca, Puebla, and as far as the Huastec region (Chinchilla Mazariegos 2010b, 2011: 112–23).

While the narratives differ significantly, they share critical details that justify their recognition as versions of each other and their parallels with ancient representations. The narratives are complex and may include many nodal subjects, among them the defeat of the primeval monsters that opposed the advent of the sun and the related explanation of the distinction between the sun and the moon—a distinction that occupies much space in the narratives and is clearly crucial in Mesoamerican cosmogony.

The distinction is variously explained. In some stories from Oaxaca and the Maya area, the moon is a girl or a woman, but that is not always the case. Very frequently, both heroes are males, although they exhibit contrasting qualities. Many versions share a passage in which, after defeating the false sun, they plucked off the monster's bright eyes—the final punishment accorded to Seven Macaw in the Popol Vuh. However, the Popol Vuh does not include a frequent passage that explains how the heroes became, respectively, the sun and the moon. Thus in Chatino and Triqui myths, the lunar hero first got the brightest eye but soon became thirsty and gave it to his brother in exchange for water (Bartolomé 1979: 25; Hollenbach 1977: 143).

Characteristically, the lunar hero needs water and enjoys the company of women. Totonac myths describe him as a *fandanguero*, a partygoer. When the time came, the sun hero ordered the animals to light a bonfire. He climbed a hill and threw himself into the flames, taking all the heat, and flew to the east, where he rose as the

FIGURE 10.2. Two Gods S—both with spotted skin—shoot a mythical bird with their blowguns. Reconstruction drawing of the "Blom Plate." Drawing by Guido Krempel 2015/2018.

sun. Meanwhile, they ran to get the *fandanguero* at the house of one of his lovers. He hurried but came late, and all he could do was roll in the ashes. Instructed by the solar hero, the animals showed him the wrong direction, to the west. Thus he became the moon (Ichon 1973: 65; Münch Galindo 1992: 290–91).

The well-known sixteenth-century Mexica versions of the origin of the sun and the moon mark the distinction between the sun and the moon in similar ways. As in the modern myths, there were two candidates with opposing personalities. The lunar hero was rich and handsome, while the solar hero was destitute and unattractive. His skin was covered with sores or pustules. The Mexica versions emphasize how the solar hero performed painful sacrifices with maguey spines while the lunar hero faked them, using red coral instruments that appeared bloodied (Sahagún 1953: 4). They say little about the lunar hero's relations with women, although the *Legend of the Suns* states that he "sang and danced like a woman" (Bierhorst 1992: 148). When it was time to perform the ultimate sacrifice, the moon hero recanted, while the solar hero threw himself into the blazing fire, from which he emerged as the sun. The specific details of each version vary, but the heroes are consistently contrasted in similar ways.

The Popol Vuh, however, departs markedly from this pattern. While they sometimes act differently, there is no emphasis on the contrast between Junajpu and Xb'alanke. Rather, the K'iche' text makes a point of describing how the heroes died in unison, throwing themselves together into the pit oven at Xibalba:

They already knew of their death. The Xibalbans were even then putting together the great heated stones in the form of a pit oven, placing large hot coals within it . . . Then they turned to face one another, spread out their arms and together they went into the pit oven. Thus both of them died there. (Christenson 2003: 178)

This peculiarity falls within the realm of López Austin's heroic subjects, and it finds explanation in terms of the political circumstances in which the Popol Vuh was written (Chinchilla Mazariegos 2017: 143–45). There is no good reason to think that ancient Maya versions were close to the Popol Vuh on this important matter, treating the solar and lunar heroes as equals. Significantly, a sixteenth-century K'iche' passage from the *Título de Totonicapán*—contemporary with the Popol Vuh—distinguished the sun and the moon heroes in terms of gender (Carmack and Mondloch 1983: 174). Gender distinctions are also common in modern Maya narratives, such as Q'eqchi' and Mopan myths in which the sun and the moon are man and wife, or versions from highland Chiapas in which the moon is a woman and the sun is her child (Thompson 1930: 132; Díaz de Salas 1963: 260). Some ancient Maya versions likely made a similar distinction, judging from the relatively frequent representations of the Moon Goddess. However, there are indications that the Classic Maya also conceived a pair of mythical heroes with contrasting personalities that bring them close to Mesoamerican solar and lunar heroes. These characters are God S and the Maize God.

THE LUNAR MAIZE GOD

Taube (1985) identified the mythical character that Coe labeled "Young Lord" in his early contributions with the Classic Maya Maize God. Several authors consider him as personifying the ideal of beauty among the Classic Maya. He is normally bedecked with abundant jewelry, and Taube (2005b) has pointed out his close association with jade, while Simon Martin (2006) has shown that he can also personify cacao. Both were major items of wealth in Mesoamerica. Abundant examples show the Maize God as a dancer, often covered in finery (figure 10.3; Taube 2009). He enjoys water and is frequently shown in the company of women, surrounded by beautiful young ladies who are naked or almost naked, immersed in water pools or seated on benches marked with water symbols (figure 10.4). The women dress him, present him with jewels, and sometimes appear to bathe him. The sexual connotations of these scenes are noticeable, especially considering that in Mesoamerica, rivers, waterholes, and other water deposits are often associated with seduction and love. In mythical narratives, sexual encounters normally occur in such places (Chinchilla Mazariegos 2010a). These scenes are strongly reminiscent of narratives

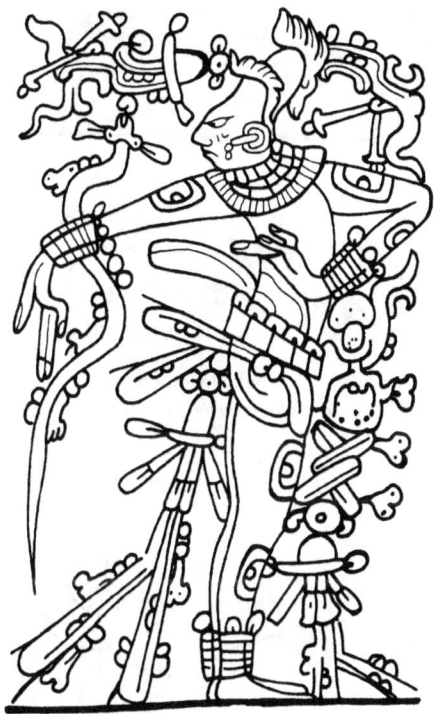

FIGURE 10.3. Dancing Maize God. Detail from Vase K6997. Drawing by the author.

FIGURE 10.4. Two naked women attend the Maize God, in an aquatic place indicated by water bands and a fish. The god's contorted pose denotes dancing. Detail from the Vase of the Paddlers, Museo Popol Vuh, Universidad Francisco Marroquín. Drawing by the author.

FIGURE 10.5. Bowl K1202. The Maize God, attended by six naked women, in the presence of God S. The phrase *och' bih*, "enters the road" refers to the god's death. Drawing by the author.

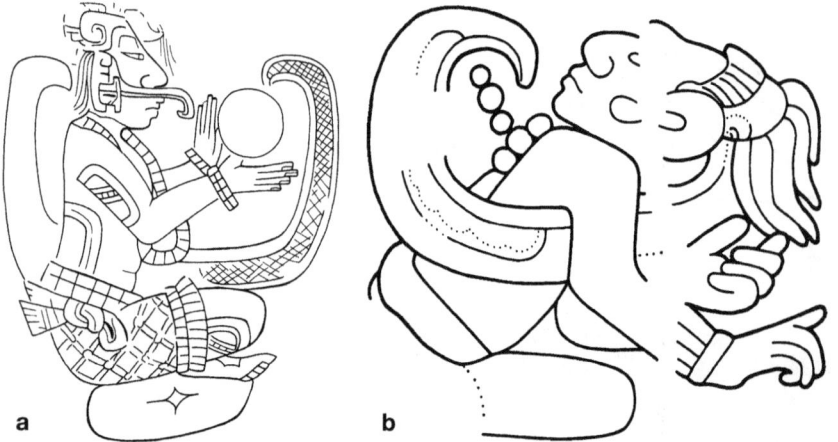

FIGURE 10.6. The Lunar Maize God. (a) Detail from conch shell trumpet, after Coe (1982: 122); (b) full-figure glyph from hieroglyphic bench, Copan Structure 9M-146. Drawings by the author.

from other regions in Mesoamerica that tell how the lunar hero spied on women or played with them while they were washing clothes (Galinier 1990: 693–99; Ichon 1973: 65).

God S and sometimes also God CH appear in some representations of the Maize God's dealings with the women, but they never participate (figure 10.5). The women accost the handsome, fair-skinned Maize God and barely look at the simple boy with the spotted skin or his companion with jaguar-skin patches on his face. Alas, there is no happy ending; the hieroglyphic captions refer to the Maize God's death. Some of the women who surround the Maize God have death markings and seem to play the role of mourners. The god's encounters with these women were not just related to his death; more likely, these encounters brought about the god's demise. This is a common trope in Mesoamerican myths; the heroes' acquiescence with the sexual demands of women marks their downfall and, very often, their death (Chinchilla Mazariegos 2017: 198–201; Graulich 1997: 178–79).

The Maya Maize God is portrayed with some frequency as a Moon God, marked with a moon sign (figure 10.6). Commenting on these portraits, several authors have suggested that he had a female aspect, overlapping with the Moon Goddess (Taube 1992: 64–68; Bassie-Sweet 2002). Gender characterization may be difficult in portraits that show only the head, but there is ample evidence that the male Maize God in his lunar aspect was distinct from the Moon Goddess. On occasion, they were portrayed together (Chinchilla Mazariegos 2011: 199–205). The ancient Maya Maize God shares features with Mesoamerican lunar heroes, to the point that there is little doubt that he belongs with them.

THE GOD WITH TAINTED SKIN

God S is markedly dissimilar to the Maize God. He is an austere hunter, and his skin marks are far from beautiful (figure 10.7). Often called "death marks," the black spots that stain his body and face can be understood as sores or pustules. They are sometimes surrounded with a red halo that makes them look like swollen abscesses containing black, putrid matter. As noted, Mesoamerican solar heroes are commonly described as suffering from grains, sores, or buboes that add to their miserable condition and cast them as opposites of the elegant lunar heroes.

God S may wear some jewelry, but his unassuming appearance, with a straw hat or a simple white headband, contrasts starkly with the Maize God's elaborate headdresses and ornaments. Coe noted that God S is sometimes shown performing self-sacrifice, which may explain his presence in a stingray-shaped sculpture from Copan that shows him in acrobatic stance at a place labeled Stingray Hill in the associated inscription (Coe 1989; Finamore and Houston 2010: 140–41). In this instance, he has jaguar attributes, which occasionally reappear in representations of both God S and God CH (Chinchilla Mazariegos 2011: 126).

The contrast between the two heroes was well established at an early date. The San Bartolo mural paintings show striking examples of God S drawing blood from his genitals, while the Maize God, not surprisingly, is surrounded by women (Saturno et al. 2005; Taube et al. 2010). His contorted posture—with the head

FIGURE 10.7. God S with straw hat. Detail from Vase K1607. Drawing by the author.

FIGURE 10.8. Vase K4479. Two naked women attend the Maize God on a bench marked with a water band, while God S turns his back, stepping out of the bench. Rollout photo by Justin Kerr. *Courtesy*, Dumbarton Oaks, Washington, DC.

turned backward—suggest that he is dancing, as is usual in Late Classic portraits, while the scroll in his mouth denotes singing. Kaminaljuyu Stela 9 shows a very similar speech scroll in the mouth of a dancer posed in a similar stance (Taube, in Finamore and Houston 2010: 234–37).

Gods S and CH sometimes witness the Maize God's affairs with the ladies without getting involved or receiving the slightest attention from them. For example, on Vase K4479, the Maize God sits between two naked ladies on a bench marked with water symbols (figure 10.8). God S turns his back to the threesome, walking away from them. Yet another example, on Vase K7268, marks a distinction between the places where the heroes appear. As usual, the Maize God appears in a watery place, receiving the attentions of three women. This elegant group contrasts with the spotted gods on the opposite side of the vase, who occupy a cave—a wild place that is well suited for their lifestyle. One of them has a jaguar-skin patch around the mouth, making this a rare case of overlap in the skin markings of Gods S and CH. While God S seems to fulfill the attributes of Mesoamerican solar heroes better than God CH, it appears that they overlapped, and both of them were contrasted with the Maize God in Classic Maya myths.

The question remains whether God S became the sun in Classic Maya narratives, and, if so, how he related with God G, the Sun God. There are no explicit portraits of God S with solar attributes; in fact, some representations suggest that he was sometimes associated with a star (Chinchilla Mazariegos 2005, 2011: 199). Classic Maya notions of the origin of the sun may have departed from other Mesoamerican myths on this important point, which requires further inquiry. Nevertheless, God S shares critical features with Mesoamerican solar heroes, including the Hero Twins of the Popol Vuh.

FINAL COMMENTS

In the preceding discussion, I departed significantly from the traditional identification of the characters represented in Classic Maya art as counterparts of the Popol Vuh heroes. Both the Classic Maya Maize God and the pair formed by Gods S and CH are best understood when compared with the broad spectrum of Mesoamerican solar and lunar heroes. Junajpu and Xb'alanke, the heroes of the Popol Vuh, are members of this group, but they are not necessarily the closest analogues; nor are they paradigmatic. Instead, they show peculiarities that should be explained in terms of the specific cultural and historical circumstances of the sixteenth-century K'iche'.

The Popol Vuh is one of the oldest written sources on Maya myths and the richest in terms of its contents and literary qualities. Yet it should not be privileged as the sole source for interpreting Precolumbian imagery. By themselves, the myths of the Popol Vuh provide insufficient models for the study of ancient Maya mythology. This chapter outlines an alternative approach, which considers both the Classic Maya artistic representations and the Popol Vuh stories as versions of widespread Mesoamerican myths and provides keys for a subtler understanding of the correspondences between ancient Maya representations and the sixteenth-century K'iche' myths.

REFERENCES CITED

Bartolomé, Miguel Alberto. 1979. *Narrativa y Etnicidad entre los Chatinos de Oaxaca.* Instituto Nacional de Antropología e Historia, Mexico City.

Bassie-Sweet, Karen. 2002. "Corn Deities and the Complementary Male/Female Principle." In *La Organización Social entre los Mayas Prehispánicos, Coloniales y Modernos: Memoria de la Tercera Mesa Redonda de Palenque,* ed. Vera Tiesler Blos, Rafael Cobos, and Merle Greene Robertson, vol. 2, 105–25. Instituto Nacional de Antropología e Historia and Universidad Autónoma de Yucatán, Mexico City.

Bassie-Sweet, Karen. 2008. *Maya Sacred Geography and the Creator Deities.* University of Oklahoma Press, Norman.

Bierhorst, John, ed. 1992. *History and Mythology of the Aztecs: The Codex Chimalpopoca.* University of Arizona Press, Tucson.

Carmack, Robert M., and James Mondloch. 1983. *El Título de Totonicapán: Texto, Traducción y Comentario.* Instituto de Investigaciones Filológicas, Centro de Estudios Mayas. Fuentes para el Estudio de la Cultura Maya 3. Universidad Autónoma de México, Mexico City [1554].

Chinchilla Mazariegos, Oswaldo. 2005. "Cosmos and Warfare on a Classic Maya Vase." *RES—Anthropology and Aesthetics* 47: 107–34.

Chinchilla Mazariegos, Oswaldo. 2010a. "Of Birds and Insects: The Hummingbird Myth in Ancient Mesoamerica." *Ancient Mesoamerica* 21: 45–61.

Chinchilla Mazariegos, Oswaldo. 2010b. "La Vagina Dentada: Una Interpretación de la Estela 25 de Izapa y las Guacamayas del Juego de Pelota de Copán." *Estudios de Cultura Maya* 36: 117–44.

Chinchilla Mazariegos, Oswaldo. 2011. *Imágenes de la Mitología Maya.* Museo Popol Vuh, Universidad Francisco Marroquín, Guatemala City.

Chinchilla Mazariegos, Oswaldo. 2017. *Art and Myth of the Ancient Maya.* Yale University Press, New Haven, CT.

Chinchilla Mazariegos, Oswaldo. 2020. "Pus, Pustules, and Ancient Maya Gods: Notes on the Names of God S and Hunahpu." *PARI Journal* 21 (1): 1–13.

Christenson, Allen J. 2003. *Popol Vuh, the Sacred Book of the Maya: The Great Classic of Central American Spirituality.* O Books, Winchester.

Coe, Michael D. 1973. *The Maya Scribe and His World.* Grolier Club, New York.

Coe, Michael D. 1978. *Lords of the Underworld: Masterpieces of Classic Maya Ceramics.* Art Museum, Princeton University Press, Princeton, NJ.

Coe, Michael D. 1982. *Old Gods and Young Heroes: The Pearlman Collection of Maya Ceramics.* Israel Museum, Jerusalem.

Coe, Michael D. 1989. "The Hero Twins: Myth and Images." In *The Maya Vase Book,* ed. Justin Kerr, vol. 1, 161–84. Kerr Associates, New York.

Díaz de Salas, Marcelo. 1963. "Notas sobre la Visión del Mundo entre los Tzotziles de Venustiano Carranza, Chiapas." *La Palabra y el Hombre: Revista de la Universidad Veracruzana* 26: 253–67.

Fash, William L., and Barbara Fash. 1996. "Building a World-View: Visual Communication in Classic Maya Architecture." *RES—Anthropology and Aesthetics* 29–30: 127–47.

Finamore, Daniel, and Stephen D. Houston, eds. 2010. *The Fiery Pool: The Maya and the Mythic Sea*. Peabody Essex Museum and Yale University Press, New Haven, CT, and London, UK.

Florescano, Enrique. 2004. *Quetzalcoatl y los Mitos Fundadores de Mesoamérica*. Santillana Ediciones Generales, S.A. de C.V., Mexico City.

Foster, George M. 1945. "Sierra Popoluca Folklore and Beliefs." *University of California Publications in American Archaeology and Ethnology* 42 (2): 177–250.

Freidel, David, Linda Schele, and Joy Parker. 1993. *Maya Cosmos: Three Thousand Years on the Shaman's Path*. William Morrow, New York.

Galinier, Jacques. 1990. *La Mitad del Mundo: Cuerpo y Cosmos en los Rituales Otomíes*. Universidad Nacional Autónoma de México, Centro de Estudios Mexicanos y Centroamericanos e Instituto Nacional Indigenista, Mexico City.

Graulich, Michel. 1997. *Myths of Ancient Mexico*. University of Oklahoma Press, Norman.

Hollenbach, Elena E. 1977. "El Origen del Sol y de la Luna-Cuatro Versiones en el Trique de Copala." *Tlalocan* 7: 123–70.

Ichon, Alain. 1973. *La Religión de los Totonacas de la Sierra*. Instituto Nacional Indigenista, Mexico City.

Incháustegui, Carlos. 1977. *Relatos del Mundo Mágico Mazateco*. Instituto Nacional de Antropología e Historia, Mexico City.

López Austin, Alfredo. 1993. *The Myths of the Opossum: Pathways of Mesoamerican Mythology*. University of New Mexico Press, Albuquerque.

López Austin, Alfredo. 1997. "Cuando Cristo Andaba de Milagros: La Innovación de un Mito Colonial." In *De Hombres y Dioses*, ed. Alfredo López Austin and Xavier Noguez, 231–54. El Colegio de Michoacán and El Colegio Mexiquense, Mexico City.

Lowe, Gareth W. 1982. "Izapa Religion, Cosmology, and Ritual." In *Izapa: An Introduction to the Ruins and Monuments*, ed. Gareth W. Lowe, Thomas A. Lee, and Eduardo Martínez Espinosa, 269–306. Brigham Young University, Provo, UT.

Martin, Simon. 2006. "Cacao in Ancient Maya Religion: First Fruit from the Maize Tree and Other Tales from the Underworld." In *Chocolate in Mesoamerica: A Cultural History of Cacao*, ed. Cameron L. McNeil, 154–83. University Press of Florida, Gainesville.

McAnany, Patricia A. 2010. *Ancestral Maya Economies in Archaeological Perspective*. Cambridge University Press, Cambridge.

Miller, Mary Ellen, and Simon Martin. 2004. *Courtly Art of the Ancient Maya*. Thames and Hudson, London.

Münch Galindo, Guido. 1992. "Acercamiento al Mito y a sus Creadores." *Anales de Antropología* 29: 285–99.

Nielsen, Jesper, and Christophe Helmke. 2015. "The Fall of the Great Celestial Bird: A Master Myth in Early Classic Central Mexico." *Ancient America* 13: 1–46.

Portal, María Ana. 1986. *Cuentos y Mitos en Una Zona Mazateca*. Instituto Nacional de Antropología e Historia, Mexico City.

Robicsek, Francis, and Donald Hales. 1981. *The Maya Book of the Dead: The Ceramic Codex*. University of Virginia Art Museum, Charlottesville.

Sahagún, Fray Bernardino de. 1953. *Florentine Codex, Book 7: The Sun, Moon, and Stars, and the Binding of the Years*, ed. Arthur J.O. Anderson and Charles E. Dibble. School of American Research, Santa Fe, NM.

Saturno, William A., Karl A. Taube, and David Stuart. 2005. *Los Murales de San Bartolo, El Petén, Guatemala*, Part 1: *El Mural del Norte*. Ancient America 7. Center for Ancient American Studies, Barnardsville, NC.

Schellhas, Paul. 1904. *Representations of Deities in the Maya Manuscripts*. Papers of the Peabody Museum of Archaeology and Ethnology 4, no. 1. Harvard University, Cambridge, MA.

Stone, Andrea, and Marc Zender. 2011. *Reading Maya Art: A Hieroglyphic Guide to Ancient Maya Painting and Sculpture*. Thames and Hudson, London.

Stuart, David, and George Stuart. 2008. *Palenque: Eternal City of the Maya*. Thames and Hudson, London.

Taube, Karl A. 1985. "The Classic Maya Maize God: A Reappraisal." In *Fifth Palenque Round Table (1983)*, vol. 7, ed. Merle Greene Robertson and Virginia Fields, 171–81. Pre-Columbian Art Research Institute, San Francisco.

Taube, Karl A. 1992. *The Major Gods of Ancient Yucatan*. Studies in Pre-Columbian Art and Archaeology 32. Dumbarton Oaks, Washington, DC.

Taube, Karl A. 2003. "Ancient and Contemporary Maya Conceptions about the Field and Forest." In *The Lowland Maya Area: Three Millennia at the Human-Wildland Interface*, ed. Arturo Gómez-Pompa, Michael F. Allen, Scott L. Fedick, and Juan J. Jiménez-Osorino, 461–92. Haworth Press, Binghamton, NY.

Taube, Karl A. 2005a. "Representaciones del Paraíso en el Arte Cerámico del Clásico Temprano de Escuintla, Guatemala." In *Iconografía y Escritura Teotihuacana en la Costa Sur de Guatemala y Chiapas*, ed. Oswaldo Chinchilla Mazariegos and Bárbara Arroyo, 35–54. U Tz'ib, Serie Reportes 1, no. 5. Asociación Tikal, Guatemala City.

Taube, Karl A. 2005b. "The Symbolism of Jade in Classic Maya Religion." *Ancient Mesoamerica* 16: 23–50.

Taube, Karl A. 2009. "The Maya Maize God and the Mythic Origins of Dance." In *The Maya and Their Sacred Narratives: Text and Context in Maya Mythologies*, ed. Geneviève LeFort, Raphaël Gardiol, Sebastian Matteo, and Christophe Helmke, 41–52. Acta Mesoamericana 20. Verlag Anton Saurwein, Markt Schwaben.

Taube, Karl A., William A. Saturno, David Stuart, and Heather Hurst. 2010. *The Murals of San Bartolo, El Petén, Guatemala*, Part 2: *The West Wall*. Ancient America 10. Boundary End Archaeology Research Center, Barnardsville, NC.

Tedlock, Dennis. 1985. *Popol Vuh: The Mayan Book of the Dawn of Life*. Simon and Schuster, New York.

Thompson, J. Eric S. 1930. *Ethnology of the Mayas of Southern and Central British Honduras*. Anthropology Series 17, no. 2. Field Museum of Natural History, Chicago.

Thompson, J. Eric S. 1970. *Maya History and Religion*. University of Oklahoma Press, Norman.

Urcid, Javier. 2008. "An Ancient Story of Creation from San Pedro Jaltepetongo." In *Mixtec Writing and Society / Escritura de Ñuu Dzaui*, ed. Maarten Jansen and Laura van Broekhoven, 145–96. Koninklijke Nederlandse Akademie van Wetenschappen, Amsterdam.

11

Beyond the "Myth or Politics" Debate

Reconsidering Late Preclassic Sculpture, the Principal Bird Deity, and the Popol Vuh

JULIA GUERNSEY

The opportunity to revisit the relationship between the text of the Popol Vuh and imagery from the Late Preclassic period is a welcome one. It necessitates engagement not only with the rich corpus of Late Preclassic iconography but also with the theoretical approaches that have driven the study of this material throughout the years. In this chapter I will focus on one motif within this broader discussion: the frequent appearance of a magnificent avian creature, typically referred to as the Principal Bird Deity and viewed by many as an antecedent to Seven Macaw of the Popol Vuh. This consideration must begin, in my opinion, by acknowledging the parallels between the imagery of these Late Preclassic monuments and the text of the Popol Vuh: they truly do exist and are provocative and productive to pursue. But one must also problematize this recognition and concede that as tempting as the parallels are, they pose challenges. Only some of the Preclassic imagery matches up well with the Popol Vuh text, and sometimes only portions of any given image correspond exactly. This is fascinating because it speaks to both patterns of continuity in ancient Mesoamerica and points of divergence (see Braakhuis 2009; Chinchilla Mazariegos 2011).

My analysis will concentrate on monuments from the site of Izapa, Chiapas, Mexico, which is located along the sloping piedmont that rises from the Pacific coastal plain and from which, on a clear day, views of the volcanic peaks of the southern Sierra Madres are clearly visible. Gareth W. Lowe, Thomas A. Lee, and Eduardo Martínez Espinosa (1982), under the auspices of the New World Archaeological

DOI: 10.5876/9781646421992.c011

FIGURE 11.1. Izapa Stela 2. Drawing by Ayax Moreno. *Courtesy*, New World Archaeological Foundation.

FIGURE 11.2. Izapa Stela 25. Drawing by Ayax Moreno. *Courtesy*, New World Archaeological Foundation.

Foundation, excavated the site between 1961 and 1965 and concluded that the vast majority of monuments were carved during the Late Preclassic Guillén phase (ca. 300–50 BCE). A detailed analysis of their iconography was completed by V. Garth Norman (1976: 94), who conjectured that the imagery on Izapa Stela 2 (figure 11.1)—which portrays two diminutive, similarly costumed individuals gesturing at the sides of a parted fruit tree into which descends a great bird—anticipated the sagas of the Hero Twins in the Popol Vuh. In a similar vein, Lowe, Lee, and Martínez Espinosa (1982: 207, caption for figure 2.2) proposed that the avian creature on Izapa Stela 25 (figure 11.2) might represent a Preclassic prototype for "the 'arrogant' Wuqub' Kaqix (7 Parrot or 7 Macaw) of the Popol Vuh" (also see Taube n.d.).

Wuqub' Kaqix, or Seven Macaw, of the Popol Vuh was the vain creature that claimed to be both the sun and the moon during the pre-Creation era of the wooden people. Prototypical versions of this avian character that appear in the Preclassic and Classic periods, however, are typically referred to as the Principal Bird Deity, a more neutral name first coined by Lawrence W. Bardawil in 1976. Bardawil's essay was the first sustained study of this avian character, which he differentiated from the plethora of beaked zoomorphs that characterize Maya art and whose symbolic significance during the Classic period had been addressed previously by scholars such as Alfred P. Maudslay (1889–1902: 63–64), Herbert J. Spinden (1975 [1913]: 60–63), Alfred V. Kidder, Jesse D. Jennings, and Edwin M. Shook (1946: 223–27), Frans Blom (1950: 81), and Linda Schele (1974: 59). Especially significant was Bardawil's (1976: 209) identification of the Principal Bird Deity as the avian aspect of the creator deity Itzamnaaj and his recognition, like that by Jacinto Quirarte (1973, 1977), that this deity complex extended back into the Late Preclassic period. Equally important was his recognition, following Schele (1974), that the bird was linked to notions of rulership and elite authority (Bardawil 1976: 207). However, it was not until the early 1980s that a correlation between the Late Preclassic avian imagery at Izapa and the story of Seven Macaw was explicitly suggested (Lowe et al. 1982; Taube n.d.). In the following decades, numerous scholars continued to analyze the relationship between the narrative of the Principal Bird Deity during the Preclassic and Classic periods and the much later Popol Vuh text (see Guernsey 2006: 95–116 for a summary of this literature).

It is essential to contextualize these studies within a debate concerning the historicity of Preclassic monuments and imagery. In her important and influential seriation of Preclassic monuments from the Pacific Coast, piedmont, and highlands of Chiapas and Guatemala, Suzanne W. Miles (1965: 237) asserted that most of the sculpture from this region was "primarily religious in function." This assessment was echoed by other scholars like Norman (1976: 4, 325–26), who dismissed any historical or political implications for the imagery at Izapa, instead describing it as a "timeless" account of deities and mythic personages (also see Miller 1974; Quirarte 1977: 265; and scholarship in which this characterization continues to be perpetuated, such as Rice 2007). These assertions contrasted with those of other academics like Michael D. Coe (1966: 61) and Tatiana Proskouriakoff (1971), who argued that Late Preclassic imagery was imbued with historical implications. For Proskouriakoff (1971: 151), imagery at Izapa interwove religious and mythic references into compositions equally concerned with sociopolitical structure and order. Interestingly, in their volume on the archaeology of Izapa, Lowe, Lee, and Martínez Espinosa (1982: 317) emphasized that the scenes on the sculpture, while teeming with mythological references, were also politically expedient, serving to

> maintain the supernatural right and means for Izapa's rulers and subjects to control
> certain lands, crops, peoples, products, and possibly their commerce. To make this

simple statement does not particularly differentiate Izapa from other sociopolitical centers—all hierarchies must struggle constantly to maintain their right to survival in the ways they choose, using all means at their disposal. The Izapa difference, already noted in the distinctive nature of its carvings (glorification of mythical events or ritual cycles, agricultural gods or "deity representatives," and allegorical weather phenomena), may finally be attributed to a concern for group (tribe or chiefdom) needs and rights, with perhaps incipient state concerns beginning to be involved. (Lowe et al. 1982: 317)

The history of the debate—whether Late Preclassic imagery that foreshadowed stories recounted in the later Popol Vuh was purely mythic in nature or imbued with sociopolitical significance—is crucial to acknowledge, especially because similar lingering deliberations continue to persist nearly a half century later. In fact, I would argue that this issue is at the heart of ongoing problems in understanding the significance of much of the Late Preclassic imagery, which continues to be interpreted primarily in mythic terms without equal emphasis paid to its social, political, and even economic import (Guernsey 2016). We need to rethink the way we have formulated arguments about Late Preclassic art and the Principal Bird Deity in particular and move beyond a "myth or politics" debate. In my opinion, stories concerning the bird throughout Mesoamerica are better viewed in cosmological terms. They engage with narrative and pictorial accounts of universal order—the stuff of myth—which are also laden with implications for the ordering of people in time and space—the stuff of politics. The term *cosmological*, as I am using it here, encompasses multimodal data—for example, mythic, political, social, economic—and is useful for thinking about how the story of the Principal Bird Deity functions on both a global/mythic level and a local/historically specific one. Before returning to this theme, however, an examination of a series of monuments at Izapa and contemporary sites that demonstrate parallels with passages from the Popol Vuh is in order.

PRINCIPAL BIRD DEITY IMAGERY IN THE PRECLASSIC AND LATER PERIODS

Lowe (in Lowe et al. 1982: 297) recognized that the scene on Izapa Stela 25 invited comparison with the Popol Vuh episode in which Seven Macaw, perched in a nance tree, was defeated by the Hero Twins, Junajpu and Xb'alanke. As translated by Allen J. Christenson (2003: 97), this passage reads:

> The twins watched for him beneath the tree, hidden in its leaves. At length Seven Macaw perched on the nance tree to feed and was shot by them. Hunahpu directed a pellet straight from his blowgun into his jaw. Seven Macaw cried out, sailing over the top of the tree and landing on the ground.

FIGURE 11.3. The Classic Maya "Blowgunner Vase." Drawing by Linda Schele. *Courtesy,* Los Angeles County Museum of Art (LACMA).

> Quickly, Hunahpu ran out to grab him. But instead Seven Macaw tore off the arm of Hunahpu.

While the bird on Stela 25 perches dramatically on some sort of staff or pole, the prototypical twin stands below, grasping the pole with one hand while his left arm appears to be severed, with blood gushing from it (Cortez 1986: 67; cf. Norman 1976: 132).

A strikingly similar vignette appears centuries later on Maya ceramics from the Classic period (Blom 1950: 81; Coe 1989: 169–71; Hellmuth 1987: figure 102; Robicsek and Hales 1981: 147, 1982: 56–57; Stone 1983: 216; Taube 1987; Tedlock 1985: 90–91). On the Blowgunner Vase (figure 11.3), for instance, a Hero Twin takes aim with his blowgun at the bird perched in a tree, much as the Popol Vuh story describes. It is a pregnant moment, *before* the shot is fired. Late Preclassic Izapa Stela 25, by contrast, focuses on a slightly later point in the narrative, presumably after Seven Macaw was targeted and, in retaliation, wrenches back the arm of Hunahpu until it is ripped from him.

The parallels between Izapa Stela 25 and a text well over a millennium later in date are uncanny. But there are also aspects of the Izapa imagery that do _not_ correspond well with the Popol Vuh text. For example, the Principal Bird Deity on Stela 25 (or anywhere else at Izapa) does not, despite the implied confrontation, appear humiliated or defeated, which is how this passage concerning Seven Macaw culminates in the Popol Vuh. Rather, the bird perches at the top of the staff held by the prototypical Hero Twin, glorious in its elaborate plumage and regalia.

There are other monuments at Izapa that, while clearly referencing some Preclassic story involving the Principal Bird Deity, bear no discernible relationship to the Popol Vuh text. Further, in several cases, they portray the bird not in purely avian form but instead as a hybrid creature with anthropomorphic attributes. I have

FIGURE 11.4. Izapa Stela 4. Drawing by Ayax Moreno. *Courtesy,* New World Archaeological Foundation.

argued at length elsewhere that the imagery on monuments such as Izapa Stela 4 (figure 11.4) portrays a Late Preclassic ruler at Izapa dressed up as and performing mythic narratives involving the Principal Bird Deity or prototypical Seven Macaw (Guernsey 2006; Guernsey Kappelman 1997, 2001, 2004). I proposed that the imagery alluded to a sort of "before and after" scenario, in which a ruler appeared in two different forms: (1) standing on a typical Late Preclassic in-turned groundline in the lower half of the composition, wearing a winged costume and the hooked beak headdress diagnostic of the Principal Bird Deity, and (2) descending above from the celestial sphere, fully transformed into the avian deity with wings spread. This interpretation was not without good evidence: Imagery from the Classic period suggests a fundamental reciprocity between the Principal Bird Deity and Itzamnaaj, one of the creator deities of the Maya. By extension, I argued that Late Preclassic rulers modeled their rituals after this mythology, portraying the same sort of reciprocity with the bird as the creator deity Itzamnaaj was known to do.

As early as 1976, Bardawil (1976: 209) had conjectured that "the Principal Bird Deity may possibly be the avian manifestation" of Itzamnaaj. Nicholas Hellmuth (1987: 201, 247) elaborated on this hypothesis, describing a *"nagual*-like" relationship between the bird and Itzamnaaj. Building off these earlier observations, Karl Taube (in Houston and Stuart 1989: n7) specifically identified the Principal Bird Deity as the co-essence of Itzamnaaj. The name of the bird during the Classic period certainly alludes to this reciprocity: In Classic period hieroglyphic inscriptions, the Principal Bird Deity is not named as Seven Macaw but instead carries the appellative *Muut Itzamnaaj*, or "Bird Itzamnaaj" (Carrasco 2005; Houston 2000: 174–75; Houston et al. 2006: 236; Taube et al. 2010: 30; Zender 2005). The bird's close relationship to the deity Itzamnaaj is further attested during the Classic period by the shared regalia worn by both. A Classic Maya polychrome vase (Kerr 7821; see Guernsey 2006: figure 5.26) with two adjacent scenes illustrates this complementarity. In one

FIGURE 11.5. Early Classic stuccoed vessel from Kaminaljuyu. After Kidder, Jennings, and Shook (1946: figure 207e).

scene, a long-lipped figure kneels before an enthroned and fully anthropomorphic Itzamnaaj. In the adjacent scene, the same long-lipped figure kneels beneath the Principal Bird Deity. An Early Classic cylindrical tripod (Kerr 3863; see Guernsey 2006: figure 5.27) emphasizes a similar duality. Itzamnaaj again appears opposite the bird, while both display wings and strikingly similar floral headdress medallions. Another avian version of Itzamnaaj wearing the same floral headdress medallion appears on the Early Classic Delataille vessel in an inverted position, legs askew as if tumbling or dancing (Hellmuth 1988: figure 4.2; Guernsey 2006: figure 5.28). The significance of performance in this iconographic complex is likewise reflected on an Early Classic stucco vessel from Kaminaljuyu (Kidder et al. 1946: 207e). Although fragmentary, the imagery portrays what appears to be another distinctly avian version of Itzamnaaj, clearly engaged in a dance or performance, replete with the wings of the Principal Bird Deity (figure 11.5; Guernsey 2006: 109).

In effect, I argued that scenes like that on Izapa Stela 4 illustrated the supernatural claims of rulers, which, in turn, provided justification for their political power. They modeled, through ritual performances like that recorded on Stela 4, the same sort of interchangeability with or ability to transform into the Principal Bird Deity as the deity Itzamnaaj. Such scenes were an integral part of Late Preclassic political rhetoric, an assertion supported by the fact that similar performances were recorded at other Late Preclassic sites where rulers also donned the costume and particularly the hooked-beak headdress of the bird. For example, the scene on Kaminaljuyu Sculpture 11 (figure 11.6) is strikingly similar to that on Izapa Stela 4 and depicts another image in which an individual, presumably a ruler, is crowned with the headdress of the bird (Guernsey 2006: 92–93). A greenstone mask with a curved beak-like element recovered from a royal burial at Kaminaljuyu provides material evidence for such costuming during the Late Preclassic period (figure 11.7) (Shook and Kidder 1952: 115, figure 81a; Shook and Popenoe de Hatch 1999: 304).

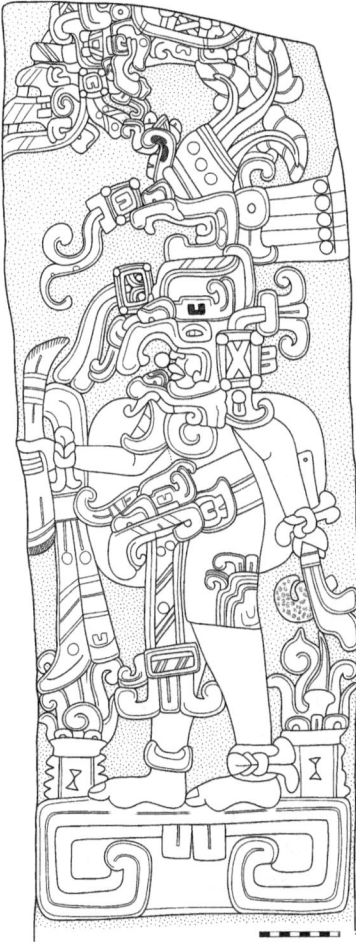

FIGURE 11.6. Kaminaljuyu Stela 11.
Drawing by Lucia R. Henderson.

Performances like those recorded on Izapa Stela 4 and Kaminaljuyu Sculpture 11 were not limited to southeastern Mesoamerica. Late Preclassic La Mojarra Stela 1, from Veracruz, portrays another individual wearing the same Principal Bird Deity headdress (Guernsey 2006: 106, figure 1.13). Such evidence indicates that the narrative of the Principal Bird Deity was invoked during the Late Preclassic period across a wide swath of Mesoamerica, including sites beyond the boundaries of the Maya region, where it was consistently related to expressions of rulership and display of the symbols and trappings of economic wealth (Guernsey 2006: 150–54).

More recently discovered material from the Maya lowland site of San Bartolo has allowed for refinement of several of my interpretations. The Late Preclassic murals of San Bartolo, as William A. Saturno and colleagues (2005; Taube et al. 2010) demonstrated, portray similar scenes involving the Principal Bird Deity. A recurring theme on the west wall of the Las Pinturas structure is the bird's descent from the sky to land in the branches of a tree (Taube et al. 2010: figure 7). This depiction at San Bartolo anticipates the imagery of the Classic period Maya Blowgunner Vase, which includes a hieroglyphic text with the verbal phrase "descends from the sky" (Zender 2005: 9–11). The San Bartolo murals make clear that through the visual reiteration of this same vignette, a story involving the "descent of the bird" was already in place by the Late Preclassic period. Stelae 2, 25, and 60 and Altar 3 at Izapa demonstrate the geographic extent of this shared narrative during the Late Preclassic period. Taube and his colleagues (2010: 12, 19–20) linked the bird's descent into a tree—which is repeated four times on the west wall of the Las Pinturas structure—to another overarching theme of the San Bartolo murals, which is the establishment of a four-part cosmology. This four-part

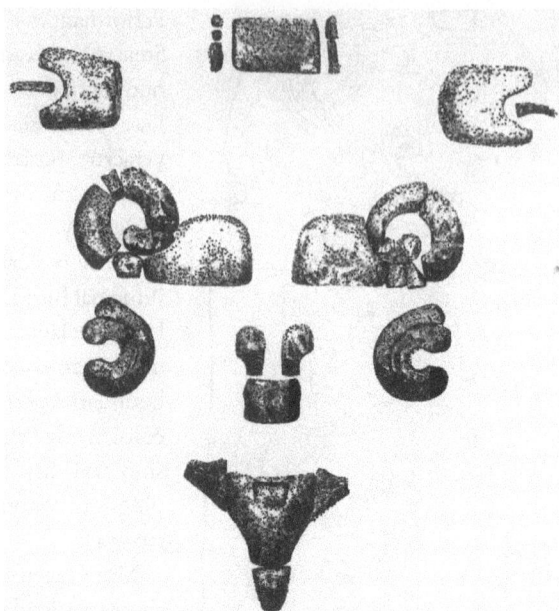

FIGURE 11.7. Greenstone mask from Kaminaljuyu Mound E-III-3 tomb. After Shook and Kidder (1952: figure 81a).

cosmology could be understood physically, as in the cardinal directions, but also temporally, as in the division of the Maya calendar with its four Year Bearers. Thus at San Bartolo, the bird's descent was linked to major cosmological ideas that governed notions of time and space or what I would suggest, following Terence Turner (1988: 243), be considered more generally as notions of proper social order.

Taube and colleagues (2010: 19, figure 12) observed that one mural fragment from San Bartolo's Las Pinturas structure Sub-1B suggests that the account of the bird at this site also included its ultimate defeat or, at the very least, its transportation-like quarry or game. They suggested that the fragmentary scene depicts a "clearly dead" Principal Bird Deity, suspended behind a Hero Twin–like figure. It is unclear to me, however, if we should read this literally, as if the bird is deceased, replete with limp legs, or whether we should understand this imagery in more symbolic terms, as if the bird is like a weighty burden or cargo whose transportation was conceptually linked to patterns of ritual, sacrifice, and renewal carried out to ensure social order. Cosmologically significant burdens, carried in backracks, are known from Classic period iconography, as in the Holmul Dancer theme that was featured on a series of polychrome vessels (Coe 1978: 94–99; Reents-Budet 1991; also see Guernsey Kappelman 1997: figure 5.7a for a possible Middle Preclassic antecedent for the bird as a bundle and Henderson 2013 for an in-depth discussion of the relationship between the Principal Bird Deity and bundles in the Late Preclassic period). In several examples, the Principal Bird Deity appears at the top of a backrack laden with mythic and dynastic information (Tokovinine 2013: 115–22). One vessel, discussed by Matthew G. Looper, Dorie Reents-Budet, and Ronald L. Bishop (2009: 120, figure 4.6 [Kerr 5123]), portrays one of the Hero Twins marked by the same black spots as in the San Bartolo mural fragment, presenting an elaborate backrack replete with a possible version of the Principal Bird Deity perched at the top. The imagery on Holmul vessels articulates the mythic underpinnings for political authority—or social order more generally—during the Classic period (Looper et al. 2009: 121).

There is evidence that during the Late Preclassic period, burdens carried on one's back were also concerned with assertions of political legitimacy. A recently discovered monument (Monument 215/217) from the site of Tak'alik Ab'aj depicts a massive, regally costumed individual bearing a "mummy bundle" on his back (Persson 2008; Schieber de Lavarreda and Orrego Corzo 2010). The "mummy bundle" is not unlike the one representing Huitzilopochtli that was carried by Aztec ancestral leaders during their legendary migration (Boone 1991). Monument 215/217 was integrated into the wall of Structure 7A during the second half of the Late Preclassic period at the same time a royal burial was placed in the same structure, which became the locus of repeated dedication ceremonies (Schieber de Lavarreda and Orrego Corzo 2010: 980). The diminutive figure transported in the bundle shares features with a series of Late Preclassic monuments portraying deceased yet still socially significant ancestors and speaks to the ways statements of lineage and ancestry were woven into assertions of political authority by Late Preclassic rulers (Guernsey 2012: 136–37).

Admittedly, the San Bartolo fragment seems not to be about lineage or ancestry per se, and the limp-legged Principal Bird Deity differs dramatically from the diminutive yet distinctly anthropomorphic figure on the Tak'alik Ab'aj monument. The bird on the fragment is not part of a more elaborate backrack assemblage, as in the later Holmul scenes; nor does it align perfectly with later Classic period imagery like that from Xupa, Chiapas, in which elites transport diminutive yet animated deities on their backs (Miller and Martin 2004: plate 48). Nevertheless, these examples seem worth mentioning, as they demonstrate that the transportation of a burden or supernatural carried a variety of meanings during the Preclassic and later Classic periods, all of which, at some level, were concerned with notions of proper social order couched in mythic terms. Rather than offer a precise, alternative interpretation for the San Bartolo mural fragment, I would merely note that the scene could be interpreted in a number of ways, several of which do *not* hinge on an understanding of the bird as literally "dead." This is important for several reasons. The vast majority of images of the bird during the Late Preclassic period portray it in a state of glory, in striking contrast to the Popol Vuh text that focuses on the bird's eventual defeat, humiliation, and death. While ruling out the possibility that the bird is indeed dead in the Late Preclassic San Bartolo fragment would be unwise, it is equally unwise to overlook the ways such a representation marks a significant departure from the known narratives concerning the bird at contemporaneous sites. The alternative interpretations I have suggested seem more in keeping with the broad contours of the bird's story, as it is known from extant Late Preclassic imagery.

THE PRINCIPAL BIRD DEITY AND SOCIAL ORDER

Other intriguing allusions to the relationship between the bird and social order appear during the Classic period. One vessel (figure 11.8) depicts the Hero Twins standing on a stepped platform or structure. Despite the fact that the Twins are armed with their blowguns, the scene does not feature a vanquished bird. Instead, as Taube (2003: 472, figure 26.5) noted, the Twins stand before "the hovering bird, now partly transformed into the powerful and aged Itzamnaaj," who still retains the wings of the Principal Bird Deity. Further to the right is a procession of animals carrying vessels, some laden with tamales. While Taube (2003) argued that this scene links the defeat of the Principal Bird Deity to the theme of mastery of the forest, I would argue that it is more concerned with the establishment of social order, which is underscored by the civilized activity of the Monkey Scribes below, who carefully record the event. It seems to be far less about the defeat of the bird than about the results of a transformative event in which an avian Itzamnaaj substitutes for the Principal Bird Deity and witnesses the presentation of gifts of food by the tamed beasts. The careful recording of the event by the Monkey Scribes merits special attention. I suggest that this act of transcription—the writing and recording of history—itself constituted a civilized act exemplary of social order in a Maya worldview. The civilized deeds function as a centripetal force in the imagery of the vessel: animals from the periphery enter the built world of order, writing, and gods. The center successfully integrates the periphery, and the animals are acculturated.

At Late Preclassic Izapa, too, although a confrontation with the bird is implied, the imagery does *not* emphasize the avian's downfall. On Stela 25, the bird appears in its glory, while the twin, with bleeding arm, gazes up at it. So, too, on Stela 2, the magnificent bird occupies the bulk of the pictorial field, wings spread wide and regalia in full display. Similarly, on Altar 3, the bird alights on a basal band with no indication of a recent rout. In these examples from Izapa, the bird's magnificence parallels that displayed on the west wall of San Bartolo.

FIGURE 11.8. Classic Maya vessel scene of forest animals presenting food and drink offerings to the Hero Twins (Kerr 3413). Photo by Justin Kerr. *Courtesy*, Barbara and Justin Kerr.

Given this situation, how can one square this Late Preclassic imagery, which overwhelmingly emphasizes the glory of the bird, to the Popol Vuh story that culminates in the defeat of Seven Macaw? Phrased in this way, the question is not resolvable. However, I suggest that by reformulating the problem, scholars can better account for the different versions of the Principal Bird narrative throughout time and space.

The story of the bird in the Late Preclassic is clearly linked to messages of proper order on a very grand scale. Scenes featuring the bird reference calendrical time, spatial organization, and mythically charged rituals of renewal and sacrifice—all things that were necessary for establishing and maintaining social order. When we see rulers garbed as the bird in the Late Preclassic, it is also clear, in my opinion, that such imagery indicates that the ruler was charged with embodying these ideals of social order.

In 1989, Michael Coe suggested that we think about certain key narratives, which first appear during the Late Preclassic period and are preserved in the much later Popol Vuh, as paradigms for proper elite behavior. Following this lead, I would argue that imagery like that on Izapa Stela 4, while invoking tales concerning the Principal Bird Deity, was doing more than retelling mythological stories: it was establishing the discourse for divinely sanctioned rulership, providing a blueprint for the actions of kings, and visualizing a system of proper social order. Images of avian performance at Izapa, Kaminaljuyu, and elsewhere portray the types of performances that I believe were once enacted in plazas, before audiences (Guernsey 2006; Guernsey Kappelman 2001, 2004). This was the visible language of high culture, civilized behavior, and elite, divinely sanctioned protocol. Rulers performed in the guise of the Principal Bird Deity to establish themselves as the earthly analogs of Itzamnaaj, the primordial creator deity. The images, to borrow the words of Jonathan D. Hill (1988: 6), illustrate that Late Preclassic rulers' assertions of power were based, at least in part, on demonstrating that they "possess[ed] some form of controlled access to the hierarchical structuring of the mythic power of liminal, neither-here-nor-there beings."

That said, this rhetoric of paradigmatic elite behavior was thoroughly grounded in myth. In fact, the two cannot be separated or tweaked apart. Susan D. Gillespie (2007: 110), following Alfredo López Austin (1973), provided an excellent discussion of the "false dichotomy" between myth and history that is often perpetuated in Mesoamerican scholarship. She invoked Terence Turner's (1988: 236) assertion that myth is productively viewed as more than a "merely passive device for classifying historical 'events' but [as] a program for orienting social, political, ritual, and other forms of historical action." She also pointed scholars toward the work of Jonathan Hill (1988: 5), who contended that myth and history are best considered as "modes of social consciousness through which people construct shared interpretive frameworks." Gillespie argued persuasively that we should think of myth and history as different ways of creating, reproducing, and transforming the same social processes (see also Akkeren 2003; Bricker 1981: 3–9; Carmack 1981: 43–74; Carrasco 2010: 608–10; Kristan-Graham and Kowalski 2007; López Austin and López Luján 2000; Marcus 1992: 8–16; Nicholson 1955; Pohl 2003; Ringle et al. 1998; Smith 2007; Umberger 2002: 88). By extension, we should understand that Late Preclassic monuments were concerned with formulating a visual repertoire through which elite conduct was situated at the nexus of myth and history and as emblematic of social order.

But—and this is of critical importance—such an understanding implies that Late Preclassic stories of the Principal Bird Deity recorded on the monuments and likely performed before audiences were by no means static. The disparities between the ways the story was told at San Bartolo and Izapa underscore this. At each of these Late Preclassic sites, particular features of a larger narrative were emphasized, modified, or sometimes neglected altogether. This could be attributed, at least in part, to different mediums or genres of expression. The murals of San Bartolo, exquisitely painted across the surface of walls, are better suited to rendering a sequence of actions and events than the carved stone monuments at Izapa. Yet as William Saturno (2009: 119) noted, the reading order of the San Bartolo murals is not self-evident. The same can certainly be said for the monuments at Izapa, which could have been approached from any number of paths or directions. Viewership was also strikingly different. The Las Pinturas structure provided an intimate setting in which the murals could be viewed, unlike the exterior spaces where the Izapa stelae were erected—at the bases of mounds, facing outward into enormous plazas. At both sites, accommodating a flexible narrative structure amenable to formulation in multiple ways may have been deliberate (see Turner 1988: 275).

Following in the same vein, while it is important to acknowledge that the over-arching story of the bird is central to both the murals of San Bartolo and the monuments of Izapa, notable differences in the way it is told are nonetheless apparent. At each site there is an image of the Principal Bird Deity dropping a twisted, serpentine cord. On Izapa Stela 25, the bird does so from a staff-like object held upright by the prototypical Hero Twin, while at San Bartolo it is from a naturalistically rendered tree. The Izapa image alludes to a confrontation between the Hero Twin and the bird, while the San Bartolo scene is included in a larger account of sacrifice and directional cosmology. Likewise, while the San Bartolo murals appear to culminate in an accession scene with "unambiguous references to kingship" (Taube et al. 2010: 84, figure 39b), none of the remaining walls at San Bartolo include anything comparable to the imagery of Izapa Stela 4, with its references to avian transformation. Late Preclassic cosmological stories such as these were elastic. They were well suited to accommodating a range of endlessly shifting sociopolitical concerns cloaked in the language of broadly shared myths (Guernsey 2010).

The repetition of the Principal Bird Deity narrative at multiple sites is significant, but perhaps no more so than the variations that are equally apparent. What we see are the loose contours of a widely shared story that factored into elite rhetoric of the time. The reason we see it throughout much of Late Preclassic Mesoamerica is because it mattered: it was expedient, probably even necessary politically, for rulers to invoke the story of the bird. It was shared but not static. It could be embellished, truncated, expanded, or manipulated to serve any number of site- or region-specific agendas.

ELITE IDENTITY, SOCIAL ORDER, AND THE POPOL VUH

Many of these same notions can be extended to the much later Popol Vuh text. Like the Late Preclassic monuments, the Popol Vuh combines mythic stories with a lived past. We find passages devoted to the retelling of ancient myths, but we also find entire sections concerning lineage and the right to rule. Likewise, concepts of cosmic order are at the heart of the Popol Vuh; it even begins with the fourfold establishment of space, much as in the San Bartolo murals or even as implied by the quadrilateral plazas at Izapa in which the monuments were displayed. In both the Late Preclassic and Postclassic periods, these narratives were undeniably mythic and deeply symbolic, but they also sanctioned the physical contours of a political site or its people. When thinking about the parallels between the Preclassic period and the

Popol Vuh, it is important to remember that myth and history do not just *represent* the past; they are structures or devices, textual as well as visual, that produce the present based on patterns from the past (following Gillespie 2007, 2008: 104; Hill 1988: 5–7; Turner 1988: 241–45). The Popol Vuh, in this sense, was rich with patterns of the past—even from the deep, Late Preclassic past—but it was also utilized to negotiate its own unique present.

As a number of scholars (Akkeren 2003; Carmack 1981: 44–74; Christenson 2003: 31; Sam Colop 2008: 15–17; Tedlock 1985: 54–65) have noted, the Popol Vuh, at one level, was about the establishment and preservation of an elite identity. It shares a remarkable similarity with the Preclassic imagery, which was also about elite social reproduction and, in particular, the rituals of kingship. This kingly identity, expressed in part through vivid imagery in which rulers performed the acts of gods or invoked the myth of the bird, seems to have been increasingly vital during the Late Preclassic period when many of the first state-level societies were forged and authority was becoming increasingly centralized in the hands of a privileged few (Guernsey 2006, 2012, 2020; Guernsey and Love 2005; Love 2011a, 2011b). Participation in this political rhetoric with neighbors—near and distant, friend or foe—may have been critical to survival in a social, political, and even an economic sense. There were massively shifting power dynamics during the Late Preclassic period, and sculpture—or monumental artistic programs more generally—gave tangible form to statements of legitimacy (Guernsey 2012: 28, 2020). So, too, was there a massive sociopolitical shift at the time the Popol Vuh was put in alphabetic form. I do not intend to imply that the sociopolitical shifts of the Preclassic period are directly comparable to those of the Postclassic period. But I do mean to suggest that at both of these junctures in the ancient past, widely shared cosmological narratives that invoked myth, political charter, and proper social order became vital to social groups concerned with negotiating their identity in the face of enormous change.

Such ancient and broadly shared stories, however, were also local and told or reformulated in unique and historically specific ways. They were "glocal," to borrow the term Roland Robertson (1992: 173–74) made famous; they were simultaneously global (or pan-Mesoamerican) and local. For example, some of the inconsistencies between the Popol Vuh and similar stories from earlier periods, competing groups, or different regions reveal conflicting political agendas (Akkeren 2003: 238–39; Braakhuis 1987; Christenson 2003; Coe 1989: 164). Ruud van Akkeren (2003: 239) observed, for instance, that the Monkey Scribes in the Popol Vuh "are presented as jealous and evil beings who are punished for their behavior," in contrast to Classic period depictions that emphasize their scribal abilities. Likewise, as both Akkeren and H.E.M. Braakhuis (1987: 30–34) noted, Bartolomé de Las Casas's (1967)

Apologética Historia Sumaria, written between 1553 and 1559, records a different version of the Monkey Twins story that is more in keeping with Classic period depictions. Akkeren associated the Las Casas version with the B'atz' lineage of Verapaz, whom he argued identified with the mythical Monkey Scribes. The K'iche' authors of the Popol Vuh, Akkeren (2000: 239) reasoned, deliberately inverted the story of the Monkey Scribes because of a "long-time conflict" with the ruling B'atz' lineage: "The authors of the Popol Wuj used the tale, too, but they intertwined their animosity with the B'atz' lineage with this Verapaz myth, making the B'atz' brothers look bad." Mythic inversions, according to Turner (1988: 258), define alien or antagonistic elements in terms of their "own internal schemata of social reproduction."

Christenson (2003: 91n152) suggested that similar dynamics explain shifts in accounts of the Principal Bird Deity/Seven Macaw. Throughout the Preclassic and Classic periods, the bird is mostly glorified. Although at times threatened, taken aim at, and perhaps even characterized as a burden (as in the San Bartolo mural fragment), for over 1,000 years the bird is nevertheless repeatedly invoked and celebrated by rulers and frequently associated with kingship and accession. But, as Christenson argued, during the Postclassic period and in the Popol Vuh specifically, these stories concerning the bird came to be associated with powerful rival lineages in Yucatan. According to the *Books of Chilam Balam*, one of the principal capitals in Yucatan, Izamal, had been founded by Kenech Kukmo ("Sun-faced/eyed Fire Macaw"), a "lord [who] was also the ancestor of a number of the principal lineages of Yucatan who worshiped him as a god" (Christenson 2003: 91n152). Izamal was eventually conquered, however, by a ruler from Mayapan, a site that Christenson argues served as the sacred city from which the ancestors of the K'iche' rulers derived their political legitimacy. As Christenson (2003: 91n152–53) concluded, "Thus this account of the boastfulness of a sun-faced/eyed macaw who declared himself to be a sun and moon god, but who ultimately fell at the hands of the ancestors of the Quichés . . . may be a mythic recollection of this historical incident." In other words, for the K'iche' lords who penned the Popol Vuh, the bird became a symbol of antagonistic lineages whose defeat and destruction were of paramount importance. As amply demonstrated by Christenson, the Popol Vuh effectively couched the political realities of the Postclassic period within an ancient story of the encounter between the bird and the Hero Twins that concerned the establishment and maintenance of social order. It is the same story but with a new twist.

I find Christenson's interpretation of the Popol Vuh story of Seven Macaw very compelling but would add that I think there is an economic aspect to its message as well. The conclusion of the passage states: "Thus the wealth of Seven Macaw was lost . . . the jewels, the precious stones, and all that which had made him proud here upon the face of the earth" (Christenson 2003: 100). The Popol Vuh makes it abundantly clear that the bird's defeat was expressed in economic terms; its defeat was equivalent to the removal of or deprivation from rare and precious items and the trappings of rulers. Significantly, this aspect of the bird—as a symbol of wealth—is well attested throughout the Preclassic and Classic periods as well. The bird is always bejeweled, wearing regalia that expressed social, political, and economic privilege (Guernsey 2006: 150–51). Late Preclassic imagery of rulers costumed as birds was undoubtedly predicated not only on a widespread set of shared beliefs and ritual behaviors but also on a shared economic interaction sphere, through which access to and control of rare and exotic goods—jade, spondylus, and the brightly colored feathers of macaws, quetzals, and other birds—was a privilege of the ruling elite. Such items were, in my opinion, the material correlate of the rituals of rulership, tangible symbols of mythically justified and supernaturally derived privilege. The iconographic overlap we see in the art was, in other words, paralleled by intersecting spheres of material exchange. The imagery also situated the ruler—as a symbol of the center and social order—within a matrix of meaning that directly invoked long-distance exchange.

During the Late Preclassic period, the economic implications of avian performance are particularly clear in the images of rulers costumed in the splendid regalia of the bird, as on Izapa Stela 4, Kaminaljuyu Sculpture 11, and La Mojarra Stela 1. They are also confirmed archaeologically by the greenstone avian mask found in the royal burial at Kaminaljuyu, a material manifestation of the relationship among exotic goods, fine craftsmanship, and the accoutrement of kings. Lucia Henderson (2013) noted that during the Late Preclassic period, the Principal Bird Deity is depicted at San Bartolo and Kaminaljuyu as the symbolic bearer of riches to the earthly world and the embodiment of abundance and wealth. Imagery of rulers costumed as the bird thus invoked this mythic precedent and provided "supernatural weight and sanction to the economic value system employed by elites to maintain power" (Henderson 2013, following Guernsey 2006: 152). The inversion of the story in which the bird loses access to these riches appears to be a Postclassic twist, rife with political overtones (Christenson 2003: 91n152) as well as economic ones. Vivid myths of the bird were subject to manipulation throughout the course of Mesoamerican history, adjusted to suit constantly changing political, social, and economic circumstances.

CONCLUDING THOUGHTS

I must admit that I have never quite understood why scholars are so surprised that the story of the Principal Bird Deity changed over the course of probably 2,000 years and hundreds of miles of arduous terrain. One should expect the story to transform over time with each retelling that was tailored to fit a unique historical situation or, perhaps better said, to reproduce a new present imbued with memories of the past. I think I would be much more alarmed if the story were presented in a monolithic fashion, seamlessly consistent through the centuries and across the miles. As Gillespie (2007: 108), following Peter Burke (1990: 279–82), advocated, scholars should guard against interpretations that are too based in literal minded-ness or a positivist approach that insists on consistent details, that overlooks rhe-torical strategies, or that deprives symbols and themes of their power to reflect, shape, and continually adapt (also see Sachse and Christenson 2005). If we could find every detail of the Popol Vuh narrative at Izapa and again at San Bartolo and again on a Classic Maya vessel and so on, in a very predictable sort of way, would we not begin to question the ability of ancient Mesoamericans to creatively adapt to locally distinct and perpetually changing historical circumstances? The fact that the story lines do *not* exactly match up speaks to ingenuity, creative adaptation, and innovative mechanisms for structuring social exchange. Such mechanisms were constantly strategically *and* poetically *and* artistically reconfigured to meet chang-ing historical circumstances throughout Mesoamerica and over the course of more than a thousand years.

In this sense, the Popol Vuh functioned in a way similar to the epic of Gilgamesh, the myth of Osiris and Horus, the works of Homer, or even the saga of King Arthur and the Knights of the Round Table—all of which, in essence, address issues of divine justice, social order, proper conduct, and balance. Coe (1989: 161) recog-nized this, as did Leonardo López Luján and Alfredo López Austin (2009: 389) who noted that, as early as the sixteenth century, Friar Bernardino de Sahagún had likened Quetzalcoatl to King Arthur and christened the Toltecs the Trojans of the New World. But one does not need to look to Mesopotamia, Egypt, Greece, or Europe for models; the myths of Quetzalcoatl or Tollan, to name only two Mesoamerican examples, seamlessly blend allegorical language with cultural codes. Nonetheless, their content, like the story of the Principal Bird Deity, varies from place to place and the imagery transforms in its details (see Cooper 1993: 12 for similar conclusions regarding ancient Mesopotamian literary traditions and their role in political legitimacy). To my mind, the extensive scholarship devoted to the mythic and historical significance of Tollan and the story of Quetzalcoatl, much of which I have benefitted from in this chapter, provides an excellent model for beginning to think about the Popol Vuh and its sociopolitical significance in Preclassic Mesoamerica.

To conclude, I would reassert that the questions we have been asking need to be reformulated a bit. Rather than scratch our heads over disparities in the story of the bird throughout time and space, we should recognize it as a polyvalent narrative whose various retellings shifted along with changing contexts of power. One needs to consider with each version "the importance of multiple actors, perspectives, and positions" rather than search in vain for a "monopoly on truth" that never existed (Lincoln 1999: 42–43). Even more important, we should explore the mechanisms that perpetuated the historical production and significance of the narrative (à la Gillespie 2007, 2008). Viewed in this manner, we are able to appreciate the remarkable continuity in the ways political legitimacy was forged, performed, and signified in imagery and text throughout the history of Mesoamerica. I would argue that the Popol Vuh is diminished if looked at only as a *guide* to the ancient past. It is that, but it is also much more; it is a guide to the *ways* the past was conceptualized and utilized by ancient Mesoamericans. Imagery from the Late Preclassic period—and the tale of the bird in particular—is integral to documenting the antiquity of certain modes of historical production and recognizing the ancient templates for civilized behavior and elite legitimation in Mesoamerica. But these data from the Preclassic to the Postclassic do not constitute an essentialized assemblage that moved through time and space in some fixed form. Rather, they constitute a fluid, flexible framework whose narratives and performative sensibilities were perfectly suited for adaptation.

The Popol Vuh is richly performative and inherently visual. As Dennis Tedlock (1985: 33, original italics) observed, at one point in the book the authors "take the role of a performer, *speaking directly to us* as if we were members of a live audience rather than mere reader[s]." In a similar vein, Akkeren (2003: 238) recognized that "many of the myths in the Popol Wuj were enacted in dance dramas," while Christenson (2003: 42), following Munro Edmonson (1982: xiii), emphasized the visual nature of the story, whose "written words were intended to conjure up an image in the mind, to give new life and breath to the gods and heroes each time the story was read." More recently, Nathan C. Henne (2012) highlighted the inherent physicality of the language used by the K'iche' authors throughout the Popol Vuh, which graphically communicates abstract or ethereal notions. For example, in the Seven Macaw saga, the arrogance of Seven Macaw is expressed as *nimarisaj rib'* "to make oneself big." The meaning of *nimarisaj rib'*, Henne argued, approximates that of the Spanish verb *engrandecer*, which is not limited solely to the negative connotations of the English words "pride" or "aggrandize." Instead, "making oneself big" also encompasses the shouldering of the burden of authority, the ability to become large enough so as not to be crushed by the weight of responsibility. While such subtle linguistic arguments are well beyond the scope of my expertise, it strikes me as significant nonetheless that the Late Preclassic imagery, with its recurring emphasis on the flamboyantly rendered and certainly larger-than-life Principal Bird Deity, parallels the visually rich nature of the Popol Vuh passages about Seven

Macaw. This recurring aesthetic trope—in which complex narratives are communicated in highly performative, visual, and physical terms—should be recognized as a crucial mechanism, or mode of historical production, that contributed to the flexible yet enduring framework we recognize as the Popol Vuh narrative, whether in poetic form or as rendered in the corpus of Preclassic monuments.

I think, to borrow a felicitous phrase from Cynthia Kristan-Graham and Jeff Karl Kowalski's (2007: 21) discussion of Mesoamerican mythic histories, that the Popol Vuh is best thought of as a long-lived strategy: the details changed through time, as did the players, the opponents, the victors, and the specific historical circumstances. But even with the changing variables and shifting storylines, the long view tells us that the overarching strategy remained effective for more than 2,000 years.

ACKNOWLEDGMENTS

I would like to thank Holley Moyes for the invitation to present this chapter at the 2012 symposium on the Popol Vuh held at the University of California, Merced, as well as the editors of this volume—Holley Moyes, Allen Christenson, and Frauke Sachse—for their efforts in bringing it to fruition. H.E.M. Braakhuis, Allen Christenson, Nathan Henne, Michael Love, Kathryn Reese-Taylor, and Stephanie Strauss graciously read earlier drafts of this essay and supplied insightful feedback and suggestions. I am also grateful to Lucia Henderson, the late Barbara Kerr, Justin Kerr, Arlene Colman, and the New World Archaeological Foundation for permission to use the drawings and photographs contained in this chapter. In addition, I would like to thank Thomas Tweed, Katie Arens, and Evan Carton for their especially helpful suggestions on a draft of this essay presented to fellow members of the Faculty Seminar on Religion in the Americas, an initiative of the College of Liberal Arts at the University of Texas at Austin, in the spring of 2013.

REFERENCES CITED

Akkeren, Ruud van. 2000. *Place of the Lord's Daughter: Rab'inal, Its History, Its Dance-Drama*. Center for Non-Western Studies Publications 91. Center for Non-Western Studies, Leiden.

Akkeren, Ruud van. 2003. "Authors of the Popol Vuh." *Ancient Mesoamerica* 14 (2): 237–56.

Bardawil, Lawrence W. 1976. "The Principal Bird Deity in Maya Art: An Iconographic Study of Form and Meaning." In *The Art, Iconography, and Dynastic History of Palenque, Part III*, ed. Merle Green Robertson, 195–209. Proceedings of the Segunda Mesa Redonda de Palenque, 1974. Pre-Columbian Art Research, Pebble Beach, CA.

Blom, Frans. 1950. "A Polychrome Maya Plate from Quintana Roo." *Notes on Middle American Archaeology and Ethnology* 4 (98). Carnegie Institution, Washington, DC.

Boone, Elizabeth Hill. 1991. "Migration Histories as Ritual Performance." In *Aztec Ceremonial Landscapes*, ed. Davíd Carrasco and William L. Fash, 121–51. University Press of Colorado, Niwot.

Braakhuis, H.E.M. 1987. "Artificers of the Days: Functions of the Howler Monkey Gods among the Mayas." *Bijdragen tot de taal-, land- and volkenkunde* (Journal of the Humanities and Social Sciences of Southeast Asia) 143 (1): 25–53.

Braakhuis, H.E.M. 2009. "The Tonsured Maize God and Chichome-Xochitl as Maize Bringers and Culture Heroes: A Gulf Coast Perspective." *Wayeb Notes* 32: 1–32. http://www.wayeb.org/notes/wayeb_notes0032.pdf.

Bricker, Victoria Reifler. 1981. *The Indian Christ, the Indian King: The Historical Substrate of Maya Myth and Ritual*. University of Texas Press, Austin.

Burke, Peter. 1990. "Historians, Anthropologists, and Symbols." In *Culture through Time: Anthropological Approaches*, ed. Emiko Ohnuki-Tierney, 268–83. Stanford University Press, Stanford, CA.

Carmack, Robert M. 1981. *The Quiché Maya of Utatlán: The Evolution of a Highland Guatemala Kingdom*. University of Oklahoma Press, Norman.

Carrasco, Michael D. 2005. "The Mask Flange Iconographic Complex: The Art, Ritual, and History of a Maya Sacred Image." PhD dissertation, Department of Art and Art History, University of Texas, Austin.

Carrasco, Michael D. 2010. "From Field to Hearth: An Earthly Interpretation of Maya and Other Mesoamerican Creation Myths." In *Pre-Columbian Foodways: Interdisciplinary Approaches to Food, Culture, and Markets in Ancient Mesoamerica*, ed. John E. Staller and Michael Carrasco, 601–34. Springer, New York.

Chinchilla Mazariegos, Oswaldo. 2011. *Imágenes de la Mitología Maya*. Museo Popol Vuh, Universidad Francisco Marroquín, Guatemala City.

Christenson, Allen J. 2003. *Popol Vuh, the Sacred Book of the Maya: The Great Classic of Central American Spirituality*. O Books, Winchester.

Coe, Michael D. 1966. *The Maya*. Frederick Praeger, New York.

Coe, Michael D. 1978. *Lords of the Underworld: Masterpieces of Classic Maya Ceramics*. Art Museum, Princeton University Press, Princeton, NJ.

Coe, Michael D. 1989. "The Hero Twins: Myth and Images." In *The Maya Vase Book*, vol. 1, ed. Justin Kerr, 161–84. Kerr Associates, New York.

Cooper, Jerrold S. 1993. "Paradigm and Propaganda: The Dynasty of Akkade in the 21st Century." In *Akkad, the First World Empire: Structure, Ideology, Traditions*, ed. Mario Liverani, 11–23. Sargon Editrice Libreria, Padova, Italy.

Cortez, Constance. 1986. "The Principal Bird Deity in Late Preclassic and Early Classic Maya Art." MA thesis, Department of Art and Art History, University of Texas, Austin.

Edmonson, Munro S. 1982. *The Ancient Future of the Itza: The Book of Chilam Balam of Tizimin*. University of Texas Press, Austin.

Gillespie, Susan D. 2007. "Toltecs, Tula, and Chichén Itzá: The Development of an Archaeological Myth." In *Twin Tollans: Chichén Itzá, Tula, and the Epiclassic to Early Postclassic Mesoamerican World*, ed. Jeff Karl Kowalski and Cynthia Kristan-Graham, 86–127. Dumbarton Oaks Research Library and Collection, Washington, DC.

Gillespie, Susan D. 2008. "Different Ways of Seeing: Modes of Social Consciousness in Mesoamerican Two-Dimensional Artworks." *Baessler-Archiv* 55: 103–42.

Guernsey, Julia. 2006. *Ritual and Power in Stone: The Performance of Rulership in Mesoamerican Izapan Style Art*. University of Texas Press, Austin.

Guernsey, Julia. 2010. "A Consideration of the Quatrefoil Motif in Preclassic Mesoamerica." *RES—Anthropology and Aesthetics* 57–58: 75–96.

Guernsey, Julia. 2012. *Sculpture and Social Dynamics in Preclassic Mesoamerica*. Cambridge University Press, New York.

Guernsey, Julia. 2016. "Water, Maize, Salt, and Canoes: An Iconography of Economics at Late Preclassic Izapa, Chiapas, Mexico." *Latin American Antiquity* 27 (3): 340–56.

Guernsey, Julia. 2020. *Human Figuration and Fragmentation in Preclassic Mesoamerica: From Figurines to Sculpture*. Cambridge University Press, New York.

Guernsey, Julia, and Michael Love. 2005. "Late Preclassic Expressions of Authority on the Pacific Slope." In *Lords of Creation: The Origins of Sacred Maya Kingship*, ed. Virginia M. Fields and Dorie Reents-Budet, 37–43. Los Angeles County Museum of Art and Scala Publishers, London and New York.

Guernsey Kappelman, Julia. 1997. "Of Macaws and Men: Late Preclassic Cosmology and Political Ideology in Izapan-Style Monuments." PhD dissertation, Department of Art and Art History, University of Texas, Austin.

Guernsey Kappelman, Julia. 2001. "Sacred Geography at Izapa and the Performance of Rulership." In *Space, Power, and Poetics in Ancient Mesoamerica*, ed. Rex Koontz, Kathryn Reese-Taylor, and Annabeth Headrick, 81–111. Westview, Boulder.

Guernsey Kappelman, Julia. 2004. "Demystifying the Late Preclassic Izapan-Style Stela-Altar 'Cult.'" *RES—Anthropology and Aesthetics* 45: 99–122.

Hellmuth, Nicholas. 1987. "The Surface of the Underwaterworld: Iconography of the Gods of Early Classic Maya Art in Peten, Guatemala." Foundation for Latin American Anthropological Research, Culver City, CA.

Hellmuth, Nicholas. 1988. "Early Maya Iconography on an Incised Cylindrical Tripod." In *Maya Iconography*, ed. Elizabeth P. Benson and Gillett G. Griffin, 152–74. Princeton University Press, Princeton, NJ.

Henderson, Lucia. 2013. "Bodies Politic, Bodies in Stone: Imagery of the Human and the Divine in the Sculpture of Late Preclassic Kaminaljuyú, Guatemala." PhD dissertation, Department of Art and Art History, University of Texas, Austin.

Henne, Nathan C. 2012. "Untranslation: The Popol Wuj and Comparative Methodology." *New Centennial Review* 12 (2): 107–49.

Hill, Jonathan D. 1988. "Introduction: Myth and History." In *Rethinking History and Myth: Indigenous South American Perspectives on the Past*, ed. Jonathan D. Hill, 1–17. University of Illinois Press, Champaign-Urbana.

Houston, Stephen. 2000. "Into the Minds of Ancients: Advances in Maya Glyph Studies." *Journal of World Prehistory* 14 (2): 121–201.

Houston, Stephen, and David Stuart. 1989. *The Way Glyph: Evidence for "Co-essences" among the Classic Maya*. Research Reports on Ancient Maya Writing 30. Center for Maya Research, Washington, DC.

Houston, Stephen, David Stuart, and Karl A. Taube. 2006. *The Memory of Bones: Body, Being, and Experience among the Classic Maya*. University of Texas Press, Austin.

Kidder, Alfred V., Jesse D. Jennings, and Edwin M. Shook. 1946. *Excavations at Kaminaljuyu, Guatemala*. Publication 561. Carnegie Institution of Washington, Washington, DC.

Kristan-Graham, Cynthia, and Jeff Karl Kowalski. 2007. "Chichén Itzá, Tula, and Tollan: Changing Perspectives on a Recurring Problem in Mesoamerican Archaeology and Art History." In *Twin Tollans: Chichén Itzá, Tula, and the Epiclassic to Early Postclassic Mesoamerican World*, ed. Jeff Karl Kowalski and Cynthia Kristan-Graham, 13–83. Dumbarton Oaks Research Library and Collection, Washington, DC.

Las Casas, Bartolomé de. 1967. *Apologética Historia Sumaria*, ed. Edmundo O'Gorman, 2 vols. Instituto de Investigaciones Históricas, Universidad Nacional Autónoma de México, Mexico City.

Lincoln, Bruce. 1999. *Theorizing Myth: Narrative, Ideology, and Scholarship*. University of Chicago Press, Chicago.

Looper, Matthew G., Dorie Reents-Budet, and Ronald L. Bishop. 2009. "Dance on Classic Maya Ceramics." In *To Be Like Gods: Dance in Ancient Maya Civilization*, ed. Matthew G. Looper, 113–50. University of Texas Press, Austin.

López Austin, Alfredo. 1973. *Hombre-dios: religión y política en el mundo náhuatl*. Universidad Nacional Autónoma de México, Mexico City.

López Austin, Alfredo, and Leonardo López Luján. 2000. "The Myth and Reality of Zuyuá: The Feathered Serpent and Mesoamerican Transformations from the Classic to the Postclassic." In *Mesoamerica's Classic Heritage from Teotihuacan to the Aztecs*, ed. Davíd Carrasco, Lindsay Jones, and Scott Sessions, 21–84. University Press of Colorado, Boulder.

López Luján, Leonardo, and Alfredo López Austin. 2009. "The Mexica in Tula and Tula in Mexico-Tenochtitlan." In *The Art of Urbanism: How Mesoamerican Kingdoms Represented Themselves in Architecture and Imagery*, ed. William L. Fash and Leonardo López Luján, 384–422. Dumbarton Oaks, Washington, DC.

Love, Michael. 2011a. "Cities, States, and City-State Culture in the Late Preclassic Southern Maya Region." In *The Southern Maya in the Late Preclassic*, ed. Michael Love and Jonathan Kaplan, 47–75. University Press of Colorado, Boulder.

Love, Michael. 2011b. "Critical Issues in the Southern Maya Region and the Late Preclassic Period." In *The Southern Maya in the Late Preclassic*, ed. Michael Love and Jonathan Kaplan, 3–23. University Press of Colorado, Boulder.

Lowe, Gareth W., Thomas A. Lee Jr., and Eduardo Martínez Espinosa. 1982. *Izapa: An Introduction to the Ruins and Monuments*. Papers of the New World Archaeological Foundation 31. Brigham Young University, Provo, UT.

Marcus, Joyce. 1992. *Mesoamerican Writing Systems: Propaganda, Myth, and History in Four Ancient Civilizations*. Princeton University Press, Princeton, NJ.

Maudslay, Alfred P. 1889–1902. *Archaeology: Biologia Centrali-Americana*. R. H. Porter and Dulau, London.

Miles, Suzanne W. 1965. "Sculpture of the Guatemala-Chiapas Highlands and Pacific Slopes and Associated Hieroglyphs." In *Handbook of Middle American Indians*, vol. 2, ed. Gordon R. Willey, 237–75. University of Texas Press, Austin.

Miller, Arthur G. 1974. "The Iconography of the Painting in the Temple of the Diving God, Tulum, Quintana Roo, Mexico." In *Mesoamerican Archaeology, New Approaches*, ed. Norman Hammond, 167–86. Proceedings of a Symposium on Mesoamerican Archaeology held at the University of Cambridge, Centre of Latin American Studies, August 1972. University of Texas Press, Austin.

Miller, Mary Ellen, and Simon Martin. 2004. *Courtly Art of the Ancient Maya*. Thames and Hudson, London.

Nicholson, Henry B. 1955. "Native Historical Traditions of Nuclear America and the Problem of Their Archaeological Correlation." *American Anthropologist* 57: 594–613.

Norman, V. Garth. 1976. *Izapa Sculpture*, Part 2: *Text*. Papers of the New World Archaeological Foundation 30. Brigham Young University, Provo, UT.

Persson, Bosse. 2008. "New Maya Olmec Archaeological Find in Guatemala." *Guatemala Times*, October 30.

Pohl, John M.D. 2003. "Creation Stories, Hero Cults, and Alliance Building: Confederacies of Central and Southern Mexico." In *The Postclassic Mesoamerican World*, ed. Michael E. Smith and Frances F. Berdan, 61–66. University of Utah Press, Salt Lake City.

Proskouriakoff, Tatiana. 1971. "Early Architecture and Sculpture in Mesoamerica." In *Observations on the Emergence of Civilization in Mesoamerica*, ed. Robert F. Heizer and John A. Graham, 141–56. Contributions of the University of California, Berkeley.

Quirarte, Jacinto. 1973. *Izapan-Style Art: A Study of Its Form and Meaning*. Studies in Pre-Columbian Art and Archaeology 10. Dumbarton Oaks, Washington, DC.

Quirarte, Jacinto. 1977. "Early Art Styles of Mesoamerica and Early Classic Maya Art." In *Origins of Maya Civilization*, ed. Richard E.W. Adams, 249–83. University of New Mexico Press, Albuquerque.

Reents-Budet, Dorie. 1991. "The 'Holmul Dancer' Theme in Maya Art." In *Sixth Palenque Round Table, 1986*, ed. Virginia M. Fields, 217–22. University of Oklahoma Press, Norman.

Rice, Prudence. 2007. *Maya Calendar Origins: Monuments, Myth, History, and the Materialization of Time*. University of Texas Press, Austin.

Ringle, William M., Tomás Gallareta Negrón, and George J. Bey III. 1998. "The Return of Quetzalcoatl: Evidence for the Spread of a World Religion during the Epiclassic Period." *Ancient Mesoamerica* 9: 183–232.

Robertson, Roland. 1992. *Globalization: Social Theory and Global Culture*. Sage, London.

Robicsek, Francis, and Donald Hales. 1981. *The Maya Book of the Dead: The Ceramic Codex*. University of Virginia Art Museum, Charlottesville.

Robicsek, Francis, and Donald Hales. 1982. *Maya Ceramic Vases from the Classic Period: The November Collection of Maya Ceramics*. University of Virginia Art Museum, Charlottesville.

Sachse, Frauke, and Allen Christenson. 2005. *Tulan and the Other Side of the Sea: Unraveling a Metaphorical Concept from Colonial Guatemalan Highland Sources*. Mesoweb, http://www.mesoweb.com/articles/tulan/Tulan.html.

Sam Colop, Enrique. 2008. *Popol Wuj: Traducción al español y notas*. Fundación Cholsamaj, Guatemala City.

Saturno, William. 2009. "Centering the Kingdom, Centering the King: Maya Creation and Legitimization at San Bartolo." In *The Art of Urbanism: How Mesoamerican Kingdoms Represented Themselves in Architecture and Imagery*, ed. William L. Fash and Leonardo López Luján, 111–34. Dumbarton Oaks, Washington, DC.

Saturno, William A., Karl A. Taube, and David Stuart. 2005. "La identificación de las figures del muro oeste de Pinturas Sub-1, San Bartolo, Petén." In *XVIII Simposio de Investigaciones Arqueológicas en Guatemala*, ed. Juan Pedro Laporte, Bárbara Arroyo, and Héctor E. Mejía, 647–55. Instituto de Antropología e Historia, Guatemala City.

Schele, Linda. 1974. "Observations on the Cross Motif at Palenque." In *Primera Mesa Redonda de Palenque: A Conference on the Art and Dynastic History of Palenque*,

Palenque, Chiapas, Part 1, ed. Merle Green Robertson, 41–61. Pre-Columbian Art
Research, Pebble Beach, CA.

Schieber de Lavarreda, Christa, and Miguel Orrego Corzo. 2010. "La escultura 'El
Cargador del Ancestro' y su contexto." In *XXIII Simposio de Investigaciones Arqueológicas
en Guatemala, 2009*, ed. Bárbara Arroyo, Adriana Linares Palma, and Lorena Paíz
Aragón, 974–91. Ministerio de Cultura y Deportes, Instituto de Antropología e Historia,
and Asociación Tikal, Guatemala City.

Shook, Edwin M., and Alfred V. Kidder. 1952. *Mound E-III-3, Kaminaljuyu, Guatemala.*
Contributions to American Anthropology and History 53. Carnegie Institution of
Washington Publication 596. Carnegie Institution, Washington, DC.

Shook, Edwin M., and Marion Popenoe de Hatch. 1999. "Las Tierras Altas Centrales:
períodos preclásico y clásico." In *Historia general de Guatemala*, vol. 1: *Epoca precolum-
bina*, ed. Marion Popenoe de Hatch, 289–318. Fundación para la Cultura y el Desarrollo,
Guatemala City.

Smith, Michael E. 2007. "Tula and Chichén Itzá: Are We Asking the Right Questions?" In
*Twin Tollans: Chichén Itzá, Tula, and the Epiclassic to Early Postclassic Mesoamerican
World*, ed. Jeff Karl Kowalski and Cynthia Kristan-Graham, 579–617. Dumbarton Oaks
Research Library and Collection, Washington, DC.

Spinden, Herbert J. 1975. *A Study of Maya Art, Its Subject Matter and Historical
Development*. Dover, New York. [Originally published in 1913 as Memoirs of the
Peabody Museum of American Archaeology and Ethnography 6, Harvard University,
Cambridge, MA.]

Stone, Andrea J. 1983. "The Zoomorphs of Quirigua, Guatemala." PhD dissertation,
Department of Art and Art History, University of Texas, Austin.

Taube, Karl A. 1987. *A Representation of the Principal Bird Deity in the Paris Codex.*
Research Reports on Ancient Maya Writing 6. Center for Maya Research, Washington,
DC.

Taube, Karl A. 2003. "Ancient and Contemporary Maya Conceptions about the Field and
Forest." In *The Lowland Maya Area: Three Millennia at the Human-Wildland Interface*,
ed. Arturo Gómez-Pompa, Michael F. Allen, Scott L. Fedick, and Juan J. Jiménez-
Osorino, 461–92. Haworth Press, Binghamton, NY.

Taube, Karl A. n.d. "The Deer and the Vulture in Classic Maya Religion." Senior honors
thesis, University of California, Berkeley.

Taube, Karl A., William A. Saturno, David Stuart, and Heather Hurst. 2010. *The Murals of
San Bartolo, El Petén, Guatemala*, Part 2: *The West Wall*. Ancient America 10. Boundary
End Archaeology Research Center, Barnardsville, NC.

Tedlock, Dennis. 1985. *Popol Vuh: The Mayan Book of the Dawn of Life*. Simon and
Schuster, New York.

Tokovinine, Alexandre. 2013. *Place and Identity in Classic Maya Narratives*. Studies in Pre-Columbian Art and Archaeology 37. Dumbarton Oaks, Washington, DC.

Turner, Terence. 1988. "Ethno-Ethnohistory: Myth and History in Native South American Representations of Contact with Western Society." In *Rethinking History and Myth: Indigenous South American Perspectives on the Past*, ed. Jonathan D. Hill, 235–81. University of Illinois Press, Champaign-Urbana.

Umberger, Emily. 2002. "Notions of Aztec History: The Case of the Great Temple Dedication." *RES—Anthropology and Aesthetics* 42: 86–108.

Zender, Marc. 2005. "The Raccoon Glyph in Classic Maya Writing." *PARI Journal* 5 (4): 6–16.

12

Blowgunners and the Great Bird at Teotihuacan

Mesoamerican Myths in a Comparative Perspective

JESPER NIELSEN, KARL A. TAUBE, CHRISTOPHE HELMKE,
AND HÉCTOR ESCOBEDO

The extensive mythic narratives documented in the Popol Vuh, the Early Colonial manuscript of the K'iche' Maya, have long been a fundamental source in attempts to interpret scenes and motifs in Precolumbian Maya iconography, among them the battle of the Hero Twins with the Great Bird as well as scenes relating the cycle of the Maize God. We thus have fairly good evidence for the continuity and survival of these core myths in the Maya area across centuries, little work has been done to document and examine the existence of similar mythic themes in Mesoamerica in general and the Central Mexican highlands in particular. In the present chapter we summarize some of our recent research at Teotihuacan (Nielsen and Helmke 2015; Helmke and Nielsen 2015; Taube 2017), showing first how the myth of the two blowgunners and their dramatic encounter with a great monstrous bird was also a local myth of major importance in the ancient metropolis; thereafter, we turn our attention to some little-studied polychromatic mural fragments from the Tetitla compound (e.g., Taube 2003; Helmke and Nielsen 2013; Staines Cicero and Helmke 2017). Known as the Pinturas Realistas, these fragments date to the late fifth to early sixth centuries and show clear influence from the Maya area. Among the fragments, we find representations of several supernatural Maya entities, including the Great Bird[1] as well as the Maize God's journey through the watery underworld (see also Taube and Ishihara-Brito 2012; Helmke and Kupprat 2016). These fascinating images provide a privileged vantage on Maya myths as reinterpreted by Teotihuacan artisans for local consumption

DOI: 10.5876/9781646421992.c012

and demonstrate that such myths played a role in the elite interaction between the Maya and Teotihuacan. Thus the Central Mexican influences that can be detected in the Popol Vuh may only be the very last examples of a long tradition of mutual sharing, exchange, and integration of mythic narratives between these two important areas of Mesoamerica.

For more than a century, the Popol Vuh has occupied a special place in Maya studies, and its use as a source for reconstructing and understanding Maya religion and mythology has not been confined to the highlands or to the Late Postclassic or Early Colonial periods. Thus the Popol Vuh is a key for interpreting Classic and Preclassic Maya imagery and even Olmec iconography, as well as aspects of Formative religion and rulership (e.g., Taube 1993; Coe 1973, 1989; Freidel et al. 1993; Guernsey 2006; Taube et al. 2010); and the myth of the Hero Twins and their victory over a monstrous bird, as well as the death and rebirth of the Maize God, were essential parts of Maya mythology for centuries. Scholars have paid less attention, however, to the ways the mythological parts of the Popol Vuh can be compared to the mythological narratives and cycles of other parts of Mesoamerica and the American continents in a wider perspective (see Nielsen and Sellner Reunert 2008; Helmke and Nielsen 2015). The two most recent editions of the Popol Vuh (Tedlock 1985; Christenson 2003) do not delve into such broader comparative issues, and it is fair to conclude that in recent decades, the myths recorded in the Popol Vuh have been conceived of as an independent expression of Maya culture situated within the broader framework of Mesoamerican culture and mythology (see, however, Bierhorst 1990: 175–80; Chinchilla Mazariegos 2011, 2017). In contrast, earlier generations of scholars attempted to describe and analyze the Popol Vuh from a comparative viewpoint (e.g., Brinton 1890; Spence 1908; Schultz 1913). Wolfgang Schultz's (1913: 70–104) study thus included a long list of mythological motifs from the Popol Vuh that he then compared to examples of myths from the Near East, Egypt, Classical Greece, Rome, India, and Japan in particular. Although such early comparative efforts were frequently embedded in now outdated and sometimes bizarre diffusionist theories, such as those put forward by Charles Étienne Brasseur de Bourbourg (see Mace 1973: 305–9), it is nevertheless remarkable how absent the insights from comparative mythology and a broad Mesoamericanist perspective have been in recent decades of scholarship focusing on the Popol Vuh. As indicated above, there is now good evidence that some of the central myths, what we refer to as core myths, documented in the Popol Vuh were shared with several other Mesoamerican cultures across time and space, among them the culture of Early Classic Teotihuacan in the Central Mexican highlands.

BLOWGUNNERS AND GREAT BIRDS AT TEOTIHUACAN
In an original study (Nielsen and Helmke 2015) and its follow-up (Helmke and Nielsen 2015) by two of the authors, it is demonstrated how the mythic motif involving the defeat of a giant celestial bird by a set of heroic twins or brothers was not confined to the Maya area but also formed an integral part of the cultural traditions of Central Mexico, Oaxaca, and the Gulf Coast. The variants of the myth narrated among such diverse Mesoamerica cultures suggests that it was a deep-seated part of Mesoamerican creation mythologies, perhaps even with precursors in the Old World (Nielsen and Sellner Reunert 2008: 52–57; Helmke and Nielsen 2015: 45–51). According to John Bierhorst (1988: 26), myths involving heroic twins can serve "as the narrative framework for a tribe's entire mythology," and indeed it seems that the victory of the monster-slaying twins or brothers was a prerequisite for the creation of humanity and the world. A pair of male twins figures prominently in mythology of the American Southwest, where they are often referred to as the War Twins due to their role as monster slayers. Thus in Zuñi mythology, they defeat a monster bird known as Knife Wing (Parsons 1939: 1043). In this regard, it is noteworthy that in the West Wall mural at San Bartolo, the Great Bird—or Principal Bird Deity, as it is also known in the literature—appears in no fewer than five scenes with wings tipped by obsidian blades or flint bifaces (see Taube et al. 2010: figure 18a; see also Helmke and Nielsen 2011: 9, figure 5).

At Teotihuacan, the myth of the bird's defeat appears in the murals of three rooms (designated as Rooms 12, 13, and 14) in the compound referred to as Zona 5A, or Conjunto del Sol at the foot of the Pyramid of the Sun and adjoining the Avenue of the Dead. Here, two human figures aim their blowguns at supernatural avian creatures representing solar entities, as indicated by their characteristic angular, stepped facial paint (Nielsen and Helmke 2015: 14–31; see also Taube 2003: 278–80, 2006: 164) (figure 12.1). They have a row of four additional bird heads on both wings, one on each knee, and one atop the tail; and they descend or fall from trees, just as Wuqub' Kaqix (Seven Macaw) was shot by the Hero Twins and collapsed to the base of his nance fruit tree.[2]

In the murals of Zona 5A, the blossoming trees are truly magical, since from each "flower" cultural items of value emerge—objects and substances that defined the civilized life at Teotihuacan, with one importantly being the mayoid Maize God, again denoting a tree of riches (fig. 12.2). However, these are not ordinary flowers, as they are entirely oval in profile with no out-flaring ends, lack petals, and bear a jagged central cleft from which the precious items emerge. Indeed, they resemble cracked eggs, and although this may seem strange for a plant, it is entirely appropriate for the gourd tree that supports the Great Bird in many images of this being in Late Preclassic and Classic period iconography.

FIGURE 12.1. Twin blowgunners from Room 13 in the Conjunto del Sol, Teotihuacan, Mexico. Drawing by Christophe Helmke.

FIGURE 12.2. Detail of tree of plenty from which the Great Bird is shot down, showing numerous objects emerging from the flowers, Conjunto del Sol, Teotihuacan. Drawing by Christophe Helmke.

In parallel to the narrative of the Popol Vuh, the final and utter defeat of the bird-monster may only have occurred once its possessions were literally "plucked," not from his body as in the Wuqub' Kaqix but from his tree of wealth. The actions of the blowgunners thus release the objects that would have been considered fundamental in defining and creating culture, just as the killing of Wuqub' Kaqix enabled the creation of the world to unfold.

It is fairly clear that the decapitation of the Great Bird constituted a source of wealth, much as if its head was a tuber or root of great abundance to be planted and sustained. The term *Jester God*—based on Linda Schele's (1974: 49–50) original insights—constitutes at least three precious, distinct headdress elements, one of these the head of the Great Bird with foliage sprouting from its crown (see Taube and Ishihara-Brito 2012; Stuart 2012). Perhaps the most celebrated example of this striking motif is the massive jadeite head from Altun Ha, Belize (figure 12.3). Although David M. Pendergast (1982: 57–59, figure 33), the original discoverer, described it as the Sun God, Stephen Houston (personal communication, 1989) noted perceptively that it is actually the head of the Great Bird with foliage atop its brow (Taube 1998: 458). The ancient rulers of Altun Ha, who bore the jadeite

FIGURE 12.3. The famous jade head from Altun Ha from Tomb 7, Structure B-4 (Belize), representing the decapitated head of the Great Bird. *Courtesy*, National Institute of Culture and History, Belize.

boulder in the crooks of their arms, thus symbolically carried the decapitated head of the Great Bird, a potent manifestation of their prowess and their affinity to the mythic Juun Ajaw, who first vanquished the avian nemesis. According to Taube (1998: 456), this avian form of the jade Jester God alludes to both the slaying and decapitation of the Great Bird and the mythic acquisition of his world tree, or *axis mundi*, by the Hero Twins—a source of immediate wealth and abundance: "Once severed from the defeated bird, this head would constitute the same form of the Jester God, a bird head sprouting a verdant tree."

In the Popol Vuh, the Great Bird succeeds in injuring the elder of the Twins, Junajpu, by tearing off his one arm, and this episode of the narrative was also of great importance to the Classic Maya, as evidenced by a stucco frieze at Tonina showing the elder Juun Ajaw overcome by the Great Bird. Stuart (personal communication, 1987) noted that Juun Ajaw is missing his left hand while the accompanying glyphic caption reads *ch'ahkaj uk'ab*, "his arm was chopped" (see Nielsen and Helmke 2015: 6) (figure 12.4a). But although the creature wears a trefoil pectoral commonly found with the Classic Maya portrayals of the Great Bird, its head is clearly serpentine, in striking contrast to conventional representations of this being and further evidencing its complexity and variant forms.

A ceramic dish discovered at a small residential group at Las Pacayas in the municipality of Sayaxche, Guatemala, features a notably similar theme, but in this case the

FIGURE 12.4. (a) Detail of Classic period stucco frieze from Tonina (Chiapas, Mexico) showing one of the Hero Twins being attacked by the Great Bird and losing his one arm. (b) Detail of one of the supernatural birds from Patio 7 at Atetelco (Teotihuacan, Mexico). Note the avian heads on the wings, knees, and tail, as well as the severed and bleeding human arm in the beak. Drawings by Christophe Helmke.

bird is clearly a scarlet macaw (Escobedo et al. 1994: 436; Chinchilla Mazariegos 2017: 148, figures 64–65). The bird holds a severed human hand in its beak, clearly from the right wrist of a youthful male, which spouts spurts of blood (figure 12.5a). Behind the wounded and yet apparently dancing human figure is a blowgun lying diagonally, clearly a form of the episode from the Popol Vuh documented for the sixteenth-century K'iche' Maya.

Representations of macaws clenching severed human arms in their beaks are not limited to the iconography of the Classic period, since a particularly telling example is also found in the Late Postclassic Madrid Codex (p. 37) (figure 12.5b), where the bird hovers above a congregation of deities amid ritual prescriptions. A very similar representation is also found in the almanac pages related to the *tonalpohualli* of the Codex Borgia (p. 2), a large precariously balanced limb in the beak of the bird (figure 12.5c). These examples seem to allude to the entire mythic narrative involving the battle with the Great Bird and testify to the widespread knowledge of the myth shortly before the Spanish Invasion.

Going back in time, the same incident is also celebrated in the imagery of the Early Classic ballcourt at Copan, featuring massive stucco macaws (Fash 1998: 230–31). It has long been recognized that this motif can be traced all the way back to Preclassic Izapa, where the Great Bird figures prominently on several monuments

FIGURE 12.5. (a) Maya blowgunner with severed arm is confronted by his enemy—a supernatural macaw. Detail of ceramic dish from the site of Las Pacayas (Peten, Guatemala). (b) Detail from the Madrid Codex wherein a macaw gnaws on a severed arm. (c) Macaw from the Codex Borgia balancing a large human arm in its beak. Drawings by Christophe Helmke.

(see Coe 1989: 162–63; Guernsey 2006: 91–116). Importantly, we now know that the inhabitants of Teotihuacan also put great emphasis on this particular episode, which may have been of significant symbolic importance in Precolumbian Mesoamerican thought. Thus Mural 1 of Patio 7 at Atetelco depicts two supernatural birds with a row of three small heads on each of the wings, the tail terminating in three other heads, and two additional ones attached to the knees (Cabrera Castro et al. 2007; Nielsen and Helmke 2015: 31–32, figure 18). Significantly, one of the birds clenches a bleeding human arm in its beak, poignantly echoing the examples from the Maya area (figure 12.4b). Nevertheless, based on current evidence, the examples from Zona 5A and from Atetelco all appear to represent the local Teotihuacan version of the myth, not emulations of a Maya myth. Other examples of the bird-man include a stunning figurine of an impersonator on display

FIGURE 12.6. Unprovenanced examples of probable impersonations of the Great Bird: (a) figurine without provenience and now in the National Museum in Guatemala City showing human figure with bird heads adorning the arms, on his belt, and on his sandals. Presumably, a removable bird-headdress, or helmet, originally belonged with the figurine. Photograph by Karl Taube. (b) Figurine fragment from highland Guatemala of an individual wearing a quetzal headdress with a distinctive tuft of feathers on his left shoulder. Photograph by Christophe Helmke.

in Guatemala City's National Museum (Chinchilla Mazariegos 2017: 144, figure 60), an unprovenanced figurine fragment from highland Guatemala (figure 12.6a, b), and a large incised Teotihuacan-style tripod with a dancing and singing figure (figure 12.7a). The latter also has a butterfly proboscis and a so-called Reptile Eye-glyph (see, e.g., Beyer 1921; Caso 1961; von Winning 1961) covering the torso, thus recalling the example from Atetelco, which has precisely the same sign on its chest. Furthermore, a Teotihuacan-style incense burner from Escuintla, on the Pacific piedmont of Guatemala, shows a descending bird-man with two smaller bird heads on its wings hovering above a row of five severed human arms that eerily hang and bleed from the lintel above the doorway to a temple-shaped incense burner (Taube 2005: 43, figures 6b-d, 7; Chinchilla Mazariegos 2010: 125–28, figures 8–9, 2011: 112–23, 2017: 144, figures 61–63; Nielsen and Helmke 2015: 32, figure 19). What is

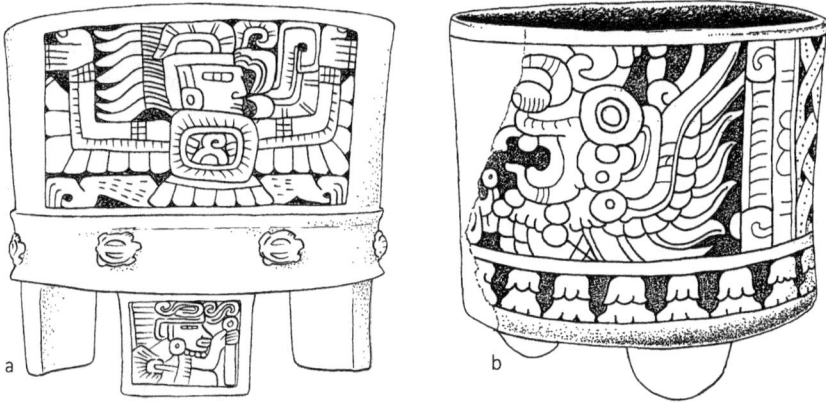

FIGURE 12.7. (a) Detail of Teotihuacan-style tripod from the Escuintla or Tiquisate region of Guatemala with human impersonator of a supernatural avian. Drawing by Christophe Helmke. (b) Partial Teotihuacan plano-relief vase portraying the Great Bird with serpent wings. Drawing by Karl Taube.

also worth noting is the one small figure to the right looking up toward the Great Bird and the clay stump that indicates that a second figure was originally placed to the left and subsequently broke off. These two human figures probably portray the same two blowgunners we saw in the murals of the Conjunto del Sol, and these representations all seem to revolve around the defining moment of a mythological narrative that is essentially the same as documented in other areas and time periods in Mesoamerica. In proposing that this narrative—centered on the defeat and slaying of a supernatural bird with solar associations or at least aspirations by two blowgunners, possibly twins—was not restricted to the Maya area but rather was a pan-Mesoamerican theme, we hypothesize that it also served roughly similar ends across Mesoamerica. The underlying meaning of the narrative was intimately linked with legitimizing strategies of the ruling lineages to create an unbroken line between themselves and the monster-slaying heroes, who through their triumph not only freed the world of a threat but also provided access to and established ordered time, creation, and civilized life.

THE PINTURAS REALISTAS AT TETITLA

Teotihuacan was one of the truly great urban centers of Mesoamerica, exhibiting a type and a degree of urbanism that was exceedingly rare in the Americas and continues to baffle modern scholars. Aside from the great complexes of monumental architecture that cluster along the Avenue of the Dead, the city's primary axis and one of the main arteries of traffic and processions, the urban fabric is defined by quadrangular compounds. These compounds can be compared to city blocks of modern cities and likewise were separated by smaller streets and passages. These essentially windowless and fortified enclosures with few entrances were probably home to extended families and attending personnel, but social differences existed, and some compounds may have housed elites whereas others were occupied by several unrelated families (e.g., Manzanilla 2004; Nielsen 2014). Of the more than 2,000 compounds that defined the urban sprawl of Teotihuacan at its height, only five dozen or so have been excavated and most of those only partially (e.g., Millon 1973; Manzanilla 2012). One of the best known of these compounds is Tetitla, located only a little over 600 m to the west of the Avenue of the Dead and 940 m southwest of the Pyramid of the Sun. This compound has the distinction of exhibiting a wide array of polychromatic murals, but, as with most such compounds at Teotihuacan, only the very lowest portions of the murals have been preserved as a result of construction practices of the ancient inhabitants themselves but also because of the farming practices in the centuries following the collapse of this great metropolis, especially plowing by the people who continued to occupy the valley in post-contact times. At Tetitla, many murals exhibit motifs that are distinctively Teotihuacano, including figurative motifs and elements of the local glyphic writing (de la Fuente 1995; Taube 2000). Yet one series of murals, known as the Pinturas Realistas, also exhibits elements drawn from the pantheon of the ancient Maya as well as glyphic texts in Maya writing (Taube 2003; Helmke and Nielsen 2013; Helmke 2017). Below, we focus on these Pinturas Realistas and, based on these fragmentary murals, delve deeper into the mythic motifs that find their origin in the Maya area to the east, particularly those pertaining to the slaying of the Great Bird.

In previous studies, Nielsen and Helmke have suggested that the myth of the Great Bird's defeat served in part to explain the origin of the headdress used in royal coronation ceremonies. Essentially, the head and feathers of the Great Bird served as a hunter's trophy, referring back to the Hero Twin Juun Ajaw, who overcame this creature in the deep mythic past, with kings inheriting the right to wear the headdress and the privileges that came with it (Nielsen and Helmke 2015: 6–8, 34–35; Helmke and Nielsen 2015: 36; see also Helmke 2010). In addition, the tail feathers and mirror assemblage adorning the abdomen of the Great Bird also probably constituted a trophy, since historical rulers wore such feathers and mirrors as part of their regalia (Taube et al. 2010: 35). Those entitled to wear the headdress and tail feathers would perhaps even have claimed descent from Juun Ajaw, the first hunter and first king. Although the Popol Vuh does not state that Wuqub' Kaqix was decapitated, there is evidence that in some versions of the myth, this was indeed what transpired. The idea that the Great Bird was eventually beheaded in some earlier variants of the story is thus corroborated by the iconography of a Late Preclassic monument from the highland site of La Lagunita in Guatemala. Monument 8 depicts the head of the Great Bird mounted on an offering tripod (figure 12.8b) comparable to those seen on the West Wall at San Bartolo (Taube et al. 2010: 22–23, figure 14a). As discussed elsewhere, a fragment (possibly from the South Wall) from San Bartolo shows the Great Bird as the quarry of the one Hero Twin (Saturno 2009: 123, figure 9; Nielsen and Helmke 2015: 8, figure 5b), and it is conceivable that eventually its head was placed on a tripod offering stand in a manner equal to that of the fish, bird, and deer shown on the West Wall, although such a scene has not been recovered.

Interestingly, Stela 60 at Izapa (Guernsey 2006: 92, figure 5.2) shows an individual seated atop what seems to be the defeated Great Bird. In light of such a bird throne, a new meaning emerges: the power of the seated ruler was directly associated with the killing and decapitation of the supernatural bird, and it is with these observations in mind that we can best understand one of the mural fragments from Tetitla (Ruiz Gallut 2002: 324–25, figure 10; Taube and Ishihara-Brito 2012). The fragment is significant, since it depicts the head of the Great Bird in typical Maya fashion but severed from the body (figure 12.8a). What is significant about the examples from La Lagunita and the Pinturas Realistas (figure 8) is that much like the jadeite head from Altun Ha, they all represent the decapitated head of the Great Bird, topped by the personification of paper (Stuart 2012). Together, this implies that they represent the head of the bird from which the primordial royal headdress was fashioned (see also Nielsen and Helmke 2015: 8). Significantly, the fragment from the Pinturas Realistas most likely decorated the eastern wall of Corridor 12a (see de la Fuente 1995: 309–10) and based on our understanding of the murals and their disposition would seem to represent an event that is later in the narrative recounted by the murals. Considering the central role of the Great Bird (in particular its head) in Maya accession ceremonies involving royal headdresses of the aforementioned Avian Jester God, it is interesting that what may be an apparent accession ceremony, also rendered according to Maya conventions, is also represented in the Pinturas Realistas fragments—albeit in the antechamber, Corridor 12 (Helmke and Nielsen 2013: 133, figure 7). The Pinturas Realistas could thus very well have included a sequence of images that made a direct visual connection between the beheading of the Great Bird and the installment of a new king—just as we know it from the San Bartolo murals.

In terms of the heads of the Great Bird depicted in profile at Tetitla, it is noteworthy that the eye is only half open, which is in contrast to most conventional portrayals of this bird in Late Preclassic and Classic Maya iconography, where it

FIGURE 12.8. The decapitated Great Bird: (a) On a mural fragment from Corridor 12a at Tetitla (Teotihuacan, Mexico). Drawing by Christophe Helmke. (b) Severed head placed on an offering tripod, Monument 8 from La Lagunita, Guatemala. Drawing by Karl Taube.

usually has the bright and shining eye also found with the diurnal Maya Sun God (see Taube et al. 2010). This half-open "lazy" eye recalls the eyes of zoomorphic mountain heads (or "*witz* monsters") denoting personified mountains in Classic Maya art, which almost invariably appear without bodies, much as if they were decapitated. In other words, the slack eye found with the Great Bird heads in the Pinturas Realistas at Tetitla also suggests that they are lifeless, severed heads. This is in striking contrast with a Teotihuacan plano-relief vessel depicting the Maya Great Bird, which has clear serpent wings as well as the solar eye (figure 12.7b). Although made locally in the region of Teotihuacan, a stucco-painted vessel in the collection of the Arizona State Museum at the University of Arizona, Tucson, portrays a Maya-style scene of an avian figure with not only the beak of the Great Bird but also the remains of the floral diadem commonly found with the Classic Maya deity. Dating to the first century BCE, the East Wall of the Pinturas Sub-1A Structure at San Bartolo portrays the Maya Sun God as a bird with clawed feet and the remains of what appears to be a Great Bird headdress, including the curving beak and floral diadem (see Taube et al. 2010: figure 21c). In addition, the roughly contemporaneous Stela 2 at Tak'alik Ab'aj depicts a flying sun god wearing the

FIGURE 12.9. Bundled figures with bird beak represented in the mural fragments of the Pinturas Realistas at Tetitla. Note the stylized flames that frame the bodies. Drawings by Christophe Helmke.

headdress of the same mythic bird (2010: figure 21b). Bundled anthropomorphic figures in the Pinturas Realistas, bearing the *ak'ab* "darkness" sign on their chest, are framed by wavy lines that may depict flames. Noteworthy is the juxtaposition of the human profiles with curved beaks resembling those of the Great Bird, likely representing avian masks, as though mortuary bundles at their immolation (Taube and Ishihara-Brito 2012) (figure 12.9).

CONCLUDING REMARKS

The lively scenes that once made up the entire Pinturas Realistas murals appear to have been peopled by a multitude of figures involved in numerous different activities, including pulque drinking (Nielsen and Helmke 2017), impersonation rituals, and, as we have seen, royal accession. The head of the Great Bird may have formed either part of a sequence illustrating the myth of its fall or possibly a reenactment of it. We now know that myths were performed and that ritual dances accompanied such reenactments, centered on the defeat of the monstrous celestial bird (see Helmke and Nielsen 2015: 36–41). Glyphic sources of the Classic period as well as ethnohistoric document sources reveal that a specific dance was devoted to the Great Bird and Junajpu and was an integral part of Maya ritual life for centuries.

As first discussed by María Elena Ruiz Gallut (2003) and Taube (2003), the Pinturas Realistas murals strongly suggest some kind of contact with ethnic Maya. Yet there is little to suggest that Tetitla was ever a Maya *barrio* or enclave comparable to the famous Zapotec enclave at Tlailotlacan (Spence 1992) and the possible nearby Michoacan enclave at the western periphery of the site (N1W5 and N1W6) (e.g., Gómez Chávez and Gazzola 2010). The imagery as well as the Maya glyphic texts were most likely produced and reinterpreted by achieved local Teotihuacan artists with a profound knowledge of Maya culture (Helmke and Nielsen 2013: 144–46). What the murals do also suggest—the motifs we have discussed here in particular—is that these mythic narratives were well-known both in the Maya area and at Teotihuacan and as such formed part of a shared pan-Mesoamerican mythology (see also Nielsen and Helmke 2013). We suspect that these motifs were selected and emphasized in their "international" setting in Tetitla (Ruiz Gallut 2003) in part because they were recognizable to the local Teotihuacan audience. In the eyes of the Teotihuacanos, they were probably reminiscent of familiar themes yet presented in a foreign and exotic manner. Thus the murals attest to the complex exchange, cross-fertilization, and, to a degree, syncretism as well as integration of cultural and religious traditions in Early Classic Mesoamerica. It is still unclear why these scenes relating to the beheading of the Great Bird and a royal accession, the life cycle of the Maize God (see Helmke and Kupprat 2016; Taube and Ishihara-Brito 2012), and Maya glyphic texts were painted precisely here, in the relatively narrow rooms at Tetitla, and we may never know. What we can say with some certainty, however, is that along with the images and artifacts from elsewhere in the ancient metropolis, they represent further evidence that the elites of the Central Mexican highlands and the Maya area were in contact during the Early Classic and that the exchange and reinterpretation of mythic narratives formed part of this dynamic intercultural setting.

Interestingly, a relief from one of the palatial compounds at Early Postclassic Tula shows the descending or falling body of the Great Bird, complete with stretched-out serpent wings and resplendent jade jewelry. Presumably, the circular hole in the center was originally intended for a tenoned sculpture representing the head of the bird, analogous to the sculpted friezes of the ballcourt at Copan (Fash 1998: 230–31). This remarkable relief exhibits a mix of Central Mexican and Maya traits and suggests that Toltec rulers continued to connect themselves with the primordial slaying of the mighty avian creature (figure 12.10). Thus just as we find Central Mexican influences and loanwords in the Popol Vuh dating to the Postclassic (e.g., Carmack 1968; Christenson 2003: 27–30), so the myths we have become accustomed to think of as originating among the Maya undoubtedly had a much more complex history and as such should be regarded as Late Postclassic K'iche' variants of a series of myth cycles and themes that had long been an established part of Mesoamerican dynastic traditions and elite culture. The slaying of the Great Bird and its associated ritual privileges along with the fundamental principles of life, death, and rebirth

FIGURE 12.10. Carved and painted relief from Tula (Hidalgo, Mexico) representing the body of the Great Bird descending from the heavens. Drawing by Christophe Helmke.

symbolized by the life cycle of the Maize God had been on the minds of generations of Mesoamericans before the K'iche' scribes put pen to paper.

ACKNOWLEDGMENTS

First and foremost, we would like to thank Allen Christenson, Holley Moyes, and Frauke Sachse for their kind invitation to contribute this chapter to the volume. Over the years of working on the documentation of Teotihuacan murals, we have received the help and insights of many but especially the members of the academic committee of the Zona Arqueológica de Teotihuacan, as well as Rubén Cabrera Castro, Sergio Gómez Chávez, Claudia María López Pérez, Miguel Morales, Monserrat Salinas Rodrigo, and Gloria Torres Rodríguez. Warm thanks to Oswaldo Chinchilla Mazariegos, Leticia Staines Cicero, María Teresa Uriarte, and Karen Bassie-Sweet for productive discussions pertaining to the iconography of Teotihuacan and the Maya. Our thanks to the New World Archaeological Foundation for information pertaining to the monuments of Izapa. We are also grateful to the Belize Institute of Archaeology, of the National Institute of Culture and History, for permission to reproduce the photograph of the jadeite head from Altun Ha.

NOTES

1. Earlier researchers termed this creature the Principal Bird Deity, and some of our colleagues have suggested that a multiplicity of different beings have been subsumed under the same heading (e.g., Bardawil 1976; Miller and Taube 1993: 137–38; Zender 2005: 9;

Bassie-Sweet 2008: 140–45; Bassie-Sweet and Hopkins, this volume). While we recognize the diverse aspects of these entities, here we regard them as regional and temporal variations of the same general avian creature, and we therefore find it useful to employ a broad designation that covers all of the cross-cultural and diachronic manifestations of these birds.

2. In terms of identifying the species of birds these supernatural avians were intended to mimic or were inspired from, it is clear that they were probably composed of traits from several different species, including the macaw and the quetzal but possibly also some raptorial bird (see Taube 2003: 278; Bassie-Sweet 2008: 140–45; Nielsen and Helmke 2015: 21).

REFERENCES CITED

Bardawil, Lawrence W. 1976. "The Principal Bird Deity in Maya Art: An Iconographic Study of Form and Meaning." In *The Art, Iconography, and Dynastic History of Palenque, Part III*, ed. Merle Green Robertson, 195–209. Proceedings of the Segunda Mesa Redonda de Palenque, 1974. Pre-Columbian Art Research, Pebble Beach, CA.

Bassie-Sweet, Karen. 2008. *Maya Sacred Geography and the Creator Deities*. University of Oklahoma Press, Norman.

Beyer, Hermann. 1921. "Algunos datos nuevos sobre el calendario azteca." *El México antiguo* 10: 261–65.

Bierhorst, John. 1988. *The Mythology of South America*. Quill William Morrow, New York.

Bierhorst, John. 1990. *The Mythology of Mexico and Central Mexico*. Quill William Morrow, New York.

Brinton, Daniel G. 1890. *Essays of an Americanist*. David McKay, Philadelphia.

Cabrera Castro, Rubén, Sergio Gómez Chávez, and Julie Gazzola. 2007. "Nuevos hallazgos de la pintura mural teotihuacana." In *Museo de murales teotihuacanos Beatriz de la Fuente*, ed. Margen Rojo S.C., Ofelia Martínez, and Blanca Coss, 137–64. Instituto de Investigaciones Estéticas, Universidad Nacional Autónoma de México, Mexico City.

Carmack, Robert M. 1968. *Toltec Influence on the Postclassic Culture History of Highland Guatemala*. Middle American Research Institute Publications 26. Middle American Research Institute, Tulane University, New Orleans.

Caso, Alfonso. 1961. "El Glifo 'Ojo de reptile.'" *Ethnos* 26 (4): 167–71.

Chinchilla Mazariegos, Oswaldo. 2010. "La vagina dentada: Una interpretación de la estela 25 de Izapa y las guacamayas del juego de pelota de Copán." *Estudios de cultura maya* 36: 117–44.

Chinchilla Mazariegos, Oswaldo. 2011. *Imágenes de la Mitología Maya*. Museo Popol Vuh, Universidad Francisco Marroquín, Guatemala City.

Chinchilla Mazariegos, Oswaldo. 2017. *Art and Myth of the Ancient Maya*. Yale University Press, New Haven, CT.

BLOWGUNNERS AND THE GREAT BIRD AT TEOTIHUACAN

311

Christenson, Allen J. 2003. *Popol Vuh, the Sacred Book of the Maya: The Great Classic of Central American Spirituality*. O Books, Winchester.

Coe, Michael D. 1973. *The Maya Scribe and His World*. Grolier Club, New York.

Coe, Michael D. 1989. "The Hero Twins: Myth and Images." In *The Maya Vase Book*, vol. 1, ed. Justin Kerr, 161–84. Kerr Associates, New York.

de la Fuente, Beatriz. 1995. "Tetitla." In *La Pintura Mural Prehispánica en México, Tomo I*, Teotihuacán, vol. 1: *Catálogo*, ed. Beatriz de la Fuente, 258–311. Universidad Nacional Autónoma de México, Mexico City.

Escobedo, Héctor L., Jorge Mario Samayoa, and Oswaldo Gómez. 1994. "Las Pacayas: Un nuevo sitio arqueológico en la región Petexbatun." In *VII Simposio de Investigaciones arqueológicas en Guatemala, 1993*, ed. Juan Pedro Laporte and Héctor L. Escobedo, 431–48. Museo Nacional de Arqueología y Etnología, Guatemala City.

Fash, William L. 1998. "Dynastic Architectural Programs: Intention and Design in Classic Maya Buildings at Copan and Other Sites." In *Function and Meaning in Classic Maya Architecture*, ed. Stephen Houston, 223–70. Dumbarton Oaks, Washington, DC.

Freidel, David, Linda Schele, and Joy Parker. 1993. *Maya Cosmos: Three Thousand Years on the Shaman's Path*. Quill, William Morrow, New York.

Gómez Chávez, Sergio, and Julie Gazzola. 2010. "Análisis de las relaciones entre Teotihuacán y el occidente de México." In *Dinámicas culturales entre el occidente, el centro-norte y la cuenca de México, del Preclásico al Epiclásico*, ed. Brigitte Faugère, 113–35. Centro de estudios mexicanos y centroamericanos, El Colegio de Michoacán, Michoacan.

Guernsey, Julia. 2006. *Ritual and Power in Stone: The Performance of Rulership in Mesoamerican Izapan Style Art*. University of Texas Press, Austin.

Helmke, Christophe. 2010. "The Transferral and Inheritance of Ritual Privileges: A Classic Maya Case from Yaxchilan, Mexico." *Wayeb Notes* 35: 1–14. http://www.wayeb.org/notes/wayeb_notes0035.pdf.

Helmke, Christophe. 2017. "El pasado es un país lejano: Un análisis epigráfico de los textos mayas de Tetitla, Teotihuacan." In *Las Pinturas Realistas de Tetitla, Teotihuacan: Estudios a través de las acuarelas de Agustín Villagra Caleti*, ed. Leticia Staines Cicero and Christophe Helmke, 110–34. Instituto de Investigaciones Estéticas, Universidad Nacional Autónoma de México, and Instituto Nacional de Antropología e Historia, Mexico City.

Helmke, Christophe, and Felix A. Kupprat. 2016. "Where Snakes Abound: Places of Origin and Founding Myths in the Titles of Classic Maya Kings." In *Places of Power and Memory in Mesoamerica's Past and Present: How Toponyms, Landscapes, and Boundaries Shape History and Remembrance*, ed. Daniel Graña-Behrens, 33–83. Estudios Indiana 9. Gebr. Mann Verlag, Berlin.

Helmke, Christophe, and Jesper Nielsen. 2011. *The Writing System of Cacaxtla, Tlaxcala, Mexico*. Ancient America, Special Publication 2. Boundary End Archaeology Research Center, Barnardsville, NC.

Helmke, Christophe, and Jesper Nielsen. 2013. "The Writing on the Wall: A Paleographic Analysis of the Maya Texts of Tetitla, Teotihuacan." In *The Maya in a Mesoamerican Context: Comparative Approaches to Maya Studies*, ed. Jesper Nielsen and Christophe Helmke, 123–66. Acta Mesoamericana 26. Verlag Anton Saurwein, Markt Schwaben.

Helmke, Christophe, and Jesper Nielsen. 2015. "The Defeat of the Great Bird in Myth and Royal Pageantry: A Mesoamerican Myth in a Comparative Perspective." *Comparative Mythology* 1 (1): 23–60.

Mace, Carroll E. 1973. "Charles Étienne Brasseur de Bourbourg, 1814–1874." In *Handbook of Middle American Indians*, vol. 13: *Guide to Ethnohistorical Sources, Part Two*, ed. Howard F. Cline, 298–325. University of Texas Press, Austin.

Manzanilla, Linda R. 2004. "Social Identity and Daily Life at Classic Teotihuacan." In *Mesoamerican Archaeology*, ed. Julia A. Hendon and Rosemary A. Joyce, 124–47. Blackwell, Malden, MA.

Manzanilla, Linda R. 2012. "Neighborhoods and Elite 'Houses' at Teotihuacan, Central Mexico." In *The Neighborhood as a Social and Spatial Unit in Mesoamerican Cities*, ed. M. Charlotte Arnauld, Linda R. Manzanilla, and Michael E. Smith, 74–101. University of Arizona Press, Tucson.

Miller, Mary Ellen, and Karl A. Taube. 1993. *The Gods and Symbols of Ancient Mexico and the Maya: An Illustrated Dictionary of Mesoamerican Religion*. Thames and Hudson, London.

Millon, René. 1973. *Urbanization at Teotihuacan, Mexico*, vol. 1: *The Teotihuacan Map, Part 1: Text*. University of Texas Press, Austin.

Nielsen, Jesper. 2014. "Where Kings Once Ruled? Considerations on Palaces and Rulership at Teotihuacan." In *Palaces and Courtly Culture in Ancient Mesoamerica*, ed. Julie Nehammer Knub, Christophe Helmke, and Jesper Nielsen, 1–16. Archaeopress Pre-Columbian Archaeology, Oxford.

Nielsen, Jesper, and Christophe Helmke. 2013. "The World in a Gourd: A Comparative Perspective on Origin Myths of the Maya and Teotihuacan." In *The Maya in a Mesoamerican Context: Comparative Approaches to Maya Studies*, ed. Jesper Nielsen and Christophe Helmke, 17–33. Acta Mesoamericana 26. Verlag Anton Saurwein, Markt Schwaben.

Nielsen, Jesper, and Christophe Helmke. 2015. "The Fall of the Great Celestial Bird: A Master Myth in Early Classic Central Mexico." *Ancient America* 13: 1–46.

Nielsen, Jesper, and Christophe Helmke. 2017. "Los bebedores de Tetitla: Representaciones del consumo ritual de pulque en los murales de Teotihuacan." In *Las pinturas realistas de Tetitla, Teotihuacan: Estudios a través de las acuarelas de Agustín Villagra Caleti*, ed.

Leticia Staines Cicero and Christophe Helmke, 135–63. Instituto de Investigaciones Estéticas, Universidad Nacional Autónoma de México. and Instituto Nacional de Antropología e Historia, Mexico City.

Nielsen, Jesper, and Toke Sellner Reunert. 2008. "Bringing Back the Dead: Shamanism and the Maya Hero Twins' Journey to the Underworld." *Acta Americana* 16 (1): 49–79.

Parsons, Elsie Clews. 1939. *Pueblo Indian Religion.* University of Chicago Press, Chicago.

Pendergast, David M. 1982. *Excavations at Altun Ha, Belize, 1964–1970,* vol. 2. Royal Ontario Museum, Toronto.

Ruiz Gallut, María Elena. 2002. "Imágenes en Tetitla: De disfraces y vecinos." In *Memoria de la Primera Mesa Redonda de Teotihuacan: Ideología y política a través de materiales, imágenes y símbolos,* ed. María Elena Ruiz Gallut, 315–29. Consejo Nacional para la Cultura y las Artes, Instituto Nacional de Antropología e Historia, and Universidad Nacional Autónoma de México. Mexico City.

Ruiz Gallut, María Elena. 2003. "El lenguaje visual de Teotihuacan: Un ejemplo de pintura mural en Tetitla." PhD dissertation, Facultad de Filosofía y Letras, Universidad Nacional Autónoma de México, Mexico City.

Saturno, William. 2009. "Centering the Kingdom, Centering the King: Maya Creation and Legitimization at San Bartolo." In *The Art of Urbanism: How Mesoamerican Kingdoms Represented Themselves in Architecture and Imagery,* ed. William L. Fash and Leonardo López Luján, 111–34. Dumbarton Oaks, Washington, DC.

Schele, Linda. 1974. "Observations on the Cross Motif at Palenque." In *Primera Mesa Redonda de Palenque: A Conference on the Art and Dynastic History of Palenque, Palenque, Chiapas, Part 1,* ed. Merle Green Robertson, 41–61. Pre-Columbian Art Research, Pebble Beach, CA.

Schultz, Wolfgang. 1913. *Einleitung in das Popol Vuh.* J. C. Hinrichs'sche Buchhandlung, Leipzig.

Spence, Lewis. 1908. *The Popol Vuh: The Mythic and Heroic Sagas of the Kichés of Central America.* David Nut, Long Acre, London.

Spence, Michael W. 1992. "Tlailotlacan, a Zapotec Enclave in Teotihuacan." In *Art, Ideology, and the City of Teotihuacan,* ed. Janet Catherine Berlo, 59–88. Dumbarton Oaks, Washington, DC.

Staines Cicero, Leticia, and Christophe Helmke, eds. 2017. *Las Pinturas Realistas de Tetitla, Teotihuacan: estudios a través de las acuarelas de Agustín Villagra Caleti.* Instituto de Investigaciones Estéticas, Universidad Nacional Autónoma de México, and Instituto Nacional de Antropología e Historia, Mexico City.

Stuart, David. 2012. "The Name of Paper: The Mythology of Crowning and Royal Nomenclature on Palenque's Palace Tablet." In *Maya Archaeology,* vol. 2, ed. Charles

Golden, Stephen Houston, and Joel Skidmore, 116–42. Precolumbia Mesoweb Press, San Francisco.

Taube, Karl A. 1993. *Aztec and Maya Myths*. British Museum Press, London.

Taube, Karl A. 1998. "The Jade Hearth: Centrality, Rulership, and the Classic Maya Temple." In *Function and Meaning in Classic Maya Architecture*, ed. Stephen Houston, 427–78. Dumbarton Oaks, Washington, DC.

Taube, Karl A. 2000. "The Writing System of Ancient Teotihuacan." *Ancient America* 1: 1–56.

Taube, Karl A. 2003. "Tetitla and the Maya Presence at Teotihuacan." In *The Maya and Teotihuacan: Reinterpreting Early Classic Interaction*, ed. Geoffrey E. Braswell, 273–314. University of Texas Press, Austin.

Taube, Karl A. 2005. "Representaciones del paraíso en el arte cerámico del clásico temprano de Escuintla, Guatemala." In *Iconografía y escritura Teotihuacana en la Costa Sur de Guatemala y Chiapas*, ed. Oswaldo Chinchilla Mazariegos and Bárbara Arroyo, 35–54. U Tz'ib, Serie Reportes 1, no. 5. Asociación Tikal, Guatemala City.

Taube, Karl A. 2006. "Climbing Flower Mountain: Concepts of Resurrection and the Afterlife at Teotihuacan." In *Arqueología e historia del Centro de México: Homenaje a Eduardo Matos Moctezuma*, ed. Leonardo López Luján, Davíd Carrasco, and Lourdes Cué, 153–70. Instituto Nacional de Antropología e Historia, Mexico City.

Taube, Karl A. 2017. "Aquellos del este: Representaciones de dioses y hombres mayas en las pinturas realistas de Tetitla, Teotihuacan." In *Las Pinturas Realistas de Tetitla, Teotihuacan: Estudios a través de las acuarelas de Agustín Villagra Caleti*, ed. Leticia Staines Cicero and Christophe Helmke, 71–100. Instituto de Investigaciones Estéticas, Universidad Nacional Autónoma de México, and Instituto Nacional de Antropología e Historia, Mexico City.

Taube, Karl, and Reiko Ishihara-Brito. 2012. "From Stone to Jewel: Jade in Ancient Maya Religion and Rulership." In *Maya Art at Dumbarton Oaks*, ed. Joanne Pillsbury, Miriam Doutriaux, Reiko Ishihara, and Alexandre Tokovinine, 134–53. Dumbarton Oaks, Washington, DC.

Taube, Karl A., William A. Saturno, David Stuart, and Heather Hurst. 2010. *The Murals of San Bartolo, El Petén, Guatemala, Part 2: The West Wall*. Ancient America 10. Boundary End Archaeology Research Center, Barnardsville, NC.

Tedlock, Dennis. 1985. *Popol Vuh: The Mayan Book of the Dawn of Life*. Simon and Schuster, New York.

von Winning, Hasso. 1961. "Teotihuacan Symbols: The Reptile's Eye Glyph." *Ethnos* 26 (3): 121–66.

Zender, Marc. 2005. "The Raccoon Glyph in Classic Maya Writing." *PARI Journal* 5 (4): 6–16.

Index

plazas, 129, 131, 132
"Polychrome Maya Plate from Quintana Roo, A"
(Blom), xiii–xiv
Popoluca, 253
Popol Vuh: authors of, 5–6; older versions
of, 3–4; origins of, 48–49, 119, 121, 143; as
performative, 286; role of, 285; translations
of, 7–10, 120
*Popol Vuh: Le livre sacré et les mythes de l'antiquité
avec les livres héroïques et historiques des
Quichés* (Brasseur de Bourbourg), 9
Poqomam, eagle terms in, 227
Postclassic period, 78, 119
power, 38, 43; political, 12, 13; and protective dei-
ties, 81–82; of speech, 44–45; of storytelling,
26–27; of women, 22–23
Preclassic period, 13, 93, 143, 296; at Cahal Pech,
94–95, 109
pregnancy, as sowing, 37, 69
Primary Standard Sequence (PSS), xv, xvi
Primordial Sea/Water, 52, 60, 129, 177
Princeton Art Museum exhibit, *Lords of the
Underworld*, xv
Principal Bird Deity (PBD), xiv, xvi, xvii, 159,
192, 211, 230, 234–35, 268, 270, 283, 287,
309–10(n1); as burden, 276–77; changes in,
284–86; depictions of, 14, *178*, 272–73, 274,
275, 277–78, 297; social order and, 278–81
procreation: light and, 66–67; maize and,
61–62; women's role in, 22–25
projectile points, and laughing falcons, 238
prophecy, history as, 120. *See also* divination;
omens
Proskouriakoff, Tatiana, 270
protector deities, 79–80, 81, 88
Provider of Sustenance Three-Leaf Paper, 203
Pseudo-E-Group, at Blue Creek, 131–32
PSS. *See* Primary Standard Sequence
psychotropic/psychoactive potions/plants, 204;
use of, 192–93, 212–14
Puebla, 227, 256
Pul Tzin, *196*, 202; headdress of, 200–201
pyramid-plaza complexes, 128, 129
pyrite mirrors, 153, 155; tessera, 147, 157

Q'alel altar, 86
Q'anjob'al, 227
Q'aq'awitz, 79, 80, 83
Q'eqchi' narratives, 255, 258

quadripartite layouts, 99–100, 102, 118, 281
Quatrefoil (Cave Monster Maw), 95
Quenon Vase, 184, 206
Quetzalcoatl, 285
Quiche', Department of, *saqirib'al* in, 80
quincunx patterns: in caches, 109, *110*, 129; in
community boundaries, 149–50
Quirarte, Jacinto, 270
Quirigua Stela C, 145
Q'ukumatz, 79, 82, 226, 227
Q'umarkaj (Utatlán), 11, 41, 58

Rabinal, on primordial dawn, 83–84
Rabinal Achi, 66, 68, 226
Rab'inaleb', 62, 77; dawning, 80–81, 83–84
rain: and intoxication, 206, 207; laughing falcon
and, 236, 238
raptors, 225, 230, 234. *See also by type*
rebellion, Cancuc, 229
rebirth/renewal, 12, 26, 27, 58, 144, 158, 204;
death and, 56–57, 70–71, 257–58; imagery
of, 189–90; Maize God and, 189–90; speech
as, 28, 29
Recinos, Adrián, xiii, 9
reciprocity, 203; maize-human, 36–37
regeneration, gods and, 45–46
religion, 11; and myth, 138–39
religious/ritual specialists, 26; divination by, 3–4.
See also ajq'ijab'
Reptile Eye-glyph, 302
resurrection, belief in, 13
Resurrection Plate, *103*; iconography on, 189–90,
206
Rilaj Mam (Maximom), 185, 207
Río Azul, Tomb 12, 232, 233
Ritual of the Bacabs, 236, 239
rituals, 3, 11, 34, 45, 77, 273; ancestor and parentage, 192–93; bloodletting, 123, 124, 159; at
Blue Creek, 130–31; in caves, 136–38, 141–42;
clustered elements, 142–43; community
protection, 149–50; curing, 209, 213; gender
and, 22–23; of Kaminaljuyu rulers, 274–75;
myth and, 138–39; renewal, 12, 26, 27, 42, 158;
as social drama, 140–41; speech in, 28–29
Roaring Creek Red pottery, 155
Román y Zamora, Jerónimo, 41
rulers, xvi; 277, 284; proper behavior and
performance, 279–80; ritual performance
of, 274–75

Topiltzin Quetzalcoatl, 49
Tortuguero Monument 6, 206
Totonac, 56, 256–57
towns, control over, 81–82
Tozzer, Alfred M., 136
Trachemys scripta elegans, 239
trees, 297; of creation, 210–12, *298*; and split
    mountain, 177–78, 183, 188. *See also* World
    Tree; *various species*
Triqui myths, 256
trophy head, Great Bird, 304
true people, maize and, 39–40
Tula, 222, 225, 308, *309*
Tulan, 226; leaving, 62, 63, 64, 78
Tulan Suywa, 58, 59, 78, 79, 225
Turner, Victor, on rituals, 140–41
Turtle-Footed Death God, 206
turtles, *158*, 239; rebirth from, 189, 190; slider
    (*Trachemys scripta elegans*), 239
twilight, in pre-Creation stories, 185–86
Tylor, E. B., 138
Tz'aqol (Framer), 78–79; and B'itol, 23, 24, 25;
    and humans, 215–16
Tz'aqol B'itol, 61
Tzeltal, 212, 138; eagle terms, 227, 228–29
Tz'ikin, 230
tzin (*tzéen*), 198, 200, 205, 206, 212
Tzolk'in anniversary, 205
Tzotzil-Maya, 38, 40, 212; eagle terms, 227, 228,
    229
Tz'utujil, 4–5, 26, 41, 43, 62, 68, 77, 185, 205;
    dawning and, 80–81; maize and, 56–57

Uaxactun, E-Group at, 105
Uhuk Chapat Men bird, 231, 232
Uk Kaan/God N, 210. *See also* God N
Uk'u'x Kaj, 52, 53, 54, 55, 193, 223–24
underworld, 54–55, 105, 138, 237; cache represen-
    tations of, *108*, 111. *See also* Xibalba
Unen Bahlam, 178
universal sustainer, Old God as, 192
University of San Carlos (Guatemala City), 9
Uspanteko, eagle terms, 227
Uto-Aztecan speakers, 59
Ux Yop Huun, 201–2

Vase K3413, deities depicted on, 254–55
Vase of the Seven Gods, 200
Vase of the Eleven Gods, 200

vases: *ahk'ab*, 206–9; Baby Jaguar on, 173–79;
    Gods S and CH on, 262–63; Headband Gods
    on, 254–56; iconographic performances on,
    179–84; Itzamnaaj on, 273–74; pictorial, xv,
    10–11, 57, *200*, 251; Snake Lady on, 187–94
Veracruz, Principal Bird Deity, 275
Verapaz, 283
Vico, Domingo de, 5–6, 38, 49
Villacorta Calderón, José Antonio, 9
vision(s), 38, 190
vultures, 223, 224, 229

Wak, 235, 237–38
War Twins, 297
water, 118, 158
waterlily, waterlily tree, 202, *211*, 211–12
Waterlily Jaguar, 181, 187, 193
water sources, watery places, 258, 260, 263
way (*uay*), 228, 229, 235
Wayeb, rituals, 158
wealth, and Great Bird, 298–99
were-jaguar imagery, 178
Western Belize Regional Cave Project
    (WBRCP), 146
Wind God, 207
witches, in Actun Tunichil Muknal, 148
witz monsters, 306
Witz Mountain, 118, 129, 176, 205
womb, primordial world as, 52–53
women: creative role of, 23–24, 34; and Maize
    God, 258, *260*, 260–61, *262*, 262–63; and
    ritual processions, 22–23
wood people, creation of, 30–31, 215
words: and knowledge, 30; in ritual context,
    28–29
world: creation of, 52–53; renewal of, 12, 26, 160
World Tree, 68, *126*, 145, 157, 159, 299
Wuk Yol Sip, 194
Wuqub' Junajpu, 55
Wuqub' Kaqix. *See* Seven Macaw

Xajil Chronicle, 80, 83
Xb'alanke, xv, 6, 55, 56, 58, 118, 144, 145, 157, 159, 206,
    212, 222, 263; death and rebirth of, 204, 257–58;
    Headband Gods and, 252, 255; and Seven
    Macaw, 271–72, *272*; and Xmucane, 236–37
Xibalba, xib'alb'a, xiii, 13, 54, 57, 144, 237;
    creation and, 117–18; death and rebirth in,
    257–58; Hero Twins in, 55, 56, 215

Contributors

JAIME J. AWE, Department of Anthropology, Northern Arizona University, Flagstaff

KAREN BASSIE-SWEET, research associate, University of Calgary, Alberta

OSWALDO CHINCHILLA MAZARIEGOS, Department of Anthropology, Yale University, New Haven, Connecticut

ALLEN J. CHRISTENSON, Department of Comparative Arts and Letters, Brigham Young University, Provo, Utah

MICHAEL D. COE, Department of Anthropology, Yale University, New Haven, Connecticut

IYAXEL COJTÍ REN, Department of Anthropology, University of Texas at Austin

HÉCTOR ESCOBEDO, Academy of Geography and History, Guatemala City

THOMAS H. GUDERJAN, Department of Social Sciences, University of Texas at Tyler

JULIA GUERNSEY, Department of Art and Art History, University of Texas at Austin

CHRISTOPHE HELMKE, Institute of Regional and Cross-Cultural Studies, University of Copenhagen, Denmark

NICHOLAS A. HOPKINS, Jaguar Tours, Tallahassee, Florida

BARBARA MACLEOD, independent scholar

HOLLEY MOYES, Department of Anthropology and Heritage Studies, University of California at Merced

JESPER NIELSEN, Institute of Regional and Cross-Cultural Studies, University of Copenhagen, Denmark

FRAUKE SACHSE, Dumbarton Oaks Research Library and Collection, Harvard Trustees

COLIN SNIDER, Department of History, University of Texas at Tyler

KARL A. TAUBE, Department of Anthropology, University of California at Riverside

www.ingramcontent.com/pod-product-compliance
Lightning Source LLC
Chambersburg PA
CBHW062107040426
42336CB00042B/2308